THE PORTABLE MBA
IN ENTREPRENEURSHIP
CASE STUDIES

The Portable MBA Series

THE PORTABLE MBA
IN ENTREPRENEURSHIP
CASE STUDIES

William D. Bygrave and
Dan D'Heilly, Editors

John Wiley & Sons, Inc.

New York • Chichester • Weinheim • Brisbane • Singapore • Toronto

Copyright © 1997 by William D. Bygrave and Dan D'Heilly.
Published by John Wiley & Sons, Inc.

ISBN 0-471-18229-X

Printed in the United States of America

10 9 8 7 6 5 4

PREFACE

This book is a collection of cases about starting and growing new ventures. It deals with entrepreneurs, their opportunities, and the resources they need to create their ventures. The book is designed to be used as a case book companion for the second edition of *The Portable MBA in Entrepreneurship*. It would be much too narrow to claim that there is one case designed specifically for the conceptual topic of each chapter. After all, starting a new business is a holistic process that cannot be conveniently compartmentalized into "classic" management disciplines, such as marketing and finance. However, each case has an emphasis. For example, "Beautiful Legs BY POST" illustrates many of the concepts in both Chapter 5, "Creating a Successful Business Plan" and Chapter 6 "Financial Projections: How To Do Them the Right Way." But the same case also raises issues dealing with the entrepreneurial process, recognizing and shaping opportunities, entry strategies, marketing, venture capital, debt, and harvesting—topics covered in Chapters 1, 2, 3, 4, 7, 8, and 14.

We carefully selected the cases so that all the important topics in *The Portable MBA in Entrepreneurship* are covered at least once. The cases contain consumer and industrial products, manufacturing and service businesses, low technology and high technology, lifestyle and high-potential firms, many different sources of financing including founders, family, friends, angels, venture capitalists, factors, credit cards, and banks. The cases are contemporary with almost every decision point occurring in the 1990s. Students relate to the entrepreneurs in the cases; hence we have selected cases about persons whom we believe provide role models of entrepreneurial behavior.

ACKNOWLEDGMENTS

We are frequently asked what puts Babson College at the forefront of undergraduate, graduate, and executive entrepreneurship education. The answer is found in the unique mix of students, alumni, faculty, friends, benefactors, and administration that make Babson College a hub of entrepreneurship education. It is this mixture that provided us with the opportunities to write the cases in this book.

First, we would like to thank the principals in the cases who allowed us to pry into their ventures and reveal their innermost secrets. Each one of them has our heart-felt thanks. In alphabetical order they are: Mike Bellobuono, Axel Bichara, Glenn Butler, Addis Dickon, Steve Duplessie, Ross Goralnick, Chris Harami, Jon Hirschtick, Eric Kaplan, Peter Lamson, Ed Marram, Kerry McGrath, Ben Narasin, Brooks O'Kane, Lisa and Bill Pernsteiner, Elizabeth Preis, Mario Ricciardelli, Greg Raiff, John Roughneen, Torrey Russell, Steve Spinelli, David Wolfe, and Neal Workman.

The Center for Entrepreneurial Studies case collection has involved the efforts of many students, alumni, faculty, administrators, writers, editors, and videographers. We are indebted to Judy Carson, Beverly Chiarelli, Gail Daniels, Kevin Ebel, Mark Ford, Michael Giorgio, Carole Guarante, George Hart, Mark Helman, Tricia Jaekle, Bob Kramer, Bonny Kerrick, Dan Lang, Bob Martin, Bill Mayfield, Georgia Papavasiliou, Jeff Selander, Joe Williams, and Scott Wipper. This has been a team effort and we are deeply indebted to the inner circle of people who have made this book possible: Andrea Alyse, Jim Foster, Jo Ann Mathieu, and Sam Perkins.

Babson College's entrepreneurship faculty have diverse backgrounds. But what makes them special is the breadth of their entrepreneurial experiences. They are entrepreneurs, consultants, board members, investors, and lawyers, who practice what they teach. We call some of them "pracademics," our term for practicing academics. Some of them have been intimately involved in producing the cases in this book . . . so intimately in fact, that Babson faculty are principals in three of the cases. Some have supervised the writing of the cases. Some have taught the cases and suggested improvements. Special thanks are due to Bill Johnston, Julian Lange, Richard Mandel, Ed Marram, Jim Nelson, Joel Shulman, Steve Spinelli, Natalie Taylor, and Jeff Timmons.

It is a pleasure to thank the benefactors whose generosity helped finance the writing of these cases. The principal source of our support was a grant from the Ewing Marion Kauffman Foundation. Additional support came from the Frederic C. Hamilton Chair for Free Enterprise and the Price Challenge Fund. It is a privilege to be associated with the late Ewing Marion Kauffman, Fred Hamilton, and Harold Price, whose entrepreneurial vision and leadership are a continuing source of inspiration.

A huge "thank you" to Ruth Mills, our editor at John Wiley & Sons. Her enthusiasm and insight into the market for trade books and textbooks has helped us shape this book and motivated us to produce the manuscript on time.

Finally, without the enthusiasm of our students we could never have found the energy to write these cases. It is the learning that students get from cases that makes it all worthwhile. They are a neverending source of ideas. We thank every one of our students, present and past.

CONTENTS

THE PORTABLE MBA
IN ENTREPRENEURSHIP
CASE STUDIES

1 JOHN ROUGHNEEN

John Roughneen turned off his computer and stared at the blank screen, which moments before had displayed the start-up menu for *Vending Tracker,* the flagship program of Streamline Business Systems. John and his partner, Glenn Butler, had founded Streamline in late 1991 to develop software for small and medium-size vending machine operators. Most of these small-business owners still managed and planned their operations and performed bookkeeping transactions by hand. Many didn't even own a personal computer. Now, in early 1993, after more than two years of development, the latest version of *Tracker* was ready for release. Complete with functions for managing inventory, calculating sales and commissions, and producing more than 40 accounting and control reports, the system incorporated numerous refinements in response to suggestions offered by prospective customers and other industry participants. The partners were confident that they had a product that met the needs of this particular market niche. However, sales had been scant and the task of achieving sufficient sales volume to propel the business forward remained a promising but elusive goal.

The previous November (1992), Glenn had given up his job at Stratus Computer to concentrate full-time on refining the software program. John, however, who was responsible for Streamline sales and marketing, had remained at his job at Pepsi. With the revised product in shape for an upcoming trade association convention, John knew that soon he would have to decide whether or not to make the leap to total involvement in, and dependence upon, the new venture. If the business were ever going to succeed, it would require John's full-time commitment. In spite of their joint optimism about the potential of the product and the business, market validation remained a large question mark. In contrast, John's position at Pepsi was secure and his long-term prospects excellent. As one of only 120 graduates selected over a two-year period to enter a special operations management training program, John had forged a promising career path. He was currently the district sales manager for eastern Rhode Island. As John pondered his situation, he turned the computer back on, "Two years from now, how many vending machine companies might be looking at this Vending Tracker menu? Twenty? Two hundred? Two thousand?"

FAMILY BACKGROUND—EDUCATION

John Roughneen was born to first-generation Irish immigrants in Lynn, Massachusetts, just north of Boston, and grew up in the town of Lakeville, near Cape Cod. John's father, "a strapper from day one," was almost 20 years old when he immigrated to Boston following an adolescence of hard work and no school in his native land. He started high school at the age most people finish and continued his education at night, graduating in his late fifties from Northeastern University. A lifetime employee of Polaroid, where John's mother also worked for 15 years, Mr. Roughneen passed on to John a single-minded determination and the belief that he could do anything:

> You have to focus all your energies in one direction. I guess the biggest thing my family ever did for me was to give me the positive attitude that you can do whatever you want once you set your mind to it.

After a high-school career replete with numerous extracurricular activities, including the class presidency his senior year, John enrolled at Worcester Polytechnic Institute (WPI), where he eventually selected a major in manufacturing engineering. John's penchant for nonacademic pursuits continued in college, initially with school-related activities, and then by starting a part-time catering business. While he believed in the value of education and graduated with distinction, John Roughneen was not one to let schoolwork and the quest for good grades interfere with the more important mission of learning and gaining experience. He had a clear perception of what success factors would determine his destiny:

> I was an average student. I knew that regardless of how much I studied I was still going to get the same job offers. I concentrated my efforts on the business while I was in school. More so than studying. I had this feeling—I just knew in my heart that I was going to achieve success with or without the extra A, so I figured I'd spend my time on the business. It turned out exactly the way I thought. I learned that it's your personality and character more than what you know. . . . It's who you are, not what you are.

INITIATION TO ENTREPRENEURSHIP

John Roughneen's first entrepreneurial venture grew out of occasional work he performed during his sophomore year for a catering company in Worcester, Massachusetts, that serviced parties at the local art museum and other high society functions. Noticing that he and fellow clean-cut students were "a big hit" with the older, well-heeled crowd who enjoyed conversing with local college kids, John polled a few of the patrons to determine their interest in hiring waiters and bartenders for smaller private parties. Based on the positive responses to this seat-of-the-pants market research, he spent $30 on business cards and set up a sole proprietorship. John established a strict appearance and dress code for his student employees to foster the clean-cut image—the college boy look—that he regarded as the key differentiating quality of his workforce. All workers had to have black pants, white button-down shirt with black bow tie, and black shoes. John supplied ties when necessary, but deducted the cost from the employee's paycheck. Training was conducted on the job, with one new freshman or sophomore accompanying several older, experienced students to learn the basic protocols of waiting and bartending.

With good connections to the wealthy cocktail party set and a clear vision of the added value his worker differentiation could provide, John found immediate success:

> It went over big because they felt they could trust you more than some other people. I guess they figured they knew the college, and they knew that these kids were coming from out of town and paying a lot of money to go to school, and thus they were probably not going to rip them off. Our workers looked clean-cut and had a good reputation.

From private parties, the business branched out into events at the Historical Society and the Antiquarian Society—societies of older rich people—and eventually into supplying workers for catering companies and even the Marriott Hotel, once for a group of parties serving 2,000 guests. Some of the work with institutions, such as the art museum, evolved into long-term contracts that continued long after John sold the business. In the spring of his junior year, John hired a student manager to run the operation when he left campus to participate in a school project in Ireland. After he returned to WPI, John kept the student manager on, satisfied that the business could succeed without his day-to-day attention and eager to avoid the "hassles" involved in rounding workers up on short notice:

> So then I hired a manager. If I was getting three dollars an hour over what I paid the workers, I gave him a dollar an hour for every person he got, and the company got two. I had a guy running the whole thing for me while I was on campus, and I was just cutting checks, managing the books. So I took it to the management level. I took it one step more.

John continued the business for several years after he graduated. Although it never made the money it had during his own tenure as manager, it did continue to provide valuable learning experiences. John dealt with expenses and headaches related to Workers Compensation and other insurance matters, and learned about incorporating the business in order to protect personal assets after he purchased a house. At one point, he envisioned a regional company with operations based at college campuses all along the East Coast. Chapters of his fraternity at other schools would provide a natural launching point and initial contacts for employees and alumni clients. Although he did start an outlet in Providence with its own manager, expansion plans fell victim to full-time responsibilities at Pepsi, other business opportunities, night school (Babson MBA program), and family life:

> I had to focus all my energies and go back to what my father taught me: be successful at one thing. So I had to get rid of this catering business because I was not making enough

money and I didn't see a clear future. I would have had to franchise to expand . . . I ended up selling it to my father. Really for no money. He bought it for a dollar. It's been going okay.

GROUNDWORK FOR A PARTNERSHIP

The project that took John to Ireland in the fourth quarter of his junior year was a social research study on entrepreneurship—a natural fit with his activities at WPI. John and two classmates went armed with six months of preparation research, an introduction to a professor in Ireland through professor Bill Bygrave of Babson College, and strong assumptions about the state of entrepreneurial endeavors and the needs of the populace. They quickly discovered that their "assumptions were pretty much 180 degrees in the wrong direction." Instead of a business community thirsting for entrepreneurial information and advice, they found one practically drowned by government business assistance programs. With their original intentions thwarted, the students regrouped and revised the project, putting together a seven-page questionnaire to administer to older students about their family business backgrounds and interest in entrepreneurship. The team developed a plan to track the group and re-interview them five years later to determine the extent of their entrepreneurial activities and to identify key indicators and/or conditions of success.

In addition to the learning experience of having to adjust procedures and objectives to respond to changing circumstances, and the benefits of exploring a society's entrepreneurial attitudes and conditions, the project provided an unexpected gain. John and one of the other project team members formed a close, working relationship that would become the foundation for a business partnership. Glenn Butler had been a lab partner with John during their freshman year, and the experience had left John with an indelible impression of Glenn's abilities. In contrast to the third team member, Glenn and John discovered that their habits and work patterns (sleeping, rising, studying) were very compatible, and the experience of spending nearly every waking hour together, working on the project for more than two months, confirmed John's earlier inclination that Glenn was the type of person he would like to have as a business partner:

> I identified early on that this guy was brilliant. He ended up graduating top of his class in electrical engineering, which is one of the harder disciplines in engineering, with high distinctions in several honor societies. He didn't get anything but A's, and in that school it is really difficult to get As in Electrical Engineering. He was a phenomenal person, and I knew that this is the type of guy that I would want to work with. I could see starting a business with him. I threw it out a few times when we were in Ireland. I can't remember how receptive he was. I remember feeling that I was more into it than he was.

GLENN BUTLER, FUTURE PARTNER

Glenn Butler was born in New Jersey, moved several times as the result of his father's corporate transfers, and finally settled in Harvard, Massachusetts, for his high school years. After 20 years in the corporate world, Glenn's father left his position as CFO at Foster Grant to purchase and operate a building supply business, which blossomed and then faded in concert with the 1980s real estate boom and bust rollercoaster. Glenn's affinity for computers dated back to his use of the IBM PC (an original model) that Mr. Butler had purchased to help run his business. Glenn was one of a few high school students doing papers on a word processor.

From Glenn's perspective, the experience in Ireland with John cemented a friendship that had been good though not especially deep during their first three years at WPI. While he lacked John's distinct memories of their freshman lab experience, he did recall many late-night, after-party meetings in which they talked long into the night. Glenn also developed a clear sense of John's character and strengths, which he saw as complementing his own:

> I'm a details guy and he's a "big picture, on the surface, go forward" guy. John had a knack. Of all the guys at WPI, it was obvious that he was the one who was really sociable and could get in there, do stuff, and sell. He had an incredible amount of energy. I'll say, "we can't do that," and he's almost shallow, letting nothing deter him. He's a straight-ahead guy. It's a great partnership.

FIRST JOBS

After graduating from WPI, both Glenn and John went to work for established companies (see Appendix). In spite of his electrical engineering major, Glenn decided against a job in computer hardware development, preferring instead the immediate feedback on creative ideas available from writing software: "You build it, you see it work and then you get to fix it really quick." Glenn turned down several offers doing digital circuit design and went to work for Stratus Computer in software engineering. A self-described happy-go-lucky guy, for whom things always seemed to fall into place, he had no grand plan in mind for where the job might lead. It was simply a chance to do exciting, enjoyable work on a completely flexible schedule that allowed sufficient opportunity to pursue other interests.

John interviewed with numerous large corporations and garnered offers from six prestigious firms: Arthur Andersen Consulting, DuPont, Westinghouse, Texas Instruments, UPS, and PepsiCo. In spite of his entrepreneurial experience and ambition to start another business, John knew exactly what he wanted from his first post-college employment: on-the-job business education. Although the Pepsi offer didn't match some of the others in compensation, John thought its training program would best serve his long-term goals:

> I really had it in my head that I wanted a training program. I felt I was putty and I needed to be molded by a good company. At first I wasn't going to work for Pepsi but . . . I interviewed with them four times. They brought me all over the country to different places. It wasn't until the very last time when I went to their headquarters in New York that I saw the manuscript (for the training program). He showed me the loose leaf manuscript of the program and said, "Here, take a look at this." I liked it. That's what the kicker was. I had a lot of job offers making a lot more money from other companies. I took this one because it had the best training program.

Pepsi's Operations Training Program accepted 60 graduates that year (1989) and 60 the next, before the company stopped running it. For the first three months, the trainees rotated through virtually every division in the company—from manufacturing to marketing—for a week at a time. After every stop, they were tested on their knowledge of the function, from production process flow to supermarket shelf location protocols. John had a bird's eye view of everything; in his week in marketing, he was on the ground floor negotiating with Star Market on Pepsi TV ads. The next three months were devoted to on-the-job training, followed by a job assignment. In spite of his manufacturing engineering background, John ended up in the distribution side of the program. He was assigned as distribution manager for New England, overseeing the operations of six locations with 300 vehicles and a $6 million budget. The real challenge was managing a dozen experienced mechanics, many of whom were the age of his father. John, a self-proclaimed "whippersnapper out of college" who couldn't do much more than change his car's oil, learned a great deal about managing people in difficult circumstances.

After a year and a half as a distribution manager, John was offered the opportunity to go into the manufacturing side of the business, with the likelihood of becoming a plant manager in three years at a "lucrative" $100,000 salary. He had also made enough connections in the company, however, to secure a job through a VP of sales. In spite of the valuable experience in distribution and the opportunities in manufacturing, John saw his future outside of operations:

> I went into sales because I knew I was going to start a company. I said, "I've got to get experience." I learned a lot, but I knew I never was going to do anything with transportation or trucks. I got into sales and that was the best move I ever made.

John did not find being a district sales manger for Pepsi a glamorous job:

> I had salesmen, route salesmen, the guys riding the trucks delivering soda for half the state of Rhode Island reporting to me. I had quotas and sales objectives and the whole bit. If I saw a place that could possibly sell soda, even if I didn't think they could sell soda I was going to try to get them to sell soda. It was crazy. I learned a lot about how products get distributed. I ended up being the sales rep that called on 7–Eleven™ stores for Rhode Island. That's when I learned about distribution channels and how to deal with franchises. That's what was key.

GENESIS OF THE ENTREPRENEURIAL VENTURE

On Tuesday, February 20, 1990, about nine months after starting their jobs at Pepsi and Stratus Computer, John and Glenn Butler met in a Dunkin' Donuts on Park Avenue in Worcester, Massachusetts. They drank coffee and committed to a common vision of the future: starting a business. It was to be the first of many meetings over the next six months, where they'd sit and hash over potential business possibilities. Initially, the field of discussion was wide open. Glenn was tremendously excited about the idea of a new-car buying service. Eventually, however, John and Glenn came to focus on computer-related business concepts. For Glenn, it was a natural extension of his formal education and work experience. For John, the interest in computers came from several sources. The summer of his junior year he had worked for EMC, manufacturing disk drives, and he had liked the company and computer industry environment. He also wanted to get away from the more mundane problems involved in a manual service business:

> So Glenn and I said, "Let's do it." We thought we were going to sell computers. We'd either make them or do something. We didn't know what we were going to do, so we kept meeting and talking. Because I was on the street meeting with people for Pepsi, selling soft drinks to basically small businesspeople, I kept on picking their brains. Asking lots of questions. What is needed out here?

John's questions and contacts with small business owners eventually led to some consulting work for Glenn. He developed a software program to facilitate the operation of a electrician's company and then automated a small supermarket. Those jobs led to the idea of providing computer services to similar small businesses. John saw that numerous mom-and-pop grocery/convenience stores and small supermarkets were in dire need of some form of computerized information systems. The partners envisioned selling computers to these businesses complete with customized software—essentially functioning as value-added resellers. As John continued talking with store owners and potential customers, he eventually became dissatisfied with the idea. While many small stores clearly needed computerization, they often lacked the basic business sophistication to understand that need and to comprehend the advantages of computer-based solutions. Moreover, many of them simply didn't have the cash to invest in a system. Although he lined up a few businesses who wanted a computer to handle some software, it never really reached the point of selling software:

> You think that just because someone is in business they make money, but it's not true. Those mom-and-pop convenience stores just don't make money. The owners are working a million hours, and the only way they are making any money is because they don't have to pay someone else. So I didn't see that there was a big market there. There are many of that type of operation but for one reason or another they aren't ready for computerization.

INTRODUCTION TO THE VENDING BUSINESS— MARKET RESEARCH

Then one day a Pepsi customer with whom John had become friends inquired about software to automate the operation of her vending machine company. As a former CPA, the woman was knowledgeable about business and accounting and knew what she wanted and what would help her run the business. Glenn and John met several times with the prospective client and hashed out an agreement to develop a totally customized software package for $550—"the best deal in America," according to John. The low price, however, came with a long turn-around time because their full-time jobs permitted only spare time work on the project. It took almost a year before the software program was operational. The partners and their client met every month, reviewing progress, discussing program needs, and refining the product. They were paid $275 at an estimated halfway point and a final $275 after they delivered the finished version in January 1992. Though the product didn't have many bells and whistles, it did "work the way they wanted it to work."

As with many custom software jobs, the question arose, "Can we sell this to other companies?" John began to explore the business potential of this niche market, following his instincts to conduct research and develop an estimate of market size. Based on a list of Pepsi's vending machine customers, he calculated the number of vending operations in three regional markets—Rhode Island, southeastern Massachusetts, and Boston—and then extrapolated from those to project the potential size of the industry and market nationwide. John's original estimate was three to four thousand small vending companies in the United States. The guess proved to be far short of the actual number, later gleaned from an industry census report, yet it was sufficient to whet his curiosity:

> I didn't know that stuff (census reports) existed. Maybe this is because of my background in engineering; you don't know how to get research unless someone teaches you. No one had ever taught me about census reports and stuff like that. Now if I go to a new market, I know what to do. I know who I would call and what I would ask for.

Along the way John discovered NAMA—National Automatic Merchandising Association—the industry association for automatic merchandising through vending machines. In the spring of 1992, John and Glenn attended a small regional association trade show in New York. To keep costs down for the suppliers and the small businesses that comprised a large portion of the membership, the affair was staged around a pool in a suburban hotel, with vendors setting up displays outside and within the poolside rooms. Though John and Glenn were surprised at the low turn-out, the 80 or more exhibitors seemed to outnumber the attendees, they used the uncrowded conditions to good advantage. Posing as a couple of eager, young business kids starting up a vending company, they picked as many brains as possible about the industry, and about industry-specific software. Only one potential competitor was at the trade show, exhibiting a software program that had been under development for six or seven years. John and Glenn were somewhat humbled, but also encouraged by what they saw:

> We were kind of taken aback. We thought that we had something pretty good but this company had worked on their program for probably six or seven years prior to this period. They had been around for about 10 years or more. They had a lot of features. Can we get up to speed fast enough? Can we compete with this? It wasn't as easy to use as ours, though. We had some merits.

The partners went back to the drawing board and added some of the features they'd seen in the competitor's product. They also continued to get feedback from the customer, who functioned as their one beta test site. By now John was regularly reviewing the trade publications and was encouraged by the relative paucity of advertisements for other software products on the market, especially products targeting small and medium-sized businesses. By his reckoning, there were only five or six companies selling vending machine software, and most of the products were aimed at larger companies that already had computer systems in place. The vending software programs of these competitors started at about $5,000 and went up to $60,000.

> They all wrote off the small guys and went after the big ones, hence they charged a lot. It just happened that we started with a small company and automated it, so we had software for small companies. We looked at what our competitors were doing and decided it made sense to stay where we were in the market.

Half a year after the regional trade show, John and Glenn were ready to take their product to the October 1992 NAMA convention, held in Washington DC. With both men holding full-time jobs, the only way they could arrange to attend the show was to use vacation time, and fortunately they both were able to schedule time-off during the convention week. They went; they set up their booth; they learned. The product, priced at a show special $995 (regular price $1295), created substantial interest. As the only software targeted at small businesses, the Streamline booth drew large crowds that were generally very receptive. Many people recognized the potential of the product to save time and reduce costs. Yet, while people were excited about the ease of use of the program, they also wanted more features, more "bells and whistles." To be really worthwhile, the product needed to be able to handle all the aspects of the vending business.

Although the show produced no immediate sales, it produced hundreds of leads. Also very important, it provided exposure for product and company, and it generated additional market research directly from potential customers. The show also gave John and Glenn the customer/market confirmation they were looking for:

> We saw people's eyes light up, "Wow. This is really good!" We said all right, this is a viable product. We are going to go forward.

REFINING THE PRODUCT

Energized by the experience and the new market intelligence, John and Glenn once again returned to the drawing board. Glenn quit his job at Stratus Computer shortly after Thanksgiving 1992 and started working to incorporate the suggestions and feedback from the Washington show. The revised product needed to be ready in time for the next major association event in April 1993, the Atlantic Coast Exposition in Myrtle Beach, South Carolina. Although Glenn recognized that there were competitors with better products, he was confident that it was "just a matter of time before we could outsmart them":

> When I made the decision to leave Stratus, John was actually more serious about the business than I was. He was the driving force. I've always been a lot more haphazard about how I live. "Yeah, whatever, sounds great to me. I'll certainly quit my job and start working on this." But it was also a big relief to leave. At that time I was burning the candle at all ends, playing in a band, doing a lot of recording—I had a company that did sound for bands—and working on the Tracker program. I was only putting in 35-hour weeks at Stratus. If you care about the people you work with, it's tough to handle

a situation like that, so I was glad to get out. I had $15,000 in Stratus stock and figured I could live off that for quite a while. No more corporate America for me.

As Glenn pursued software development full-time, John followed up on the leads from the Washington convention, which eventually produced the first three sales, and continued with other marketing and sales tasks. By that time he was far enough along the learning curve in his job at Pepsi that he had developed an efficient routine which allowed him to complete his work in a fairly standard 40-hour week, leaving some time for Streamline. As the April exposition approached, however, and Version 2.5 of Vending Tracker neared completion, he knew that soon he was going to have to decide whether or not to commit full-time to the business.

Working out of their homes throughout this start-up phase, John and Glenn were able to keep business expenses down to about $500 a month, mainly for phone lines, promotional materials, and office and computer supplies. They also took full advantage of opportunities for free publicity. By early 1993, John was starting to develop good relationships with the editors of several trade publications, and Streamline was able to build market awareness through a series of articles, favorable product reviews, and press releases. The success of this free exposure obviated the need to spend cash on advertising. Trade shows were the other major expense for the business, costing about $3,000 (close to the trade show rule-of-thumb of three times the booth fee). In addition to the fee of $900, other show expenses included travel, booth presentation materials, special promotional literature, and mailings to potential customers.

Thus far, John and Glenn had financed the start-up costs with savings and earnings from their other jobs. When Glenn left Stratus Computer in November 1992, he had sufficient savings to carry him through the program refinement process. John had gotten married in 1991 at about the time he and Glenn started talking about going into business, and he and his wife had purchased a three-family house in Rhode Island the next year, where they lived in the top floor unit. Although the rent covered most of the mortgage, the purchase had depleted John's savings and he was wary about relying on his wife's income to support them if he left Pepsi prematurely. Cash flow would be tight unless sales picked up quickly. Moreover, in spite of John's confidence in the venture, his wife was less sanguine about its prospects, "I would say that she believes in me, but I don't think she has 100 percent confidence that this product or this market is the best one."

Also adding to the difficulty of John's decision was his situation at Pepsi, where a long successful career looked promising and lucrative:

> The next step was a pretty cushy job: regional sales manager or marketing manager. I'd make good money and get a company car, but it was probably two years away.

PREPARATION QUESTIONS

1. Has Glenn made a good career move?
2. Should John quit Pepsi and join Glenn full-time?
3. What factors did you contemplate as you considered questions 1 and 2?

APPENDIX: RESUMES

JOHN H. ROUGHNEEN

Professional Experience

PEPSI-COLA COMPANY, Cranston, Rhode Island

District Sales Manager (November 1990 to present)
Responsible for establishing and achieving sales objectives within an 875 account customer base with annual revenues in excess of $5 million.

- Coordinate sales execution.
- Conduct corporate level buyer calls.
- Design marketing strategies.
- Control promotional spending and market equipment placement.

Distribution Team Manager (June 1989 to November 1990)
Responsible for the annual delivery of 6 million soft drink cases. Financial responsibility of $2.3 million relating to the repair and maintenance of 300 vehicles.

EMC CORPORATION, Hopkinton, Massachusetts

Manufacturing Engineer (June 1988 to March 1989)
Liaison between the marketing, sales and design teams for the introduction and manufacturing of prototype memory and disk drive enhancements for Hewlett Packard, IBM, DEC, Prime, and Wang compatible computer systems.

COLLEGE ESSENTIALS, Worcester, Massachusetts

Owner (October 1987 to September 1990)
Founded agency to supply waiters, bartenders, and valets for catering companies and private parties. Annual revenues of $45,000.

Education

Worcester Polytechnic Institute, Worcester, Massachusetts
Graduated with distinction in May 1989 - BS Manufacturing Engineering

Babson College, Babson Park, Massachusetts
Candidate for Masters in Business Administration

References available upon request.

GLENN BUTLER

Professional Experience

STREAMLINE BUSINESS SYSTEMS, Barrington, Rhode Island

Co-Owner and VP of Systems Development (November 1990 to present)
Responsible for:

- Design and development of software programs and computer code.
- Customer technical support.
- Technical support of sales and marketing.

STRATUS COMPUTER, Marlborough, Massachusetts

Computer Software Engineer (June 1990 to November 1992)
Responsible for:

- UNIX development.
- Designing user interfaces.
- Coordinating user support services.

Education

Worcester Polytechnic Institute, Worcester, Massachusetts
Graduated with high distinction in May 1989—BS Electrical Engineering

References available upon request.

2 SCOTT TOMPKINS

At the beginning of April 1987, two students walked into Professor Ron Ditchin's office at Bessemer College and introduced themselves. They were Scott Tompkins and Rachel Waller. Scott's friends had suggested that he should talk to Ron Ditchin about his ideas for opening a travel agency on the Bessemer campus. Ron invited them to share their ideas with him.

Over the next three weeks, Ron discussed the new business idea with Scott on several occasions. Scott's enthusiasm seemed boundless. However, Scott's father and mother were somewhat less than enthusiastic. Scott's father had expressed his concerns in a letter to Ron (see Exhibit 2.1). After Ron read the letter, he wondered how he should handle the situation. He also mused over his new sedate life as an academic.

BESSEMER COLLEGE

Bessemer College was an increasingly well-known western business school with approximately 1,500 undergraduates, 250 full-time MBA students, and 1,300 part-time MBA students. There were about 100 full-time faculty members. It was in Hillsborough, California, about 15 miles from San Francisco. Barrons rated it as highly competitive. Students at Bessemer could major in entrepreneurial studies as well as traditional subjects. Bessemer College had a worldwide reputation as a leading school in entrepreneurship education and research. Its entrepreneurial studies group had five full-time faculty members.

This case was prepared by Professor William Bygrave. Copyright © 1987 Babson College. All rights reserved. Names and locations have been changed. However, information relevant to case analysis remains unaltered.

EXHIBIT 2.1   Robert Tompkins letter of concern.

April 30, 1987

Professor Ronald C. Ditchin
Bessemer College
Hillsborough, CA 92126

CONFIDENTIAL

Dear Professor Ditchin:

Thank you for the interest, support, encouragement, and advice that you have given Scott in his pursuit of becoming an entrepreneur.

I am very proud of Scott. He has grown from an average high school student to an outstanding college student who tackles his studies with vigor. It was not long ago that Scott hesitated to step into a library. Now, he not only spends hours in the Bessemer library, but in the search for data on any area that interests him, he visits Stanford and Berkeley libraries.

Scott got a job with Bear Stearns in Boston last summer that was eagerly sought by many other students. He did such a good job that the manager of the San Francisco office of Bear Stearns heard about him and called him to work part time in the San Francisco office to set up cost control systems for their office.

Last fall, I suggested to Scott that it would be a good practical experience to try setting up a small business. He worked on a program of providing client investment analysis for stock brokers but dropped that after finding that a few brokers were not receptive.

During a discussion at home during the Christmas break, an on-campus travel agency was suggested. Scott pursued this by talking to you and other professors and found out about the travel agency business plan put together by graduate students.

Scott claims that you told him that the plan was viable, that by pushing the administration, they could get office space in Fenn Hall, that it was possible for them to raise venture capital to finance the operation, and they should be able to get some of Bessemer's business by pushing Jerry Kyoto. Now, Scott is all fired up and totally committed. He put out a survey and within two days, he has received over 400 responses. Needless to say, he is excited. Then he calls me this morning all upset. He got a C in last week's Economics test. This business is interfering with his studies and that is a big problem.

I think it is great to help and encourage students to start businesses. However, there should be a policy to strictly limit the scope of any such business so it should not interfere with a student's studies. Secondly, the emphasis on starting a business should be first on gaining the experience of creating a viable business plan and more important, the actual start-up and operation of the business.

The extent of Scott's work on this project has been to read several books and to conduct the survey. He has got the names of several Bessemer alumni in the travel business in the San Francisco area.

I have raised the following questions and suggestions to which Scott responds that I am negative and not supportive:

1. Have you discussed your idea with any people in the travel business? (He has never been in a travel agency.)

2. How are you going to operate a full-fledged business and go to school? (He is going to hire a full-time professional manager to run the business.)

3. Why don't you limit the scope of the business to something you can reasonably handle while going to school, like starting with only airline tickets? (No answer.)

EXHIBIT 2.1 *(Continued)*

4. Why don't you talk to Bessemer alumni in the travel business about your opening a satellite operation on campus in affiliation with them? (No answer.)

5. How are you going to handle the financing of the business? (Venture capital.)

   Scott is under the impression that you have encouraged him to go full speed ahead and he is smart and determined and unrealistic and he will succeed, but now is not the time.

   He is talking of staying at Bessemer for the summer, going to summer school, and working on the plan. I asked where he was going to get the money to pay for summer school and housing? He doesn't know. And how is he going to replace the $3,500 that he can make on his summer job that is needed for school expenses? (No answer.)

   Enough of a rambling father. What I would like you to do is speak to Scott. Tell him that we had a good discussion and as a result, you would advise him to go home for the summer, work on the business plan, complete all the research (in particular, talk to people in the travel business), and work at Bear Stearns or at a travel agency in Boston. And tell him that he can always speak to you on the phone if he wants to discuss the business plan and that he should get some rest and relaxation during the summer and return to school in the fall with a clear head, a tan, and a complete business plan.

   Thank you for your cooperation.

Yours truly,

Robert Tompkins

Professor Ron Ditchin

Ron Ditchin joined Bessemer in the fall of 1985 as a visiting associate professor. A brief biographical sketch is shown in Exhibit 2.2. As well as teaching three entrepreneurship courses each semester (a normal teaching load at Bessemer), Ron was also the academic coordinator of the entrepreneurial studies program, the faculty advisor to the Bessemer Entrepreneurial Exchange, and an active scholar specializing in venture capital. After his first semester at Bessemer, he was asked to stay, so he resigned from Hayward College, where he had been a tenure-track associate professor.

   In his first 18 months at Bessemer, he published three articles in refereed journals; he presented competitive papers at two national meetings; he presented two invited review papers; he was invited to join the Entrepreneurship Teaching Committee of the Academy of Management; he published two book reviews; and he was a reviewer of papers submitted for the Academy of Management Annual Meeting.

   Bessemer demanded excellent teaching and placed great importance on that when considering faculty for promotion and tenure. Based on student evaluations and his annual review with the chairman of the department, Ron felt that students and fellow faculty were satisfied with his teaching. He also knew that his name had been one of those submitted by students for the "Teacher of the Year" award, but he had not won it.

   Ron, who had a doctorate in applied mathematics, was enrolled in the DBA program at San Francisco University. He had originally enrolled in a DBA program

EXHIBIT 2.2   Resume.

RONALD C. DITCHIN

Ronald C. Ditchin, BA (Harvard, 1959), MS, PhD (Brown, 1964), MBA (Santa Clara, 1979) is a visiting associate professor of management and academic coordinator of the entrepreneurship program at Bessemer College. His scholarly interests include entrepreneurship, emerging technologies, venture capital, and organizational change. His recent research has focused on the flows of venture capital to highly innovative technological companies. In 1984, he and a partner founded and started up the IHS Data Base Service.

Before he began his academic career in 1979, Dr. Ditchin did basic research on the structure of DNA molecules, founded a venture capital backed start-up, and managed a division of a NYSE company. His company received a hi-tech award for developing one of the hundred most significant technical products that were introduced in the U.S.A. in 1976. He has marketed technological products worldwide. He is the author of a textbook and several papers on experimental biophysics.

His consulting includes strategic planning for technology companies. Among his recent clients are 3M, Hewlett-Packard, Intel, Beckman, and Syntex.

to learn the research methodologies of the social and business sciences. But he found that Bessemer expected him to complete his DBA degree before it would grant him tenure-track rather than visiting status. In January, he had passed his comprehensive exams and was planning to write his dissertation over the summer of 1987.

SCOTT TOMPKINS: A TRAVEL AGENCY START-UP

Ron had never met Scott or Rachel before they walked into his office. Scott and his partner had come to Ron to seek advice about the possibility of becoming entrepreneurship majors. This was their sophomore year, so they would need to take their first required entrepreneurship course in the fall if they wanted to earn majors in that subject. Ron explained the requirements for the entrepreneurship major and encouraged them to consider it. He told them that in one of their required courses they would have to write a business plan for a start-up company.

Scott told Ron that they wanted to start a travel agency on campus. Ron asked what had become his standard opening question to students who told him they were going to open a new venture: What do you know about _____ ? In this case, travel agencies.

"Well, we travel a lot. I live in Boston," Scott responded.

"Has either of you ever worked in a travel agency?" Ron asked.

"No."

"Do your parents or a close friend have an agency, or do they work in the travel business?" Ron asked.

"No."

"Well, I'm not saying that you always need to have worked in a business before you start a similar one, but we do know that approximately 90 percent of all businesses are started by people with experience in the same industry. . . . And by experience, I don't mean as customers. For example, I see lots of students who want to start a fast-food chain. I always ask them if they have worked in McDonald's or a similar restaurant. If they haven't—which is usually the case—I tell them to get a job in a fast-food restaurant, and then come back to see me. One student actually did that last semester. He was hired by the local McDonald's. He became friends with the regional manager who is responsible for selecting new franchisees and helping them open their restaurants. In two months, he learned enough to write a plan for opening his own fast-food restaurant. Another student walked into this office and told me he had this great idea for a fast-food restaurant. I asked him the same question. He told me he had worked in a Burger King. He had hated every minute. He had quit at the end of his first day. He said he couldn't stand fast food. I told him to forget about becoming a fast-food entrepreneur."

"So you think we should work for a travel agent?" Scott asked.

"Definitely. Get a job with an agency in the Boston area this summer. Ask lots of questions. Find out as much as possible about all aspects of the business. Come back to see me in the fall. I will be glad to help you write a business plan."

"But this opportunity won't wait that long. And anyway, we have only two more years at Bessemer. We want to start this agency so that it is in place by the beginning of the fall semester," Scott replied.

"I think you should talk to a couple of MBA students who wrote a business plan for a campus travel agency. They were students in MG 501: Entrepreneurship. They are graduating next month so they will not actually open the agency, but the numbers were quite encouraging. Here are their names. Tell them that I suggested that they talk to you."

"Thanks. We will talk to them. Is there anything else we should do?" Scott said.

"Well, first of all, get a job with a travel agency this summer. But you could make some preliminary inquiries. Talk to Jerry Kyoto. He is head of all administrative matters. He is one of the most powerful persons on this campus. He insists that we all buy tickets for college travel from Hillsborough Valley Travel. He objects if we buy them anywhere else, even though it is better for Bessemer's cash-flow when we buy tickets on our personal credit cards. He could tell you how much Bessemer spends each year on official travel. What's more, Bessemer has offices on campus that can be rented by for-profit businesses. You will need one of those. Jerry is in charge of them. You will need some capital. Where will that come from? Telephone John Herbacek at International Charter. His company is one of the largest charter travel businesses in the United States. He founded it when he was a few years out of the Stanford MBA program. He came to talk to our students last year. He was really innovative in the way he raised his initial capital. Tell him I suggested you should talk to him."

"Thanks very much for your help. We will talk to those MBA students and Jerry Kyoto," Scott said.

"O.K. Come and see me at any time. If I am not here call me at home," Ron replied.

Spring Fever

A couple of weeks later, Ron bumped into Rachel on the campus.

"How are your plans for a travel agency going?" Ron greeted her.

"Scott and I are not getting along so well at the moment," she replied.

"I'm sorry to hear that. I tell my students that a sure way of testing the strength of a relationship is to start a business," Ron said with a smile.

As he walked away, Ron thought to himself, "That's the end of another idea for a student business. On this campus, they come and go faster than student romances during spring break." So he was quite surprised when he received a call from Scott on Friday, April 24, asking if he could come to the office to discuss his plans for the campus travel agency.

"Could you wait until final exams are over in about 10 days?" Ron asked.

Ron was extremely busy. He had a very intense 10-day period ahead of him. On Monday in Vancouver, he was addressing the Financial Research Foundation of Canada on venture capital for high-tech start-ups. He was flying to Vancouver on Sunday morning so that he could have lunch with the parents of an MBA student at a new restaurant that they had started six-months earlier. He was planning to return to San Francisco on Monday night, and after he had taught his class on Tuesday, he was flying to Boston for a three-day research conference on entrepreneurship at the University of Cape Cod, where he was presenting a paper. He had to prepare two presentations, one after-lunch talk, and review some drafts of students' business plans before he left for Vancouver on Sunday morning.

Scott continued, "This is really urgent. Jerry Kyoto was very discouraging. But we are going ahead anyway. We must see you today."

"O.K. Come on over. I can give you about 15 minutes at the most," Ron responded.

"Well," Ron thought, "I suppose I can always work on the plane and at the airport."

The Travel Agency

A few minutes later, Scott walked into the office with another student. Scott greeted Ron and said, "Professor Ditchin, I would like you to meet Mario Ricciardelli. He is going to be my partner in the travel agency."

Scott began, "Since we talked, I have put in a lot of work on the travel agency. I met with your MBA students. They are convinced there is enough business to support a travel agency on the Bessemer campus. But they wouldn't let us see their business plan. In addition, we have talked to some travel agencies about their helping us to set up an office on the Bessemer campus. They have been helpful."

He continued, "But Jerry Kyoto was very discouraging. He says there is no available space that we can rent on campus."

Ron said, "That's funny. He was very encouraging when my MBA students talked to him, I wonder what has changed his mind?"

"Well, he mentioned that he wants to have a travel agency on campus by next January. We suspect he intends to work a deal with Hillsborough Valley Travel," Scott replied. "He mentioned that there would be space in the new Student Center, which is opening early in 1988. But we can't wait until then. We want to open our agency in September."

"How much capital will you need and where will you get it?" Ron asked.

"We don't think that will be a problem. We are planning to talk to a few people who might be interested in investing. Do you know Andy Brown? He recently came to talk to the students. One of his customers invested $30,000 in his student business," Scott responded. "I'm going to stay in San Francisco for the summer to get this business started. Will you be able to help me?"

"Well, I will help you as much as possible. I will be on campus during May and parts of June. In July and August, I will be at my cottage in Carmel. I go there to write. I usually visit the campus once every two or three weeks during those two months."

Ron said, "Have you got a summer job with a travel agency?"

"No, not yet, but we are planning to do so."

"We are surveying faculty, administrators, and students to determine how much travel business we will get from the campus. We would like you to fill out this draft questionnaire and recommend any changes. We have already shown it to a statistics professor."

ROBERT TOMPKINS: SOME FATHERLY ADVICE

On Tuesday afternoon, April 28, Ron was working frantically in his office before he left to catch a flight to Boston. He had to read a revised copy of a paper that had been accepted for publication and had to be returned to the editor; speak with some students about the draft copies of their business plans; pick up the slides from Media Services and put them in the correct sequence for his talk to the research conference at the University of Cape Cod on Thursday; return about half-a-dozen phone calls; call the SBA; and clear his desk of paperwork that had accumulated on Monday. He had been mildly annoyed at lunch when, during a conversation between Ron and a colleague, he had mentioned that he was leaving for Boston that night, and the undergraduate dean had commented, "another junket."

He was with two seniors when his phone rang, "This is Robert Tompkins, Scott's father. He is the student who you are encouraging to start a travel agency on campus. I was at Bessemer this weekend. I visited your office on Monday, but you were not on campus. I left a message that I would like to get together with you in Boston this week."

Ron replied, "I would like to meet you. I'll be in Boston tomorrow at the University of Cape Cod research conference. Let's get together at the conference. Let's set up a date and a time."

"There's no need. I am a Bessemer alumnus and have been invited to attend that conference to meet the Bessemer faculty who are coming to the conference. I will find you there. However, before you leave for Boston, I would appreciate your talking to Scott about two things: (1) Limiting the scope of the planned travel business to something feasible for a full-time college student, (2) His tentative plans for staying in San Francisco for the summer, working at a travel agency and working with you on a business plan.

"Scott's concept of the travel business has included setting up a regular full-service agency on campus with an experienced manager. I would really like Scott to gain the experience of planning and starting and operating a business, but it is important that he has the guidance from you to limit the scope of the business to what is practical financially and time wise. A student like Scott who is so strongly motivated should certainly be encouraged in his endeavors. What is important here is the experience the student can get from planning the business AND successfully working the plan, no matter how small.

"Professor Ditchin, it gets very emotional when I make suggestions to Scott about his business plans, so I would appreciate your encouraging him to limit the scope of his plans and return home for the summer."

"Robert, I will try to get a hold of him right away. I will definitely speak to him before I leave for Boston. I am sorry that I was not in the office yesterday. I would have liked to talk to you and Scott together. I look forward to meeting with you at the University of Cape Cod," Ron said.

Ron rang Scott's number but there was no reply. He finished talking to the students. There were four others waiting. Sometime later, Scott entered Ron's office.

"We must talk. Your father just called me. He wants you to return home to Boston for the summer."

"I know. He doesn't want me to start this business. But he's not to blame. He should understand. He has started five businesses—all successful. It's my mother. She can't bear the thought of me being away from home for the summer."

"Your father said you need to work to help pay for your education. Is that critical?" Ron asked.

"We're not rich. But we are comfortably-off middle-class. It is not a matter of my not coming back to school if I don't earn as much money as I did last year at Bear Stearns. I am staying in San Francisco to start this business."

"How about your grades? Do you have any problems? Your father is quite concerned," Ron said.

"No problem. I have better than a 3 GPA. (2 is required to graduate, and 4 is the maximum possible)."

"Well, I will meet your father in Boston and talk to him. Does he realize you can get academic credit for doing this?" Ron said.

"Tell him this is a good idea and he should encourage me to do it. It won't cost him a penny. He has already said he won't help me financially with the business. Have a nice trip to Boston. See you next week."

THE MERMAID RESTAURANT, HYANNIS

On Thursday evening, April 30, Ron was relaxing over a cocktail at the Mermaid Restaurant, where the conference dinner was being held. Just before the dinner was to be served, Robert Tompkins came up to Ron and introduced himself and his wife and younger son, who was a senior in high school. They were a very pleasant family. They chatted with Ron for about 15 minutes.

During the conversation, Ron tried to be reassuring about Scott. Mrs. Tompkins said that Scott was calling them frequently. There had been five calls during the last 24 hours. She was trying to find a summer course in Boston that would help Scott to learn more about the travel business. She had found one, but Scott had announced that he would come home for May, return to San Francisco for June and July, when Professor Ditchin would be available to help him with his plan, and then return home for August. The Tompkins weren't too pleased with that idea.

Robert explained that they had been at Bessemer on Monday to show his younger son the campus. Robert and his son had met with John Welch, the president of Bessemer, on Monday. Robert also mentioned that he had talked to Jerry Kyoto, who was a classmate of his in the Bessemer class of 1958. He said he hadn't seen Jerry in almost 30 years.

As Ron and the Tompkins were saying good-bye, Robert handed Ron a letter marked confidential (Exhibit 2.1). He told Ron to read it later.

BESSEMER COLLEGE, MONDAY, MAY 4—JUST ANOTHER DAY AT THE OFFICE

As Ron walked into his office at 8:15 A.M., he wondered when he would have time to call Scott Tompkins. Ron had returned to San Francisco from Boston on the evening flight so that he would have all of Saturday and Sunday at home. As soon as he walked through the door on Friday night, his wife told him that two students had telephoned and wanted him to return their calls. At lunchtime on Saturday, the student who was the executive vice president of the Bessemer Entrepreneurial Exchange had phoned to tell him that Carol Leitch, the part-time administrator of that organization, had undergone major surgery at Stanford Medical Center on Thursday. The surgery had been successful, but she would not be back at work this semester. In the afternoon, a member of the Alumni Board had telephoned to discuss an important matter. A student had phoned to ask for help because he was unable to reconcile the balance sheet with the income statement in the business plan he was writing. In the early evening, another student phoned to ask if she could postpone her business plan by two days so that she could incorporate some new, important information.

On Sunday, Ron had worked for about eight hours on the preparation of his teaching materials. There were two more telephone calls from students—the last one at 10:15 P.M. That evening, he and his wife, Jane, had watched a TV movie on the life of Henry Ford. Ron was editing an article at the same time. At one stage, Henry Ford said to his wife, "I love you." To which Mrs. Ford had retorted, "No Henry, you haven't loved anyone for 20 years. You only love your company." Jane had commented sarcastically to Ron, "And isn't that the truth. Just like someone I could name."

Ron usually arrived at Bessemer at 7:15 A.M. Today, he had not arrived until 8:15 A.M. because he had attended a breakfast with two of his fellow entrepreneurial studies faculty to discuss funding for research with a prospective sponsor. He had an exam that started at 8:30 A.M. He checked his telephone messages for anything that was urgent. One message was from the president of a small high-tech firm who had interviewed five of Ron's students for the position of administrative assistant to the president. He had narrowed his choice to two candidates and wanted to discuss them with Ron over lunch. Ron left a message for his secretary to call the president and tell him that the only possible time he could meet was 1:30 P.M. to 2:30 P.M.

The rest of his day was going to be busy. The exam would last until 1:30 P.M. He had appointments with students from 2:30 P.M. until 4:00 P.M. Then at 4:00 P.M., he was meeting with an alumna who was seeking Ron's advice about a small business she had started.

It was 5:00 P.M. when he finally found time to telephone Scott Tompkins. They agreed to meet for breakfast the next day. At 5:30 P.M., Ron's youngest daughter telephoned to ask him to pick her up at the high school at 6:00 P.M. As he drove along the Bayshore Freeway, he reflected on his day. The exams had gone well. He was pleased with the business plans that the students had presented. He was almost certain that he had secured a job for one of his students. But he was very frustrated because he had not been able to read most of the pile of mail on his desk; he had not phoned the SBA about next week's presentations; he had yet to arrange for a part-time instructor to teach the MBA entrepreneurship course in the second summer session; he had not returned telephone calls to at least half-a-dozen persons, including a senior manager at Ernst & Young in Los Angeles, which was one of his clients; he had not talked to the executive vice president of the Bessemer Entrepreneurial Exchange about the newsletter that was overdue because of the administrator's operation; and he wondered what else he had left undone.

"I must be crazy," he thought. "I am working longer hours than when I started my first high-tech company in 1970. Of course, it is not as stressful, but nor am I 32 years old anymore." That evening he was working at his computer and pondering what he should do about Scott, specifically, and about his own situation, generally, when the phone rang at 9:45 P.M.

"Hello, this is Pedro Ramirez. I am about to get my funding for the business. I have a final meeting with the investors on May 12. We could be cutting metal by June."

In the fall semester, Pedro had written a business plan for a high-tech start-up in Ron's MBA class. Several times over the last four months, Pedro had asked Ron for advice about the plan and its funding. Ron had a nice chat with Pedro. As he put the phone down, he said to himself, "That's what makes it all worthwhile. If Pedro gets his money, it will be the second plan from that class that has been funded."

Before falling asleep, Ron began to wonder about his breakfast meeting the next morning with Scott. "What will I do about Mr. Tompkins letter? What should I say to Scott?"

3 JACK SPRAT'S RESTAURANT

In November of 1995, Chris Harami, nascent entrepreneur, and soon-to-be founder of Jack Sprat's Restaurants, pondered his year-old business plan. The plan was a work-in-process, but he hoped to open the first Jack Sprat's Restaurant during the summer of 1996. Chris wondered how to best ensure success.

During the course of his research, he had discovered that many restauranteurs used consultants to launch new restaurant concepts.° People in the industry agreed that using a consultant was usually a good idea. However, hiring a consultant was expensive, and the seed money was coming from his father—a financially secure (but very conservative and not rich) physician. He had retainer bids from consultants between $50,000 and $150,000 and they all proposed rewriting the business plan as the first order of business. The consultant that Chris selected was Arlene Spiegel. She was enthusiastic about the concept and submitted the low bid.

Chris had written a professional-quality business plan in graduate school, then wrote and rewrote the plan for Jack Sprat's, so the value he saw in hiring a consultant was centered on building a successful team, and less on the business plan rewrite. Chris believed that Jack Sprat's could someday be a hot IPO and he wanted Arlene on the team to make sure it would happen, but his father did not understand the need. Was his father trying to micromanage the venture, or was this a role Chris wanted him to play? And did Chris really need a consultant to overhaul his plan, or was he just avoiding the leap into action? It was clear that they needed to conserve

---

This case was prepared by Mark Helman and Dan D'Heilly under the direction of Professor William Bygrave. Copyright © 1996 Babson College. All rights reserved.
° In the restaurant industry, new operations are usually designed around a single theme (e.g., American west steakhouse, home-cooking, ethnic). The theme is combined with the type of restaurant (e.g., fine dining, casual, fast food) and referred to as the "concept."

their scarce resources for the road ahead, but this might actually be a very conservative move.

CHRIS HARAMI

A connoisseur of fine cuisine and a cooking enthusiast, Chris had contemplated owning a restaurant from an early age. Now, at age 28, he was ready to move. His role models were his aunt and uncle who had been in the restaurant business since the 1960s. He liked the lifestyle:

> It was very social, almost like being in show business—they were celebrities. They were always talking to customers and they received a lot of recognition in the community. For years, my parents talked about opening a restaurant, but they never got into the details. It was always a distant, foggy dream.

Chris was overweight as a youth, and he consciously worked to control his weight as an adult. He was prone to the "yo-yo" weight-loss syndrome. He would diet and lose weight, then go off the diet and regain his original size. Chris was determined to lose weight, so he exercised regularly and vigorously. Unfortunately, his exercise program only offered a partial solution to his weight-loss problem. He felt and looked better, but didn't drop much weight.

Chris worked part-time in several restaurants while attending Pace University in New York City (Exhibit 3.1). He fell in love with the business and decided that he would someday open his own restaurant. Chris graduated with a business degree in 1990 and lived at home following college.

Things changed suddenly at the Harami's household when a stress test on his father revealed severe coronary blockage. His father, a physician, needed open-heart surgery. Afterwards, Dr. Harami was put on a diet low in fats, sodium, and cholesterol, and high in fiber. In support of this new lifestyle, the whole family changed the way they ate. Chris' exercise routine combined with his new diet reduced his waist size from 38 to 33. He was sold on the benefits of a healthy diet.

MBA: CREPE DU JOUR, S'IL VOUS PLAIS

In 1992, Chris enrolled in the Babson Graduate School of Business to "obtain the knowledge necessary to become a successful entrepreneur." One of his classes was New Venture Creation, a course where students formed teams to write business plans. In that class, his five-person team created a business plan for a chain of French quick-service restaurants (QSR) they called "Crepe du Jour." In the course of creating the business plan, Chris learned a great deal about success and failure in the restaurant business. Chris graduated in May 1994 with the intention of starting a chain of Crepe du Jour QSRs with his French team-member, Michael Tapiro.

As they continued to develop their plan, a negative trend became unmistakable: Their idea was not being well-received by industry analysts. The standard reaction to

EXHIBIT 3.1   Resume.

CHRISTOPHER C. HARAMI

Experience

Fall 1994   NEW ENGLAND BOOK COMPONENTS   HINGHAM, MA

Marketing Consultant
- Performed market research study to determine size and value of market.
- Forecasted financial and marketing impact of eleven key industry segments.
- Assisted management in defining key success factors and strategic focus.

1993   FLIGHT LTD.   KRASNODAR, RUSSIA

Trade Consultant
- Provided framework for Flight Ltd. to become an international trading entity, and supplier of goods to government level buyers.
- Developed strategic business plan to export Russian products to the West.
- Initiated contact and assisted in negotiating first successful import contracts between Flight Ltd., and Greek international trading firm.

1991–1992   CSM TRADING   WAYNE, NJ

Owner/ Manager
- Founded and managed an import/export company which specialized in high end consumer products.
- Imported high quality woolen goods from Australia and New Zealand.

1990–1991   LIBBYS CORPORATION   PATERSON, NJ

Restaurant Manager
- Managed restaurant with annual sales of over $1 million.
- Led team of 15 employees.

1990   PIZZA AND MORE   WAYNE, NJ

Restaurant Manager
- Managed full service Italian restaurant.
- Managed in-house computer system.

1989   BENNIGANS   WAYNE, NJ

Server
- Waited tables and insured quality presentation of meal.

1986–1987   THE ROOST   SAN JOSE, CA

Cook
- Cooked fast food meals for college students in campus foodservice facility.

Education

1992–1994   BABSON GRADUATE SCHOOL OF BUSINESS   WELLESLEY, MA
Master of Business Administration degree, May 1994. Concentrations in International Marketing, Entrepreneurship.

Fall 1993   NORWEGIAN SCHOOL OF MANAGEMENT   OSLO, NORWAY
Exchange program, concentrations in Euromanagement, Energy-management European business technique.

1987–1990   PACE UNIVERSITY   NEW YORK, NY
Bachelor of Business Administration, June, 1990. Concentration in International Marketing.

their idea was, "Crepes?!" They did additional research on the history of French restaurants in America and the idea lost momentum as they found a trail of failed French restaurants with precious few success stories. For example, the Magic Pan, a crepe restaurant chain similar to their concept, had failed in the mid-1980s. By the end of summer, they decided to defer to the wisdom of the experts. Michael trekked back to France, and Chris re-invigorated his job search.

RUSSIAN (CAREER) ROULETTE

In spite of his desire to start a restaurant empire, Chris kept his resume current and almost took a position with Deloitte & Touche in Russia. He had spent the summer working in Krasnowdar while in graduate school. He loved the adventure, and the feeling that he was making a difference in the world.

Babson College belonged to a consortium of graduate schools and consulting firms called the MBA Enterprise Corporation, a nonprofit placement organization assisting businesses to grow in the former Soviet Union and in other developing countries. It was through this agency that Chris received an offer from Deloitte & Touche following graduation. This position required an 18-month commitment beginning in February 1995. He was torn between this chance to work abroad for a top consulting company, and his desire to pursue his entrepreneurial dream.

JACK SPRAT'S: HIGH-POTENTIAL OPPORTUNITY OR WISHFUL THINKING?

In the fall of 1994, Chris found himself talking with a friend, John Farmian, about working out and eating healthy. During the course of the conversation, John commented that it would be great to have a restaurant that served healthy *and* tasty fast food. Chris knew immediately that this was an idea worth exploring, "It was so obvious. There was nothing at all filling that niche in the restaurant industry." With a new start-up vision in focus, and the preliminary research going well, he turned down the consulting opportunity in Russia.

Chris and John decided to become partners. They were friends and fellow Babson alumni, and both felt they could get access to family money with a well-designed business plan. John had the additional motivation of wanting to stay in the United States. He was a Turkish national in Boston on a student visa—their restaurant would sponsor his green card. Soon they were at work on a business plan for a low-fat/fat-free, gourmet-quality QSR.

With the basic concept in place, they began to think of names for their new venture. While lying in bed one evening, Chris happened to remember the words to "Jack Sprat," the Mother Goose nursery rhyme—eureka!

> Jack Sprat could eat no fat, his wife could eat no lean;
> And between the two of them, they licked the platter clean.

Although Chris and John developed the idea together, John was a somewhat reluctant partner. From the beginning, Chris led the investigation and contributed most of the ideas. Within six months, the partnership was finished. Chris told John that he would have a job waiting for him at Jack Sprat's if it ever came together:

> Little by little, it seemed John's enthusiasm was fading. It was hard to get him to sit down and talk about the business. We talked to a few architects together, but it was really over pretty quickly. After a while, I realized that I was the one with the entrepreneurial fever. After that, I recruited other friends and classmates, but no one was ready to commit.

ON THE ROAD BENCHMARKING FAT-FREE AMERICA

Chris' research quickly uncovered a large and expanding low-fat/fat-free products segment in the prepared goods market (i.e., the low-fat/fat-free products segment). Foodservice was one of the largest business segments in the nation, with sales of just under $300 billion, in 1994. Of that, the fast-food market was nearly $100 billion, which represented 33 percent of the total "eat away from home" food sales. In addition, they found that the American fat-free and lite packaged goods market was $24.8 billion in 1993, and it was estimated that it would reach to $29.5 billion in 1994. Projections called for steady growth at about 5 percent per year into the near future.

He also found some low-fat/fat-free restaurants in California and Florida, but they were more reminiscent of the counterculture health food movement of days past than the concept Chris was developing.

In February 1995, Chris went to Los Angeles, California, to see a couple of successful low-fat/fat-free restaurants. First, he visited Sprouts, a small, full-service restaurant, with about 60 seats and a take-out counter. Chris said, "The food was marginal and the portions were skimpy. Why have small portions when it's low-fat/fat-free food?" Chris visited another Californian restaurant called Juicers. It was started in 1989 by a professional bicyclist who was frustrated by the lack of healthy food in restaurants. His smoothies (blended drinks made with fruit and yogurt) were popular among friends, so he opened a QSR. By 1995, he had 30 to 40 restaurants in the Los Angeles area.

Chris also traveled to Boca Raton, Florida, to visit a local restaurant chain called Healthy Way. This was another successful low-fat/fat-free restaurant that did not impress him. "I was even less impressed (but perhaps more excited) about Healthy Way because it was so simple. It was very cheaply put together, yet it was very successful." The success of these restaurants led Chris to believe that he had discovered a gap in the market. "Each of the restaurants had major flaws, so I thought, 'If these places are successful, I'll have a real winner when I do it right.'"

> The only restaurants even similar to our idea seemed like something left over from the seventies. You know the type, granola restaurants with bean sprout-avocado sandwiches, and wheat juice cocktails. Our idea was not anything like those, in fact, the only similarity was that both emphasized healthy eating.

Another Restaurant Chain? Yes!

In March 1995, Chris attended The Northeast Foodservice Exhibition at the World Trade Center in downtown Boston. Many vendors were selling quality low-fat/fat-free products: sauces, precooked entrees, desserts, and so on. These vendors told Chris there was phenomenal demand for low-fat/fat-free packaged products. When asked if they thought there was a need for a low-fat/fat-free restaurant chain, they responded with a resounding "Yes."

Chris also contacted the Boston branch of the Small Business Administration in April of 1995. There Chris met Maximilian Charm, an SBA consultant who had a chain of Burger King franchises. As a successful QSR owner, Max was enthusiastic about the potential of Chris' idea. He told Chris that the reason most restaurants failed was not because of an inherent flaw in the restaurant business, but rather because their owners did not plan thoroughly enough before launching the business (this was especially true for the mom-and-pop operations). Max argued that restauranteurs who have done the research and put together a quality business plan usually succeed. He urged Chris to return when the business plan was complete, because there was a good chance that he could arrange for an SBA-guaranteed loan.

The largest annual food trade show in the world was the National Restaurant Show. In May 1995, it was held at Chicago's McCormack Place and vendors at the show met Chris' plan with enthusiasm. One vendor, Skinny Cow Inc., a provider of private-labeled low-fat/fat-free cheese for companies like Alpine Lace and Healthy Choice, was particularly helpful. They referred Chris to a consultant with experience in QSR chain start-ups, and an interest in low-fat/fat-free foods, Arlene Spiegel. Following the Chicago show, Chris was convinced that this was a great business opportunity. Now he asked, "How are we going to do it?"

Jack Sprat's Business Plan

From the beginning, Chris' plan called for creating a national chain of restaurants; he wanted it to be a high-potential venture. The chain would have two basic types of restaurants: stand-alone and hosted QSRs. The key differences between the two types of restaurants were (1) size, (2) location, (3) menu selection, and (4) customer base—both would be quick service restaurants.

Stand-alone restaurants would be larger with more menu variety, and they would be situated in high traffic locations. They would use typical QSR locations such as busy urban street corners, strip malls, and shopping complexes. Stand-alones had to pull customers into the store "off of the street." By contrast, hosts would supply customer-traffic for hosted stores.

Hosted stores would have fewer menu items and be smaller than stand-alone restaurants. They would also be located within larger institutions such as in the lobby of a hotel. The goal was to have these scaled-down, "express" versions in each city that had Jack Sprat's stand-alone operations. The origin of the hosted location idea was Chris' aunt and uncle, the restaurant owners. They had been approached about opening hosted locations in local healthcare establishments and Chris speculated that he could find hosts in health-conscious organizations (e.g., hospitals, gyms, schools).

Chris planned to have the first two restaurants operational in 1996, a standalone and a host location. This would be followed by a quick expansion once the prototypes proved the concept. The restaurants would not need to payback the investment to prove the concept, simply generating positive cash flow would demonstrate attractiveness (Exhibits 3.2 and 3.3). He was told that if the first locations succeed, financing will not be a problem for the rest:

> You have to pay your dues before outside money shows up. But if you bring a successful new concept to the market, investment money will come knocking on your door.

Anticipating rapid growth, Chris planned to outsource some operational departments once the company began to grow. He thought that food preparation in particular, could be macromanaged with maximum tradeoff satisfaction. Given the right criteria, an outside vendor could maintain high quality standards while reducing management complexity:

> I wanted to create something like a virtual franchise. Many aspects of the business could be outsourced to stay in control, while allowing us to expand rapidly. I wanted to make everything basically idiot-proof. A lot of people thought there would have to be a chef on-site. No. Not at all. Of course, an executive chef would be on staff or retainer to create the recipes, but he would not be there each day preparing food. The

EXHIBIT 3.2   Estimated start-up costs.

Sources of funds		Uses of funds	
Seed money	$ 25,000	Equipment	$115,000
Start-up funding (loans/equity)	460,000	Furniture and fixtures	80,000
SBA guaranteed loan	75,000	Leasehold improvements	45,000
		Construction	50,000
		Working capital	35,000
		Pre-opening expenses (training)	5,000
		Consulting expenses	25,000
		Opening inventory—supplies	10,000
		Architect—engineering services	15,000
		Management salary—Pre-opening	15,000
		Legal fees	10,000
		Signage	8,000
		Marketing expenses	15,000
		Lease and utility deposits	7,000
		Location consulting	5,000
		Brokerage fees	5,000
		Accounting fees	5,000
		Graphics	10,000
		Development expenses	35,000
		Contingency	65,000
Total	$560,000	Total	$560,000

EXHIBIT 3.3   Estimated monthly pro forma income statement, May 31, 1997 to May 31, 1998.

	May	Jun.	Jul.	Aug.	Sept.	Oct.	Nov.	Dec.	Jan.	Feb.	Mar.	Apr.	Total
Total revenues	$75,431	$70,200	$67,669	$61,425	$70,200	$71,550	$63,788	$58,556	$56,194	$51,975	$63,788	$65,138	$775,914
CGS—food	18,858	17,550	16,917	15,356	17,550	17,888	15,947	14,639	14,049	12,994	15,947	16,285	193,979
Gross profit	$56,573	$52,650	$50,752	$46,069	$52,650	$53,663	$47,841	$43,917	$42,146	$38,981	$47,841	$48,854	$581,936
General and administrative													
expense	5,000	5,000	5,000	5,000	5,000	5,000	5,000	5,000	5,000	5,000	5,000	5,000	60,000
Rent	6,000	6,000	6,000	6,000	6,000	6,000	6,000	6,000	6,000	6,000	6,000	6,000	72,000
Management expense	5,666	5,666	5,666	5,666	5,666	5,666	5,666	5,666	5,666	5,666	5,666	5,666	67,992
Employee wages	16,595	15,444	14,887	13,514	15,444	15,741	14,033	12,882	12,363	11,435	14,033	14,330	170,701
Wage related	4,000	4,000	4,000	4,000	4,000	4,000	4,000	4,000	4,000	4,000	4,000	4,000	48,000
Depreciation expense	3,268	3,268	3,268	3,268	3,268	3,268	3,268	3,268	3,268	3,268	3,268	3,268	39,216
Amortization expense	833	833	833	833	833	833	833	833	833	833	833	833	9,996
Insurance expense	500	500	500	500	500	500	500	500	500	500	500	500	6,000
Marketing expense	—	1,000	1,000	1,000	2,000	1,000	1,000	500	500	500	1,000	1,000	10,000
Accounting/legal	—											15,000	15,000
Real estate taxes	800	800	800	800	800	800	800	800	800	800	800	800	9,600
Net profit	$13,911	$10,139	$ 8,798	$ 5,488	$ 9,139	$10,855	$ 6,741	$ 4,968	$ 3,216	$ 979	$ 6,741	$(7,544)	$ 3,431
Interest expense	625	617	609	601	592	584	576	567	559	550	541	532	6,953
Pretax profit	13,286	9,522	8,189	4,887	8,547	10,271	6,165	4,401	2,657	429	6,200	(8,076)	66,478
Current income tax	3,720	2,666	2,293	1,368	2,393	2,876	1,726	1,232	744	120	1,736	(2,261)	18,614
Profit after tax	$ 9,566	$ 6,856	$ 5,896	$ 3,518	$ 6,154	$ 7,395	$ 4,439	$ 3,169	$ 1,913	$ 309	$ 4,464	$(5,814)	$ 47,864
Dividends	—	—	—	—	—	—	—	—	—	—	—	—	—
Adjustment to retained earnings	$ 9,566	$ 6,856	$ 5,896	$ 3,518	$ 6,154	$ 7,395	$ 4,439	$ 3,169	$1,913	$ 309	$ 4,464	$(5,814)	$ 47,864

trend was for almost everything to come pre-made. A foodservice supplier would use our recipes to make our food. Our staff would just heat it up. Prior to that, when we are just beginning, we would make food in-house, then hourly staff would work for just a few dollars an hour to assemble meals. No chef would be on site (and on the payroll) each day. This is one reason why efficiently planned operations were so critical.

Chris knew that location is a key consideration for a foodservice business. Boston had a relatively health-conscious, trendy, and educated population; perfect for the Jack Sprat's concept. He noted that many successful chains had started here— Boston Market, Pizzeria Uno, and Au Bon Pain, to name a few. Also, Chris found it easier and cheaper than trying to get started in New York City. Real estate in New York City was twice as expensive as Boston.

To reach his target customer, he wanted to locate Jack Sprat's in prime business districts, with a strong concentration of professionals and higher income wage earners. Sites would be preliminarily selected using the following general guidelines, then additional demographic and psychographic criteria for the typical customer in the area would be applied:

- Heavy lunch and dinner traffic.
- Dense target consumer-base close to the site.
- Close proximity to main shopping areas and travel routes.
- Heavy foot or road traffic.
- Positioning on the "going home" side of traffic, so consumers can stop by on their way home from work conveniently.
- Availability of a suitable 1,500 to 3,000 square foot location.

Chris was also considering locating near existing restaurants that catered to the same target consumer as Jack Sprat's. This way he would get the benefit of the demographic research conducted by a large chain for no cost at all:

> This is exactly what Burger King does. If you notice, Burger King is nearly always located very near McDonald's. McDonald's does the research and Burger King just follows them right to a new location.

In April 1995, a place in Boston, on Newbury Street, went up for sale. The customer in that area of Boston seemed to fit with Chris's concept. But the price was extremely high at about $225,000 for essentially buying some used physical equipment from the previous restaurant and the lease agreement. Two factors dampened Chris's enthusiasm for this site: (1) He thought it might be too trendy, where passersby would perhaps be more tempted by the boutique restaurants of the area, and (2) Back Bay is a historic district, strictly limiting the dynamics of businesses there. Renovations, innovative designs, fancy signs, and so on were all subject to guidelines set by local committees—they might not let Chris implement his business plan.

Chris contacted several real estate brokers to inquire about potential sites. He was told that before he signed a contract for a site, he should have his business plan complete, and all the financing ready. This would prevent him from wasting money on a location for months before he was ready to begin building. They also told him that locations for his type of QSR concept were not that hard to find. Chris decided to stop location shopping until the business plan was done.

Expansion Strategy

Short-Term Goals

Chris' immediate goal was to develop a base of operations, from which further growth could be established. Funding for the construction and operation of the first Jack Sprat's facility would come partially from his family and the rest from outside sources. During its initial period of operation (3 to 6 months), Chris had plans, subject to obtaining further financing and the success of the original location, to begin construction of additional facilities. Chris wanted to have additional Jack Sprat's open within a year of launching the initial location.

He did not know exactly how fast he would be able to grow, but he knew that similar chains had grown very quickly after their initial rollout. For example, Boston Market had expanded to 21 sites in its first two years of existence, and Bertucci's had grown to 20 sites in its first six years.

Long-Term Growth

To capitalize on what he felt would be tremendous market demand, and Jack Sprat's position as first-to-market with this concept, Chris established an aggressive expansion plan. Funding for the expansion would be derived from long-term bank debt, a second round of (nonfamily) equity, and Jack Sprat's cash flow (see Exhibits 3.2 and 3.3).

During the initial phase, store locations would be clustered in Boston for marketing efficiencies. As media purchases spread awareness of the concept into neighboring towns, other cities in New England would be targeted. Next, Jack Sprat's would be located throughout the Northeast, and finally to more distant areas. Chris was confident that Jack Sprat's would be operating nationally by the year 2005. He felt that demand was great enough to support hundreds, and maybe thousands of locations.

Chris felt that there were many options for rapid growth: company-owned and operated locations, strategic partnerships, franchising, and selling or licensing the concept. Chris did not think that the method of expansion needed to be established immediately, as long as the issues involved with remote ownership and management were considered in the business design. The current problem was getting the business plan finished in such a way that this expansion would be relatively easy when the time arrived.

Financing the Vision

Shortly after developing Jack Sprat's first business plan summary and deciding not to pursue the Russian opportunity, Chris contacted entrepreneurship professor Bill Bygrave for advice. In addition to advice, Bygrave put Chris in touch with potential angel investors. A group of local doctors had called him with a similar restaurant idea.

They often recommended low-fat, no cholesterol diets, but it was hard for their patients to find healthy food in restaurants. Over the phone, the doctors liked Chris and his idea, so they set up a formal meeting. Chris put together a presentation to sell the concept, but the meeting faltered for reasons unrelated to the idea: The doctors had expected Chris to be older and more experienced. A dialog continued for a couple of months, but ultimately, the doctors weren't interested.

Thinking back to his entrepreneurial finance class, Chris looked for ways to get free consulting. He tried to make a deal with the dean of a culinary university, Johnson and Wales. Chris proposed an internship project where Johnson and Wales students would get experience in leading-edge restaurant development work. They would help develop recipes, a menu, and the restaurant layout. The dean indicated that the school did not endorse projects, but that he would be willing to do it himself for standard consulting fees. Several other culinary institutions responded in the same way— once there was an established business, they welcomed internship opportunities, but they were not interested in supporting start-ups

It was time to find out what resources Chris' family were going to contribute. First, he presented the idea to the family's restaurant experts: his aunt and uncle. They liked it; in fact, they had been approached about similar ideas a couple of times. One was a consortium of local hospitals who wanted a low-fat/fat-free menu for heart patients. Another was a critical care facility that wanted to host a low-fat/fat-free restaurant. They were not interested in either venture at the time, but it provided evidence of a demand for this type of restaurant. They encouraged Chris to move forward and recommended the investment to Chris' father, Dr. Harami, but they did not offer financial support due to a recent expansion of their own restaurant that ran into seven figures.

Dr. Harami knew a great deal about nutrition, but when Chris told him about Jack Sprat's, he didn't understand, "If you want to be in foodservice, why don't you just open a hamburger joint?" From this initial discussion in the fall of 1994, until the family meeting in the summer of 1995, Chris actively sought to assuage his father's concerns and gain his support for the venture.

Finally, Dr. Harami, Mrs. Harami, and their three sons gathered for a meeting to decide if this would be a good use of the family money. Out of this meeting came a few key decisions. First, they decided to invest $250,000. Second, they would all serve on the board of directors. Third, Chris' younger brothers, Steve, age 26, and Matt, age 24, would actively participate in the planning and management of Jack Sprat's Restaurants. Steve had an MBA from Rutgers University and restaurant experience and Matt was eager to learn. Finally, Dr. Harami would determine when the time was right to make the investment. This was an open-ended commitment: Dr. Harami could decide that the timing was never right. He was concerned that Chris did not have enough practical experience to pull this off. Chris filed the incorporation papers on August 17, 1995.

Wanted: QSR Training Program

The day after the family meeting, Chris saw an ad in a local paper announcing the planned opening of a new Chicago Jake's restaurant. Chicago Jake's was a national chain of quick service restaurants. Chris thought that he would get good experience helping an established chain open a new location and learn many things he would need to know for his own business. He also remembered his father's concerns about practical experience, and called to ask for a job at the new store.

Chris told the store manager that he wanted to learn the business so that he could open his own QSR chain. The store manager was nonplused, but wanted to hire him anyway, "I need people who can speak English for the grand opening, but I can't hire an MBA who wants to open his own restaurant." So he had Chris interview with his boss, the regional manager, who agreed to hire him if he would commit to staying 90 days. The regional manager agreed to provide on-the-job training in how to open and run a new fast-food restaurant. He would be a floater, involved with all aspects of the business.

He was initially assigned to two stores that were already open. First, Chris worked in a low-income area store, then he worked in a high-income area store. The differences between the two were fascinating, "These stores were laid-out and operated in completely different ways, and I got to learn both operations."

Next, he went to the new store a week before the grand opening. Chris helped install equipment and organize the launch. Once open, he helped troubleshoot and run it; Chris learned all aspects of managing the new restaurant. "I saw the good, the bad, and yes, the ugly. . . . It was a great experience." Chris stayed more than two months—until a new manager decided that it was time for him to go.

Wanted—QSR Guru

By this point, Chris was convinced that Jack Sprat's was a winner. Research supported it, industry insiders embraced it, and he had the support of his family, but he was still worried about his lack of experience. If anything, the two months with Chicago Jake's served to underscore how much he didn't know:

> There were so many things which the layman would never think of. To create a single dish, you need about 20 ingredients. Then to actually cook it, put it together, hold it properly, and serve it perfectly, there's a lot of different equipment that you need. It requires an efficient step-by-step process, and, as a layman, you don't know these things. These days it's a science, and I worry about being able to do it right the first time, because with my limited funding I cannot afford to make too many mistakes.
>
> We had a great idea and we'd done our homework, but none of us had ever built a restaurant chain from scratch. That made me nervous because we were betting the farm on this venture. I wanted as much probability of success as I could possibly get. I wanted a guru, somebody who knew all the ins and outs, had the network, knew the suppliers, and could help me bring this concept to reality.

Chris wanted to hire a consultant, he felt that having a well-respected consultant help him execute his plan would offer a much greater probability of success, but his father did not. Chris' aunt and uncle had not used one, and their restaurant was a success, so Dr. Harami couldn't see why his business-degreed son needed a consultant. To compound matters, Dr. Harami asked around, and he did not know of anyone who had used a restaurant consultant.

Undeterred, Chris requested a list of restaurant consultants from the National Restaurant Association. He was pleased to find Skinny Cow's referral, Arlene Spiegel, on this list. He contacted consultants based in Boston and New York City, where the first restaurants would be located. Most of the consultants sent "impressive, but distant proposals." They did not seem to be enthusiastic about the "lean gourmet" concept. Also, they were all very expensive, ranging from $50,000 to $150,000 for a business plan rewrite.

All the firms had similar qualifications and experience. Chris checked their references, and all came back with high praise. After meeting with numerous consultants, Chris chose Arlene Spiegel's company, Market Discoveries, Inc. He gave six reasons for choosing her:

1. Good interpersonal chemistry.
2. A high level of involvement in health food issues.
3. Her enthusiasm for the Jack Sprat's concept.
4. The unsolicited referral from Skinny Cow.
5. An excellent resume and references (he called them all).
6. A negotiated price (she agreed to sign-on for $25,000)

Arlene Spiegel, Food Consultant

Arlene Spiegel was recognized as one of the nation's leading foodservice specialists. She had won awards for achievements in foodservice, food and menu development, and food and beverage merchandising for many major fast-food companies including McDonald's, Burger King, and KFC. She also developed and re-engineered the in-house dining services for Chase Manhattan Bank, Marriott, and Holiday Inn, as well as developing branded concepts for Coca-Cola, Chock Full O' Nuts, and others. In addition, her expertise included facilities planning, brand development, procurement, staffing, training, and promotion. For her many achievements, she was named the "Foodservice Woman of the Year" in 1982, and in 1987 she received the prestigious Pacesetter Award for her innovations in foodservice marketing.

Arlene recently joined forces with four other foodservice professionals to form the IBM Foodservice Consulting Consortium. This group, sponsored by IBM, offered consulting services to IBM's restaurant clients. IBM was the largest vendor of restaurant POS systems. In addition to restaurants, Arlene had done a lot of work for hospitals and the medical community.

DECISION POINT

On the one hand, Chris thought his father was ready to move forward. But on the other hand, Dr. Harami didn't want to spend precious resources to have a consultant rewrite Chris' "MBA-informed business plan." His father insinuated that the desire to hire a consultant might be a sign that Chris didn't have enough confidence in the

Jack Sprat's concept. Chris was left with a tough decision; he wanted to hire Arlene, but if he insisted, Dr. Harami might get cold feet and decide that the timing was not yet right for funding the venture.

Chris felt that the window of opportunity for Jack Sprat's was open now, and he didn't want to risk another delay.

PREPARATION QUESTIONS

1. Should Chris insist on hiring Arlene Spiegel?
2. Evaluate Jack Sprat's Restaurant as a high-potential venture.
3. Evaluate Chris' progress to date.
4. What advice would you give Dr. Harami?

4 INTERNET FASHION MALL, LLC

After meeting with his lawyers to discuss the latest draft of the partnership agreement, Ben Narasin, CEO and founder of the Boston Prepatory Company (BPC), a men's fashion firm, pondered the future of Internet Fashion Mall (IFM, *fashionmall*, or *fashionmall.com*). "We have an opportunity to dominate the Internet fashion market, but we have to get through the lawyers to make it happen."

Fashionmall.com was probably the most important fashion site on the web in February 1996. The traffic at Ben's Web site averaged over 200,000 hits a day (see Exhibit 4.1), and his clients included leading magazines and fashion houses (see Exhibit 4.2 for a list of *fashionmall* clients). However, the primary reason Ben's site was pre-eminent was that he was a pioneer. There were single-brand sites and multiple-brand, online-service cybermalls (see Exhibit 4.3 for explanation of selected terms), but so far, there was no other cybermall focused on fashion. Ben contemplated his opportunity as he gazed out the window of his fashionable Madison Avenue office:

> As in many areas of business, timing is everything. In my view, there are only two times you will get involved in the Net: you can either be too early or too late. Those of us who have been too early will be there when the time is right. By then it will be too late for competitors.
>
> But one of the biggest risks in this venture is that we may be too far ahead of the market. My clients think of the fashionmall as another outlet for public relations, but I don't want to be another item in the PR budget. Of course, I can't blame them; no one is really selling fashion on the Internet yet.
>
> By the time the Web makes it into the sales budget, it will be too late to grab market share. Then we'll have to fight in the trenches for every client. The Web is

This case was prepared by Beverly Chiarelli and Dan D'Heilly under the direction of Professor Julian E. Lange. Funding provided by the Ewing Marion Kauffman Foundation. Copyright © 1996 Babson College. All rights reserved.

37

EXHIBIT 4.1 *Fashionmall.com* traffic.

Date	Number of hits	Pages viewed	Unique IPs
Jul. 1995	77,000	15,000	3,000
Aug. 1995	68,000	4,000	3,000
Sept. 1995	126,000	8,000	2,000
Oct. 1995	239,000	23,000	3,000
Nov. 1995	324,000	80,000	10,000
Dec. 1995	450,000	115,000	17,000
Jan. 1996	508,000	137,000	14,000
Feb. 1996	1,042,000	218,000	38,000

The table shows traffic data rounded to the nearest thousand. The number of hits represents the total number of pages and graphic files requested by visitors at *fashionmall.com* in a given month (one visitor may count more than once). Pages viewed represents the total number of HTML pages. A unique IP number is a server that connects to *fashionmall.com*. It may register one or more page hits in a single visit (the total number of visitors may include repeat visitors), so IPs more accurately represent the number of computers that have linked to *fashionmall.com*.

developing so fast that every hour I invest in positioning the *fashionmall* today is worth 10 hours tomorrow. I can't wait until the Internet is commercially viable to create the fashion mall of the future—I have to be aggressive now. A shake-out is coming, and I don't want to be roadkill on the information superhighway.

Ben's strategy for staying at the forefront of Internet fashion had several components: using and developing leading-edge technology, establishing relationships with leading brands and fashion leaders, and creating traffic through the mall. These initiatives stretched Ben's team to the breaking point, "I think about bringing on a partner every day," he thought. "I need more resources, but I never had a partner with BPC and I just don't like the idea of someone else with P&L authority at my company."

BEN NARASIN

At the age of 12, Ben Narasin began his first business brokering comic books. He borrowed $50 from his father, an IBM executive, and bought exhibit space at a local show. To his father's surprise, Ben came home with a tidy profit and his first entrepreneurial

EXHIBIT 4.2 Fashion vendors with IFM storefronts, 2/96.

Houndtooth	Due Per Due
Sigrid Olsen	River Sharpe
Suit Club	Winston
Boston Prepatory Co.	Faces of Time
Pendleton	Cole Haan
Briars	Alden of Camel

EXHIBIT 4.3   Explanation of selected technical terms.

At-home shopping	Purchasing items from home through any one of several channels: direct mail (including catalog shopping), infomercials, telemarketing, or by computer. The consumers in this new market segment were called at-home or storeless shoppers.
Search engines	A type of Internet software that classifies, catalogs, and retrieves the location of information on the Web in response to user queries.
Browser	A software application that allows the user to interact with Internet information.
Cybermall	An online shopping site in which a group of merchants showcase their goods and services at a common Web site.
Electronic storefront	An electronic "page" of information that describes and shows products and processes orders.
Hits	The number of times a page is down-loaded from a Web site.
Homepage	The primary page of electronic information for a Web site. It can be supplemented by subsequent pages of information and be linked to other sites.
Hypertext	Highlighted text in a homepage that provides electronic links to other online pages. Clicking on this text transfers the viewer to another page.
Multimedia	Using multiple media (print, video, sound, and graphics) within one presentation to communicate information.
Web site	A collection of electronic pages linked to a homepage.
World Wide Web	A hypertext browsing and searching system on the Internet that has electronic links to multimedia files.

success. By the time he was 17, Ben's comic book inventory was valued at $100,000. By high school, he had developed an interest in fashion, so he took a part-time job at a haberdashery.

Ben majored in entrepreneurial studies at Babson College. As an undergraduate, he started a profitable diamond wholesale business, but discovered that he did not enjoy dealing in diamonds, so he sold his inventory. Ben decided that his next business would be in an industry that better suited his interests.

Upon graduating in 1986, Ben Narasin founded a men's fashion firm, the Boston Prepatory Company (BPC), with less than $20,000. His first design breakthrough was the "original panel shirts" which were worn by the character "Woody" on the television show, *Cheers*.

The 12-employee company used all natural materials and manufactured all of its products in the United States. BPC positioned its products as high-quality, affordable sportswear with a unique and fun look.

BPC produced and branded private label merchandise for some of the country's leading clothiers and catalogs including Macy's, Nordstrom, Land's End, The Limited, Ann Taylor, and Abercrombie & Fitch.

Ben believed that building brand recognition was the key to being successful in an industry dominated by giants such as Ralph Lauren and Calvin Klein. Ben talked to *Inc.* magazine in 1987:

> When you have a brand, you own equity in something tangible. The advertising we do is purely for brand awareness. Retailers like to have awareness built by the manufacturer. They like to see advertising reinforcement. We gear our campaigns around two ideas. One, we make fun clothes, and two, we make American clothes. That's the look I want to own. It is a personal goal of mine to develop a brand.

Twice the company was named to the *Inc. 500* list of fastest growing companies, rising from number 416 in 1986 to 57 in 1987, with revenues of approximately $4 million. Over the next six years, BPC sales ranged between $1.5 million and $4 million, and revenues were declining. Ben was disappointed that he could not move his brand into the upper tier of fashion companies. He attributed this disappointment to the difficulty of building brand image. It was difficult to reposition BPC once the apparel industry had categorized his label, and with industry resistance, repositioning and building mass-market brand recognition on a small-company budget was next to impossible. In 1993, a year in which BPC generated over $1 million in revenues, Ben spent over $100,000 on advertising and public relations.

THE APPAREL INDUSTRY

According to the 1994 U.S. Industrial Outlook, the fashion and apparel industry grew at about the same rate as inflation during the first half of the 1990s (see Exhibit 4.4). The apparel industry was dominated by a handful of large companies (Exhibit 4.5) which manufactured offshore, sold enormous volumes with low gross margins, and kept mass-market prices low.

There were a number of forums for designers to promote their ideas to the apparel industry. The trade press reported on runway shows, exhibitions, trade shows, seminars, and conferences. Retail buyers avidly followed these mediums to uncover trends in consumer fashion. Since this coverage was mostly paid for by fashion houses, designers with the largest promotional budgets consistently received the best media coverage. This system was hard on small designers seeking a niche in the mass market. In both 1994 and 1995 there were over 12,000 apparel companies that declared Chapter 11.

EXHIBIT 4.4   Apparel industry trends: Retail sales (in billions).

Nondurable goods	1991	1992	1993	1994
General merchandise	$228	$247	$280	$320
Apparel	97	105	108	112

Source: U.S. Industrial Outlook 1994—Retailing.

EXHIBIT 4.5   Top ten apparel companies by annual sales (ranked by profitability).

Company name	Five-year average profit margin	1995 Revenues (in millions)	Percent increase in sales	Percent increase in net income
1. Tommy Hilfiger	10.8%	$ 478.1	58.6%	88.9%
2. St. John Knits	10.7	161.8	24.1	64.6
3. Jones Apparel	8.9	776.4	21.8	27.7
4. Nautica	8.0	247.6	24.2	54.1
5. Liz Claiborne	7.5	2,081.6	3.8	−9.2
6. Russell Corp.	7.2	1,152.6	10.1	−4.4
7. Superior Surgical	7.0	135.2	1.9	−1.6
8. Garan	7.0	141.3	−1.2	−10.3
9. Fruit of the Loom	6.8	2,403.1	11.0	−4.9
10. Hampshire Group	6.3	112.5	N/A	N/A

Source: Bobbin Blenheim Media Corporation, June, 1996 and Compact Disclosure, Inc., 1996.

Similarly, consumers received fashion information from a variety of sources: television and radio advertising, magazines, billboards, exhibitions, in-store displays, and television programming. All these media reflected the trends supported by the large fashion houses. However, the direct sales trend began to be felt in the early 1980s, as catalogs and television infomercials became more attractive to consumers, and several new brands (e.g., Land's End) were subsequently established.

Companies in the apparel business sold their products through a variety of channels; however, most mass-market business was conducted in retail stores—department stores, discount stores, manufacturers' outlets, and boutiques—primarily in downtown shopping districts, large retail malls, and strip malls. Kurt Salmon Associates, a management consulting firm specializing in retail and consumer products, surveyed consumers in 1995, and reported that people increasingly viewed shopping as a stressful experience—53 percent of respondents said they were shopping less to save time and 70 percent bought almost all of their merchandise on sale. In response to the survey, most consumers said they had about a 50/50 chance of actually finding the item they wanted to purchase in a store. Given the rise in price-sensitive, time-pressed, and unsatisfied consumers, retailers were striving to make the shopping experience more entertaining and successful for the consumer. Kurt Salmon Associates predicted retailers would lose marketshare to nonstore retailing, which will grow from approximately 10 percent to over 50 percent of total retail sales by the year 2010.

In the early 1980s, at-home shopping channels emerged to compete with retail locations for apparel-shopping dollars. Initially through catalogs, designers and manufacturers began to communicate directly with the consumer, bypassing traditional retail channels. Following the success of catalogs, television (e.g., Home Shopping

Network) became an established direct-sales avenue for the at-home shopping market by the early 1990s.

However, the at-home shopping segment continued to evolve, and Internet shopping was considered a threat. Mastercard International conducted a survey for the National Retail Federation in 1996, and found that 46 percent of the people surveyed responded that they would be less likely to buy from mail-order sources if they started shopping online.

While at-home shopping represented a growth segment in the market, many consumers were uninterested in buying apparel at home (see Exhibit 4.6). They wanted to see, touch, and wear a garment before making a purchasing decision. For many other consumers, however, hectic lifestyles combined with the "satisfaction guaranteed" credo of all reputable at-home shopping channels made shopping for clothes from home a low-risk, high-reward experience that many people enjoyed. At-home apparel shopping was projected to be a $10 billion industry by the year 2010. This growth was expected in part from the newest at-home distribution channel—the Internet.

The 1994 *U.S. Industrial Outlook* predicted that the years 1995 to 2000 would see a surge in the number of teenagers and young adults embracing electronic shopping channels and interactive television. The demographics were in favor of an increase in Internet shopping, because 15 percent of the people with computers at home described fashion as one of their interests (see Exhibit 4.7). In 1994, Ben Narasin discovered the Internet.

A BRIEF HISTORY OF THE INTERNET

The Internet began as a project called ARPANET in 1969. It was started by the Department of Defense in an attempt to increase the reliability of the telecommunications networks linking military-research contractors, several of which were universities. The Internet was designed with dynamic rerouting capabilities, so that when a link was disrupted (presumably by a Russian bomb), it would be automatically re-established through a different line. The ARPANET was very successful,

EXHIBIT 4.6   Shopping channel demographics.

	Catalog shoppers	TV shoppers	Online shoppers
Median household income ($000)	$49	$45	$66
Average age of purchaser	43.0	43.2	41.6
At-home shopping industry	93%	6%	1%
Revenue per demographic ($000,000)	$53,010	$3,648	$342
Percentage that graduated college	n/a	29%	64%

Source: Interactive Consumer, May 1995; Discount Store News, February 21, 1994.

EXHIBIT 4.7 Lifestyle profiles—users of personal computers.

	Households	Percentage of PC users
Home life		
Subscribe to cable TV	24,820,818	70.4%
Home furnishing/decorating	8,285,358	23.5
Good life		
Gourmet cooking/fine foods	7,368,680	20.9
Fashion clothing	5,359,040	15.2
Fine art/antiques	4,548,133	12.9
High-tech activities		
Use an IBM compatible	29,545,235	83.8
Own a CD player	24,327,222	69.0
Use an Apple/Macintosh	8,673,184	24.6
Home video games	5,041,729	14.3

Source: Simmons Research Bureau, Inc., 1994

and every major university in the United States eventually joined the network. However, the network became more difficult to manage as the traffic volume increased.

Communications on the Internet were almost entirely in the not-for-profit realm until the 1980s. The Internet was created for scientists, researchers, and other highly skilled professionals with special information needs. Users typed computer commands and the Internet retrieved text-only files from distant computers. Everything changed in 1991, when the World Wide Web was introduced by the European Laboratory for Particle Physics (CERN). Suddenly, the Internet had an application with mass-market potential.

With the Web, users could access multimedia information on another computer anywhere in the world. In addition to improved content, the Web was easier to use. It was entertaining, user-friendly, and anyone with a telephone line and some inexpensive computer equipment could "surf the Web."

Several large commercial networks had developed alongside of the ARPANET system to help manage the traffic. Some networks were developed by organizations such as IBM and SPRINT, and others by specialist companies such as UUNet. By the mid-1990s, these commercial networks had taken over managing the Internet.

The Web accessed information through hypertext functions. Hypertext lets users move from one document to another by clicking on hyperlinks (highlighted words or images) with a software program called a *browser*. Netscape was the most popular browser, with an 87 percent market share in January 1996. Another key feature of hypertext was its ability to describe what was inside files—it made finding information easy. The Web was a revolutionary advancement and its growth was nearly exponential through the early 1990s (see Exhibit 4.8).

Exhibit 4.8   Internet hosts.

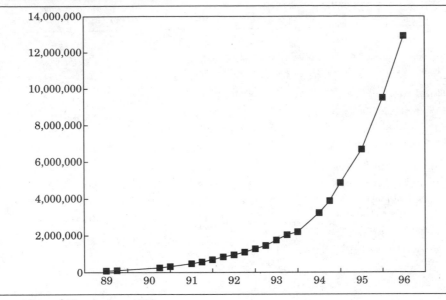

Source: General Margin, Inc., 1996.

Unfortunately, the Web's revolutionary technology was traveling on an infrastructure created for less information-rich communications systems. Multimedia information had the potential to slow Internet connections to a crawl, and slow Web connections were boring. While solutions to this problem appeared to be within reach in the mid-1990s, the entertainment potential of the Web appeared limited by the U.S. information infrastructure.

WORLD WIDE WEB DEMOGRAPHICS

The Web was often described as "organized anarchy." With users selectively anonymous and geographically dispersed, the Internet offered little certainty about who was doing what. This uncertainty was illustrated by disparities among analysts' projections concerning online population and commerce.

Depending on which analysts were surveyed, the online population was anywhere between 7 and 43 million adults in 1996 (see Exhibit 4.9 for a survey of online population estimates). One thing that most experts agreed upon was the rate of growth. The American Internet User Survey released in January 1996 by the FIND/SVP Emerging Technologies Research Group reported that over half of all Internet users began using their first Internet application in 1995, and that 61 percent of all users expected their personal use to increase in 1996.

In 1995, the majority of Internet users were men (65% according to FIND/SVP and 74% according to Forrester Research); however, more women were using the Internet than before, and women compared favorably in frequency of usage. Internet users were also primarily young: 32 percent were under 30, 28 percent were between 30 and 39, 27 percent of the Internet users were between 40 and 49, and 13 percent were over 50 according to the FIND/SVP report.

According to analyst ActivMedia, Internet sales from August 1994 to August 1995 were approximately $118 million. Another analyst, Jupiter Communications, reported Web sales for 1995 at $43 million, and $72 million for the first six months of 1996, but projected sales of $249 million for the last six months of 1996. See Exhibits 4.10, 4.11, and 4.12 for revenue projections through the year 2000.

One system for classifying companies analyzed Web sales volume and product type: 21 percent of the sites with online commerce had sales over $10,000 and 39 percent sold consumer products. Of the consumer product companies, 7 percent sold clothing on the Web. Nielsen Media Research projected total online sales for 1996: $140 million for computer hardware and software, $126 million for travel services, $85 million for entertainment, and $46 million for apparel.

EXHIBIT 4.9   Range of online, Internet, and WWW statistics, 1994–1996.

Users (millions)	Description	Source	Date
43.0	Adults use online services	Yankelovich Partners	8/96
50.0	Adults (16+) have access to the Net	Nielsen Media	8/96
35.0	Adults (16+) use Internet and online services	Intelliquest	7/96
36.7	Adults have accessed the Internet	Fairfield Research	7/96
10.4	Use the Internet	Boardwatch	6/96
7.6	Computers hooked up to the Internet	Network Wizards	5/96
23.5	World Wide Web users	IDC	5/96
9.6	Online households in the U.S., 1995	Jupiter Communications	4/96
15.0	Subscriptions to online services	Simba	3/96
7.0	Home Internet use	The NPD Group	3/96
9.0	Internet and WWW users in 1995	Morgan Stanley	2/96
9.5	Use online services	Find/SVP	1/96
10.0	Or less use the Internet	Dr. Donna Hoffman	1/96
37.0	Have access to the Internet	Nielsen Media	11/95
5.8	Adults connected to the Internet	O'Reilly & Assoc.	9/95
8.6	Internet users	Forrester Research	9/95
9.1	Subscribe to AOL, Compuserve, Prodigy, MSN		9/95
6.7	Households accessing online services	INTECO	8/95
40.0	Use the Internet	"Launching a Business on the Web"	8/95
28.5	Adults online	Yankelovich Partners	5/95
16.0	U.S. Internet users	Management Forum International	9/94
25.0	People use the Internet	Common Knowledge	1993–1996

Source: New Networks Institute, 1996. Gathered at http://www.newnetworks.com/statsexecsum.htm

EXHIBIT 4.10   Online revenue projections.

	1996	2000
Subscription services	$120 million	$1.0 billion
Retail sales	518 million	6.6 billion

Source: Jupiter Communications.

A NEW VISION: THE INTERNET FASHION MARKET

Ben realized that the Internet medium was nearly ideal for BPC. He could control his message and communicate directly with the public to achieve better PR for less money. And it had home run potential: if the world decided his Web site was cool, BPC could become a very hip brand. Ben reflected on the potential impact of the Web on the fashion industry:

> Part of the value I see in the Web is that it can tilt the power toward the more fashionable designers and manufacturers, and away from those that simply have more money.

Ben began setting up a Web site for BPC in late 1994, and procured the services of a local Internet Access Provider for Boston Prepatory's home page—$300/month in rent was less expensive than hiring someone to maintain an in-house Web server. As he researched the Internet and the World Wide Web, he became increasingly excited by the possibilities. The technology was still not easy or fast enough for the mass market, but he thought that was temporary. The combination of interactive communications, high-quality graphics, and potentially universal accessibility convinced Ben that the Web would become a major new fashion sales and distribution channel. He came to believe that the Internet would change the way people lived and conducted business. Ben wanted to start working on the Web full-time, but there was considerable risk for BPC. Ben did not have a professional manager in place and he thought that BPC might collapse without his hands-on management.

He was also concerned about the ripeness of the opportunity. How long would it be before Internet and Web technology was ready for the mass market? And what about his niche of the mass market—how much of the better-lifestyle population was into high tech and the Internet? Ben had set up a Local Area Network (LAN) at BPC, and he was a sophisticated computer user; but he was no programmer, and Internet

EXHIBIT 4.11   Online revenue projections by types of providers.

	2000
Internet services	$9.0 billion
Consumer content providers	2.8 billion
Business content providers	5.6 billion

Source: Forrester Research.

EXHIBIT 4.12   Internet advertising.°

	1995	1996	2000
Frost & Sullivan	N/A	$ 85 million	$5.5 billion†
Jupiter Communications	$43 million	312 million	5.0 billion
Hambrecht & Quist	12 million	30 million	3.8 billion
Simba	N/A	200 million	1.97 billion

° All reports published in 1996.
† Forecast for the year 2002.

technology was beyond his technical competency. In addition, Ben was not independently wealthy, so he didn't want to pursue a venture that would lose too much money before reaching break-even. Ben could live without income if BPC went downhill, but he would have to decide how much of his personal net worth he was willing to gamble on a leading-edge, start-up company.

When the BPC web site was up and running in the summer of 1994, Ben took the plunge and launched a new venture, the Internet Fashion Mall, with Boston Prepatory as its charter store. He envisioned a virtual shopping mall where shoppers could browse and purchase goods from the comfort of their own home computers. Ben wanted *fashionmall.com* to attain an important place in the world of fashion. Ben outlined his thoughts in the Fashionmall Business Plan:

> My mission is to expand the ways in which the fashion industry does business. *Fashionmall.com* will reach into all aspects of the "better fashion lifestyle," touching on the entire fashion-self, from clothing and accessories to lifestyle luxuries and home designer goods. I am positioning my Web site to be a meta-repository for better fashion products and content, targeted at both businesses and consumers across the globe. I want to create a place:
>
> - Where people interested in current fashion trends, fashion news, and better lifestyle products will visit.
> - That people will visit often because it changes regularly.
> - That will be recognized in both traditional and non-traditional media as a *must-see* site.
> - That will serve as a resource for the fashion industry (for example, access to media kits, artwork and industry news).
> - Where retailers and apparel manufacturers will sell products.
> - Where consumers will feel comfortable purchasing products.

The Competition

When Ben launched IFM in 1994, market data was limited. According to Modem Media, $50 million in sales were made at online subscription services' cybermalls in 1993, and about 90 percent of these sales came through Prodigy and CompuServe. The top 10 (out of 150 total) consumer merchants generated 80 percent of the revenue. The largest merchants generated an average of $3 million annually from online sales, while medium-sized firms earned about $500,000 and small merchants around $80,000.

The first few cybermalls were developed by commercial online service companies—CompuServe, Prodigy, and America Online (AOL). By 1995, CompuServe's Electronic mall had over 130 companies selling products and services online. The cost for vendors to join this cybermall was $25,000 plus 2 percent of sales. In January 1995, AOL unveiled a new cybermall package. For $300,000 per year, retail companies could have AOL develop an online area in its Marketplace section with multimedia capacity, market-research reports, transactional capabilities, and AOL would create a separate home page for the Web, however, its success was limited.

In some ways, *fashionmall* competed with television-shopping at an infomercial service like QVC and catalog-shopping with a vendor like L.L. Bean, because television and catalogs sold consumer fashion items to people in their homes. *Fashionmall* was different from the infomercial vendors because the consumer could look for what they wanted, when they wanted it, on the Internet. Catalog shoppers also controlled content and timing, but they had a very different shopping experience. Catalogs were mobile, and consumers often shopped while comfortably reclined in a favorite chair, not while sitting in front of a television or computer. On the other hand, the content in catalogs was dated, static, and of limited entertainment value. CD ROM catalogs also competed with *fashionmall.com*, but CD-ROMs became quickly dated and had not yet caught the market's attention. Magazines and other fashion content-providers were also indirect competitors of *fashionmall.com*. They were also prospective competitors or clients when they decided to establish a presence on the Internet.

Because *fashionmall.com* was a multimedia, customized experience, Ben thought that direct competition also had to be online. Most Internet sites with fashion content were small, poorly capitalized, focused on one brand or category, or did not have a fashion focus, so Ben thought that he had little direct competition in early 1996. There were sites that discussed designers and fashion trends, but did not sell products, and there were sites that sold products, but did not offer a variety of vendors. There were no cybermalls focused solely on fashion.

Ben saw successful cybermalls developing in other industries, so he believed that it would happen in the fashion industry as well. The Home Shopping Network, for example, established The Internet Shopping Network (ISN) to sell computer hardware and software online in the summer of 1994, and had sales of $200,000 for the month of January 1995. By that October, ISN had sales of $1.2 million, and was projecting over $12 million in sales for 1996. Ben had the fashion field to himself, but he wondered, "How long do I have before a major player builds a fashion cybermall and this becomes a real battle?"

If You Build It, They May Come

Fashionmall.com was the first web site dedicated to fashion. Ben reasoned that it gave *fashionmall* a competitive advantage to get out in front early and set the pace.

He also thought that if smaller designers like BPC were going to attract traffic to a homepage, it would be through strength in numbers. When any one designer with a storefront at *fashionmall.com* generated public interest, all storefronts would benefit from increased traffic at the mall. Ben believed that creating a mall made sense:

> As *fashionmall.com* brands itself as a place for "hot" products, it becomes a hot cyber-mall, and consumers learn to come to *fashionmall* to find fashionable products. As retailers and apparel manufacturers see more investment in industry-specific cybermalls, they will recognize that single-company sites are not sufficient to build Web traffic.

Ben talked to friends in the industry and got a couple of them to sign onto *fashionmall.com.* He also began to attract people interested in fashion to his site (see Exhibit 4.13). It was time to get organized and develop tactical objectives. Ben drafted goals in five categories:

1. Increase the number of storefront rentals (fixed fee, percentage of sales, and a combination).
2. Increase the number of consumer memberships (with transaction information).
3. Increase the number of pages delivered per month.
4. Improve presentation technology.
5. Develop relationships in the fashion industry.

EXHIBIT 4.13   IFM search engine requests for the week of 2/20/96.

Hits	Inquiry	Hits	Inquiry	Hits	Inquiry	Hits	Inquiry
430	calvin	407	klein	189	donna	153	karan
117	hilfiger	110	dkny	99	armani	95	tommy
78	nautica	74	lingerie	70	gucci	68	boss
63	girbaud	63	chanel	58	hugo	53	underwear
53	dolce	52	versace	49	nude	46	shoes
44	oldham	43	karen	43	dresses	42	todd
42	jeans	41	polo	43	&	37	klien
37	cole	36	pendleton	35	lauren	35	jobs
33	prada	33	karl	33	kani	32	ralph
32	mossimo	30	liz	28	and	26	valentino
25	skirts	25	johnson	25	gaultier	24	guess
24	clothes	23	the	23	paul	23	fashion
23	claiborne	22	pantyhose	22	crawford	21	scarves
21	republic	21	clothing	21	anna	20	panties
20	moschino	20	models	19	nike	19	couture
19	banana	18	sui	18	smith	18	runway
18	leather	18	haan	18	diesel	18	anne
17	hats	17	gabbana	17	boots	16	women's
16	wear	16	suits	16	shirts	16	replay
6	marcus	16	levi	16	gap	16	exchange
16	cindy	16	cigars	16	burberrys	15	women

A hot product would generate traffic to the mall, but so would advertising. Ben set to work selling electronic storefronts in the cybermall and quickly realized that retail customers were required to attract trade clients. Ben began advertising aggressively and successfully pulled retail traffic into the *fashionmall*. He tried to establish the *fashionmall's* reputation by developing an industry and consumer presence in newspapers, magazines, and other media. This included advertising and public relations coverage in *GQ, Details, Rolling Stone, Net Guide, Wired,* a TV Video Release, the *Wall Street Journal, CNN, NBR,* and *USA Today.* Clients' advertising also began to boost this effort. For example, Pendleton and Sigrid Olsen tagged their own advertising with the *fashionmall.com* Internet address in numerous magazines including *Sports Illustrated, Life,* and *Vogue.* Finally, Ben bought space on over 20,000 billboards in New York City. Ben recalled the strong response:

> When we planned our media campaign, we hoped to pull 50,000 hits a week, but we had 100,000 hits the week after our ads dropped in November!

The emergence of *fashionmall.com* created a media stir. Examples of the company's publicity include an article on the front page of *The Wall Street Journal,* a notice in *USA Today,* and television profiles on *CNN, Managing with Lou Dobbs, and the Nightly Business Report.*

In an effort to reduce the cost of promotion and at the same time gain media coverage, *fashionmall* occasionally produced video news releases (VNR) for television on specific fashion topics. The *fashionmall* kept its costs down by partnering with clients who participated in the VNR by paying a portion of the production cost in exchange for being featured in the company's piece. A VNR costing $15,000 to produce reached over five million viewers through televised news features in late 1995.

Ben also focused his resources on online advertising and key-word sponsorships. Other "better lifestyle" sites offered hyperlinks to *fashionmall.com* in exchange for nominal fees. Ben found that some sites justified the expenditure, but most did not. Key-word sponsorships were more expensive but more predictable because they were akin to buying traffic. Ben paid key-word sponsorship fees to ensure that *fashionmall.com* was listed first when a user searched for the words *fashion* and *fashions* on the search engines of several indexing services, including Infoseek, Lycos, Yahoo!, and Alta Vista.

Although clients wanted traffic, a gross traffic-tally was only partially useful: traffic-count was an insufficient gauge of customer activity. For example, if 5 million users accessed the *fashionmall* through 10 different hubs, Ben could only know for certain that 10 users had actually visited the mall. Further, traffic-counts provided no demographic data. Initially, Ben required visitors to register before they could visit the *fashionmall*; however, many people refused and others entered incorrect information. So Ben went to voluntary registration, and only 4 percent chose to answer his survey. He anticipated that *fashionmall* would know its customers better when he installed new technology that offered customers more fun and convenience if they registered.

The *fashionmall's* user registrations showed that 60 percent of its users were male. Of the total registered base, 49 percent were 17 to 27, 31 percent were 28 to

40, 16 percent were 41 or older, and 4 percent were less than 16 years old. Studies showed that women and men shopped differently on the Web, so Ben geared his site toward men's preferences: "quick hits" and men's products. Women tended to browse longer before making a purchasing decision. According to industry pundits, the trend was for more women to surf the Web, but he intended to develop the site based on customer feedback.

Fashionmall planned to offer every customer a personal attendant called a "Fashion Assistant." This interactive software agent would be programmed with a unique style chosen by the shopper as their desired "attitude." Fashion Assistants would know every item available in the mall and would combine that information with the shopper's registration profile, purchasing information, and search-engine history to help make shopping at the Internet Fashion Mall a very enjoyable experience. Ben thought that Fashion Assistants would be a compelling reason to shop at *fashionmall.com:*

> What will make the *fashionmall* appealing is that the mall will be different every time you visit, and it will be different for every person who visits. On your first visit to *fashionmall.com,* you will choose a Fashion Assistant, like Rugged Rob or Preppy Paul, and register your personal profile. Based on that profile, your Fashion Assistant will suggest interesting places for you to visit. We will provide our visitors with excellent service—they will tell us what they want and we will find it for them, or at least we'll know what we're missing. Our objective will be to provide content with a point of view, because it will make us a unique and fun place to visit. In the future, media will change, but content will always be required, and we will be there as the deliverer of fashion content.

DESIGNING *FASHIONMALL.COM*

Ben believed that many fashion-industry communication forums would eventually be replicated on the Internet, because of the Web's multimedia potential. Ben anticipated that the scope of his Web site content would increase on an ongoing basis. Although he called his Web site a "mall," Ben believed that the mall metaphor was too limited. He anticipated that one of the *fashionmall*'s ultimate roles would be as a provider of fashion content and as a bulwark against fashion monopolists.

Designing for the Internet was not like designing for other media. Technical issues were more critical, and a radically different perspective was required. This was multimedia: Ben planned to have video clips of runway models and live interviews with fashion designers:

- Content could be audio, video, graphics, text, or some combination of the four.
- Content delivery occurred at differing speeds, depending on the receiving technology.
- Content also looked different depending on the receiving technology.
- The technology was interactive, so the designer had to prepare content for non-linear browsing controlled by the consumer.
- The attention span of consumers was notoriously short.

**Exhibit 4.14   Internet Fashion Mall homepage, http://www
.fashionmall.com.**

While Web pages had a magazine-like quality (see Exhibits 4.14 and 4.15), the design was more like an architect's three-dimensional blueprint complete with drawings for the plumbers and electricians. This demanded a new skill set and perspective. Content had to be captivating in order for customers to repeatedly visit a Web site. Yet designers who knew how to use multimedia tools also had to understand the limitations of the technology displaying the content. For example, customers using the latest version of Netscape™ browsers were able to view certain types of graphic information, such as tables, that looked incoherent on earlier versions of Netscape™

**Exhibit 4.15   Internet Fashion Mall: Media, http://www.fashionmall
.com/media.html.**

software. As Ben looked out the conference room window, he reflected on finding talent:

> Finding people who understand and can design for this medium is hard, but recruiting them is next to impossible. There is an enormous demand for people with these talents, so they tend to be very well taken care of by their current employers.

MAKING MONEY ON THE WEB

Dealing with revolutionary technology in an emerging segment of a mature market, Ben targeted both business-to-consumer and business-to-business clients. Manufacturers, designers, retailers, trade media, and catalog marketers were all courted to join the *fashionmall*. The business-to-consumer market required something like an outlet store for manufacturers so they could communicate directly to consumers. In addition to online transactions and telling customers about local outlets and corporate news, clients could benefit from highly targeted market research. For the business-to-business market, *fashionmall* provided an inexpensive and fast way for manufacturers and designers to show their lines to retail buyers, and for the retail buyers to preview new products.

To create a place with leading-edge content, Ben pursued strategic relationships with a variety of fashion industry organizations and experts. He wanted to host an online advice column, up-to-the-minute trade show information, and online "breaking news" features for fashion magazines.

The list price for a *fashionmall* storefront was a $2,000 monthly fee for a minimum one-year period. This package gave the client ten Web pages. However, as a start-up in a relatively unproved medium, that list price didn't mean much. Ben experimented with various pricing models and offered special pricing to desirable clients. As a result, most clients ended up paying a combination of

1. A discount for signing up early,
2. Barter, and
3. Commissions on sales.

Ben planned to keep pricing flexible through the end of 1996.

> I want to use a rental business model to determine pricing for our fashion partners. Fashion partners will pay a flat monthly "rent" for an electronic storefront plus a percentage of sales transactions. As sales grow, I expect the bulk of our revenue to come from transactions. But right now, I'm mainly trying to make skeptics into believers.

In the *fashionmall* business plan, Ben projected income from licensing the fashion assistant technology, advertising (see Exhibit 4.16), promoting online contests, and a consumer discount club, but the biggest potential payoff seemed to come from selling market research data. Ben planned to build a data warehouse of demographic information by tracking shoppers and their Fashion Assistants through the mall. *Fashionmall* clients were given demographic and traffic reports as part of their membership in the *fashionmall*. This would help them to understand what market segments

EXHIBIT 4.16 Projected revenues by product.

Revenue streams	Pricing	Contribution
Site rentals per site	$10,000	90%
Monthly fee	5,000	90
Sales commissions		10
Distribution center		25
Service resales (EDI)		50
Communications marketing		85
Database information sales		70
Product sales		35–50
Advertising banners		90
Consumer added value programs (per person/per year)	25	90

were interested in their products, and how well their products might do in comparison to others. Unlike traditional test-market methods, *fashionmall* clients could test a product's viability by placing it on the *fashionmall* before incurring production and distribution costs. By noting consumer interest online, clients had more insight into a product's potential in the retail marketplace. Ben described his plans for cross-selling information:

> When some guy buys ties, the guy who sells shirts is going to want his name—the direct marketing potential is enormous. I want to hire a salesperson to expand the mall's scope and include sports and home areas. It's all about serving the better-lifestyles consumer. Once this gets rolling, it could go in all kinds of directions.

Ben began presenting his business plan to anyone in the trade who would listen. Ben conducted a wide variety of seminars highlighting the Internet and *fashionmall.com.* He presented to executives at The CIT Group, Israel Discount Bank, Rosenthal and Rosenthal, and Republic (4 major factor and banking firms involved in the apparel business). He also made presentations to Chemical Bank, the American Apparel Manufacturers Association (AAMA), Fashion Roundtable, and the Strategic Research Institute. His presentation to the AAMA was very successful; the audience feedback forms showed a 95 percent approval rating and heavy demand for further information and direct follow-up. In his presentations, Ben described the many benefits of having a storefront at *fashionmall.com:*

- Up-to-date information on the latest fashion news and trends.
- Fast, convenient shopping 24 hours a day, 7 days a week.
- A wide selection of clothing and accessories at one site.
- Access to fashion industry experts to answer questions.
- Secured, online purchasing as well as traditional telephone, e-mail, or fax ordering.

Eventually, Ben caught the eye of Bruce Strzelczyk and Thomas Bruno, partners at Richard A. Eisner & Co. (see Exhibit 4.17), a leading management consulting

EXHIBIT 4.17   Richard A. Eisner & Associates—services.

Internet consulting services	For Web page development as well as the application of sophisticated database/information management technologies.
Telecom	For advanced telecommunications support.
Firewall and security	For protection of existing systems while connected to the Net.
Data warehousing/data mining	For development of high-end database applications.
Distribution	For the creation of entire distribution centers to support order volume.
Tax specialists	For sales tax and related issues specific to the Internet.
Industry-specific accounting	For accounting and financial issues related to conducting apparel business on the Internet.

firm with many clients in the fashion industry. Bruce's areas of expertise were retail and the Internet, and Tom was primarily an information technology consultant (see Exhibit 4.18), so when they sat down with Ben, they asked some very pointed questions. Ben was thrilled—these guys really understood what he was trying to do. But it was more than the insightful discussion that impressed Ben; he liked these guys. In the space of two weeks, they decided to collaborate on *fashionmall.com*. Ben needed resources—money, technology, and personnel (see Exhibit 4.19)—and Eisner needed to provide Internet services to its fashion industry clients. They began working together immediately, leaving the details to their lawyers. Ben moved into Eisner's suite on Madison Avenue, received $130,000 in cash for marketing and computer programming, and split the time of new hires who would help with peak periods at Eisner and work for the *fashionmall* as needed. Ben described the working relationship in glowing terms:

> We have a unique collaboration that is one part in a high potential venture and the other a mature consulting firm. We work together when hiring staff, when preparing presentations, and with introductions. I need more resources, and they need an Internet project.

Eisner made its staff of technical and functional professionals available to *fashionmall.com*. This meant that Ben had access to expertise in information technology, accounting and tax services, and in-depth fashion industry experience.

The Partnership

Ben walked from the window back to the conference table and thought about his dilemma. Ben wanted to form a partnership with Eisner, but he wasn't sure he could accept what their lawyers demanded. On the other hand, this might be a matter of survival:

> I want to take this venture public, but I need funding in order to build on our lead position and be ready for an IPO. I'm looking for $2 to $2.5 million in the first round; are

EXHIBIT 4.18 Biographies.

Ben Narasin, Internet Fashion Mall, LLC, President (Age 30)

Ben brings a strong background in the apparel business as well as technology expertise. He oversees the company's management and has overall responsibility for business development and generation of leads. He functions as the primary promoter and is the primary media relations representative.

Prior to serving as the President of IFM, he founded and managed Boston Prepatory Company (BPC). BPC produced private-label merchandise for some of the country's leading fashion companies. As the CTO of BPC, Ben was responsible for all of the firm's hardware and software, including creating and maintaining the company's LAN and other networking systems. Ben occasionally writes about technology and the Internet for *Inc.* magazine's *Technology Quarterly* and for *Online* magazine. His personal achievements include receipt of an Effie award for advertising.

Thomas Bruno, RAE, Management Consultant (Age 34)

Tom, an RAE principal, is the leader of the firm's information technology practice that includes four major areas: Internet Consulting Services, Client/Server, Operations Management, and Telecommunications. He specializes in strategic technology planning, business performance, and the application of advanced technology. He is knowledgeable in most processing architectures, a broad range of enabling technologies, many leading business solutions, and various communications architectures including the Internet. In addition to his responsibilities as a practice leader, Tom takes an active role in client projects involving strategic planning activities.

Tom has participated in the development of financial and operational systems for clients across a range of industries including media and entertainment, professional services, travel, hospitality, and a variety of manufacturing and distribution companies. He actively participates in various technology and industry associations, and is a member of the Conference Board's Information Technology Executive Council.

Bruce J. Strzelczyk, CPA, RAE Management Consultant (Age 44)

Bruce, an RAE Partner, has extensive consulting and accounting experience in representing apparel, textile, and retail companies in obtaining and maintaining financing, SEC matters, purchase and sale of companies, corporate restructuring, strategic planning, and due diligence. He is actively involved in the firm's Internet consulting and corporate-finance practices, providing strategic planning assistance to Internet and technology-related companies.

Prior to joining RAE, Bruce was a partner in Arthur Andersen's Middle Market practice; prior to that, he was partner-in-charge of the apparel, textile, and retail practice at Laventhol & Horwath. Bruce is a member of the Financial Management Committee and the Membership Committee of the American Apparel Manufacturers Association. He is also active in the Intimate Apparel Association, the Fashion Roundtable, the Business Credit Club, and the Glen Rock Jaycees.

EXHIBIT 4.19   Pro forma financials.

	Six months ending 12/31/96 $(000)	Year ending 12/31/97 $(000)	Year ending 12/31/98 $(000)
Revenue:			
Fixed rent	$ 22	$ 1,312	$ 4,654
Percentage rent	0	4	5,045
Credit card processing	0	151	4,053
Distribution center	0	213	4,818
Management wings	2	23	49
Gold card membership fees	0	13	287
Commission on coop ads	0	30	30
Consulting referral fees	1	12	27
Total revenues	$ 25	$ 1,758	$18,962
Variable costs:			
Credit card costs	0	101	2,702
Distribution center costs	0	183	4,130
Expenses:			
Advertising/Marketing/Promotion	360	932	4,154
Sales	176	489	1,422
Technology	394	1,073	1,767
Overhead	42	337	305
Interest income	(27)	(40)	(39)
Total costs and expenses	$ 945	$ 3,075	$14,440
Pretax income (loss)	(920)	(1,316)	4,522
Income taxes	0	0	914
Net income	$(920)	$(1,316)	$ 3,608

Assumptions

1. Revenue assumptions are driven by expected growth in the number of sites. Management forecasts that there will be 63 net new sites by June 30, 1997, a further 167 net new sites by June 30, 1998, and a further 114 net new sites by December 31, 1998. All of these figures are net of a 20% annual nonrenewal factor. The sites operated by the company are excluded from the forecasts due to the nature of the special arrangements made with the early clients.
2. 60% of all sites are assumed to be manufacturers and the rest are assumed to be retailers. Through December 31, 1996, half of the sites are assumed to pay a fixed rent against 7% of sales and the remainder are assumed to pay percentage rent only. From January through June 1997, half of the percentage rent sites are assumed to pay fixed rent against 7% of sales, and starting in July 1997, all sites are assumed to pay fixed rent against 7% of sales. The fixed rent is forecast at $1,000 per month for manufacturers and $500 per month for retailers through December 1996; thereafter the fixed rent increases to $2,000 per month for manufacturers and $1,000 per month for retailers.
3. The forecast number of units sold per vendor increases from 8 per month in July 1996 to 75 per month in June 1997 and 3,000 per month in December 1998. 30% of all sites are expected to be operated as marketing sites only that sell no products. The forecast includes a 30% reserve on all sales for returned merchandise.

(Continued)

EXHIBIT 4.19   *(Continued)*

4. The company will charge its vendors a 3% credit card processing fee on all product sales. The cost of the related services is assumed to be 2% of sales.
5. The company will provide fulfillment services through a contracted distribution center for some of its vendors. It is assumed that 30% of net sales will be shipped through the distribution center with revenue of $7 per order and cost of $6 per order.
6. Management wings are forecast to sell $25,000 per year worth of merchandise in the first 12 months of operations and $50,000 per year thereafter. The company will earn half of the gross margin earned by the operators of the management wings, which is forecast at 40% of sales. IFM expects four management wings by June 1997 and six by December 1998.
7. The company expects that 0.5% of its customers each month will purchase a gold card membership for $25 which will entitle the holder to promotions, discounts, and contests sponsored by the vendors.
8. The company will earn a 15% commission on coop advertising in magazines and other publications sponsored by the company's vendors. Management expects 10 pages in each of 1997 and 1998 at $20,000 per page.
9. The company earns a fee for any consulting business referred to RAE, at rates ranging between 5% and 10% of billing.

Expenses

1. Public relations agency, marketing materials, promotions, video news releases, online key-word sponsorship and trade shows are each budgeted to increase 10% per annum.
2. Media purchases are budgeted at $700,000 for the twelve months beginning September 1996 and at 20% of revenue each month thereafter.
3. Sales staff is budgeted to receive a 5% increase in salary each year. Half of base salary is considered a draw against commission of 10% of site rental fees. Additional sales staff is assumed to be paid commission only, at 10% of site rental fees.
4. Benefits are calculated at 15% of all the company's salaries and commissions. An additional 20% of all the company's salaries are paid to RAE to cover general and administrative expenses such as rent, utilities, telephone, and accounting services.
5. Outsourcing and nonpayroll research and development are budgeted to increase 10% annually.
6. Additional technical staff is budgeted at $35,000 per person. The number of people is determined in each month by the number of man-months required to create new sites and maintain existing sites.
7. RAE receives 10% of total revenue, net of commissions earned, through December 1997.
8. Pro forma income taxes are calculated at 40% after operating losses commencing in July 1996.

Balance Sheet

1. All revenue is assumed to be collected in the month earned, other than advertising commissions and referral fees, which are assumed to be collected in 60 days.
2. Capital expenditures are budgeted at $75,000 per quarter commencing July 1996 and at $100,000 per quarter commencing July 1997. Fixed assets are depreciated over 5 years.
3. Accounts payable is assumed to be paid in 30 days for all costs other than salary, commissions, benefits, and G&A expenses paid to RAE.

these the best guys to get the job done? They don't do IPOs, but I think they have the finance industry network and reputation to be credible raising that kind of capital.

Besides, Eisner has already contributed $130,000, we share staff, and I'm committed to sharing some of the proceeds from the IPO—it would be tricky to walk away now. So far we have made a lot of progress on the partnership agreement, but Eisner's lawyers are taking a tough line. They want the right to control my management hires, where and when I get money, and what technology I develop. I'm just not sure it's worth it.

I'm trying to move away from sales so I can focus more on relationships with opinion leaders with access to content, but I can't. I need to hire another salesman who can pull in more fashion partners. I also need better technology to make sure the *fashionmall* experience is something people tell their friends about—but everything takes money. I'm worried, we have a good pull-position but how do I make sure I get return customers? I've got to have more resources now!

If they could just allow me to retain control, I would sign today. I really need a partner, but I have to be thinking about the 2nd, 3rd, and 4th rounds of financing. I don't want to give up control so early in the game.

PREPARATION QUESTIONS

1. How do you judge the market for revolutionary technology or products? How can you tell if the market is ready for you? How do you measure the risk?
2. Who is Ben's competition?
3. Is *fashionmall* an apparel company or a software company?

5 NEVERFAIL COMPUTING

THANKSGIVING WEEKEND, 1994

Tim Delaney, the founder and CEO of Neverfail Computing (a provider of fault-tolerant hardware systems), was with his wife and child at home, but he was preoccupied with events across town where his CFO and partner, Ted Jones, was negotiating for venture capital. Tim asked Ted to handle the negotiations that weekend, but it was hard to stay away. At stake were the terms and covenants that would bind Neverfail to its venture partners. Sales in October and November were awful, and they needed cash soon or things could get messy.

TIM DELANEY

Tim, the oldest of four children, was raised in a San Francisco suburb. He graduated from high school in 1980, and spent a year performing manual labor in an industrial factory before attending college. His experience with physical labor steeled his determination to go to college and get a job where he would be paid for thinking.

Tim graduated in 1985 from Bessemer College in Hillsborough, California. He majored in entrepreneurship and marketing. As part of his education, Tim and a classmate, Dan Hopkins, developed a business plan in Professor Ditchin's entrepreneurship class and submitted it to the Bessemer College Business Plan Contest. They won top honors and the $5,000 cash prize.

This case was prepared by Dan D'Heilly with assistance from Kevin Ebel under the direction of Professor William Bygrave. Copyright © 1995 Babson College. All rights reserved.

Tim was introduced to the computer industry during a senior-year marketing class assignment, when he accompanied Bill Deane on a sales call for R&A Computing. R&A Computing, then a $50 million computer component reseller, sold physical storage for large computers. During that meeting, Bill convinced the customer to trade 64MB of IBM physical memory for 128MB of "generic" R&A Computing physical memory. Essentially, Bill bartered the R&A computer board for the IBM board. The manufacturing cost of R&A's 128MB board was about $6,000, and it resold the IBM 64MB board for $100,000. The gross profit on this deal was $94,000. Tim was impressed, "In a little over an hour, we made two sales calls and Bill earned $11,000 in commission. I decided right then and there to build a career in this industry."

THE INDUSTRY: PHYSICAL STORAGE IN COMPUTERS

Three near-revolutionary trends in physical storage created a business opportunity for Neverfail in the early 1990s:

1. The increase in computer memory capacity and requirements;
2. The move from proprietary to open systems; and
3. The move from centralized to decentralized computing systems.

However, these decentralized, open, high-capacity systems didn't work very well. Centralized systems very rarely failed; decentralized ones failed regularly.

The capacity of computer hardware to store data had undergone continual improvement. Historically, disk capacity doubled every 18 months. As a result, powerful new software applications were written that generated more data, and thus, the supply and demand for physical storage grew.

A second trend in physical storage was the move from proprietary to open-system architecture. Prior to the late 1980s, large computer firms such as IBM, Digital, and WANG designed proprietary systems that were not compatible with systems from other vendors. Because they had to buy propriety components, clients were referred to as an original equipment manufacturer's (OEM) "captive base." As a result, each major OEM created a unique computer niche market where its proprietary systems required customized components.

As computers became more of a commodity product, consumers demanded nonproprietary systems that used standards common to all vendors—open-system products. All OEMs began moving toward open-system product lines. The transition to open systems occurred rapidly because the product-development cycle time was only nine months by the early 1990s.

The third trend was the move away from centralized computing solutions (i.e., mainframe systems) and toward flexible and inexpensive distributed computing environments (i.e., local area networks (LANs) and wide area networks (WANs)). Business was migrating from mainframes to PCs. The total installed base of LAN servers was projected to increase at an average annual rate of 42 percent through 1995. This change was made possible by enormous strides in capacity and computing power in desktop PCs.

Part of the historic success of centralized systems stemmed from their ability to share hardware and software. However, distributed computing systems had that same resource-sharing advantage; printers, modems, fax machines, databases, communications, and other software could be used by any computer on the network. Furthermore, distributed-computing hardware was less expensive than centralized-system hardware. When decentralized systems were compared to centralized systems, hardware savings were often in the 50 to 70 percent range. However, maintenance of the new systems was usually much more costly, and quality control posed a potential problem.

NEW TECHNOLOGY: FAULT-TOLERANT, HOT-REPLACEABLE SYSTEMS

With increased dependence on distributed computing came two major problems: increased downtime (low data availability) and faulty information (poor data integrity). If data retrieved from computer storage were the same as the data that went into the computer, there was a high level of data integrity. When data were unintentionally altered by operations within the machine, data integrity was compromised.

Data integrity was ensured by creating fault-tolerant systems. RAID (Redundant Arrays of Inexpensive Disks) technology was one of the most popular types of fault-tolerant systems. Basically, RAID technology created and stored a back-up copy of the data on a separate disk at the same time that the original was stored. Then, when a disk failed, redundant data on the nonfailed disks were used to recreate the data of the failed disk. No data were lost despite hardware failure.

RAID technology was first developed by IBM in the 1970s, but found popular use in the late 1980s, after a group of researchers at the University of California at Berkeley published an article suggesting broad new applications. Most physical storage systems developed by Neverfail were based on RAID technology.

Data availability was the second serious vulnerability of decentralized mass storage systems—did a computer operate when it was needed? If everyone was working on computers and the computers failed, then the company failed until the computers were working again. This problem was addressed by creating systems with redundant components that could fail and be replaced while the system remained on—"hot-replaceable" or "hot-pluggable" systems. Data availability required being able to exchange the failed unit without turning the system off. All of Neverfail's products were hot-pluggable.

When clients were sophisticated enough to demand solutions to ensure data integrity, they generally wanted solutions for data availability, too. Beginning in late 1992, the hottest products in the computer mass storage industry were those that combined RAID and components that could be replaced while the computer was in operation. This niche was the focus of Neverfail's marketing and development.

The total market for RAID technology was based on the demand for mass storage. The installed capacity of mass storage systems in 1993 was 9,512TBs,° while the

---

° Terabyte = one thousand Gigabytes; Gigabyte = one thousand Megabytes.

installed RAID base was only 596TBs. There was a very large potential market for RAID technology.

Competition

Through the mid-1990s, the RAID industry was dominated by proprietary manufacturers who focused service and sales on their own installed base. Consumers usually standardized on one computer manufacturer, so competition between manufacturers for RAID business was rare. For example, SUN rarely sold mass storage to IBM customers.

Systems vendors—led by IBM ($209 million) and DEC ($205 million), with Compaq, Tandem, Data General, SUN, and Silicon Graphics all competing at the next tier—captured over 60 percent of the RAID market in 1993. However, their share was expected to drop to under 50 percent by 1996 as independent vendors—the leader at the end of 1993 was EMC ($315 million)—captured an increasing share of the market. During these same years, industry revenue was projected to grow from $2 billion to $10.4 billion.

The disk drive array/RAID market outpaced the growth in LAN installations in 1994. In 1993, fewer than 100 companies offered disk drive arrays, but by the end of 1994, there were 154 companies offering them, most with some type of RAID technology. There were also fast-developing markets for other systems to safeguard network operations.

Neverfail focused on hardware solutions for Silicon Graphics' captive base, so Silicon Graphics was its primary competitor. The dominant third party competing in Silicon Graphics' marketplace was EMC; all other independent vendors were insignificant by comparison. Yet neither EMC nor Silicon Graphics was focused on the Silicon Graphics mass storage upgrade market. Both competitors were gearing up for the open-systems market and they treated Silicon Graphics' captive base as an after-thought. Neverfail had an opportunity to grow without arousing powerful competitors.

R&A COMPUTING, 1985–1989

During college, Tim's part-time job at Bessemer College paid $9/hr, but he wanted to work in the mass storage market. He asked R&A for a job. It was only willing to pay him $6/hr to be a telemarketer. Tim took the pay cut:

> There weren't any guarantees, but I paid for my own training by working as a telemarketer. I had a job waiting with R&A Computing when I graduated.

Upon graduation, Tim worked as a sales representative. He enjoyed figuring out the angles and taking on the old IBM salesmen. It was a formative time for building skills, industry knowledge, and contacts. For example, he met future Neverfail partner Kevin Brady at R&A.

After a year and a half, Tim grew frustrated with company management. He thought they were missing major opportunities. In fact, R&A Computing was

floundering—at one point it almost ran out of cash. When he was recruited by Byteway Computers, a local computer reseller, Tim was ready to leave R&A.

BYTEWAY COMPUTERS, 1989–1991

Tim joined Byteway Computers as a salesman, but he saw beyond its traditional market of brokering used Silicon Graphics equipment. He soon added third-party storage
components to the company's product list. This was a new market for Byteway, and it
soon became a major revenue source. Tim was its top salesperson within a year and
was promoted to sales manager. Over the next 18 months, the company tripled in size
from $7 million in 1989, to a projected $21 million for 1991.

However, he felt increasingly frustrated by senior management's lack of enthusiasm for his initiatives. He persuaded three other employees to leave Byteway with
him and start a new company to pursue a quasi-manufacturing idea that Byteway had
rejected. Tim began writing a business plan (based on the plan he wrote at Bessemer
College) to prepare for this opportunity. However, Byteway heard about the planned
start-up, and the four would-be entrepreneurs were summarily fired.

Unfortunately, Tim wasn't ready to start the new venture. Their plan was to
produce open-system SCSI [pronounced: scuzzy] devices: low-cost, low-tech, and
low-margin, but with excellent volume potential. This required capital and distribution channels that weren't immediately available.

They considered boot-strapping the new business, but the timing was wrong.
Tim's wife was two months pregnant with their first child, and he didn't want to start
a new company at a time when she needed a lot of attention. He was also not ready for
the financial risk. He jumped at an offer to bring his team and their idea to Axionic
Development, where he would create a new SCSI business unit. As division manager,
Tim would have complete P&L responsibility.

AXIONIC DEVELOPMENT, 1991–1993

Axionic Development had over 250 employees and $60 million in annual revenues.
This was a firm with a strong computer storage product line and an excellent distribution system. Tim was recruited by Kevin Brady, a friend from his days at R&A
Computing. Axionic wanted Tim to create and manage a new mass storage division
that it could move through its distribution network. Kevin needed managers he could
trust because the foundation of his distribution network was integrity. Axionic provided warranty and nonwarranty after-market support for the distributor's customer-
base, and Kevin knew that Tim would do what he said he would do.

Tim's department did not engineer new products. It was a revenue center focused on generating cash and earnings:

> They left me alone. I used a different business model, grew my own salesforce, and
> started manufacturing. We reverse-engineered products, then sold them for half of
> what the competition was asking.

Tim's mass storage division was very profitable. It asked customers for problems, then created systems that solved them. Tim's unit was producing revenue at $15 million annualized when problems caught up with Axionic Development.

In 1990, Axionic Development had some of the best technology in the world, $27 million cash in the bank, and no debt. The founder and CEO was a brilliant engineer but a poor manager. Resources were squandered on nonrevenue-producing projects, perks, and technically elegant projects that didn't solve customer's problems. Axionic also lacked sales savvy. Tim characterized its sales approach as "order taking and tech support."

When the world caught up with Axionic Development's leading-edge products in 1993, its R&D didn't have another "world's best product," so there were no more orders waiting to be written. In early 1993, two groups emerged from Axionic Development to start their own companies; one was led by Tim Delaney, the other by Axionic's former CEO.

NEVERFAIL COMPUTING

The exodus from Axionic Development occurred during the last week of February 1993. Four staff members and three managers cofounded Neverfail Computing. They started a new market-driven company specializing in fault-tolerant, hot-replaceable mass storage systems that used open-systems architecture.

Neverfail Computing designed and marketed computer storage peripherals for the workstation, minicomputer, and network file server markets. Neverfail's products included proprietary fault-tolerant storage subsystems, communications controllers, and other off-the-shelf storage products that were designed to provide mass storage capacity for mid-range and large computer systems in the financial, medical, manufacturing, and telecommunications markets.

The Management Team

The founding team was composed of three industry professionals—two managers from sales and marketing and one from engineering. Tim Delaney, chief executive officer, was joined by Kevin Brady as president and chief operating officer and by Richard Murdoch as vice president of engineering and operations. All three had held management positions at leading firms in the computer industry for at least three years, and, perhaps most important, they had moved as a team from Axionic Development.

Kevin Brady was Axionic Development's distribution manager from 1988 to 1993. Prior to joining Axionic, Kevin worked for R&A Computing from 1982 to 1988. R&A Computing was where Tim and Kevin met and became friends.

Richard Murdoch directed Axionic Development's engineering department from 1988 to 1993. Prior to joining Axionic, Rick was the director of customer support at Silicon Graphics for five years.

However, the team was still incomplete; they needed a finance manager. Kevin's best friend from high school, Ted Jones, had a strong background in finance. Tim and

Kevin had recruited him, but Ted was not willing to leave Citibank where he was a vice president responsible for several loan portfolios, until Neverfail was more established. He consulted part-time for the first nine months and joined full-time as chief financial officer and vice president of finance in December 1993.

Corporate Strategy

The underlying idea behind Neverfail's plan was a broad vision about the future of the computer industry. Tim explained their position:

> In corporate America today, everything except physical labor is done on a computer. Our first and overriding goal was fault-tolerant data management, storage, and availability. Computers were becoming easier to use and more important for running almost everything. At the same time, their circuitry was becoming more complex and loss from downtime [elapsed time that a computer is inoperable] more critical, thus completely fault-tolerant data management systems had to evolve soon. We planned to be there when it happened.
>
> We didn't want to be a hardware company, a software company, or a network company. We wanted to be a data management company defined by niches that sprang from our evolving R&D skills. As the revolution to fault-tolerant systems unfolded, there would be a huge market. We anticipated that our biggest problem would be focusing our resources.

Neverfail's strategy also centered on the idea that the computer market would change too rapidly to be product-driven. As Tim Delaney stated:

> For long-term success, computer companies had to be market-driven. We sold what the marketplace wanted by asking customers, "What would make your life easier?" We just wanted to make products that solved problems.

Another pillar of Neverfail's strategy was to develop products using open-system standards. It avoided using proprietary components whenever possible. The benefit of using open-system standards was improved speed to market and adaptability. As Tim remarked:

> We had some of the best stuff in our market in 1994, but that wouldn't always be true—things moved too fast in computer mass storage. Major change was predictable, but the direction wasn't, so we were constantly preparing for change.
>
> We used open systems so that the company could thrive regardless of who won a particular development battle over protocols or standards. As a result, I needed only three weeks of redevelopment time when a better widget came out. We developed products that worked with interchangeable components. We also avoided inventing anything that we could buy. That way we shortened cycle times while creating products that solved specific problems.

Product History

Neverfail's personnel had technical expertise in mass storage and RAID technology. Their first products were fairly low-tech SCSI systems—mass data storage—that could be produced without a large infrastructure. They knew the product, they knew the distributors, and the market was under-supplied (partially as a result of Axionic Development's demise), so they were able to get orders from distributors. Because the basic idea behind RAID technology was fault tolerance and data security, consumers tended to look for name-brand awareness when they bought RAID systems. By representing Neverfail products, distributors extended their credibility to the young company. This was also critical for Neverfail's entry into the market.

Customers wanted computers that didn't break, so Neverfail's second product used a RAID configuration. They had created (reverse-engineered) a low-end RAID product at Axionic Development, so they improved on that design and offered a basic RAID product for the low-end market. However, they still needed products for more sophisticated systems.

Neverfail had to expand beyond the high-volume, low-margin SCSI drive market because this was a cash intensive business. A little profit required a lot of cash flow. Their largely self-financed operation needed better margins to survive. Better margins were one of the major reasons to develop a RAID product line.

The Neverfail team developed a product for an emerging niche in RAID technology, the mid-range, high-tech market. RAID technology was initially a feature only available in high-end products. It was very complex and expensive. Neverfail licensed, then adapted, Data General's mid-range UNIX RAID system, Clariion, for the Silicon Graphics market. This low-cost, high-tech RAID system could be built for a fraction of what traditional high-end RAID systems cost.

As a result, Neverfail was one of the first mid-range RAID providers for Silicon Graphics. Typically, high-end systems were sold, installed, and serviced by the OEM, but this mid-range system was simple and inexpensive enough to be sold through distributors, and Neverfail had excellent distribution channels.

Their next product was a component that connected RAID SCSI storage systems to the servers° that run distributed computing networks. It fit squarely into their SCSI storage systems and used RAID technology. Neverfail was well on its way to producing a complete fault-tolerant system, it only lacked one product—the server.

Servers ran distributed computing systems. By December 1994, Neverfail's R&D was focused on producing a hot-pluggable, fault-tolerant server which would serve data generically to all types of systems. This would give them a complete open-system, hot-tolerant product line and an entree into the larger, non-Silicon Graphics mass storage market.

A financial expectation was imposed on all R&D projects—each new component would pay its own way. As Ted Jones stated:

> We sold every component of our R&D along the way. The goal was to get into the server market. How do you do that? There were certain building blocks you needed within the system. Our first product was the first block, the second was the second block, and so on. We funded our R&D with sales.

° A server is any computer used to control the activities of a local or wide area network (LAN or WAN). The server usually housed the database and other application software used by all computers on the network, as well as sophisticated software for managing network operations.

FINANCING NEVERFAIL COMPUTING

Contacts, Friends, and Family

The founding employees had offered the only source of start-up capital. Neverfail got a $48,000 loan from two employees, and each Neverfail employee used personal savings for living expenses while the company became a going concern. Between February and October of 1993, no one received a paycheck. (See Exhibits 5.1, 5.2, and 5.3.)

Their survival plan consisted of two parts: (1) leveraging industry relationships to generate cash, beginning with the first month of operations, and (2) spending no money. For example, they rented an old factory building because the rent was $1 sq/ft and because it didn't require a deposit.

Their ability to nurture relationships with the industry's three biggest distributors was critical to their success. During fiscal 1994, three distributors and one leasing company provided almost all of Neverfail's revenue. Tim's Axionic Development division had supplied distributors with SCSI drives in January, so offering to supply them from Neverfail in February seemed like a reasonable proposition.

The distributors had many Axionic customers who no longer got technical support from Axionic. These were potentially angry customers. Neverfail offered free customer support for old Axionic hardware if the distributors would carry its products and help supply it with operating capital (e.g., vendor credit).

Structuring the deal was key because of Neverfail's cash shortage—it couldn't afford to buy raw materials. Distributors had orders *and* the raw materials needed to fulfill those orders, so Neverfail proposed to use the same distributor for both halves of each deal. If a distributor sold the raw materials and then received the finished goods, the monetary transaction would wait until the whole deal was finished. Tim called this financing method "contra-funding."

> For the first six months, the distributors gave us contra-funding: they carried us by "selling" us components that we assembled and "sold" back to them—except no money changed hands until they paid us the difference between the component's price and the finished product's price. These deals were all financed by the distributors—they just gave us the gross profit when we gave them the finished goods.

Neverfail shipped products two weeks after unlocking its warehouse doors. As Tim recalled:

> These were low-end, low-margin, slap-it-together SCSI drives. No infrastructure was required, and there was no value-added engineering. It just required access to the market, and we had access through our distributors.

Because of its reliance on contra-funding, even when Neverfail generated an order, the order went directly to one of its distributors, because distributors were financing its deals. It took nine months to get out of the contra-funding cycle and start paying directly for raw materials. At that point, CFO Ted Jones recalls continuing to leverage the distributor's receivables and payables, but in a different way:

> We began discounting distributors for quick paying, but we typically paid our vendors in 45 days, so that their cash could fund our new deals. They were still the major capital source for Neverfail.

EXHIBIT 5.1   Neverfail statement of stockholders' equity.

For the Year Ended March 31, 1994

| | Convertible preferred stock number of $.01 par | | Common stock number of $.01 par | | Additional paid-in capital | Accumulated deficit | Total stockholders' equity |
	Shares	Value	Shares	Value			
Balance as of March 31, 1993	—	—	4,795,000	$47,960	—	$ (47,960)	—
Sale of convertible preferred stock, net of issuance costs	550,000	$5,500	—	—	$535,747	—	$ 541,247
Sale of common stock	—	—	401,500	4,015	—	—	4,015
Repurchase and retirement of common stock	—	—	(44,000)	(440)	—	—	(440)
Net loss	—	—	—	—	—	(369,584)	(369,584)
Balance as of March 31, 1994	550,000	$5,500	5,153,500	$51,535	$535,747	$(417,544)	$175,239

EXHIBIT 5.2   Neverfail balance sheet—March 31, 1994.

ASSETS
Current assets:

Cash	$ 50,161
Accounts receivable	406,648
Inventories	356,941
Total current assets	$ 813,750

Property and equipment (at cost):

Machinery and equipment	88,252
Furniture and fixtures	14,772
Total property and equipment	$ 103,024
Less accumulated depreciation	(18,792)
Total property and equipment	$ 84,232
Other assets	2,598
Total assets	$ 900,580

LIABILITIES AND STOCKHOLDERS' EQUITY
Current liabilities:

Accounts payable	$ 403,556
Accrued expenses	112,010
Demand notes payable to stockholders	31,815
Amount due to stockholder	177,960
Total current liabilities	$ 725,341

Stockholders' equity:

Convertible preferred stock, $.01 value[1]	5,500
Common stock, $.01 par value[2]	51,535
Additional paid-in capital	535,747
Accumulated deficit	(417,544)
Total stockholders' equity	$ 175,239
Total liabilities and stockholders' equity	$ 900,580

[1] Issued and outstanding—550,000 shares.
[2] Issued and outstanding—5,153,500 shares.

Angel Financing

Two of the three Neverfail partners were former employees of the successful R&A Computing; in fact, COO Kevin Brady was one of its first employees. Kevin called the retired cofounder of R&A Computing, George Lawrence, when Neverfail was seeking members for its board of directors. He called George in June, again in July, and they finally talked in August.

The partners met with George in September and asked for his help. He had succeeded with a start-up computer company, and they knew his advice could be invaluable. They worried that he would think they were just after his money, so they told him flat-out, "We want your help, not your money." In fact, they continued to refuse his financial assistance until George literally said, "What's wrong with my money?"

EXHIBIT 5.3   Notes to financial statements, FYE 3/31/94.

(3) STOCKHOLDERS' EQUITY

  (a) *Convertible Preferred Stock*

  The Board of Directors has authorized the issuance of 2,000,000 shares of preferred stock, of which 500,000 shares are designated as convertible preferred stock. The preferred stockholders have the following rights and privileges:

  Voting

  The holders of the convertible preferred stock will vote with the common stockholders as a single class on all matters, with one vote for each share held.

  Conversion

  Each share of outstanding preferred stock is convertible at any time into one share of common stock. The conversion of preferred stock is automatic upon the closing of a private or public offering of its securities by the Company, resulting in net proceeds of at least $2,000,000 to the Company.

  Liquidation

  The holders of the convertible preferred stock have preference and priority over common stockholders and any other preferred stockholders upon liquidation of the Company.

  (b) *Common Stock Repurchase Agreements*

  Certain of the Company's common stockholders are subject to agreements that allow the Company to repurchase any unvested common stock for $.01 per share upon termination, as defined. A total of 4,420,000 shares are subject to these repurchase rights, which expire ratably over periods ranging from three to four years. As of March 31, 1994, no shares subject to repurchase were vested.

  (c) *Stock Option Plan*

  In May 1994, the Board of Directors granted incentive stock options to purchase 300,000 shares of common stock to certain employees with an exercise price of $.50 per share. The options vest over four years.

(6) SALE OF PREFERRED STOCK SUBSEQUENT TO MARCH 31, 1994

  (a) *Convertible Preferred Stock*

  Subsequent to March 31, 1994, the Company sold 400,000 shares of convertible preferred stock resulting in total proceeds to the Company of $400,000. These shares of convertible preferred stock have the same rights and privileges as those convertible preferred shares described in Note 3(a).

  (b) *Series B Convertible Redeemable Preferred Stock*

  On December 30, 1994, the Company sold 1,000,000 shares of Series B convertible redeemable preferred stock (Series B preferred stock) at $1.50 per share. In connection with the financing, the Company designated the convertible preferred stock (as described above and in Note 3(a)) as Series A convertible preferred stock (Series A preferred stock). The Series B preferred stock has the following rights and privileges:

  Voting

  The holders of the Series B preferred stock will vote with the Series A preferred stockholders and common stockholders as a single class on matters, with one vote for each share held. Upon the occurrence of certain events, as defined, the Series B preferred stockholders will vote as a separate class.

(Continued)

EXHIBIT 5.3 *(Continued)*

Conversion

Each share of outstanding Series B preferred stock is convertible at any time into an equal number of shares of common stock at the option of the holder. The conversion of Series B preferred stock is automatic upon the firm commitment of an initial public offering of the Company's common stock, resulting in gross proceeds of at least $7,000,000 and a price of at least $3.75 per share.

Liquidation

Holders of Series B preferred stock are subordinate to Series A preferred stockholders and have preference and priority over common stockholders upon liquidation of the Company. In the event of liquidation, the Series B preferred stockholders shall be paid $1.50 per share plus a portion of any additional distributions, as defined.

Redemption

Series B preferred stockholders have the option to have all of their outstanding shares redeemed by the Company for cash on or after December 30, 2001. The holders of Series B preferred stock shall be paid cash equal to the greater of the fair market value per share or the original purchase price plus all dividend declared but unpaid at the redemption date.

He participated in Neverfail's second placement by purchasing $250,000 worth of preferred stock, and in the first week of October, the seven founders received their first paychecks. They were also able to expand their sales staff for the first time.

Over the next year, George provided over a million dollars in debt and equity capital. He invested a total of $650,000 in preferred stock at $1 per share, and acted as banker when a large deal needed funding. Once a contract was signed, George acted as a factor and bought the account receivable. This allowed Neverfail to sign contracts that its own financial situation couldn't support.

As George was being courted, the partners were introduced by a board member to an investor from Seattle. He was Neverfail's first outside investor, and he made an initial placement of $50,000. He made a second placement of $100,000 a year later, bringing his total investment to $150,000. His shares were also purchased at $1 per share.

There were other potential "angel" funding sources. The chairman of a major manufacturing company was interested, and a couple of family friends talked about investing, but nothing else worked out.

Besides, the company was profitable from the first month of operations, and they were successfully boot-strapping growth from cash flow and creative financing. They weren't eager to begin giving equity away before the company's value increased.

Venture Capital

The search for venture capital began with a six-minute presentation at an American Electronics Association venture capital conference. Tim wasn't looking for an immediate cash infusion, but his lawyers suggested it would be good preparation for the inevitable fund-raising and IPO meetings to come.

After the six-minute presentation, each company's executives were assigned to a meeting room. Three or four VCs stopped by to talk with Tim, Kevin, and Ted.

Palo Alto Capital called Neverfail after the conference, but didn't pursue the discussion. However, they contacted Pacific Ridge Capital partner Leo Frank to tell him about Neverfail Computing. Leo met with Tim and Ted for two hours to get a feel for the potential fit.

Tim gave Leo an overview of Neverfail Computing, the future of the computer industry, and how they were positioned to prosper. Leo decided to invest early money in Neverfail at that first meeting. As Ted recalled:

> What Leo cared about was that seven guys did $2 million in their first year with only $45,000 in outside capital during the first seven months. We said we'd do $6 million in year two, and we were on track to do it. He said "OK, I believe." From then on, it was about negotiating the specific details. (See Exhibits 5.4, 5.5, and 5.6.)

Neverfail conveyed a relaxed, casual negotiating attitude. They maintained that they weren't all that interested in raising capital. As Tim recalled, "We told him that we didn't need or want anything and wouldn't know what we'd do with the money if we had it."

Despite their air of disinterest, the Neverfail partners stated from the beginning that any deal had to be signed by December 31, 1994. They didn't want the process to drag on. After that date, everything would be open to renegotiation.

As serious negotiations began, and the Neverfail partners conceded that they needed venture capital, George became their ace in the hole. "We don't need your money enough to do a bad deal—because we've got George."

But in fact, urgency was developing because Neverfail Computing faced a cash crunch. Sales weren't meeting fourth-quarter goals—Neverfail ended the fourth quarter 30 percent under plan—so the company needed money to finance deals and continue its rapid growth. George was approached for a short-term loan, but he

EXHIBIT 5.4   Neverfail statement of operations.

For the Year Ended March 31, 1994

Revenue	$2,238,151
Cost of revenues	1,523,514
Gross margin	$ 714,637
Operating expenses	
S, G, & A	987,544
R & D	94,362
	$1,081,906
Loss from operations	(367,269)
Interest expense	2,314
Net loss	$ (369,584)

EXHIBIT 5.5   Neverfail statement of cash flows.

For the Year Ended March 31, 1994

Cash flows from operating activities:	
Net loss	$(369,584)
Adjustment to reconcile net loss to net cash used in operating activities:	
Depreciation and amortization	18,792
Changes in assets and liabilities	
Accounts receivable	(406,648)
Inventories	(356,941)
Accounts payable	403,556
Accrued expenses	112,010
Net cash used in operating activities	$(598,815)
Cash flows from investing activities:	
Purchases of property and equipment	(103,024)
Increase in other assets	(2,598)
Net cash used in investing activities	$(105,622)
Cash flows from financing activities:	
Amount due to stockholder	177,960
Notes payable to stockholders	31,815
Proceeds from sale of common stock	4,015
Purchase and retirement of common stock	(440)
Net proceeds: sales of convertible preferred stock	541,247
Net cash provided by financing activities	$ 754,598
Net increase in cash	50,161
Cash, start	0
Cash, end	$ 50,161

wasn't happy about increasing his investment because of missed sales goals. Neverfail really needed a fresh source of financing.

Valuation

Pacific Ridge Capital opened negotiations in October by stating that Neverfail was worth $0.05/share. Tim countered that they were worth $20/share because George and the Seattle investor had purchased shares at $1/share in 1993, and that was before they exceeded their sales and profitability goals for FYE March 31, 1994. Pacific Ridge maintained that the early round investors overpaid, "You were worth $0.25 at best." Both sides searched for justifications for their price.

The Neverfail team was nervous about dealing with a venture capitalist, so they used a negotiating precaution that Ted had learned at the bank:

> I wanted to have a witness to all conversations, because I'd seen terms changed during negotiations that the affected party didn't notice. I'd seen that tactic used intentionally before, so I tried to have a second witness on the telephone whenever possible.

EXHIBIT 5.6 Neverfail pro forma income statement–FYE 3/31/95.

| | Quarter | | | | FYE |
	1	2	3	4	3/31/95
Net sales	$984	$1,298	$1,711	$2,141	$6,134
Material costs:					
Begin inventory	280	333	371	489	280
Purchases	638	805	1,122	1,373	3,937
Ending inventory	333	371	489	612	612
Total material cost	$585	$ 766	$1,004	$1,250	$3,605
Gross material margin	399	532	708	891	2,529
G.M.M.%	41%	41%	41%	42%	41%
SG&A expenses:					
R&D	$ 18	$ 18	$ 18	$ 18	$ 74
Payroll	194	206	206	206	814
Manufacturing equipment	7	7	7	7	29
Depreciation	0	0	0	0	0
Rent and leases	14	17	19	22	72
Insurance	15	18	20	24	78
Travel and entertainment	25	36	36	36	133
Net shipping	7	10	12	14	43
Equipment	7	7	7	7	29
Telephone	10	12	14	17	53
Postage	2	4	6	7	19
Office supplies	5	5	7	10	26
Utilities	22	29	32	38	122
Marketing	7	10	12	14	43
Other miscellaneous	16	0	0	0	16
Finance expense	0	0	0	0	0
Sales commissions	36	65	86	43	230
Total SG&A	$387	$ 444	$ 483	$ 465	$1,779
EBT	$ 11	$ 88	$ 224	$ 426	$ 750

At this point, the Neverfail partners increased the pressure on Pacific Ridge by meeting with another venture capital suitor, Golden Bear Investments. They were introduced by Professor Ditchin, who looked at Pacific Ridge's first offer and suggested that Leo might not be serious about doing a deal. Discussions with Golden Bear Investments didn't progress very far, but it reassured Tim that they were on the right path.

Negotiations with Pacific Ridge got more serious in early November. Pacific Ridge moved up to $0.75, and Neverfail moved down to $2; these share prices valued Neverfail at $3 million and $12 million, respectively. Ted described the negotiations:

> We were on the phone, and we all wanted to do a deal, but Leo was nowhere near where we needed him to be. He moved up to slightly more than a dollar, but we

couldn't let our shares go for that, because we sold our shares for a buck last year. I decided to create a spreadsheet that would value the firm, given different assumptions. With this table, I could ask Leo for his assumptions, then give him our value using his own numbers. This was a tactic I used to analyze and negotiate acquisitions I financed for the bank. I wanted to know what we were worth in real time while we were negotiating on the phone.

I created the spreadsheet with different rates of return (IRR) and cash flow assumptions and ran a discounted cash flow analysis. Then Leo and I went down a list of valuation issues. I asked about assumptions, "Could you buy into an annual growth of 40 percent from 1995 to 1999?" He said "Yes." I asked what IRR he needed, and he said 50 percent annually over five years. We also agreed on a terminal value. I said "OK, if you accept those assumptions, we're worth over $3 a share. According to a standard discounted cash flow valuation formula, I'm giving it to you a dollar short at $2." Leo replied, "But I just can't do that."

This was a turning point in the negotiations, because now there was a line in the sand. Maybe he wasn't going to give us what the valuation said we were worth, but now it was his job to tell us why.

Tim and Leo reached an agreement in principle during the second week in November: (1) Neverfail was worth $9 million, or $1.50 a share; (2) the total Pacific Ridge investment would be at least $1 million; (3) covenants would be minimal; and (4) the deal would be signed by December 31.

Pacific Ridge's lawyers hastily drew up a statement of terms and conditions (see Exhibit 5.7). They were in a big hurry, because six weeks wasn't enough time to do a thorough due diligence, and they couldn't get started on that until after the covenants were completed. Time was very limited.

When Ted, Tim, and Kevin looked at the first draft of the terms and conditions, they were shocked. There were all kinds of obscure legalisms, and they remembered fears and warnings about venture capitalists. November was almost over, the verbal agreement sounded good, but the first hard copy wasn't even in the ballpark. They asked Ted to get the best deal he could in marathon negotiations over the coming four-day weekend. Those 96 hours would determine whether the money was going to be worth the price, because there was no way the paperwork for this million-dollar deal could be wrapped up in less than a month.

THANKSGIVING WEEKEND 1994: TERMS AND CONDITIONS

Ted recalled his thoughts going into that weekend's negotiations:

> We were very cautious. We'd been hearing from all our contacts that VCs would find a way to take more than you think they're taking. We kept waiting for the other shoe to drop, and every time there was a misunderstanding, our first reaction was, "This is it, they're trying to pull a fast one."

There were two deal points in particular that Neverfail didn't like:

1. A 20 percent accruing annual dividend.
2. On-demand IPO registration rights.

EXHIBIT 5.7   Term sheet agreement.

November 15, 1994:

TERM SHEET AGREEMENT
between
PACIFIC RIDGE CAPITAL
and
NEVERFAIL COMPUTING COMPANY

I. SECURITIES

A. Pacific Ridge ("The Investor") will lead a transaction in which the Investor and its Investor Group (the "Investor Group") will purchase a total of $1.04 million face amount of newly issued Convertible Preferred Stock (the "Preferred Stock") of Neverfail Computing Company ("The Company"). The Convertible Preferred Stock will be convertible into 13% of the outstanding fully-diluted common shares at the time of issuance, including any shares allocated or to be allocated to option pools during the life of the investment. The Preferred Stock will have an accruing dividend of 20% per annum which will be deferred and then paid upon sale, merger, or liquidation of the Company or redemption of the Preferred Stock. In the event of any initial public offering (IPO), liquidation, sale, or winding up of the Company, the holders of the Preferred Stock shall be entitled to receive, in preference to the common stockholders, an amount equal to the purchase price plus the greater of (1) any accrued but unpaid dividends or (2) the pro-rata share of any remaining proceeds, treating the Preferred on an as-if-converted basis. The Preferred Stock will be subject to redemption at the holder's option in years 7, 8, and 9 at the greater of fair market value or cost. In the event of an IPO in which over $10 million in new capital is raised and the offering price is at least 3 times the conversion price of the Preferred Stock, the Preferred Stock will automatically convert to Common Stock.

B. Pacific Ridge understands the fully-diluted capitalization of the Company to be 6 million common share equivalents, including 700,000 employee shares and options which have been reserved or are planned to be issued during the term of this investment. Based on that number, Pacific Ridge will purchase Preferred Stock convertible into 666,667 common shares at an initial conversion price of $1.50 per share and 133,333 common shares at an initial conversion price of $.30 per share. This price will be adjusted for splits, stock dividends, etc., and will have standard weighted-average anti-dilution protection.

II. USE OF PROCEEDS

A. The proceeds of the financing will be used for general working capital purposes and the repurchase of founders' stock of 133,333.

III. BOARD OF DIRECTORS' RIGHTS

A. Board Seat:
The Investor will have the right to appoint a member to the Board of Directors. Direct travel costs incurred by the Investor's appointed Board members for the purpose of attending the Board meetings and conducting other Company business will be borne by the Company.

B. Compensation Committee:
The compensation for the members of the management team will be at a reasonable level (industry standard), and if in dispute, will be referred to a committee of the Board of Directors, comprised of one management team member, the Investor Group's representative, and a third-party director.

(Continued)

EXHIBIT 5.7   *(Continued)*

IV. REGISTRATION RIGHTS

A. Rights:

The Investor Group will have on-demand registration rights and consecutive pig-gyback registration rights. All sales of stock will be pro-rata in proportion to own-ership, subject to underwriter's limitations.

B. Expenses:

The Company will pay all expenses in connection with the demand and piggyback offerings.

V. VOTING RIGHTS

A. Securities shall have voting rights as if converted to Common Stock, and will vote as a class on major corporate transactions (merger, dissolution, sale of assets, etc.).

VI. PREEMPTIVE PURCHASE AND SALE RIGHTS

A. Preemptive Rights:

The Investor Group will have preemptive rights to maintain its pro-rata equity ownership in future private equity financings at market value at the time of financing.

B. Side-by-side Rights

The Investor Group will have a right-of-first-refusal and side-by-side selling rights on the sale of stock by management and major shareholders. The side-by-side sell-ing rights will provide that the Investor Group will receive their pro-rata share in any sale by a management shareholder.

VII. COVENANTS

A. Monthly financial information will be provided to the Investor Group within 30 days of the end of each month. An annual budget will be provided to the Investor Group prior to each fiscal year end. Annual audit by an accounting firm of national recognition selected by the Board of Directors will be provided within 90 days of year end.

B. The Company will make its best efforts to maintain life insurance in the amount of $_____ million on the lives of _____ , _____ , and _____ .

C. The Company will neither pay dividends on Preferred or Common Stock, nor re-purchase Common Stock, nor repurchase Common Stock, nor repay shareholder loans so long as the Preferred Stock is outstanding. A majority in interest of pre-ferred shareholders may waive these provisions.

D. The reasonable due diligence expenses, legal fees, and closing costs of the Investor Group will be paid out of the proceeds of the financing.

E. The Company and the principal shareholders will grant the Investor Group repre-sentations and warranties which are standard in agreements of this kind. In partic-ular, all of the officers of the Company will be asked to certify the accuracy of the financial statements prior to closing.

VIII. CLOSING

A. Subject to the completion of the final due diligence, the closing of this transaction will be on or before December 30, 1994.

B. Closing is conditioned upon satisfactory agreements being reached with the Com-pany's lenders.

EXHIBIT 5.7   (Continued)

    C. Upon acceptance of this term sheet, the Investor Group will commit substantial resources to a due diligence review of the Company and the preparation of legal documents relating to this transaction. In consideration of such commitment by the Investor Group, the Company agrees that, during the period between acceptance of this term sheet and the closing date specified in Section VIII, Paragraph A, it will not enter into or continue any discussions with any third party, either agent or principal, concerning a possible investment, initial public offering, merger, acquisition, or other financial accommodation.

    D. The Company agrees to provide the Investor Group with the information necessary to complete a final due diligence review satisfactory to the Investor Group. The Investor Group and the Company agree that they will use their best efforts to negotiate in good faith the terms of definitive documentation incorporating the provisions of this Term Sheet Agreement, and the Company agrees that it will make its personnel and business records available to the Investor Group and its representatives during normal business hours.

AGREED AND ACCEPTED:

Neverfail Computing   Pacific Ridge

BY: _____   BY: _____

DATE: _____

There was also a discussion point that could be a problem—Pacific Ridge wanted independent, super-voting rights for its preferred series B stock that would provide ratification authority on many business matters. It also wanted a veto on mergers and acquisitions under most circumstances.

Ted considered their dilemma. Even if they negotiated a deal that weekend, there would be little time for Pacific Ridge's due diligence investigation and for drafting the contract. If they didn't conclude the deal that weekend, there was no way that the deal could be signed by the new year, period.

They knew they could go back to George for short-term financing if necessary, but realized that his money was relationship-based, and that it was time to bring professional money into the venture. They also realized that within 12 months, an additional investment of $3 to $5 million would be required, and having a foot in the venture capital community would be important at that time.

PREPARATION QUESTIONS

1. What are the qualities of Neverfail that attract venture capitalists?
2. Examine the valuation of Neverfail:

   Assume that Pacific Ridge Capital expects to realize an IRR of at least 40 percent per year over five years on this round of investment. What does this imply for the future sales and income of Neverfail? Bear in mind that there will probably be another round of investment in about 12 months.

3. Appraise the conditions on the term sheet from the perspective of both Pacific Ridge Capital and Neverfail.

4. Why does Neverfail insist on signing the deal before the new year?

6 JON HIRSCHTICK'S NEW VENTURE

August 1994, twelve months after Jon Hirschtick left a great job to launch a new venture in the software industry, SolidWorks, the deal was looking good. The seed capital discussions had shifted into high gear as soon as Michael Payne joined the SolidWorks team. After working on the deal for nine months, Axel Bichara, the Atlas Venture vice president originating the project, finally got a syndicate excited about it: Atlas Venture, North Bridge Venture Capital Partners, and Burr, Egan, Deleage & Co. presented an offer sheet to SolidWorks two weeks after Michael was on board.

This process was particularly interesting because Jon and Axel had worked together for most of the past eight years. They met at MIT in 1986 and cofounded Premise, Inc., a Computer Aided Design (CAD) software company, in 1987. After Premise was bought by Computervision, they joined that team as managers. Now, they sat on opposite sides of the table for Axel's first deal as the lead venture capitalist.

Jon and the other founders thought the valuation and terms were fair, but the post-money° equity issue was unresolved. They had to decide how much money to raise. Did they want enough capital to support SolidWorks until it achieved a positive cash flow, or should they take less money and attempt to increase the entrepreneurial team's post-money equity?

If they took less money now, they could raise funds later, when SolidWorks might have a higher valuation. But they would be gambling on the success of the development team and the investment climate. If their product was in beta testing

---

This case was written by Dan D'Heily and Tricia Jaekle under the direction of Professor William Bygrave. Funding provided by the Ewing Marion Kauffman Foundation and the Frederic C. Hamilton Chair for Free Enterprise Studies. Copyright © 1995 Babson College. All rights reserved.
° Post-money valuation: the value of a company's equity after additional money is invested.

with high customer acceptance, raising more money would probably be fast and fun, but if they hit any development snags, the process could take a lot of time and yield a poor result.

JON HIRSCHTICK: 1962–1987

Jon grew up in Chicago in an entrepreneurial family. He fondly remembers helping with his father's part-time business by traveling to stamp collectors' shows across the Midwest. In high school, he was self-employed as a magician.

The entrepreneurial impulse continued during his undergraduate years. Jon recalls the Blackjack team he played with at MIT:

> We raised money to get started. At the same time, we developed a probabilistic system for winning at Blackjack. The results were amazing! We tripled our money in the first six months, doubled it during the next six months, and doubled it again in the next six months. We produced a 900% annualized return.
>
> I learned a useful lesson: you really can know more than the next guy, and make money by applying that knowledge. We tackled Blackjack because people thought it was unbeatable; we studied it, and we won. The same principle applies to entrepreneurship. Opportunities often exist where popular opinion holds that they don't.

Jon's introduction to CAD came from a college internship with Computervision during the summer of 1981. Computervision was one of the most successful start-up companies to emerge during the 1970s. By the early 1980s, it dominated the CAD market.

After earning a master's degree in mechanical engineering (M.E.) at MIT, Jon managed the MIT CAD laboratory. He supervised student employees, coordinated research projects, and conducted tours for visitors.

AXEL BICHARA: 1963–1987

Axel was born in Berlin and attended a French high school. In 1986, while studying at the Technical University of Berlin for a master's degree in mechanical engineering, he won a scholarship to MIT. Axel had worked in a CAD research lab in Germany, and he selected the CAD laboratory for his work-study assignment at MIT.

EARLY CAD SOFTWARE

CAD software traces its roots to 1969 when computers were first used by engineers to automate the production of drawings. CAD was used by architects, engineers, designers, and other planners to create various types of drawings and blueprints. Any company that designed and manufactured products (e.g., Ford, Sony, Black & Decker) was a prospective CAD software customer.

An Entrepreneurship Class: January 1987

Visitors to the MIT CAD lab often complained about problems that Jon knew he could solve. He enrolled in an entrepreneurship class to write a business plan for a CAD start-up company, Premise, Inc. Jon described the decision to quit his job and start a company.

> I once heard Mitch Kapor° use a game show metaphor to describe the entrepreneurial impulse. He said, "Part of the entrepreneurial instinct is to push the button before you know the answer and hope it will come to you before the buzzer." That's what happened for us: we didn't know how to start a company, or how to fund it, but Premise got rolling, and we came up with answers before we ran out of time.

Jon and Axel were surprised and delighted to find each other in the entrepreneurship class. They had worked together for the past month on a project at the CAD lab, and they decided to become partners in the first class session. Axel recalled:

> It was a coincidence that we enrolled in the same class, but it was clear that we should work together. Jon had had the idea for a couple of months, and we started work on the product and the business plan immediately.

Axel took the master's exam at MIT in October 1987, and at Technical University of Berlin in July 1988. He was still a student at both universities when he and Jon started Premise. Axel graduated with highest honors from both institutions.

Premise, Inc.: 1987–1991

Premise went from concept to business plan to venture capitalist-backed start-up in less than six months. As Axel remembered:

> The class deadline for the business plan was May 14. On June 1, we had our first meeting with venture capitalists, and by June 22, we had a handshake deal with Harvard Management Company for $1.5 million. We actually received an advance that week. It was much easier than it should have been, but the story's 100 percent true.

In the first quarter of 1989, Premise raised its second round of capital. Harvard Management and Kleiner Perkins Caufield & Byers combined to finance the product launch. The product shipped in May to very positive industry reviews, but sales were slow. Premise's software didn't solve a large mass-market problem. As Jon later recalled:

> I've seen successful companies get started without talent, time, or money—but I've never seen a successful company without a market. Premise targeted a small market. I had a professor who said it all, "The only necessary and sufficient condition for a business is customers."

By the end of 1990, the partners had decided that the best way to harvest Premise was an industry buyout. They hired a Minneapolis investment banking firm

---

° Mitchell Kapor founded Lotus Development Corporation.

to find a buyer. Wessels, Arnold & Henderson was considered one of the elite investment banking firms serving the CAD industry. Premise attracted top-level service providers because of the prestige of its venture capitalist partners. Jon explained:

> Several bankers wanted to do the deal, and a big reason was because they wanted to work with our venture capitalists. We had top venture capitalists, and that opened all kinds of doors. This is often under-appreciated. I believe in shopping for venture capital partners.

Wessels, Arnold & Henderson were as good as their reputation. As Axel recalled:

> We sold Premise to Computervision on 7 March 1991. Computervision bought us for our proprietary technology and engineering team. It was a good deal for both companies.

Computervision: 1991–1993

As part of the purchase agreement, Jon and Axel joined the management team at Computervision. They managed the integration of Premise's development team and product line for one year before Axel left to study business in Europe. Jon stayed on after Axel's departure.

Revenues for the Premise team's products grew 200 percent between 1991 and 1993, and perhaps as important as direct revenue, their technology was incorporated into some of Computervision's high-end products. In January 1993, Jon was promoted to director of product definition for another CAD product. He stayed in this position for eight months. After two years at Computervision, he was ready for new horizons. He resigned effective 23 August 1993. (See Exhibit 6.1 for excerpts from his Letter of Resignation.)

After a holiday in the Caribbean, Jon purchased new computer equipment, called business friends and associates, and began working on a business plan. He didn't have a clear product idea, but his market research suggested that the time was ripe for a new CAD start-up.

CAD SOFTWARE MARKET IN THE 1990s

By the 1990s, the hottest CAD software performed a function called solid modeling. Solid modeling produced three-dimensional computer objects that resembled the products being built in almost every detail. It was primarily used for designing manufacturing tools and parts. Solid modeling was SolidWorks' focus.

The key benefits driving the boom in solid modeling were:

1. Relatively inexpensive CAD prototypes could be accurate enough to replace costly (labor, materials, tooling, etc.) physical prototypes.
2. The elimination of physical prototypes dramatically improved time-to-market.
3. More prototypes could be created and tested, so product quality was improved.

However, not all CAD software could manage solid modeling well enough to effectively replace physical prototypes.

EXHIBIT 6.1   Excerpts from Jon Hirschtick's letter of resignation from Computervision (CV).

This is my explanation for wanting to leave CV. . . . The other day you asked me whether I was leaving because I was unhappy, or whether I really want to start another company. <u>I strongly believe that it is because I really want to work on another entrepreneurial venture.</u> I want to try to build another company that achieves business value . . .

I am interested in leaving CV to pursue another entrepreneurial opportunity because I seek to:

1. <u>Be a part of business strategy decisions.</u> I want to attend board meetings and create business plans, as I did at Premise.
2. <u>Select, recruit, lead, and motivate a team of outstanding people.</u> I believe that one of my strengths is the ability to select great people and form strong teams.
3. <u>Represent a company with customers, press, investors, and analysts.</u> I enjoy the challenge of selling and presenting to these groups.
4. <u>Work on multidisciplinary problems: market analysis, strategy, product, funding, distribution, and marketing.</u> I am good at cross-functional problem-solving and deal-making.
5. <u>Work in a fast-moving environment.</u> I like to be in a place where decisions can be made quickly, and individuals (not just me) are empowered to use their own judgment.
6. <u>Work in a customer-driven and market-driven organization.</u> I find technology and computer architecture interesting only as they directly relate to winning business. I want to focus on building products customers want to buy.
7. <u>Have significant equity-based incentives.</u> I thrive on calculated risks with large potential rewards.
8. <u>Be recognized for having built business success.</u> I measure "business success" by sales, profitability, and company valuation; I want to directly impact business success. Recognition will follow. I admit that this ego-need plays a part in my decision.

Summary

I've decided I want to work on an entrepreneurial venture . . . . This is more a function of what I do best than any problems at CV . . . . I don't have any delusions about an entrepreneurial company being any easier. I know first-hand that start up companies have at least as many obstacles as large established companies—but they are the obstacles I want.

Note: Underlines in original.

Most vendors offered CAD software based on computer technology from the 1970s and 1980s. IBM, Computervision, Intergraph, and other traditional market leaders were losing market share because solid modeling required software architecture that worked poorly on older systems.

As one of the industry's newest competitors, Parametric Technology Corp. (PTC) was setting new benchmarks for state-of-the-art solid modeling software. (It was an eight-year-old company in 1994.) CAD was a mature and fragmented industry with many competitors, but PTC thrived because other companies tried to make older technology perform solid modeling functions.

Worldwide mechanical CAD software revenues were projected at $1.8 billion for 1995, with IBM expected to lead the category with sales of $388 million. PTC was growing over 50 percent annually and had the second highest sales, with $305 million in projected revenue. Industry analysts predicted 3 percent to 5 percent revenue growth per year, with annual unit volume projected to grow at 15 percent. The downward pressure on prices was squeezing margins, so many stock analysts thought that the market was becoming unattractive. However, PTC was trading at a P/E of 35 in 1994.

AXEL AFTER COMPUTERVISION: 1992–1994

After five years in the United States, Axel decided to attend an MBA program in Europe. From his experiences at Premise and Computervision, he had become intrigued with the art and science of business management and he was ready for a geographic change.

INSEAD was his choice. Located in Fontainebleau, an hour south of Paris, INSEAD was considered one of the top three business schools in Europe. The application process included two alumni interviews, and one of Axel's interviewers was Christopher Spray, the founder of Atlas Venture's Boston office. Atlas Venture was a venture capital firm with offices in Europe and the United States. It had $250 million under management in 1994.

Since Axel had a three-month break before INSEAD started, Chris asked him to consult on a couple of Atlas Venture's projects. Axel found he enjoyed evaluating business proposals "from the other side of the table." He graduated in June 1993 and joined the Boston office of Atlas Venture as a vice president with responsibility for developing high-tech deals.

Axel reflected on the relationship between business school training and venture capital practice:

> I was qualified to become a venture capitalist because of my technical and entrepreneurial background; business school just rounded out my skills. You do not need a bunch of MBA courses to be a successful venture capitalist. Take finance, for example, I learned everything I needed from the core course. People without entrepreneurial experience who want to be venture capitalists should take as many entrepreneurship courses as possible.

JON FOUNDS SOLIDWORKS: 1993–1994

Jon's business plan focused on CAD opportunities. He explained:

> I knew that this big market was going through major changes, with more changes to come. From an entrepreneur's perspective, I saw the right conditions for giving birth to a new business. I also knew I had the technical skills, industry credibility, and vision needed to make it happen. This was a pretty rare situation.

SolidWorks' product vision evolved slowly from Jon's personal research and from discussions with friends. He was careful to avoid using research that Computervision

EXHIBIT 6.2   Competitive positioning grid.

	Computer aided drafting and add-ons	Production solid modeling
Low-end		
Windows	Autodesk	SolidWorks
˜$5K per station	Bentley	
VAR channel	CADKEY	
High-end		
UNIX	Applicon	PTC
˜$20K per station	CADAM	
Direct sales		

Source: Solidworks' business plan, 1994.

might claim as proprietary. He was concerned about legal issues, because he would be designing software similar to what Computervision was trying to produce. Axel explained:

> Both Computervision and SolidWorks wanted to produce a quality solid modeling product. Solid modeling technology was still too difficult to learn and use. Only PTC's solid modeling software really worked well enough. The rest made nice drawings but could not replace physical prototypes for testing purposes.

There were only 50,000 licensed solid modeling terminals in the United States, and most of them belonged to PTC, but there were over 500,000 CAD terminals. There were two main reasons PTC did not have a larger market: (1) its products required very powerful computers, and (2) it took up to nine months of daily use to become proficient with PTC software. Solidworks' goal was to create solid modeling software that was easier to learn, and modeled real-world parts on less specialized hardware (see Exhibit 6.2).

This vision was not unique in the industry. Many CAD companies were developing solid modeling software, and the low-end market was wide open. SolidWorks' major advantage was its ability to use recent advances in software architecture and new hardware platforms—it wasn't tied to antique technology. Attracting talented developers was Jon's top priority.

Teambuilding

Jon's wife, Melissa, enthusiastically supported his decision to resign from Computervision. Jon explained:

> Some spouses couldn't deal with a husband who quits a secure job to start a new company. Melissa never gave me a hard time about being an entrepreneur.

Jon described his priorities in October 1993 when he decided to launch SolidWorks:

I knew I needed three things: good people, a good business plan, and a good proof-of-concept.° I needed a talented team that could set new industry benchmarks, but there was no way I could get those people without a persuasive prototype demonstration.

The venture capitalists wanted a solid business plan, but that wouldn't be enough. They wanted a strong team. I needed fundable people who were also CAD masters. Venture capitalists couldn't understand most complex technologies well enough to be confident a high-tech business plan was really sound, so they looked at the team and placed their bets largely on that basis. If the proof-of-concept attracted the team, then the team and the business plan would attract the money. I needed a team that could create the vision and make venture capitalists believe it was real.

Jon worked on finding the team and developing the proof-of-concept concurrently; but the proof-of-concept was his first priority. He worked on it daily. In his search for cofounders, Jon talked to dozens of people.

Recruiting posed another dilemma—how to get people to work full-time without pay, while the company retained the right to their output? He resolved this problem by creating consulting agreements that gave SolidWorks ownership of employees' work and made salaries payable at the time of funding. As it turned out, this arrangement lasted nine months. Jon described his approach to recruiting.

I always paid for the meal when I talked with someone about SolidWorks. I wanted them to feel confident about it, and that meant that I had to act with confidence. The deal I offered was: no salary, buy your own computer, work out of your house, and we're going to build a great company. I'd done it before, so people signed on.

Axel described Jon's management style as, "visionary, he's a talented motivator, and a strong leader."

ROBERT ZUFFANTE: CAD ENGINEER/CONSULTANT

A major development in 1993 was the addition of super-star consultant Bob Zuffante as manager of proof-of-concept development. Jon needed time to write the business plan and recruit his team. He had been working on the prototype for over a month when Bob took over development. Jon recalled the situation.

I hadn't seen him since we were students together at MIT, but when I thought about the skills I needed, my mental rolodex came up with his name. I always thought about working with him again. We talked in late November, and about a month later, he began work on the prototype.

Bob knew Jon and Axel from MIT where he earned a master's degree in mechanical engineering. He had worked in the CAD industry for over ten years and had managed a successful consulting business. His arrival at SolidWorks allowed Jon to focus on other pressing issues.

° "Proof-of-concept" is a term that refers to a computer program designed to illustrate a proposed project. Also referred to as a "prototype," it is used for demonstration purposes and it is limited but functional in ideal circumstances.

SCOTT HARRIS: CAD MARKETER

Scott Harris worked at Computervision for eleven years, where he managed development and marketing activities. Most notably, Scott was the founder and manager of Computervision's product design and definition group. He also managed the eleven-person solid modeling development group, and acted as technical liaison between Computervision's customers and R&D engineers.

Scott was let go by Computervision during a large-scale lay-off. He was skeptical when Jon first told him about the SolidWorks vision, but he became a believer after seeing a proof-of-concept demonstration. Scott stopped looking for a job and started working full-time for SolidWorks almost immediately. Scott was impressed, "The prototype was the embodiment of a lot of the things I was thinking about. This was the way solid modeling should perform."

Scott started with SolidWorks about six weeks after Bob signed on. He became involved in the marketing sections of the business plan and in the product definition process. He ran focus groups, conducted demonstrations for potential customers, and analyzed the purchasing process. He kept the development team focused on customer needs—how did customers really use CAD software, and what did they need that current products lacked?

THE BUSINESS PLAN

When Bob came on in January, Jon turned to the business plan with a passion. The plan went through a number of versions as Jon and his advisors wrestled with key issues such as positioning, competitive strategy, and functionality. By the end of March, the plan was polished enough for Jon to show it to venture capitalists. Axel recalled:

> Jon and I decided that the business plan was ready to show in April, so I scheduled a presentation at Atlas. Jon gave the presentation to Barry [Barry Fidelman, Atlas general partner] and myself—market, team, and concept. Overall, Barry was encouraging, but not excited. He thought Jon's story was not crisp enough; it was he was looking for money to take on some very large companies; and the CAD market was not that attractive. It was a rocky start.

INITIAL FINANCING ATTEMPTS

In addition to negotiating with Atlas Venture, Jon met with other venture capital firms and rewrote the business plan several times. Axel described the rationale behind this process.

> If you talk to too many people and you do not make a good impression, it will be much harder to get funding, because the word on the street will be, "this deal will not fly." Meet with 4 or 5 venture capitalists at most, then revise the plan if you are not getting the right response. After each major revision, show it again to the lead venture partner.

While there were promising discussions with several venture capitalists, Atlas did not want to be the sole investor, and SolidWorks did not win support from other venture capitalists during the spring or summer.

Jon was contacted by an established CAD software company in May 1994. It wanted to acquire SolidWorks—essentially the development team and the prototype. The proposal was attractive; it included signing bonuses and stock. Scott recalled his excitement.

> This was a big shot in the arm. It meant that other industry insiders respected our vision and talent enough to put up their money and take the risk. This was like a cold bucket of Gatorade on a hot day.

Jon stopped seeking venture capital for about a month while he considered the buyout offer. If the offer was a boost to morale, the way the team rejected it was even more meaningful. Jon talked to each person (several other programmers had joined during the spring), and they were unanimous in wanting to continue towards their original goal. Affirming their commitment reinvigorated the team.

TURNING POINT: MICHAEL PAYNE, CAD COMPANY FOUNDER

The most significant advance that summer began with a due diligence meeting set up by Atlas Venture. Atlas wanted the SolidWorks team to meet its agent, Michael Payne, who had recently resigned from PTC. Michael had cofounded PTC, the number one company in CAD software. He was one of the most influential people in the industry.

Michael had grown up in London. He earned his bachelor's degree in electrical engineering from Southampton University and his master's degree in solid-state physics from the University of London. He came to the U.S. and worked many years for RCA designing computer chips. Michael continued his education at Pace University, where he earned an MBA. His senior CAD development experience began in the 1970s when he ran the CAD/CAM design lab at Prime Computer. He was subsequently recruited by Sam Geisberg, the visionary behind PTC. Michael recalled their first meeting in 1986, "Sam had some kind of crazy prototype, and I said, "Hey, we can do something with that. This is what we should be working on."

PTC was founded in 1986 with Michael as vice president of development, and within five years the company had created a new set of CAD industry benchmarks. For FY 1994, PTC sales were just under $150 million, it earned a pretax profit margin over 40 percent, and realized a market capitalization° of $2 billion. Michael's reputation as a development manager was outstanding. Remarkably, PTC had never missed a new product release date, and it released products every six months. This was considered a near-impossible feat in software development. He left PTC in April 1994 during a management dispute, about two months before the due diligence meeting with SolidWorks.

° The value of the company established by the selling price of the stock times the number of shares outstanding.

Jon had never met Michael, but knew by reputation that he was a tough character. The SolidWorks team was worried about two possibilities: that Michael would say
they were on the wrong track, or that he might take their ideas back to PTC. Jon recalled the meeting.

> Bob and I were on one side of the table and Michael and Axel on the other. I decided to
> gamble on a dramatic entrance. Before we told him anything about SolidWorks, I asked
> Michael to show his cards. I asked him to tell us what he thought were the greatest op-
> portunities in the CAD market. Michael mentioned many of the things we were target-
> ing. I couldn't imagine a better way to start the meeting.
>   We presented our plan and prototype. Michael asked us a lot of tough, confronta-
> tional questions. Afterwards, he told Atlas Venture, "These guys have a chance." Com-
> ing from him, that was high praise.

The due diligence meeting was also the beginning of a dialogue between
Michael and Jon about joining SolidWorks. Over the next couple of months, Michael
decided to join the team. Jon described the synergy between them.

> You almost couldn't ask for two people with more different styles, but we got along well
> because we were united in our philosophy and vision. We found that our stylistic dif-
> ferences were assets; they created more options for solving problems.

Michael talked about his motivation for joining the SolidWorks team.

> I couldn't go work for a big company because I didn't have any patience for petty poli-
> tics. A start-up was my only option. The larger the company, the more focused it would
> be on internal issues rather than on making a product that customers would buy. Cus-
> tomers don't care about technique, they care about the benefits of the technology.
>   Jon focused on CAD features that I knew customers wanted, and he had a proto-
> type demonstrating that he could do it. It was quicker and easier than what was on the
> market. Being able to develop it was another matter. They still had to build it. Imple-
> mentation, that's where I would be useful. I told them, "Give me whatever title you
> want, I just want to run development."

TEAM ADJUSTMENTS

Michael's arrival created an imbalance in the SolidWorks team, and it took time to
sort it out. In fact, Michael didn't join the team until the last week in August. Jon described his thoughts about team cohesion.

> When I decided to start SolidWorks, I had three goals:
>   1. Work with great people,
>   2. Realize the vision of a new generation of software, and
>   3. Make a lot of money.
>
>   We didn't go looking for Michael Payne, but when he came along it was an easy
> decision. It can be hard to bring in strong players, but if those are your three goals, the
> decision falls out of the analysis rather naturally.
>   Bob and I had to give up the reins in some areas so Michael could come on board.
> We weren't looking for a top development manager because we thought we already had
> two. The change took some getting used to, but it was clearly the right thing to do.

Jon focused on team building, and Michael became the development manager. There were still big talent gaps, especially in sales and finance, but those positions could be filled when they were closer to the product launch. Michael was satisfied, "We didn't have a vast team, but you don't start out with a vast team, and we had a terrific nucleus."

SEPTEMBER 1994

Atlas arranged for Jon to talk with venture firms interested in joining the investment syndicate. The team met with Jon Flint of Burr, Egan, Deleage & Co. and Rich D'Amore of North Bridge Venture Capital Partners. After completing their due diligence investigations, both firms joined the syndicate. Jon Hirschtick recalled the situation.

> I was pleased that Jon Flint and Rich D'Amore decided to invest. I had met Jon many years earlier and thought very well of him. Rich also impressed me as a very knowledgeable investor. Both had excellent reputations and I looked forward to having them join our board.

An offer sheet was presented to SolidWorks two weeks after Michael officially joined the SolidWorks management team. Now the team had to decide how much money they really wanted. Michael's last venture, PTC, only needed one round of capital, and this team wanted to go for one round, too. SolidWorks' monthly cash burn rate was projected to average about $250 thousand, and they planned to launch the product in a year, so they needed $3 million for development. Sales and marketing would also need money; they decided that $1 million should be enough to take them through the product launch to generating positive cash flow. To that total, they added a $500,000 safety margin. SolidWorks asked Atlas to put together an offer sheet based on raising $4.5 million.

SolidWorks received the offer sheet during the first week of September. It gave a $2.5 million pre-money valuation with a 15 percent post-money stock option pool (the pool of company stock reserved for rewarding employees in the future). These terms were fairly typical for a first round deal, but the SolidWorks team didn't like what happened to their post-money equity when they ran the numbers.

PREPARATION QUESTIONS

1. Why has this deal attracted venture capital?
2. Can the founders optimize their personal financial returns and simultaneously ensure that SolidWorks has sufficient capital to optimize its chance of succeeding? What factors should the founders consider?
3. How can the syndicate optimize its potential return? What factors should it consider?
4. After you have answered questions 2 and 3, structure a deal that will serve the best interests of the founders, the company, and the venture capital firms.

7 BEAUTIFUL LEGS
BY POST

"This is *Vogue*, we would like to write a story about your new company." It was a dream come true for Elizabeth Preis and Dickon Addis founders of Beautiful Legs BY POST, which was a London-based mail-order business selling quality tights to professional women throughout the U.K. Their company had started trading on October 10, 1995, only one day before the phone call from *Vogue*. They knew that publicity in one of the premier fashion magazines in the U.K. would give a tremendous boost to their fledgling venture.

Since graduating in July with MBA degrees from INSEAD (The European Institute of Business Administration in France), Elizabeth and Dickon worked hard to implement the business plan that they wrote as classmates. Each had invested £5,000 to launch Beautiful Legs BY POST. With that seed money, they had printed a catalog, purchased a mailing list, found a supplier of tights, and completed a mailing of 4,000 catalogs. They had not yet paid themselves any salary, and had not budgeted to do so until December, when they would begin to draw modest salaries. Their plan called for a mailing of 80,000 catalogs in November to be followed by two mailings of 20,000 catalogs each in January and February. To finance those mailings they needed to raise £110,000 in the next month or so.

THE CONCEPT

After graduating from Wellesley College in 1991, Elizabeth joined Bloomingdales department store in New York as an assistant department manager, specializing in

This case was prepared by William D. Bygrave. Case writing support was provided by the Ewing Marion Kauffman Foundation and the Frederic C. Hamilton Chair for Free Enterprise. Copyright © 1996 Babson College. All rights reserved.

Career Collections. By the time she left the store in 1994 to study at INSEAD, she was a department manager for the European Designer Collections with average monthly sales of $800,000. She managed a team of two assistants, twelve sales associates, and two stock associates. In addition to her management responsibilities, she was buying/purchasing in Bloomingdales own private label division. About half her total time at Bloomingdales was occupied with buying. As she thought about her future, Elizabeth was enthusiastic about retailing:

> There is just no other industry that combines all the things that I love so much. It's fast; it's marketing; it's a little bit of style.

In January 1994, Elizabeth had written a report on mail order, with an emphasis on the repeat purchaser. She thought that in comparison with the U.S. industry, mail order in Europe, especially for high quality products, was underdeveloped. She thought there were plenty of opportunities for new firms to enter that industry in Europe. From her experience at Bloomingdales, she knew that she ought to pick a product that was found on the first floor of department stores because, in general, it was a high margin item, it had virtually zero return rate, and it was an impulse buy. Among the products that she considered were women's tights.

While on a skiing vacation in late February, Elizabeth had fallen and injured her knee so severely on the first day on the slopes that she had to stay in her hotel for the next six days. While her friends were skiing, she spent the time thinking about her future career.

Developing the Concept

When Elizabeth returned to INSEAD, she shared her ideas for a mail-order business with her classmates enrolled in a new ventures course in which groups of students write business plans. Dickon Addis, a classmate, had identified a gap in the marketplace for mail order in Europe, specifically in the U.K., his home country. After graduating from the London School of Economics in 1984, Dickon had built a successful career in accounting. When he applied to INSEAD, he was the financial controller of a firm with 400 employees. As he thought about his business concept, Dickon recognized that because he lacked retailing experience and would need to team up with a retailing person if his idea was to have credibility. He asked Elizabeth to join him. Together, they agreed that tights would be the perfect item for a mail-order business specializing in high-quality products. As Elizabeth put it:

> Tights don't break, they go through the letter box, customers don't try them on before they buy them, and more importantly, with mail order we can establish a relationship with the customer so we can leverage the database.

From March until they graduated in July, Elizabeth and Dickon worked diligently on a business plan for their new venture, Beautiful Legs BY POST. Their research indicated that the U.K. was the best country to locate their business. What's more, Dickon had a home in London, and although Elizabeth had never lived in the U.K., she was willing to move there. So in August, Elizabeth rented an apartment in

London that would also serve as the first office for their new company. Over the next three months they implemented their business concept. In the process, they refined the initial business plan that they had written at INSEAD (see Exhibit 7.1 on pages 96–142). On October 11, the same day that *Vogue* telephoned, they printed the latest version of their plan. This was the document that they would show to potential investors.

As they waited for orders from their first mailing, they wondered what the response rate would be, what the average size per order would be, and what percent of initial customers would reorder. Would they be able to raise the financing that they needed in the next two months if they were to stay on track? How could they get more free publicity? In the next few months, they expected to learn whether Beautiful Legs BY POST was a viable business.

PREPARATION QUESTIONS

1. Use the Timmons' opportunity-people-resources framework to evaluate this new venture.
2. Would you invest in this venture? List the reasons for your decision.
3. What are the purposes of this business plan?
4. How well does the plan fulfill those purposes?
5. Can you recommend any improvements to the business plan?
6. Are Elizabeth and Dickon realistic about fund raising?
7. What might happen if they fail to raise £110,000 in the next 30 days?

online?

Exhibit 7.1   Beautiful Legs BY POST business plan.

1. Executive Summary

1.1. The Team

We have a perfectly matched management team. Marketing skills and retailing buying experience are complemented by financial experience and logistics skills. Dickon Addis is the Director of Finance and Operations. Elizabeth Preis is the Director of Marketing and Purchasing.

Dickon Addis, aged 33, qualified in 1987 as a Chartered Accountant while working at Arthur Andersen & Co., London. Subsequently, he gained five years practical experience as the Financial Controller in two companies, one of which was publicly traded. He has experience in designing and implementing accounting, stock control and budgeting systems. At YRM plc he played an active part in the formation of the company's business plan.

Elizabeth Preis, aged 26, has built her retail experience through managing front-line operations at Bloomingdale's, a premier New York department store. She then gained retail buying knowledge as Assistant Buyer in the private label department through buying stock for all fifteen stores. She was then promoted to the Department Manager, where she managed a team of 16 people. She achieved department sales of $800,000 per month and was recognised as managing the "Best Department of the Store".

1.2. The Business

A mail-order business targeted at the professional woman and specialising in tights

- Professional women have higher disposal incomes, but they have less time to shop. This makes them an ideal market for a mail order catalogue to target.
- Work tights are part of the professional woman's work "uniform". They are regularly purchased. Professional women are estimated to buy around 35 pairs per year.
- The mail-order business in Europe is following the American trend of targeting higher income consumers through "specialogues" that offer a limited range of products, which match their customers' needs.

1.3. The Business Opportunity

- Tights have an average retail margin of over 40%.
- Tights are a replenishment item that requires regular purchases. This reduces the cost of acquiring business since a large percentage of sales will be to existing customers.
- 85% of respondents to our April 1995 survey of executive women expressed a willingness to purchase tights by mail-order.
- Our surveys found that perceived quality is dependent on price. Tights should be of sufficient quality to match the rest of their professional wardrobe.
- High quality tights are only available from department stores and high end variety stores. Time-pressed professional women must either waste valuable time purchasing this basic item, or buy lower quality tights.
- They are an ideal mail-order product. Tights are lightweight, small and non-breakable, making them easy to post.

Exhibit 7.1 *(Continued)*

- Our market research has shown that women are not brand loyal when buying tights. This allows us to potentially enter the market with a new brand. Doré Doré, a well-known quality French supplier, has agreed to supply us tights in packaging with our own private label.

1.4. Strategy

Our overall strategy is to start by targeting professional women living in the larger cities of Britain, where there is a higher density of women working in the financial and service sectors. In the first year, we will target customers by catalogue. We will rent names of potential clients from list brokers. We will encourage all existing customers to pass our catalogue to friends and colleagues. In the second year, leveraging the experience gained in Britain, we will begin to target the rest of Northern Europe.

The first mailing totalled 4,000 catalogues. This mailing allowed us to test our concept and logistics, and provide us a clearer indication of response rates.

The next mailing will be in early November when we will send out 80,000 catalogues. Smaller postings of 20,000 will take place in January and February. The mail shots in the first year will concentrate on the United Kingdom. We estimate our active client base to be 2,600 by the end of the first year.

In the second and third years, we plan to send out 220,000 catalogues to   Continental Europe. We estimate our client base to be 6,800 active customers by the end of the third year.

During this time we will experiment with a number of different forms of catalogues and special offers in order to test which method is the most effective. Special offers will include: giving away a free hosiery wash bag, offering a free pair with the purchase of two others, and offering a free trial pair of tights.

1.5. Competitors

There are currently no mail-order houses selling only tights. A number of general catalogues do include tights, but this is not their focus.

Our main competitors are the traditional retail channels, department stores, groceries and variety stores (for example Marks & Spencer). Department stores stock the whole range of prices and brands. Their drawback is that, since tights are needed so frequently, the customer often has to go to the store just to buy tights. Grocery stores do not have this drawback. However, since they aim to sell in high volumes to the mass market customer, their quality is lower. Variety stores have tried to address both the convenience and the quality issues. However, even at the high end their quality is still lower that what is desired by many respondents to our survey.

1.6. Competitive Advantage

We will have the advantage of being the first mover. We will be the first to locate the buyers of high quality tights and will be able keep them by offering an efficient and reliable service through the Monthly Order Program. For a new entrant, since many potential customers will be our customers, their "hit-rates" will be reduced. This means that the cost of acquiring clients becomes prohibitive. New entrants cannot gain market share through price reductions since quality is perceived to be reflected in price.

If a very strong entrant enters the market, this gives us the opportunity of exiting the market by selling the business to the entrant. Our mail list will be very valuable since it contains proven

(Continued)

Exhibit 7.1   *(Continued)*

buyers of a premium product through mail-order. An analysis of our data will give the entrant the characteristics of these buyers.

1.7. The Economics

The key information is as follows:

- The average selling price (including VAT) per unit is £7.60. The standard work tight (15 denier appearance) will be sold at £7. The other two styles, a 10 denier appearance and a microfiber 30 denier style, will be sold £6 and £11, respectively. The average cost per unit is £3.88 and the packing and fulfilment costs are approximately £2.50 per order (this includes a new catalogue to be passed onto a colleague). We expect to sell in units of four and charge an average of £2 postage and handling. This gives a gross margin per order of £9.86.

- The cost of each catalogue including postage is approximately 77p.

- Fixed costs are marginal. They will include costs such a lease of computers, office space, salaries and other marketing costs. We have budgeted administration costs' totalling £66,000 in the first year. This includes directors' salaries totalling £37,500, which start being paid after the completion of the test mailings.

1.8. Financial Summary

	Year ending 31 August 1996 £'000	Year ending 31 August 1997 £'000	Year ending 31 August 1998 £'000
Revenue	363	1,130	1,684
Gross margin	113	369	553
Mail shot costs	99	175	192
Administration	66	154	165
Earnings before interest and taxes	(52)	40	196
Income after tax and interest	(55)	40	150
Net operating Cashflow	(61)	58	201
Net cash balance	27	85	286
Net working capital	8	(10)	(61)
Shareholders' equity	35	75	225
Active customers	2,622	4,829	6,795

1.9. The Exit Strategy

We seek to have a saleable business by the end of the third year. The potential purchaser is likely to be a trade buyer, either from the hosiery or mail-order business. Hosiery companies are currently fighting for market share and this would give them another distribution channel

Exhibit 7.1 *(Continued)*

closer to the customer. A mail-order house would be interested in our client base since it will contain names of active purchasers of a quality item. These names could be used to launch new products.

1.10. Proposed Offering

The offering will comprise of Ordinary Shares (£1 par value) and short-term debenture stock. Under the business plan's assumptions, there will be one round of financing. We are asking outside investors to purchase 20% of the company for £80,000, and to loan £30,000 in the form of debenture stock that will repayable in six months.

On the basis of the projections and assuming a price earnings' ratio on exit of seven times, we estimate that the rate of return for our investors will be approximately 60% per annum.

(Continued)

Exhibit 7.1 *(Continued)*

---

2. The Management Team

We believe that the most important element supporting the feasibility of *Beautiful Legs by post* is the diversity of proven skills offered by the management team. While both have strong analytical and commercial backgrounds, each has expertise specific to their role. Dickon Addis has financial experience and logistics skills. These are balanced by Elizabeth Preis's marketing skills and retail experience.

Dickon Addis and Elizabeth Preis have demonstrated their ability to work as a team during the formation of their business plan. This was achieved despite the pressures imposed on both of them in completing INSEAD's rigorous course work.

The separation of responsibilities was one of the easiest decisions given the team's skills. Dickon Addis will be the Director of Finance and Operations. Elizabeth Preis will be the Director of Marketing and Purchasing.

2.1. Dickon Addis, Director of Finance and Operations

Dickon Addis, aged 33, qualified in 1987 as a chartered accountant while working for Arthur Andersen & Co., London. During his three years at Arthur Andersen & Co., his clients included a building society, an insurance broker and a life assurance company.

In January 1988, he joined ADS Office Systems Limited, an office equipment supplier as the Financial Controller. By redesigning and implementing a new accounting system, he halved the finance team to 15 members. He also reduced the time taken to produce monthly management accounts from 20 to 9 working days. He helped to implement a new stock control system which reduced stock levels, while simultaneously reducing delivery lead times.

After ADS, he spent three years as the Financial Controller for YRM plc, a building design consultant. YRM plc is a firm of building design consultants, which has a full listing on the London Stock Exchange. Here he worked with the board in formulating and managing the company's business strategy. He redesigned the budgeting and forecasting process. He also identified the need for and assisted in the implementation of a cost cutting program that reduced the company's cost base by 25%.

Other experience includes a three month assignment in 1994 with a firm of strategy consultants advising a venture capitalist in the evaluation of the market opportunities in potential acquisitions.

He graduated with an MBA from INSEAD in July 1995. He received a B.Sc. in Economics from The London School of Economics in 1984.

2.2. Elizabeth Preis, Director of Marketing and Purchasing

Elizabeth Preis, aged 26, has built her retail experience both through managing front-line operations at Bloomingdale's, a premier New York department store.

She joined Bloomingdale's in 1991 as an Assistant Department Manager in charge of fifteen sales and stock associates. After only nine months, she was promoted to Assistant Buyer for the "Better Casual Collections". Along with the buyer, she sourced from suppliers and purchased stock for the merchandising of the private label program in all fifteen stores. In addition to merchandising responsibilities, she developed and executed seasonal marketing, and financial projections for this area.

Exhibit 7.1   *(Continued)*

In 1993 she was promoted to Department Manager for the high fashion "European Designer Collections". She managed a team of two assistants, and fourteen sales and stock associates. She achieved department sales of on average $800,000, always surpassing the sales target. As a result she was recognised as managing the "Best Department of the Store" having realised a 15% increase in sales during the Holiday 1993 season.

She graduated with an MBA from INSEAD in July 1995. In 1991, she received a BA in Economics and French from Wellesley College, Massachusetts. As part of her degree course she spent six months at the University of Copenhagen having been accepted into their International Business Studies' program.

2.3. Directors' Compensation and Share of Ownership

During the three month test phase both directors are forgoing all compensation. On completion of the first round of financing the directors will each be paid a basic salary of £25,000 per annum with no benefits-in-kind. This is significantly lower than the market level which INSEAD graduates command.

Until the first round of financing, each director will own 50% of *Beautiful Legs by post*, having each made an equity investment of £5,000.

(Continued)

Exhibit 7.1 *(Continued)*

3. The Niche Opportunity

3.1. The Distribution Channel: Direct Mail

The inevitable development of direct distribution of product, from supplier to customer, has started to change European retailing. The United States has successfully developed today's form of direct mailing from yesterday's method of mass mailing. All American catalogues are now product specific, for example only casual clothing, or only houseware supplies. As a result, all US catalogues are concise "specialogues". The last US general merchandise catalogue, the Sear's Catalogue, was withdrawn in 1994. This is a sharp contrast to European styled catalogues that are dominated by general merchandise catalogues. For example Freeman's and Littlewoods have catalogues with more than a thousand pages and are offering a full range within all product categories.

We now see American companies expanding into Europe and targeting a market with sophisticated methods of direct marketing. Successful American catalogue houses such as L. L. Bean, Land's End, and J. Crew have entered the European market. Recently a number of British catalogues have been launched aimed at the professional women. Kingshill has recently received a lot of attention in the press with three catalogues selling designer outerwear, clothes for professional women and accessories.

In 1991 average per capita sales through mail-order was 100 ECU in Europe. This is less than half of the 211 ECU spent in the United States.

Direct mail offers relatively low start-up and fixed costs when compared to more traditional forms of retailing. Free-standing, high rent stores are replaced with flexibly leased low rent warehouse space. Commissioned sales associates and hourly stock people are replaced with telephones and fax machines accepting orders, and data entry clerks and packers to prepare the packages. The only "front-office" of a mail-order house is the catalogue.

3.2. The Customer: Professional Women

More European women are working in paid employment than ever before. Total North European women's employment increased from 39 million in 1981 to 45 million in 1991. This is an increase of 16%. In Germany and France the number of women in the service and business sectors grew by 29% in the 10 years to the early 1990s. (Comparative data is not available for the United Kingdom, due to change in the basis of calculation.) This trend has several positive effects for a mail-order business. There are higher disposable incomes, either individually or within household unit. Women have less free time in which to spend their money. Finally, more women in the workforce are now required to dress professionally.

Our target customers are professional women who wear tights on a regular basis to work. Thus they are likely to work in either the service or financial sectors. Our April 1995 survey indicated that our customer will buy on average 25 to 45 tights a year in an average lot size of four pairs. According to Marketing Intelligence March 1995 industry studies, 22.4% of Britain's full-time working women were "heavy users", purchasing 5 or more pairs of tights each month. 29.3% were considered to be "medium users", purchasing three or four pairs of tights each month. In contrast, The Economic Intelligence Unit found that total British consumption per head is 17.9 units per year. In Germany it is 16.8 units and similarly in France it is 16.4 units. Based on this information, our average of 33 units per annum is a reasonable figure.

Exhibit 7.1 *(Continued)*

Marketing Intelligence industry report, March 1995, reports that professional women must buy durable tights that will not snag or ladder. Our target customer more than any other customer profile was more likely to prefer Lycra-based tights, a standard requirement for quality. Working women, married women, women with children and AB socio-demographic types were the strongest supporter of such Lycra-based products.

Outerwear fashions are a major influence of the type of hosiery purchased. The outerwear ranges for 1995 show a move away from the casual look to a more glamorous look of soft tailoring and high heeled shoes. The recent trend towards shorter skirts has led to tights gaining a higher market share since stockings are more impractical for work. While knee-highs may be worn with long skirts, leggings and tailored trousers, the predominant work basic remains the full leg tight. In 1994, 82% of all hosiery sold were tights and 8% were knee-highs.

Our April 1995 survey shows that in our target market 70% of respondents stated "Quality" as their most important purchase criteria when buying tights. "Price" is considerably lower in importance, with 49% stating it as their second most important influence and 21% stating it is their third and least most important.

Our target customer currently buys tights from the department store, carrying a better than average quality product, or from variety and grocery stores, presumably from the higher quality selections. Although only 7% of all hosiery sold in the United Kingdom is through the relatively high end department stores, this still represents 25 million pairs annually.

85% of our surveyed target market said that they would consider buying through mail-order, provided there was the opportunity to try the product, and that there were no problems with delivery or returns.

3.3. The Product: Work Tights

Women's work tights are a regularly purchased necessity. Even the best hosiery lasts no more than 10 washings before the nylon breaks down. Tights are similar to basic men's work shirts, in that they are part of the professional's uniform and they need to be bought regularly. Both James Meade and Thomas Pink recognised this basic demand and built successful mail-order operations serving this market. However, unlike men's shirts, tights require more frequent purchases. This is due to two reasons. Firstly, men's shirts can still be worn despite slight wear and tear while any slight imperfection, a "ladder", in any part of women's hosiery makes a pair of tights totally unwearable. Secondly, cotton shirts last longer than a pair of nylon tights.

Our goal is to access the European women professional market and to be the exclusive supplier of our client's work hosiery. Given this specific and highly selective niche, we have found that our customers have similar tastes for tights despite national borders (see Survey Results, page 14). They have to conform to a certain dress style that emphasises skirt suits as opposed to trouser suits. While the fashions of the suits themselves may be country specific, the styling of hosiery is consistent across Europe.

Retail mark-up and total mark-downs taken are the two most important components of the final gross margin figures. The Economic Intelligence Unit has found that retail mark-ups average at least 40% for all ranges of women's hosiery. Mark-downs of aged goods are virtually non-existent, since the styles remain constant over time. Tights are a standard quality product for which the manufacturers have had to concentrate on quality control; thus we expect returns, due to faulty product, to be minimal. Additional Doré Doré guarantees their product and will take back faulty product.

(Continued)

Exhibit 7.1 *(Continued)*

Our range includes only four sizes. Styles and colours are limited in the professional context. Work tights are plain, and the styles are defined by the density (denier). The colours are limited to black, blue and tan. This will allow us to stock three styles, in four sizes, with five colours.

Tights are the ideal mail-order product. They are lightweight (35 grams per pair including packaging). They are small enough to be packaged compactly and therefore deliverable to individual homes via letter boxes. Although fragile in fabrication, they are non-breakable.

Tights cannot be tried on prior to purchase, even in traditional retailing. Therefore mail-order is not at a disadvantage to a traditional retailer.

From our market survey, we can conclude our target market is not purchasing basic work tights at reduced prices, nor are they purchasing "multi-packs". Had these women been purchasing during the sales, we would have seen greater evidence of bulk buying (i.e. six or more pairs purchased at one time). This is further supported by our market survey where only 30% stated that price was their first criteria in choosing which tights to purchase.

There is a relative constant need to buy tights. Thus each mailing list can be evaluated immediately after its first mail shot, and not after additional second or third mailings. By contrast, the purchasing cycle in clothing is far more irregular. For example, March is typically a strong month for spring sportswear sales, but forecasting revenue in March is difficult. Factors, such as weather, holiday schedules and individual shopping attitudes, determine someone's purchase. Locating a potential client may take a year's worth of mailings before catching the customer with all variables acting in the cataloguer's favour.

Exhibit 7.1   *(Continued)*

4. Our Product Portfolio

4.1. The Range

We aim to cover the full range of working needs. This will be the lower end of premium quality-tights, on par with Calvin Klein, Donna Karan and Christian Dior.

We will not supply hosiery that tends to be bought for special occasions nor the styles that are bought infrequently. These are usually bought along with another purchase (for example, an expensive pair of tights will be bought along with a new evening dress).

We will have three styles;
- Classic sheer (The standard working tights with a 15 denier appearance)
- Ultra-sheer tights (10 denier appearance)
- Thicker microfiber tights (30 denier)

We will have five colours;
- Black and near black
- navy blue
- two different tans

There will be the four sizes.

4.2. The Supplier

We have chosen a well-known French hosiery company founded in 1819 called Doré Doré to be our supplier. They have a number of advantages compared to the others that we considered.

- They are willing to supply marketing material, such as samples and discounted products.

- They are able to supply goods in small lot sizes. Production runs with special packaging require a minimum order of 2,000 units as opposed to the industry average of 24,000 units.

- They have an excellent reputation for quality, especially in France.

- They are willing to supply us on a weekly basis.

- Lead times are short. They can deliver within 5 working days of receiving an order, and the transportation time is less than 24 hours.

- They wish to enter the British fine gauge hosiery market. They are established as high quality suppliers of men's and children's socks.

- We have negotiated credit terms of 60 days, with a discount of 2.75% for payment within 30 days.

- They supply socks to other mail-order companies and thus have experience of our industry.

(Continued)

Exhibit 7.1   *(Continued)*

5. Competitive Advantages

Our competitive advantage is being able to offer quality tights at a fair competitive price through a convenient distribution channel.

The sources of our competitive advantage are: first movers advantage and targeted mailing lists.

We will have the advantage of being the first mover. We will be the first to locate the buyers of high quality tights and will be able keep them by offering an efficient and reliable service through the Monthly Order Program. For a new entrant, since many potential customers will be our customers, their "hit-rates" will be reduced. This means that the cost of acquiring clients becomes prohibitive. New entrants cannot gain market share through price reductions since quality is perceived to be reflected in price. General interest from being the first mail-order company specialising in tights will give us free publicity opportunities. This cannot be repeated by new entrants.

These advantages can be sustained in the short to medium term through generating customer loyalty by offering excellent service at an excellent value. As the client base increases, we will increase our buying power and will be able to reduce the cost prices and thus increase our margins.

The tights' business is faced by two potential entrants. The most likely entrant is a major manufacturer, such as Sara Lee of Chicago, or one. of the large independent European manufacturers. In our discussions with suppliers, Golden Lady said that they had considered mail-order. They had not pursued this, since as a manufacturer they believed that they should concentrate on designing and manufacturing new high quality products, rather than diverting resources to retailing.

Exhibit 7.1   *(Continued)*

6. Market Research

Our market research consisted of careful analysis of the three critical points of this business:

- the hosiery market
- mail-order developments in Europe
- employment trends among professional women

In conducting our research, we used a variety of both primary and secondary data.

6.1. Survey Results

In an effort to better understand the hosiery needs of this target segment, we distributed a survey to all 710 women INSEAD alumnae currently residing in Europe. The alumnae were asked to return the pre-addressed questionnaire card. It is important to note that no incentive was offered; not even return postage was included. We did this to track the true response rate, rather than an offer induced one. It can be argued that an "INSEAD to INSEAD" survey may be inflated due to like associations. However, we aim to instil a similar association in pitching our service as "woman to woman.".

Of the 710 survey cards, we received 231 responses representing a 33% "hit rate." 85% of those respondents stated that they would consider purchasing hosiery by post, given a high level of guaranteed quality, ease in ordering and speed in delivery.

We received 74 responses from the United Kingdom and 67 responses from France. This represented a response rate of 33% and 29% respectively. We sent out fewer surveys to Germany, Switzerland, and the other Northern European countries, but the response rate was on average 45%. In addition, these countries were proportionally more positive in their responses, with Germany 100% receptive to the concept. Southern Europe, primarily Italy, Spain, and Portugal, demonstrated a lower response rate, and was less receptive to our concept. The average response rate was 25% and only 33% were interested in buying through mail-order. This information has directed us to concentrate our initial entry strategy on Northern Europe. Other factors involved in this decision included reliable domestic postal services, and relatively higher priced hosiery.

	Response Rate	Receptive Rate
France	29%	88%
United Kingdom	33%	89%
Germany	50%	100%
Switzerland	42%	94%
Total Target Market	33%	85%

Perhaps the strongest information we gained from this survey was the purchase pattern similarities among alumnae across countries. Responses to hosiery colour preferences demonstrate this point quite clearly. Asked what percentage of their wardrobe was black, navy [blue], or other in autumn and winter as opposed to spring and summer, each nationality within our target market responded almost identically.

(Continued)

Exhibit 7.1   (Continued)

		France %	UK %	Germany %	Switzerland %	Total %
Autumn	Black	59	58	64	62	58
and Winter	Navy	12	14	14	19	14
	Other	27	27	22	19	28
	Not stated	2	1	0	0	0
Spring and	Black	16	23	23	23	20
Summer	Navy	15	13	12	15	14
	Other	61	59	55	61	60
	Not stated	8	5	10	1	6

Similarly, although perhaps not as simply obvious as the previous example, is the relative importance for each factor (quality, price and brand) are in the customer's purchasing decision. In each case, "quality" was the strongest influence with approximately 70% of respondents, regardless of country stating it to be their first priority. "Price" was the second most important criteria for 49% of respondents. "Brand" was third and least important criteria for 60% of respondents.

These trends are confirmed with the March 1995 Marketing Intelligence report that states that for age groups' 25-54, there appears to be little brand loyalty. 15% of the 1,181 British women who responded stated "Brand" as the first purchase criteria. In their survey, Lycra (a recognised assurance of quality) is a significant factor in their purchasing decision. On average 47% responded that Lycra was their first purchase criteria. This supports the hypothesis that our particular niche can be targeted across borders, and not confined to one national market. Such information is crucial to our ultimate goal of establishing a catalogue house serving the entire Northern European up-scale professional woman market.

6.2. Interviews

Thierry Weber, Director of Marketing for France's third largest catalogue house CAMIF, was interviewed on 12 April 1995 by Elizabeth Preis. According to him, the European mail-order is currently going through an "Americanising trend." Speciality product specific catalogues are becoming increasingly popular, and are aimed at more financially sound target segments. Supporting this are the many acquisitions by the large catalogue houses of smaller speciality catalogues. Otto Versand, of Germany, owns ten separate catalogue houses, including speciality catalogues. La Redoute, of France, controls not only a 1200+ page general catalogue, but also more than a dozen "specialogues" such as "Jardin de Florimon" and "Enfant". These trends toward Americanised cataloguing are expected to continue. We aim to enter the market immediately, before the market becomes saturated with specialogues. Using the United States as an example, "first mover" catalogues still continue to dominate the catalogue market, despite the many new entrants.

6.3. Independent Market Research

Shopping in the major French and UK department stores, variety outlets, discount stores, and grocery channels enabled us to better understand the range of products and prices offered.

Exhibit 7.1 *(Continued)*

The retail market for tights can be broken into three broad ranges;

1. The low end, these are sold for between £0.35 to £1.25. These contain from between zero to 19 % Lycra. They have few extras such as having a fully shaped leg, cotton gussets or reinforced toe. They are packed in simple boxes.

2. Middle range, these are sold for between £1.25 to £7.50. These contain on average 15 % Lycra. The higher end varieties have many extra features to add to their quality. They are wrapped around card that is then inserted into a plastic bag along with a cardboard insert. The insert has a picture and a description of the product. Sara Lee has launched a new premium brand, the "Donna Karan" range starting at £10 per pair.

3. High end, these are sold for anything up to £25. To the uninformed, there is little to distinguish them from the middle range products. Well-known brands include Wolford of Austria and Chantall Thomass of France.

The price of the tights seems therefore to be correlated to the quality. No market share will be gained in drastically under-cutting traditional outlets since this will lower the perceived quality of the product.

6.4. Third Party Research - Hosiery Market

We consulted trade and business articles, Marketing Intelligence reports, and Economic Intelligence Unit (EIU) reports highlighting recent trends in the hosiery industry.

According to the March 1995 Marketing Intelligence report "Stockings and Tights" that studied the UK market trends, the hosiery market has been difficult over the last few years but is expected to improve. With the introduction, and immediate success of Lycra in 1989, total sales value increased, while volume decreased. Manufacturers were able to charge higher prices for this innovative material, but fewer units were sold each year due to its longer-lasting wear.

Recent fashions have also adversely affected the total hosiery market. However the extent to which it affected the professional market cannot be determined as such studies do not separate professional use versus non-professional use. Specifically, high denier (the industry measurement of tight density) hosiery was extremely popular in the early 90's as fashions emphasised heavy fabrications and monochromatic matte fashion looks. These trends have now begun to swing back to lighter colours and more feminine styles. For Autumn, skirts will be increasingly important. The fashion of wearing trousers will decrease in both the professional and recreational contexts. Due to this, hosiery is expected to increase in sales volume. Value, however will remain high, as women have come to appreciate and mandate Lycra-based tights for both work and recreation.

The EIU has studied the hosiery sectors of each of our key markets: Hosiery in France, November 1994; Hosiery in the UK, January 1994; Knitted underwear, hosiery and swimwear in Spain, November 1994. Their studies further support the Marketing Intelligence report, and substantiated our primary data findings.

(Continued)

Exhibit 7.1   *(Continued)*

6.5. Third Party Research - Mail-order Industry

Various studies have been conducted on the mail-order industry, both at the Pan-European level, as well as country specific. In 1993, The Euromonitor published a complete Market Direction Report on Mail-order and Home Shopping highlighting the following socio-demographic trends:

- an increase in dual income families increasing total household disposable income

- an overall ageing population, placing stronger emphasis on the added value of convenience

- although somewhat loosened, strict store opening hours are dictated by government authorities

These three general trends support not only our chosen distribution channel, mail-order, but also the specific product and market we have chosen to target.

Exhibit 7.1 *(Continued)*

7. Competitors and Substitutes

7.1. Competitors

There are currently no mail-order catalogues selling quality tights. In the United States there are a number of companies that only sell slightly "irregular" tights, but these are all imperfect. In Europe a number of catalogues offer tights as an accessory. However these are not aimed at the professional woman, they are either thick tights for outdoor use (L. L. Bean), or the lacy style sold in lingerie catalogues.

Our targeted customer currently buys her tights from department stores, groceries and other convenience stores, and variety stores (for example Marks & Spencer).

Department stores stock the whole range of quality and have a wide range of brands. Floor space was divided fairly evenly between the two product categories. However the range is often too wide. This results in customers constantly changing brand and may be confused by so many similar products. The main draw back of buying from a department store is that a separate purchase needs to be made. Tights cannot be purchased along with other necessities. In the UK, 7% of all tights were bought through department stores in 1994. This represents 25 million pairs.

Groceries and convenience stores have the advantage that the customer does not need to make a separate purchase in order to buy tights. They can be purchased along with the weekly shopping. Product packaging included both individual pairs and multi-packs. The disadvantage is that the quality is not necessarily as high as she may wish. Groceries are trying to combat this by selling better fitting and higher quality styles. The range is from low to middle range. In the UK, 36% of all tights were bought through groceries' stores in 1994.

Variety stores, like Marks & Spencer, have tried to address the above disadvantages. They have a wider range of quality, a single brand (Marks & Spencer's own label), and the ability to purchase tights along with either other clothing items or even food. In the UK, 28% of all tights were bought through variety stores in 1994. Marks & Spencer has acknowledged the demand for high quality tights by launching the "Italian collection" at £4 per pair.

7.2. Substitutes

There are no real substitutes for tights. Stockings could be considered but they represent a decreasing percentage of hosiery. They represented 10% of all hosiery units sold in 1994, down from 15% in 1990. This trend is unlikely to be reversed given the convenience of wearing tights and the requirements of current fashions (shorter less bulky skirts). Hold-ups have never caught on due to technical difficulties of making them stay up without being too tight.

The main area of risk in this area is if women start wearing more trousers and more casual clothes to work. This appeared to be happening in the late eighties, but the trend has been reversed especially amongst professional women.

(Continued)

Exhibit 7.1   *(Continued)*

8. Marketing plan

The launch will be conducted as follows:

8.1. 9 October 1995

First mailings posted. Until a mailing has actually been sent out, it is impossible to predict the "hit-rate". We, therefore, sent out a total of 4,000 catalogues. Two thousand names and addresses have been acquired through our network of friends and business associates. We have rented 2,000 names to test the response rates from a rented mailing list. The names have been selected using the following criteria; women, professionals or senior management, earning over £25,000 and living in London.

Our promotional activities range from offering a free pair of tights, a special offer (buy two, and get one free), a gift (for example, a hosiery bag), to offering no incentives.

This test mailing will also allow us to gauge whether orders will be received by post, telephone or fax. The fulfilment house can then adjust the number of telephone lines and operators accordingly.

8.2. Late October 1995

Assuming that the test proves that the business is viable, we will continue the earlier discussions with potential investors in order to raise £110,000. Several potential investors have already been identified and expressed interest.

8.3. November 1995

Beautiful Legs by post will send out an 80,000 mail-shot in early November. The names and addresses will be rented from a number of list houses. This is to test the different sources and to maximise the spread across professions and companies. Potential sources of mailing lists are; the professional bodies such as the Institute of Chartered Accountants and The Law Society. Alumnae from schools such as INSEAD, and Wellesley College, names acquired through lifestyle interviews, subscriptions, department stores and existing high-end mail-order customers.

8.4. General Strategy

In the first year we will concentrate on the British market. This is to allow us to perfect our marketing and logistic experience before launching into other Northern European countries, especially Germany.

Having built the client base we will encourage our clients to recommend *Beautiful Legs by post* to their friends. We will achieve this through quality service, sending a new catalogue and price list with every order and asking our clients to recommend *Beautiful Legs by post* to their friends. Open communication is vital to the success of this business. In every delivery, our phone number and fax number will be included.

All our marketing material will emphasise the quality of our product and the convenience of the distribution channel. We will encourage first time orders with free trials or special offers, and guarantee to accept all returns without question and with refund of postage.

Exhibit 7.1   *(Continued)*

8.5. Pricing

Our product will be priced at the high end of the middle range. Thus it will be priced at the top end of the mass market brands. This appeals to quality conscious mass market consumers as well as value conscious upmarket consumers. Our market surveys have shown that consumer can differentiate between the quality of £7 pair as opposed to a £2 pair. More importantly we have found that a significant percentage is willing to pay £7 a pair.

8.6. Brand Name

We intend to have our own brand name, yet leverage the reputed quality of Doré Doré.

The potential draw backs of having our own brand name are brand recognition and a minimum quantity order size required for private label. Brand recognition is unlikely to be a problem. Our survey showed that only 15% of respondents chose brand as their number one influencing decision. 19% of respondents used brand name as the second criteria for choosing their tights. As our supplier is eager to build their British business, minimum order quantities are at a mere 2,000 units per style.

(Continued)

Exhibit 7.1   *(Continued)*

9. Logistics and Administration

We will seek to minimise all fixed costs by contracting out wherever possible. Thus we have contracted out catalogue fulfilment, order processing, data management, and order fulfilment. Marketing, the key to our success will be handled in-house. Catalogue design and product sourcing will remain totally under the founders control.

9.1. Fulfilment and Order Processing

All fulfilment and order processing are contracted-out. We will use one fulfilment house to cover all functions from the direct catalogue mailings, order processing, to sending out the product. We have chosen a company called Marketlink Marketing Communications Limited (MMC). They are able to provide a very flexible fulfilment service. They are able to staff up at short notice, using a number of experienced packers who would work on a piecemeal basis. We will be using the Heathrow site.

9.2. Delivery

All deliveries will be via UK's Royal Post, as well as the respective national postal carriers of our countries of business. Eventually, we anticipate organising time-definite deliveries through courier services once minimum parcel levels are met. Initially the orders will be filled the day after the order is taken and delivery by post will take an additional two to three days. Thus the customer will receive the order in just three to four days.

9.3. Offices and Staffing Requirements

Since the work carried out by the company is limited, total staff employed directly will be limited to the two founders. The offices for the short term will remain in one of the founder's homes, though we are considering renting a small office.

9.4. Business Location

The business will initially be only based in the United Kingdom. The reasons are simple:

- The United Kingdom enjoys one of the lowest corporation tax rates in Europe.

- Due to problems renting European mailing lists, initially a large percentage of our client base will be in the United Kingdom and will be concentrated around London.

- The postage rates are the low (due to the weaker purchasing power of the pound against DM related currencies).

As the business grows and we perfect the British "template", we will locate a subsidiary in a country where foreign language speakers can be hired cheaply. Alternatively satellite offices can be opened in each country in which we have a sufficient customer base. The choice will depend on the cost effectiveness of re-routing regional toll-free numbers against the extra overhead and administration costs of having satellite offices.

Exhibit 7.1 *(Continued)*

10. Business Economics

10.1. Gross Margins

Supplier price lists and publicly available market surveys (i.e. Mintel, and The Economic Intelligence Reports) show that the hosiery business enjoys margins of 40%. This occurs across brands, price ranges and distribution outlets. We will charge £7 for the standard work tights (15 denier appearance), £6 for the 10 denier appearance ultra-sheer tights and £11 for the microfiber 30 denier semi-opaque tights. We expect to have an average retail price (including VAT) of £7.60, giving a revenue per unit in the UK of £6.47. The revenue in the rest of Europe will depend on the prevailing VAT rate and whether we have sufficient turnover to be registered for VAT.

The average cost per unit (excluding VAT) is expected to £3.88.

Tights are lightweight and small. It is a perfect product for posting. They weigh approximately 35 grams including packaging. A standard package is 16 cm by 21 cm by 0.5 cm. Mailing and packaging costs will total approximately £2.50 per order. 50p for post and £2.00 for order handling and packaging (this includes a new catalogue costing 25p, which can be passed onto a colleague). We will charge an average of £2.00 for postage and handling.

We expect to have an average order size of 4 units (the initial order size will be smaller at 3 units). Thus the gross margin per UK order will be £9.86.

10.2. Acquiring Customer Costs

The main advantage of supplying tights, rather than other products through mail-order, is that tights are a repeat purchase item. Thus the business needs only to secure an initial sale and repeat sales will naturally follow.

New customers can be acquired in two ways; using rented mailing lists and sending out a catalogue, and through encouraging our client base to recommend *Beautiful Legs by post* to a friend. Renting mailing lists can be very expensive if the "hit rate" is low. Thus, we will target customers through first renting the lists of professional bodies such as the Institute of Chartered Accountants and The Law Society. Secondly, we will target women living in urban areas that are likely to have a high concentration of professional women. In London this will cover areas such as Knightsbridge, Belsize Park, Hammersmith, Clapham and South Kensington.

"Word of mouth" is the most cost effective and credible method of acquiring new clients. This assumes *Beautiful Legs by post* will have adequately satisfied a client in the first place, but this is vital in order to secure a repeat purchase. We plan to encourage "word of mouth" recommendations by periodically targeting our client base using incentives as well as sending out catalogues with every order.

10.3. Repeat Purchases

Since over 75% of all orders will be by existing customers, orders will be placed without us having had to send out a mail shot. This significantly reduces the costs of obtaining a sale. We are also supplying a necessity, rather than encouraging clients to buy a luxury, thus the costs of encouraging clients to make repeat purchases are also reduced.

Exhibit 7.1   *(Continued)*

10.4. Break-even Analysis

The cost of a mailing is £773 per 1,000 catalogues sent. (This is broken down as follows; mailing list rent £120, fulfilment £141, catalogue £250, envelope £42, postage £220.) Thus if our "hit-rate" is 1.5%, the cost of acquiring one client is £51.53.

Since the margin per order is £9.86, we start to make money when our client places their fifth full value order. (A customer is estimated to order on average over eight times per year.)

Below is an example of an active client who receives an inducement valued at £1.60 on her first order of three pairs, and then subsequently buys in order lots of four pairs.

(Cost)/revenue per client acquired	Order 1	Order 2	Order 3	Order 4	Order 5	Order 6
Mailing	(51.53)	0.00	0.00	0.00	0.00	0.00
Gross margin	5.67	9.86	9.86	9.86	9.86	9.86
Per order	(45.86)	9.86	9.86	9.86	9.86	9.86
Cumulative	(45.86)	(36.00)	(26.14)	(16.28)	(6.42)	3.44

The financial projections assume that each month 5% of the client base returns to purchasing tights from other sources.

10.5. A Seasonal Business Requires Low Fixed Costs

The business is seasonal. Sales will be the highest during the autumn and winter. They will tail off during the spring and will be the lowest during the summer. Therefore *Beautiful legs by post* must constantly seek to ensure that all its costs are variable and that it has low fixed costs. This will allow the business to maintain its net margins throughout the seasons.

Fulfilment (inserting of catalogues or tights into envelopes), data management and order processing will be contracted out and thus variable.

10.6. Cash Management

Payment will be made by credit card. Credit card companies will normally settle their accounts within five working dates. However for the first year, until we have a proven track record, Midland Bank will pay us after thirty days. This gives them security in the event that fraud is committed either by our customers or ourselves. This is standard practice.

We have negotiated the following payment terms with our supplier. Standard terms are 60 days, however we will receive a 2.75% discount if we pay within 30 days. Since stock can be ordered weekly and our stock-keeping-units are limited to 48, our stock levels will be minimal.

The warehousing, data management and fulfilment services will be contracted-out. Therefore there is no requirement to rent space and enter into any long term contractual obligations. Computer equipment and other office equipment will be rented, when necessary. There are negligible fixed assets.

Exhibit 7.1   *(Continued)*

11. Risk factors

We believe that all potential investors should be aware of the following risk factors relating to their investment in the Company. However, it should be noted that investors are advised to conduct their own risk assessment of the Company's prospects.

11.1. Mail Shot "Hit Rate"

As in all mail-order businesses, the "hit rate" is probably the most crucial factor. A mail-order house has no way of estimating this rate, until it actually sends out letters and starts to receive orders. Our market survey generated a 33% response rate. 85% of these respondents said that they were willing to try buying tights through mail-order.

We will target all mail shots carefully, initially aiming at the professional woman living in city centres. We will heavily target areas that have a high concentration of professionals. We are looking for customers who would normally buy from department stores or who buy the higher quality tights in groceries and variety stores.

In our financial model we assumed that 1.5% of recipients of a catalogue will place an order and become regular customers.

Below is a table that shows the effect of different "hit rates".

Hit rate	Earnings before interest and taxes 1996 £ `000	Earnings before interest and taxes 1997 £ `000	Earnings before interest and taxes 1998 £ `000
1%	(89)	(79)	17
1.5%(as in financial model)	(55)	40	196
2%	(22)	151	363
2.5%	12	263	533

Financial year end is 31 August

11.2. "Friend of a Friend" Rate

A good service will generate referrals. On average women recommend good value products or services to two other women. *Beautiful Legs by post* will be recommend by satisfied customers of its service. Encouraging this will be our cheapest and most effective way of generating new clients.

In our financial model we have assumed the following "friend of a friend rates". This is the number of friends introduced per month by a client base of 100. In the first year the rate is 15, the second year is 10 and in the third year is 5. (To balance for the new clients being introduced we have assumed that our customer base will reduce through wastage by 5% every month.)

Below is a table that shows the effect of different "friend of a friend rates". The hit rate is assumed to be 1.5%.

(Continued)

Exhibit 7.1   *(Continued)*

Friend of a friend rate (Year 1, 2, 3)	Net income/(loss) 1996 £ `000	Net income/(loss) 1996 £ `000	Net income/(loss) 1996 £ `000
5, 5,5	(80)	(56)	52
10, 10, 5	(69)	(13)	116
15, 10, 5 (As in model)	(55)	40	196
20, 10, 5	(40)	107	304

Financial year end is 31 August

11.3. Strong Entrant into the Mail-order Hosiery Market

There is a risk that a strong entrant such as Pretty Polly (a subsidiary of Sara Lee of Chicago) will enter the market. This is likely if they believe that *Beautiful Legs by post* is successful. All Sara Lee's hosiery subsidiaries constantly introduce new products in order to gain market share. This is not detrimental to the investment since this will give us the opportunity for an earlier exit route. Any entrant will want to purchase our list of proven customers, thus saving them the expense and risk or starting a new direct mail business themselves.

11.4. Exit price

We plan to have a saleable business after three years of operation. A potential purchaser would be a trade buyer wanting to purchase a new distribution channel, which has direct contact with their customers. Given the Earnings before interest and tax for year 3 is £196,000, we would expect a trade sale price of 7 times earnings before interest and taxes, thus giving a total price of £1,372,000.

The risk is that a trade purchaser will prefer to start their own business rather than buy an existing business. However, we believe that because we will have already identified members of a valuable segment (professional women buying quality products), they will want to purchase our customer base in order to expand on our knowledge.

Exhibit 7.1 *(Continued)*

12. Assumptions Used in Financial Model

We have used the following assumptions in formulating the financial projections (see appendix A). While we have sought to ensure that the financial projections are substantially accurate, potential investors should conduct their own analysis of the future prospects of the business. The attention of potential investors is also drawn to the discussion of risks that may affect the business.

12.1. General

- All data has not been adjusted for inflation. Inflation is currently below 3 % in the United Kingdom and is projected to remain at low levels.

12.2. Sales

- We have assumed an average unit sale price (including VAT) of £7.60, both in the United Kingdom and continental Europe.

- Customers will place an average trial order of 3 units, and all repeat orders will have an average lot size of 4 units.

- Customers will order with the following frequency: 100% of all customers will order once a month in the winter months (November to February). 75% will order once a month during the Spring (March to May) and Autumn (September and October). Only 20% will order once a month in the Summer (June to August).

- We will have to collect value-added-tax on all sales. We have assumed a value added tax of 17.5% in the United Kingdom and an average of 20% in continental Europe. (We have to register for VAT in each country once we have reached their VAT threshold, until that time we have to charge British VAT)

- Current customers will introduce new clients to *Beautiful Legs by post* at an initial rate of 15 new clients a month per 100 existing customers. This will reduce to 10 per 100 in the second year and 5 per 100 in the third year.

- We will lose 5% of our customer base every month.

12.3. Cost of Sales

- We have assumed an average unit cost price (excluding VAT) of £3.63. This is based on our current negotiations with our suppliers.

- All stock fulfilment will be carried out by MMC. We have based our costs on a quotation received from MMC on 11 September 1995.

12.4. Mail Shot Costs

We currently employ four different forms of mail shots;

- Free trial pair of tights, with no obligation to make a purchase
- Free pair provided the customer buys two pairs
- Gift inducement, such as a free hosiery wash bag with the first order
- No inducement

(Continued)

Exhibit 7.1 *(Continued)*

12.5. Administration Costs

- These have been calculated on a line item basis and include salaries of the two directors. Other marketing costs covers marketing activities other than direct mail shots. Such activities would be a launch event to generate awareness amongst innovators and a follow-up letter to our existing customer base. Credit card charges have been assumed to be 2.48% of sales revenue, including value added tax. Other staff represent the cost of data input temporary staff from MMC, who would answer queries.

12.6. Corporation Tax

- We have assumed a rate of 25%, payable six months after the financial year end. We have assumed that all expenses are allowable for tax purposes and losses can be carried forward.

12.7. Working Capital

- We will maintain an average stock level of representing 2 weeks' stock plus 10%. This low level can be achieved by weekly replenishment orders.

- Payment will be by credit or debit card only. For the first year, trade debtors represent one month of sales. Thereafter, trade debtors represent one quarter of the previous month's sales.

- Corporation tax is payable six months after the financial year end, 31 August.

- Value added tax is payable quarterly. This represents amounts collected on sales less value added tax charged on purchases.

- Stock will be paid 60 days after delivery, as already agreed with Doré Doré.

- Accounts payable to suppliers is calculated at either 30 days or immediate. Fulfilment costs and catalogues are 30 days; Postage is paid immediately.

12.8. Capital Expenditure

- To minimise cash outlays, all equipment, if required, will be leased.

Exhibit 7.1 (Continued)

	Sep-95 Autumn	Oct-95 Autumn	Nov-95 Winter	Dec-95 Winter	Jan-96 Winter	Feb-96 Winter	Mar-96 Spring	Apr-96 Spring	May-96 Spring	Jun-96 Summer	Jul-96 Summer	Aug-96 Summer	Year 1
Free pair with 1st order	0	1,380	40,000	0	10,000	10,000	0	0	0	0	0	0	61,380
Cold mail shots Catalogue	0	2,000	39,900	0	9,900	9,900							61,700
Cold mail shots free pair	0	620	100	0	100	100							920
Reminders	0	0	0	0	349	459							808
Total	0	4,000	80,000	0	20,349	20,459	0	0	0	0	0	0	124,808
Number of free pairs-ms	0	388	63	0	63	63	0	0	0	0	0	0	575
Number of free pairs-F of f		0	0	0	0	0	0	0	0	0	0	0	0
First time orders-free pair		0	10	2	0	2	2	0	0	0	0	0	16
First time orders-Catalogue		30	600	0	150	150	0	0	0	0	0	0	930
Free pair with 1st order		22	600	0	150	150	0	0	0	0	0	0	922
First time orders-F of f		0	8	190	209	275	261	278	295	84	82	80	1,762
Number of repeat orders			26	661	1,363	1,651	1,593	1,839	1,955	554	566	554	10,762
Total orders	0	52	1,244	853	1,873	2,228	1,856	2,117	2,250	638	648	635	14,393
UK	0	47	1,119	768	1,685	2,005	1,671	1,905	2,025	574	583	571	12,953
Continental Europe	0	5	124	85	187	223	186	212	225	64	65	63	1,439
Total lights sent out	0	544	3,820	3,220	7,044	8,397	7,162	8,191	8,706	2,467	2,508	2,458	54,515
Purchased	1,000	1,835	3,460	5,514	7,856	7,298	7,728	8,474	5,274	2,490	3,587	6,154	60,669
Brought forward		1,000	2,292	1,932	4,226	5,038	3,939	4,505	4,788	1,357	1,380	2,458	0
Carried forward	1,000	2,292	1,932	4,226	5,038	3,939	4,505	4,788	1,357	1,380	2,458	6,154	6,154
Client base	0	52	1,267	1,396	1,836	2,321	2,468	2,622	2,786	2,731	2,676	2,622	2,622

(Continued)

Exhibit 7.1 *(Continued)*

Profit & Loss Account

	Sep-95	Oct-95	Nov-95	Dec-95	Jan-96	Feb-96	Mar-96	Apr-96	May-96	Jun-96	Jul-96	Aug-96	Year 1
Revenue-UK	0	780	18,380	18,744	39,766	47,644	41,691	47,681	50,680	14,359	14,601	14,309	308,635
Revenue-continental Europe	0	85	2,000	2,039	4,326	5,183	4,536	5,188	5,514	1,562	1,589	1,557	33,578
Postage (exc. VAT)		0	57	1,445	2,671	3,271	3,149	3,596	3,822	1,083	1,100	1,078	21,273
Total Revenue	0	865	20,437	22,228	46,763	56,099	49,377	56,465	60,016	17,004	17,289	16,944	363,487
													100.0%
Cost of tights	0	605	14,564	12,480	27,059	32,304	27,759	31,748	33,744	9,561	9,722	9,527	209,073
Packaging	0	10	243	166	365	434	362	413	439	124	126	124	2,807
Catalogue (1 x A4 folded)	0	13	309	212	466	554	462	527	560	159	161	158	3,579
Acknowledgment insert	0	3	83	57	125	149	124	141	150	43	43	42	960
Inducements repeat orders	0	0	5	132	273	330	319	368	391	111	113	111	2,152
Inducements new orders	0	83	1,948	307	815	924	421	444	472	134	131	128	5,808
Postage-UK	0	23	549	376	826	983	819	934	992	281	286	280	6,347
Postage-continental Europe	0	3	73	50	110	131	109	124	132	37	38	37	846
Packers & warehouse	0	68	1,622	1,112	2,442	2,906	2,421	2,761	2,935	832	845	828	18,772
Gross Margin £	0	57	1,041	7,334	14,283	17,384	16,581	19,005	20,200	5,723	5,825	5,708	113,142
Gross Margin %		6.6%	5.1%	33.0%	30.5%	31.0%	33.6%	33.7%	33.7%	33.7%	33.7%	33.7%	31.1%
Mail shots & reminders													
Mailing list	0	480	9,600	0	2,400	2,400	0	0	0	0	0	0	14,880
Fulfillment	0	564	11,270	0	2,867	2,882	0	0	0	0	0	0	17,582
Catalogue (1 x A4 folded)	0	995	19,896	0	5,061	5,088	0	0	0	0	0	0	31,040
Envelope	0	168	3,360	0	855	859	0	0	0	0	0	0	5,242
Postage	0	880	17,600	0	4,477	4,501	0	0	0	0	0	0	27,458
	0	3,086	61,726	0	15,659	15,730	0	0	0	0	0	0	96,202
Free tights													
Tights	0	1,502	242	0	242	242	0	0	0	0	0	0	2,229
Packaging	0	39	6	0	6	6	0	0	0	0	0	0	58
Catalogue (1 x A4 folded)	0	96	16	0	16	16	0	0	0	0	0	0	143
Fulfillment	0	505	82	0	82	82	0	0	0	0	0	0	750
Postage	0	0	0	0	0	0	0	0	0	0	0	0	0
	0	2,142	346	0	346	346	0	0	0	0	0	0	3,179
													0.9%
Operating margin	0	(5,172)	(61,030)	7,334	(1,722)	1,308	16,581	19,005	20,200	5,723	5,825	5,708	13,761
Operating margin %		(598.0%)	(298.6%)	33.0%	(3.7%)	2.3%	33.6%	33.7%	33.7%	33.7%	33.7%	33.7%	3.8%

	Sep-95	Oct-95	Nov-95	Dec-95	Jan-96	Feb-96	Mar-96	Apr-96	May-96	Jun-96	Jul-96	Aug-96	Year 1
Administration													
Telephone	200	260	440	340	340	340	340	340	340	340	340	340	3,960
Other marketing		1,000	1,500										2,500
Other stationary	325					500							825
Office rental	0	125	125	125	200	200	200	200	200	200	200	200	1,975
Computer costs	1,450												1,450
Travel	100	100	100	100	100	100	100	100	100	100	100	100	1,200
Advisors	275	0	1,000		1,000								2,275
Credit card charges	0	25	537	649	1,366	1,638	1,442	1,649	1,753	497	505	495	10,614
Other staff		350	350	350	350	350	350	350	350	350	350	350	3,850
Directors' salaries				4,167	4,167	4,167	4,167	4,167	4,167	4,167	4,167	4,167	37,500
	2,350	1,860	4,112	5,731	7,522	7,295	6,599	6,805	6,909	5,653	5,662	5,651	66,149
EBIT	(2,350)	(7,032)	(65,142)	1,604	(9,244)	(5,987)	9,983	12,199	13,291	70	163	57	(52,388)
Interest (OD & debenture)	0	0	0	(500)	(500)	(500)	(500)	(500)	(500)	0	0	0	(3,000)
Earnings before tax	(2,350)	(7,032)	(65,142)	1,104	(9,744)	(6,487)	9,483	11,699	12,791	70	163	57	(55,388)
Corporation tax	0	0	0	0	0	0	0	0	0	0	0	0	0
Earnings after tax	(2,350)	(7,032)	(65,142)	1,104	(9,744)	(6,487)	9,483	11,699	12,791	70	163	57	(55,388)

(Continued)

Exhibit 7.1 (Continued)

Cash flow

	Sep-95	Oct-95	Nov-95	Dec-95	Jan-96	Feb-96	Mar-96	Apr-96	May-96	Jun-96	Jul-96	Aug-96	Year 1
Inflows													
Revenue	0	0	865	20,437	22,228	46,763	56,099	49,377	56,465	60,016	17,004	17,289	346,543
VAT-UK	0	0	137	3,226	3,508	7,380	8,853	7,792	8,911	9,471	2,683	2,728	54,688
VAT-continental Europe	0	0	17	401	437	919	1,102	970	1,109	1,179	334	340	6,808
	0	0	1,018	24,064	26,173	55,062	66,054	58,139	66,485	70,666	20,022	20,358	408,039
Outflows													
Cost of Sales													
Tights	195	49	3,876	7,114	13,410	21,373	30,448	28,286	29,953	32,846	20,443	9,649	197,400
Packaging	0	3	249	166	371	441	362	413	439	124	126	124	3,059
Acknowledgment insert	0		83	57	125	149	124	141	150	43	43	42	960
Postage-UK	0	23	549	376	826	983	819	934	992	281	286	280	6,347
Postage-continental Europe	0	3	73	50	110	131	109	124	132	37	38	37	846
Packers	0	68	1,622	1,112	2,442	2,906	2,421	2,761	2,935	832	845	828	18,772
Marketing													
Mailing list	0	480	9,600	0	2,400	2,400	0	0	0	0	0	0	14,880
Fulfillment (mail shots)	0	564	11,270	0	2,867	2,882	0	0	0	0	0	0	17,582
Postage	0	880	17,600	0	4,477	4,501	0	0	0	0	0	0	27,458
Envelopes (Catalogue)	0	0	168	3,360	0	855	859	0	0	0	0	0	5,242
Catalogue (1 x A4 folded)	1,244	0	21,140	0	6,218	6,218	0	0	0	0	0	0	34,818
Fulfillment (free tights)	0	505	82	0	82	82	0	0	0	0	0	0	750
Inducements	0	83	1,954	440	1,088	1,254	740	812	863	245	244	239	7,961
Postage (free tights)	0	0	0	0	0	0	0	0	0	0	0	0	0

Administration

											Total
Telephone	200	260	440	340	340	340	340	340	340	340	340	3,620
Other marketing costs	0	1,000	1,500	0	0	0	0	0	0	0	0	2,500
Other stationary/	325	0	0	0	0	500	0	0	0	0	0	825
Office rental	125	125	125	200	200	200	200	200	200	200	200	1,975
Computer costs	1,450	0	0	0	0	0	0	0	0	0	0	1,450
Travel	100	100	100	100	100	100	100	100	100	100	100	1,100
Advisors	275	0	1,000	0	1,000	0	0	0	0	0	0	2,275
Credit card charges	0	25	597	649	1,366	1,638	1,442	1,649	1,753	497	505	10,119
Other salaries	350	350	350	350	350	350	350	350	350	350	350	3,850
Directors' salaries	0	0	4,167	4,167	4,167	4,167	4,167	4,167	4,167	4,167	4,167	37,500
VAT (quarterly settlement)			(5,770)			8,501			11,291			14,021
VAT (paid on inputs)	322	8,723	1,915	5,129	5,654	6,181	5,810	6,150	6,073	3,906	2,013	53,381
Corporation tax												0
	3,394	78,848	17,098	45,350	58,348	57,859	45,880	48,420	58,681	31,585	18,874	468,690
Fixed assets												
Computers	0	0	0	0	0	0	0	0	0	0	0	0
Financing												
Equity	10,000	80,000	0	0	0	0	0	0	0	0	0	90,000
Interest (OD & debenture)	0	0	(500)	(500)	(500)	(500)	(500)	(500)	0	0	0	(3,000)
Debt	0	30,000	30,000	0	0	0	0	0	(30,000)	0	0	87,000
	10,000	80,000	29,500	(500)	(500)	(500)	(500)	(500)	(30,000)	0	0	87,000
Net cash flow	6,606	(2,184)	36,465	(19,677)	(3,786)	7,695	11,759	17,565	(18,015)	(11,563)	1,484	26,349
Cumulative	6,606	4,422	40,887	21,210	17,424	25,119	36,877	54,442	36,427	24,865	26,349	26,349

(Continued)

125

Exhibit 7.1 *(Continued)*

Balance Sheet

	Sep-95	Oct-95	Nov-95	Dec-95	Jan-96	Feb-96	Mar-96	Apr-96	May-96	Jun-96	Jul-96	Aug-96	Year 1
Fixed assets													
Cost	0	0	0	0	0	0	0	0	0	0	0	0	0
Depreciation	0	0	0	0	0	0	0	0	0	0	0	0	0
	0	0	0	0	0	0	0	0	0	0	0	0	0
Current assets													
Stationary													
-Packaging (card etc.)	195	195	195	195	195	195	195	195	195	195	195	195	195
-Catalogue (1 x A4 folded)	1,244	139	1,058	846	1,521	2,081	1,619	1,093	533	375	214	56	56
Tights	3,876	8,884	7,488	16,381	19,528	15,268	17,461	18,559	5,258	5,347	9,527	23,852	23,852
Debtors	0	1,018	24,064	26,173	55,062	66,054	58,139	66,485	70,666	20,022	20,358	19,950	19,950
Cash	6,606	2,251	4,422	40,887	21,210	17,424	25,119	36,877	54,442	36,427	24,865	26,349	26,349
	11,921	12,487	37,227	84,481	97,516	101,021	102,533	123,209	131,095	62,366	55,158	70,402	70,402
Current liabilities													
Overdraft	0	0	0	0	0	0	0	0	0	0	0	0	0
Corporation tax	0	0	0	0	0	0	0	0	0	0	0	0	0
VAT	(505)	(674)	(5,770)	2,030	5,199	8,501	2,581	6,791	11,291	(3,055)	(3,894)	(2,899)	(2,899)
Accounts payable - tights	3,876	10,990	20,525	34,783	51,821	58,735	58,239	62,799	53,289	30,093	23,552	37,754	37,754
Credit card charges	0	25	597	649	1,366	1,638	1,442	1,649	1,753	497	505	495	495
Accounts payable - others	900	1,528	6,400	440	2,295	1,799	440	440	440	440	440	440	440
	4,271	11,869	21,751	37,902	60,680	70,673	62,702	71,678	66,773	27,974	20,603	35,790	35,790
Net current assets	7,650	618	15,476	46,579	36,835	30,349	39,832	51,531	64,322	34,392	34,555	34,612	34,612
Debentures	0	0	0	(30,000)	(30,000)	(30,000)	(30,000)	(30,000)	(30,000)	0	0	0	0
Net Assets	7,650	618	15,476	16,579	6,835	349	9,832	21,531	34,322	34,392	34,555	34,612	34,612
Capital													
Equity	10,000	10,000	90,000	90,000	90,000	90,000	90,000	90,000	90,000	90,000	90,000	90,000	90,000
Profit and loss	(2,350)	(9,382)	(74,524)	(73,421)	(83,165)	(89,651)	(80,168)	(68,469)	(55,678)	(55,608)	(55,445)	(55,388)	(55,388)
	7,650	618	15,476	16,579	6,835	349	9,832	21,531	34,322	34,392	34,555	34,612	34,612

	Sep-96 Autumn	Oct-96 Autumn	Nov-96 Winter	Dec-96 Winter	Jan-97 Winter	Feb-97 Winter	Mar-97 Spring	Apr-97 Spring	May-97 Spring	Jun-97 Summer	Jul-97 Summer	Aug-97 Summer	Year 2
Free pair with 1st order	30,000	40,000	0	0	20,000	20,000		0	0	0	0	0	110,000
Cold mail shots Catalogue	29,900	39,900	0	0	19,900	19,900		0	0	0	0	0	109,600
Cold mail shots free pair	100	100	0	0	100	100		0	0	0	0	0	400
Reminders		871	1,154	1,131	1,109	1,237							5,502
Total	£0,000	80,871	1,154	1,131	41,109	41,237	0	0	0	0	0	0	225,502
Number of free pairs-ms	63	63	0	0	63	63	0	0	0	0	0	0	250
Number of free pairs-F of f	0	0	0	0	0	0	0	0	0	0	0	0	0
First time orders-free pair	14	2	2	0	0	2	2	0	0	0	0	0	22
First time orders-Catalogue	450	600	0	0	300	300	0	0	0	0	0	0	1,650
Free pair with 1st order	450	600	0	0	300	300	0	0	0	0	0	0	1,650
First time orders-F of f	79	105	138	136	133	148	163	160	157	154	151	148	1,672
Number of repeat orders	2,037	2,339	4,137	4,687	4,594	4,802	3,991	4,149	4,067	1,063	1,042	1,021	37,929
Total orders	3,030	3,646	4,278	4,822	5,327	5,562	4,157	4,310	4,224	1,217	1,193	1,169	42,924
UK	2,424	2,916	3,422	3,858	4,262	4,442	3,326	3,448	3,379	973	954	935	38,631
Continental Europe	606	729	856	964	1,065	1,110	831	862	845	243	239	234	4,292
Total tights sent out	11,189	13,338	16,970	19,154	20,637	21,522	16,462	17,079	16,740	4,713	4,619	4,527	166,950
Purchased	12,371	15,336	18,171	19,970	21,124	18,739	16,801	16,892	10,125	4,662	6,605	10,517	171,313
Brought forward	6,154	7,336	9,334	10,534	11,350	11,837	9,054	9,393	9,207	2,592	2,541	4,527	6,154
Carried forward	7,336	9,334	10,534	11,350	11,837	9,054	9,393	9,207	2,592	2,541	4,527	10,517	10,517
Client base	3,484	4,516	4,526	4,435	4,947	5,450	5,343	5,236	5,131	5,029	4,928	4,829	4,829

(Continued)

Exhibit 7.1 (Continued)

Profit & Loss Account

	Sep-96	Oct-96	Nov-96	Dec-96	Jan-97	Feb-97	Mar-97	Apr-97	May-97	Jun-97	Jul-97	Aug-97	Year 2
Revenue-UK	55,244	65,591	87,813	99,109	104,911	109,487	85,184	88,372	86,621	24,389	23,902	23,424	854,047
Revenue-continental Europe	13,523	16,056	21,496	24,261	25,681	26,802	20,852	21,633	21,204	5,970	5,851	5,734	209,064
Postage (exc. VAT)	3,586	4,142	7,247	8,173	8,012	8,390	7,042	7,305	7,160	2,062	2,021	1,981	67,121
Total Revenue	72,353	85,789	116,556	131,544	138,604	144,680	113,078	117,310	114,985	32,422	31,774	31,138	1,130,232
													100.0%
Cost of tights	43,125	51,457	65,777	74,239	79,747	83,176	63,808	66,196	64,885	18,269	17,904	17,546	646,130
Packaging	591	711	834	940	1,039	1,083	811	840	824	237	233	228	8,370
Catalogue (1 x A4 folded)	753	907	1,064	1,199	1,325	1,381	1,034	1,072	1,051	303	297	291	10,675
Acknowledgment insert	202	243	285	321	355	370	277	287	282	81	80	78	2,862
Inducements repeat orders	407	468	827	937	919	960	798	830	813	213	208	204	7,586
Inducements new orders	1,588	2,090	225	217	1,173	1,201	265	256	251	246	241	237	7,991
Postage-UK	1,188	1,429	1,677	1,890	2,088	2,177	1,630	1,689	1,656	477	467	458	16,826
Postage-continental Europe	356	429	503	567	626	653	489	507	497	143	140	137	5,048
Packers & warehouse	3,952	4,755	5,579	6,290	6,948	7,242	5,422	5,621	5,510	1,587	1,555	1,524	55,983
	52,163	62,489	76,772	86,602	94,220	98,242	74,533	77,299	75,768	21,556	21,125	20,703	761,471
Gross Margin £	20,190	23,300	39,784	44,942	44,384	46,438	38,546	40,010	39,218	10,866	10,649	10,436	368,761
Gross Margin %	27.9%	27.2%	34.1%	34.2%	32.0%	32.1%	34.1%	34.1%	34.1%	33.5%	33.5%	33.5%	32.6%
Mail shots & reminders													
Mailing list	7,200	9,600	0	0	4,800	4,800	0	0	0	0	0	0	26,400
Fulfillment	8,453	11,393	163	159	5,791	5,809	0	0	0	0	0	0	31,768
Catalogue (1 x A4 folded)	14,922	20,113	287	281	10,224	10,256	0	0	0	0	0	0	56,082
Envelope	2,520	3,397	48	48	1,727	1,732	0	0	0	0	0	0	9,471
Postage	13,200	17,792	254	249	9,044	9,072	0	0	0	0	0	0	49,610
	46,295	62,294	752	737	31,586	31,669	0	0	0	0	0	0	173,332
													15.3%
Free lights													
Tights	242	242	0	0	242	242	0	0	0	0	0	0	969
Packaging	6	6	0	0	6	6	0	0	0	0	0	0	25
Catalogue (1 x A4 folded)	16	16	0	0	16	16	0	0	0	0	0	0	62
Fulfillment	82	82	0	0	82	82	0	0	0	0	0	0	326
Postage	0	0	0	0	0	0	0	0	0	0	0	0	0
	346	346	0	0	346	346	0	0	0	0	0	0	1,382
Operating margin	(26,450)	(39,339)	39,032	44,205	12,452	14,423	38,546	40,010	39,218	10,866	10,649	10,436	194,048
Operating margin %	(36.6%)	(45.9%)	33.5%	33.6%	9.0%	10.0%	34.1%	34.1%	34.1%	33.5%	33.5%	33.5%	17.2%

	Sep-96	Oct-96	Nov-96	Dec-96	Jan-97	Feb-97	Mar-97	Apr-97	May-97	Jun-97	Jul-97	Aug-97	Year 2
Administration													
Telephone	520	420	420	420	420	420	420	420	420	420	420	420	5,140
Other marketing	2,500				2,500	1,000							5,000
Other stationary	500												1,500
Office rental	200	200	200	200	200	200	200	200	200	200	200	200	2,400
Computer costs	0	0	0	0	0	0	0	0	0	0	0	0	0
Travel	300	300	300	300	300	300	300	300	300	300	300	300	3,600
Advisors		2,500											2,500
Credit card charges	1,905	2,259	3,370	3,464	3,650	3,810	2,978	3,089	3,028	854	837	820	29,766
Other staff	350	350	350	350	350	350	350	350	350	350	350	350	4,200
Directors' salaries	8,333	8,333	8,333	8,333	8,333	8,333	8,333	8,333	8,333	8,333	8,333	8,333	100,000
	14,609	14,363	12,673	13,068	15,754	14,414	12,581	12,693	12,632	10,457	10,440	10,423	154,106
EBIT	(41,058)	(53,702)	26,359	31,137	(3,301)	10	25,964	27,318	26,586	409	208	12	39,942
Interest (OD & debenture)	0	0	(32)	0	0	0	0	0	0	0	0	0	(32)
Earnings before tax	(41,058)	(53,702)	26,327	31,137	(3,301)	10	25,964	27,318	26,586	409	208	12	39,910
Corporation tax	0	0	0	0	0	0	0	0	0	0	0	0	0
Earnings after tax	(41,058)	(53,702)	26,327	31,137	(3,301)	10	25,964	27,318	26,586	409	208	12	39,910

(Continued)

Exhibit 7.1 (Continued)

Cash flow

	Sep-96	Oct-96	Nov-96	Dec-96	Jan-97	Feb-97	Mar-97	Apr-97	May-97	Jun-97	Jul-97	Aug-97	Year 2
Inflows													
Revenue	71,209	82,430	108,864	127,797	136,839	143,161	120,979	116,252	115,566	53,063	31,936	31,297	1,139,391
VAT-UK	10,301	11,586	15,301	17,962	19,233	20,121	17,004	16,339	16,243	7,458	4,489	4,399	160,435
VAT-continental Europe	2,469	3,245	4,286	5,032	5,387	5,636	4,763	4,577	4,550	2,089	1,257	1,232	44,524
	83,979	97,261	128,451	150,790	161,459	168,918	142,745	137,168	136,359	62,610	37,682	36,928	1,344,350
Outflows													
Cost of Sales													
Tights	13,902	23,852	47,950	59,442	70,431	77,402	81,875	72,632	65,122	65,475	39,246	18,068	635,399
Packaging	597	717	834	940	1,045	1,089	811	840	824	237	233	228	8,395
Acknowledgment insert	202	243	285	321	355	370	277	287	282	81	80	78	2,862
Postage-UK	1,188	1,429	1,677	1,890	2,088	2,177	1,630	1,689	1,656	477	467	458	16,826
Postage-continental Europe	356	429	503	567	626	653	489	507	497	143	140	137	5,048
Packers	3,952	4,755	5,579	6,290	6,948	7,242	5,422	5,621	5,510	1,587	1,555	1,524	55,983
Marketing													
Mailing list	7,200	9,600	0	0	4,800	4,800	0	0	0	0	0	0	26,400
Fulfillment (mail shots)	8,453	11,393	163	159	5,791	5,809	0	0	0	0	0	0	31,768
Postage	13,200	17,792	254	249	9,044	9,072	0	0	0	0	0	0	49,610
Envelopes (Catalogue)	0	2,520	3,397	48	48	1,727	1,732	0	0	0	0	0	9,471
Catalogue (1 x A4 folded)	17,409	21,140	0	2,487	12,435	12,435	0	0	2,487	0	0	0	68,393
Fulfillment (free tights)	82	82	0	0	82	82	0	0	0	0	0	0	326
Inducements	1,996	2,558	1,052	1,155	2,092	2,161	1,063	1,086	1,065	459	450	441	15,577
Postage (free tights)	0	0	0	0	0	0	0	0	0	0	0	0	0
Administration													
Telephone	340	520	420	420	420	420	420	420	420	420	420	420	5,060
Other marketing costs	0	2,500	0	0	0	2,500	0	0	0	0	0	0	5,000
Other stationary	0	500	0	0	0	0	1,000	0	0	0	0	0	1,500
Office rental	200	200	200	200	200	200	200	200	200	200	200	200	2,400
Computer costs	0	0	0	0	0	0	0	0	0	0	0	0	0
Travel	100	300	300	300	300	300	300	300	300	300	300	300	3,400
Advisors	0	0	2,500	0	0	0	0	0	0	0	0	0	2,500
Credit card charges	495	1,905	2,259	3,070	3,464	3,650	3,810	2,978	3,089	3,028	854	837	29,440
Other salaries	350	350	350	350	350	350	350	350	350	350	350	350	4,200
Directors' salaries	8,333	8,333	8,333	8,333	8,333	8,333	8,333	8,333	8,333	8,333	8,333	8,333	100,000
VAT (quarterly settlement)	(2,899)			16,404			23,369			18,160			55,033
VAT (paid on inputs)	9,415	13,524	10,082	12,726	18,399	20,142	16,122	14,385	13,474	12,009	7,410	3,695	151,381
Corporation tax						0							
	84,869	124,641	86,139	115,352	147,252	160,913	147,202	109,630	103,608	111,259	60,038	35,070	1,285,972
Fixed assets													
Computers	0	0	0	0	0	0	0	0	0	0	0	0	0
Financing													
Equity	0	0	0	0	0	0	0	0	0	0	0	0	0
Interest (OD & debenture)	0	0	(32)	0	0	0	0	0	0	0	0	0	(32)
Debt	0	0	0	0	0	0	0	0	0	0	0	0	
	0	0	(32)	0	0	0	0	0	0	0	0	0	(32)
Net cash flow	(890)	(27,380)	42,280	35,439	14,207	8,005	(4,457)	27,539	32,751	(48,649)	(22,356)	1,859	58,347
Cumulative	25,459	(1,922)	40,359	75,797	90,004	98,009	93,552	121,091	153,842	105,193	82,837	84,695	84,695

Balance Sheet

	Sep-96	Oct-96	Nov-96	Dec-96	Jan-97	Feb-97	Mar-97	Apr-97	May-97	Jun-97	Jul-97	Aug-97	Year 2
Fixed assets													
Cost	0	0	0	0	0	0	0	0	0	0	0	0	0
Depreciation	0	0	0	0	0	0	0	0	0	0	0	0	0
	0	0	0	0	0	0	0	0	0	0	0	0	0
Current assets													
Stationary													
-Packaging (card etc.)	195	195	195	195	195	195	195	195	195	195	195	195	195
-Catalogue (1 x A4 folder)	1,774	1,878	528	1,534	2,405	3,186	2,154	1,082	2,519	2,216	1,919	1,629	1,629
Tights	28,435	36,178	40,831	43,594	45,880	35,294	36,408	35,687	10,048	9,847	17,546	40,762	40,762
Debtors	21,343	25,306	34,382	38,603	40,885	42,378	33,356	34,604	33,918	9,564	9,373	9,185	9,185
Cash	25,459	0	40,359	75,797	90,004	98,009	93,552	121,091	153,842	105,193	82,837	84,695	84,695
	77,205	63,557	116,294	160,323	179,369	179,164	165,655	192,658	200,522	127,014	111,869	136,466	136,466
Current liabilities													
Overdraft	0	1,922	0	0	0	0	0	0	0	0	0	0	0
Corporation tax	0	0	0	0	0	0	0	0	0	0	0	0	0
VAT	3,603	5,515	16,404	10,942	17,480	23,369	4,224	10,946	18,160	(6,175)	(7,868)	(5,961)	(5,961)
Accounts payable - tights	71,892	107,393	129,874	147,833	159,277	154,508	137,754	130,597	104,721	57,314	43,671	66,365	66,365
Credit card charges	1,905	2,259	3,070	3,464	3,650	3,810	2,978	3,089	3,028	854	837	820	820
Accounts payable - others	6,340	6,617	768	768	4,947	3,452	720	720	720	720	720	720	720
	83,651	123,705	150,115	163,007	185,354	185,139	145,676	145,352	126,629	52,713	37,359	61,944	61,944
Net current assets	(6,446)	(60,148)	(33,821)	(2,684)	(5,985)	(5,975)	19,989	47,307	73,893	74,301	74,510	74,522	74,522
Debentures	0	0	0	0	0	0	0	0	0	0	0	0	0
Net Assets	(6,446)	(60,148)	(33,821)	(2,684)	(5,985)	(5,975)	19,989	47,307	73,893	74,301	74,510	74,522	74,522
Capital													
Equity	90,000	90,000	90,000	90,000	90,000	90,000	90,000	90,000	90,000	90,000	90,000	90,000	90,000
Profit and loss	(96,446)	(150,148)	(123,821)	(92,684)	(95,985)	(95,975)	(70,011)	(42,693)	(16,107)	(15,699)	(15,490)	(15,478)	(15,478)
	(6,446)	(60,148)	(33,821)	(2,684)	(5,985)	(5,975)	19,989	47,307	73,893	74,301	74,510	74,522	74,522

(Continued)

Exhibit 7.1 (Continued)

	Sep-97 Autumn	Oct-97 Autumn	Nov-97 Winter	Dec-97 Winter	Jan-98 Winter	Feb-98 Winter	Mar-98 Spring	Apr-98 Spring	May-98 Spring	Jun-98 Summer	Jul-98 Summer	Aug-98 Summer	Year 3
Free pair with 1st order	40,000	40,000	0	0	20,000	20,000							120,000
Cold mail shots Catalogue	39,900	39,900	0	0	19,900	19,900							119,600
Cold mail shots free pair	100	100	0	0	100	100							400
Reminders		1,485	1,756	1,721	1,686	1,803							8,450
Total	80,000	81,485	1,756	1,721	41,686	41,803	0	0	0	0	0	0	248,450
Number of free pairs-ms	63	63	0	0	63	63	0	0	0	0	0	0	250
Number of free pairs-F of f	0	0	0	0	0	0	0	0	0	0	0	0	0
First time orders-free pair	6	2	2	0	0	2	2	0	0	0	0	0	14
First time orders-Catalogue	600	600	0	0	300	300	0	0	0	0	0	0	1,800
Free pair with 1st order	600	600	0	0	300	300	0	0	0	0	0	0	1,800
First time orders-F of f	145	178	211	207	202	216	230	226	221	217	212	208	2,472
Number of repeat orders	3,751	4,129	6,629	7,128	6,987	7,147	5,715	5,839	5,723	1,496	1,466	1,436	57,446
Total orders	5,102	5,509	6,842	7,335	7,789	7,966	5,947	6,064	5,944	1,712	1,678	1,644	63,532
UK	3,572	3,856	4,789	5,134	5,453	5,576	4,163	4,245	4,161	1,198	1,175	1,151	57,179
Continental Europe	1,531	1,653	2,052	2,200	2,337	2,390	1,784	1,819	1,783	514	503	493	6,353
Total tights sent out	19,121	20,718	27,154	29,133	30,417	31,106	23,557	24,031	23,554	6,632	6,499	6,369	248,292
Purchased	19,999	24,258	28,243	29,840	30,796	26,954	23,818	23,769	14,247	6,559	9,294	11,959	249,734
Brought forward	10,517	11,395	14,935	16,023	16,730	17,108	12,956	13,217	12,955	3,648	3,575	6,369	10,517
Carried forward	11,395	14,935	16,023	16,730	17,108	12,956	13,217	12,955	3,648	3,575	6,369	11,959	11,959
Client base	5,939	7,022	6,884	6,746	7,211	7,669	7,517	7,367	7,220	7,075	6,934	6,795	6,795

Profit & Loss Account

	Sep-97	Oct-97	Nov-97	Dec-97	Jan-98	Feb-98	Mar-98	Apr-98	May-98	Jun-98	Jul-98	Aug-98	Year 3
Revenue-UK	83,574	90,803	122,944	131,906	136,078	139,137	105,658	108,805	106,643	30,027	29,426	28,838	1,114,900
Revenue-continental Europe	35,071	38,105	51,592	55,353	57,104	58,413	44,758	45,659	44,752	12,601	12,349	12,102	467,860
Postage (exc. VAT)	6,590	7,284	11,568	12,406	12,160	12,454	10,055	10,257	10,053	2,896	2,838	2,781	101,341
Total Revenue	125,235	136,193	186,104	199,665	205,342	210,065	161,471	164,721	161,448	45,523	44,613	43,721	1,684,101
													100.0%
Cost of tights	73,871	80,063	105,249	112,921	117,655	120,326	91,307	93,145	91,294	25,705	25,191	24,687	961,411
Packaging	995	1,074	1,334	1,430	1,519	1,553	1,160	1,183	1,159	334	327	321	12,389
Catalogue (1 x A4 folded)	1,269	1,370	1,702	1,824	1,937	1,961	1,479	1,508	1,478	426	417	409	15,800
Acknowledgment insert	340	367	456	489	519	531	396	404	396	114	112	110	4,235
Inducements repeat orders	750	826	1,326	1,426	1,397	1,429	1,143	1,168	1,145	299	293	287	11,489
Inducements new orders	2,161	2,208	340	330	1,284	1,309	371	361	354	347	340	333	9,738
Postage-UK	1,750	1,890	2,347	2,516	2,672	2,732	2,040	2,080	2,039	587	576	564	21,792
Postage-continental Europe	900	972	1,207	1,294	1,374	1,405	1,043	1,070	1,048	302	296	290	11,207
Packers & warehouse	6,655	7,185	8,923	9,567	10,159	10,389	7,757	7,909	7,752	2,233	2,188	2,145	82,862
	88,692	95,952	122,883	131,797	138,517	141,655	106,702	108,828	106,665	30,347	29,740	29,145	1,130,923
Gross Margin £	36,544	40,241	63,221	67,368	66,825	68,409	54,769	55,894	54,783	15,176	14,873	14,575	553,178
Gross Margin %	29.2%	29.5%	34.0%	34.0%	32.5%	32.6%	33.9%	33.9%	33.9%	33.3%	33.3%	33.3%	32.8%
Mail shots & reminders													
Mailing list	9,600	9,600	0	0	4,800	4,800	0	0	0	0	0	0	28,800
Fulfillment	11,270	11,479	247	242	5,873	5,886	0	0	0	0	0	0	35,000
Catalogue (1 x A4 folded)	19,896	20,265	437	428	10,367	10,396	0	0	0	0	0	0	61,790
Envelope	3,360	3,422	74	72	1,751	1,756	0	0	0	0	0	0	10,435
Postage	17,600	17,927	386	379	9,171	9,197	0	0	0	0	0	0	54,659
	61,726	62,693	1,144	1,121	31,962	32,038	0	0	0	0	0	0	190,684
Free tights													
Tights	242	242	0	0	242	242	0	0	0	0	0	0	969
Packaging	6	6	0	0	6	6	0	0	0	0	0	0	25
Catalogue (1 x A4 folded)	16	16	0	0	16	16	0	0	0	0	0	0	62
Fulfillment	82	82	0	0	82	82	0	0	0	0	0	0	326
Postage	0	0	0	0	0	0	0	0	0	0	0	0	0
	346	346	0	0	346	346	0	0	0	0	0	0	1,382
Operating margin	(25,528)	(22,798)	62,077	56,747	34,517	36,025	54,769	55,894	54,783	15,176	14,873	14,575	361,112
Operating margin %	(20.4%)	(16.7%)	33.4%	33.4%	16.8%	17.1%	33.9%	33.9%	33.9%	33.3%	33.3%	33.3%	21.4%

(Continued)

Exhibit 7.1 (Continued)

Profit & Loss Account

	Sep-97	Oct-97	Nov-97	Dec-97	Jan-98	Feb-98	Mar-98	Apr-98	May-98	Jun-98	Jul-98	Aug-98	Year 3
Administration													
Telephone	600	500	500	500	500	500	500	500	500	500	500	500	6,100
Other marketing	2,500				2,500	1,000							5,000
Other stationary	500												1,500
Office rental	200	200	200	200	200	200	200	200	200	200	200	200	2,400
Computer costs	0	0	0	0	0	0	0	0	0	0	0	0	0
Travel	300	300	300	300	300	300	300	300	300	300	300	300	3,600
Advisors		2,500											2,500
Credit card charges	2,975	3,235	4,420	4,742	4,877	4,989	3,835	3,912	3,835	1,081	1,060	1,038	40,001
Other staff	350	350	350	350	350	350	350	350	350	350	350	350	4,200
Directors' salaries	8,333	8,333	8,333	8,333	8,333	8,333	8,333	8,333	8,333	8,333	8,333	8,333	100,000
	15,758	15,418	14,104	14,426	17,061	15,673	13,519	13,596	13,518	10,765	10,743	10,722	165,301
EBIT	(41,286)	(38,216)	47,974	52,321	17,457	20,353	41,251	42,298	41,265	4,412	4,130	3,854	195,811
Interest (OD & debenture)	0	0	0	0	0	0	0	0	0	0	0	0	0
Earnings before tax	(41,286)	(38,216)	47,974	52,321	17,457	20,353	41,251	42,298	41,265	4,412	4,130	3,854	195,811
Corporation tax	0	0	0	(1,329)	(4,364)	(5,088)	(10,313)	(10,574)	(10,316)	(1,103)	(1,032)	(963)	(45,083)
Earnings after tax	(41,286)	(38,216)	47,974	50,992	13,093	15,264	30,938	31,723	30,949	3,309	3,097	2,890	150,728

Cash flow

	Sep-97	Oct-97	Nov-97	Dec-97	Jan-98	Feb-98	Mar-98	Apr-98	May-98	Jun-98	Jul-98	Aug-98	Year 3
Inflows													
Revenue	101,711	133,453	173,626	196,275	203,923	208,884	173,620	163,909	162,267	74,505	44,840	43,944	1,680,956
VAT-UK	12,669	16,445	21,395	24,185	25,128	25,740	21,354	20,197	19,995	9,181	5,525	5,415	207,269
VAT-continental Europe	5,864	7,856	10,274	11,614	12,067	12,360	10,274	9,699	9,602	4,409	2,653	2,600	99,312
	120,243	157,755	205,295	232,075	241,117	246,984	205,237	193,805	191,864	88,094	53,019	51,959	1,987,537
Outflows													
Cost of Sales													
Tights	25,602	40,762	77,517	94,023	109,468	115,658	119,365	104,474	92,318	92,127	55,220	25,422	951,959
Packaging	1,001	1,083	1,334	1,430	1,525	1,560	1,160	1,183	1,159	334	327	321	12,414
Acknowledgment Insert	340	367	456	489	519	531	396	404	396	114	112	110	4,235
Postage-UK	1,750	1,890	2,347	2,515	2,672	2,732	2,040	2,080	2,039	587	576	564	21,792
Postage-continental Europe	900	972	1,207	1,294	1,374	1,405	1,049	1,070	1,048	302	296	290	11,207
Packers	6,655	7,185	8,923	9,567	10,159	10,369	7,757	7,909	7,752	2,233	2,188	2,145	82,862
Marketing													
Mailing list	9,600	9,600	0	0	4,800	4,800	0	0	0	0	0	0	28,800
Fulfillment (mail shots)	11,270	11,479	247	242	5,873	5,889	0	0	0	0	0	0	35,000
Postage	17,600	17,927	366	379	9,171	9,197	0	0	0	0	0	0	54,659
Envelopes (Catalogue)	0	0	3,422	74	72	1,751	1,756	0	0	0	0	0	10,435
Catalogue (1 x A4 folded)	22,383	22,383	0	2,487	12,435	12,435	2,487	0	2,487	0	0	0	77,097
Fulfillment (free tights)	82	82	0	0	82	82	0	0	0	0	0	0	326
Inducements	2,912	3,034	1,666	1,756	2,681	2,739	1,514	1,529	1,498	646	633	620	21,227
Postage (free tights)	0	0	0	0	0	0	0	0	0	0	0	0	0
Administration													
Telephone	420	600	500	500	500	500	500	500	500	500	500	500	6,020
Other marketing costs	0	2,500	0	0	0	2,500	0	0	0	0	0	0	5,000
Other stationary	0	500	0	0	0	0	1,000	0	0	0	0	0	1,500
Office rental	200	200	200	200	200	200	200	200	200	200	200	200	2,400
Computer costs	0	0	0	0	0	0	0	0	0	0	0	0	0
Travel	300	300	300	300	300	300	300	300	300	300	300	300	3,600
Advisors	0	0	2,500	0	0	0	0	0	0	0	0	0	2,500
Credit card charges	820	2,975	3,235	4,420	4,742	4,877	4,989	3,835	3,912	3,835	1,081	1,060	39,782
Other salaries	350	350	350	350	350	350	350	350	350	350	350	350	4,200
Directors' salaries	8,333	8,333	8,333	8,333	8,333	8,333	8,333	6,333	8,333	8,333	8,333	8,333	100,000
VAT (quarterly settlement)	(5,961)			33,963			38,534			25,651			92,188
VAT (paid on inputs)	14,021	17,416	16,223	19,731	26,167	27,755	23,792	20,618	18,882	16,870	10,398	5,171	217,050
Corporation tax	0	0	0	0	0	0	0	0	0	0	0	0	0
Fixed assets													
Computers	0	0	0	0	0	0	0	0	0	0	0	0	0
Financing													
Equity	0	0	0	0	0	0	0	0	0	0	0	0	0
Interest (OD & debenture)	0	0	0	0	0	0	0	0	0	0	0	0	0
Debt	0	0	0	0	0	0	0	0	0	0	0	0	0
Net cash flow	1,664	4,501	76,143	50,021	39,693	33,002	(10,237)	41,020	50,688	(64,288)	(27,496)	6,573	201,283
Cumulative	86,359	90,860	167,003	217,024	256,717	239,719	279,482	320,501	371,189	306,901	279,405	285,978	285,978

(Continued)

135

Exhibit 7.1 (Continued)

Balance Sheet

	Sep-97	Oct-97	Nov-97	Dec-97	Jan-98	Feb-98	Mar-98	Apr-98	May-98	Jun-98	Jul-98	Aug-98	Year 3
Fixed assets													
Cost	0	0	0	0	0	0	0	0	0	0	0	0	0
Depreciation	0	0	0	0	0	0	0	0	0	0	0	0	0
	0	0	0	0	0	0	0	0	0	0	0	0	0
Current assets													
Stationery													
-Packaging (card etc.)	195	195	195	195	195	195	195	195	195	195	195	195	195
-Catalogue (1 x A4 folded)	2,831	3,563	1,425	1,660	1,775	1,817	2,825	1,317	2,325	1,900	1,482	1,073	1,073
Tights	44,166	57,887	62,106	64,844	66,312	50,219	51,230	50,212	14,138	13,855	24,687	46,352	46,352
Debtors	37,019	40,258	55,012	59,021	60,699	62,095	47,731	48,691	47,724	13,457	13,188	12,924	12,924
Cash	86,359	90,860	167,003	217,024	256,717	289,719	279,482	320,501	371,189	306,901	279,405	285,978	285,978
	170,571	192,764	285,742	342,743	385,698	404,044	381,462	420,916	435,571	336,307	318,957	346,523	346,523
Current liabilities													
Overdraft	0	0	0	0	0	0	0	0	0	0	0	0	0
Corporation tax	0	0	0	1,329	5,693	10,781	21,094	31,668	41,984	43,087	44,120	45,083	45,083
VAT	8,821	16,246	33,963	16,687	27,974	38,534	5,660	15,086	25,651	(8,566)	(10,827)	(8,024)	(8,024)
Accounts payable - tights	118,279	171,540	203,491	225,126	235,024	223,840	196,792	184,445	147,348	80,643	61,446	82,376	82,376
Credit card charges	2,975	3,235	4,420	4,742	4,877	4,989	3,835	3,912	3,835	1,081	1,060	1,038	1,038
Accounts payable - others	7,260	6,722	874	872	5,051	3,556	800	800	800	800	800	800	800
	137,335	197,743	242,748	248,757	278,619	281,701	228,181	235,912	219,618	117,045	96,598	121,273	121,273
Net current assets	33,236	(4,980)	42,994	93,986	107,079	122,343	153,281	185,005	215,953	219,262	222,360	225,250	225,250
Debentures	0	0	0	0	0	0	0	0	0	0	0	0	0
Net Assets	33,236	(4,980)	42,994	93,986	107,079	122,343	153,281	185,005	215,953	219,262	222,360	225,250	225,250
Capital													
Equity	90,000	90,000	90,000	90,000	90,000	90,000	90,000	90,000	90,000	90,000	90,000	90,000	90,000
Profit and loss	(56,764)	(94,980)	(47,006)	3,986	17,079	32,343	63,281	95,005	125,953	129,262	132,360	135,250	135,250
	33,236	(4,980)	42,994	93,986	107,079	122,343	153,281	185,005	215,953	219,262	222,360	225,250	225,250

Exhibit 7.1   *(Continued)*

Exhibit 7.1   *(Continued)*

As a way to
THANK YOU
for your support earlier this year, enjoy a
FREE
pair of tights with our compliments.

Telephone by *31 October* and receive a complimentary pair of
Classic Sheer Tights in Black,
shipped to you free of charge.
No purchase necessary.

With this gift, we wish to thank you individually.
Thus, we regret this offer is non-transferable.

Exhibit 7.1 *(Continued)*

Beautiful Legs
BY POST

3 October, 1995

Dear

As a busy professional woman, I appreciate services that save time without compromising quality. This is precisely why Beautiful Legs by Post has been created: to offer fellow working women only the highest quality department store tights without the inconvenience of department store shopping. Our ultimate goal is to give you exceptional quality at an exceptional value, with the service you deserve.

The perfect tight has as much to do with the way it fits and feels as it does with the way it looks. That is why each style in our collection is completely sheer to waist and includes such features as double covered Lycra, reinforced toe, flat-lock seams and full gusset.

Beautiful Legs by Post is supplied exclusively by Doré Doré of France. This family-run company has been in operation since 1819 and is highly regarded for its unsurpassed quality. The subtle shades of colours available are designed to perfectly complement your working wardrobe. Yet, the detailed workmanship means your tights will feel as wonderful as they look. It is no wonder why so many French women choose Doré Doré as their favoured brand.

Purchasing by post means no more wasted time in the crowded tights section of your local department store. Purchasing by post means finding your size in stock, even of that perfect shade of neutral, so especially important this autumn. Purchasing by post means prompt and discreet deliveries to your office, or conveniently through your letter-box at home. You can even create a customised order to be shipped free of charge each month when you become a Monthly Order Program Member.

I hope you accept this invitation to try Beautiful Legs by Post. I feel confident that our tights will meet your expectations. However, if they should not, we will certainly accept their immediate return and your account will be fully credited.

I look forward to serving you soon.

Yours sincerely,

Elizabeth Preis
Marketing Director

Beautiful Legs by Post Limited
Unit 15, Haslemere Heathrow Estate
The Parkway, Hounslow
Middlesex TW4 6NF
Telephone: 0181 759 0915; Fax: 0181 759 4730

(Continued)

Exhibit 7.1 *(Continued)*

ADDIS Dickon

Date of birth	19 February 1962
Nationality	British
Address	
	London NW3 6YA
	United Kingdom

WORK EXPERIENCE

1995-present   **Beautiful Legs by post** - Mail-order house   London
Founder and Director

1990-1993   **YRM plc.**- Building design consultants -Staff 400   London
Financial Controller responsible for the day to day management of all functions of
the finance department; managed a team of six.
• Assisted the board in formulating and managing the company's business strategy.
• Identified the need for and assisted in the structuring and implementation of a
  cost cutting program that reduced the company's cost base by 25%.
• Redesigned the budgeting and forecasting processes resulting in stronger
  commitment from department managers to attaining budgeted results.
• Managed the day to day relationship with the company's bankers and taxation
  authorities.

1988-1989   **ADS Office Systems Ltd.**- Office equipment supplier-Staff 150   London
Financial Controller responsible for the production of all financial management
information, credit control, cash management and payroll.
• Designed and implemented new accounting and reporting systems: reduced the
  finance team by 50% to 15 members: reduced the time taken to produce monthly
  management accounts from 20 to 9 working days.
• Assisted in the development of the company's business plan that altered the
  company's strategy from short-term customer relationships to earning long-term
  customer loyalty.

1984-1987   **Arthur Andersen & Co.** - Auditors and tax advisors   London
Audit Senior responsible for planning, controlling and reviewing audit teams for
various clients including a building society, an investment bank, an insurance
broker and a life assurance company.

EDUCATION
1994-1995   **INSEAD**, Fontainebleau, MBA Program
1984-1987   **Institute of Chartered Accountants in England and Wales**
            (Qualified with first time passes in 1987)
1981-1984   **London School of Economics,** London, BSc.(Hons.) Economics

LANGUAGES   English (mother tongue), French (proficient), Spanish (basic)

OTHER EXPERIENCE
1994   3 month assignment with a firm of strategy consultants evaluating   London
            market the opportunities of potential acquisitions for a venture capitalist.
1990   Two months travelling with faculty members from a Shanghai University.   China
1980-1982   Summer work experience in two stockbrokers and a hotel.   Hong Kong
1981   Travelled throughout South East Asia and India.

Exhibit 7.1 *(Continued)*

PREIS, Elizabeth L.

Date of birth	21 April 1969
Nationality	American
Address	
	London SW10 9RG
	United Kingdom

WORK EXPERIENCE

1995-present

Beautiful Legs by post - Mail-order house   London
Founder and Director

1991-1994

BLOOMINGDALE'S   New York
Subsidiary of Federated Department Stores

1993-1994

Department Manager, "European Designer Collections" (7 months)
- Achieved monthly department sales averaging $800,000
  from a stock of $5 million in high-end women's couture fashions
- Managed a team of two assistants, twelve sales associates, and
  two stock associates.
- Recognised as managing "Best Department of the Store" having
  realised a 15% sales increase over plan during three month period.

1992-1993

Assistant Buyer, "Better Casual Collections" (18 months)
- Developed and executed seasonal marketing, financial, and
  merchandising strategies for private label fashion department.
- Sourced suppliers and handled preliminary negotiations over price
  and payment terms.
- Managed internal stock levels with an average stock of $1.6 million.
- Designed a private shopping event targeted to New York
  working women.

1991-1992

Assistant Department Manager, "Career Collections" (9 months)
- Managed a team of fifteen sales and stock associates.
- Developed and implemented a store-wide appreciation program for
  both sales associates and executives.
- Initiated Fall 1992 and 1993 on-campus pre-recruiting
  information sessions.

EDUCATION

1994-1995

INSEAD, Fontainebleau   France
MBA Programme

1987-1991

Wellesley College, Massachusetts   USA
BA in Economics and French

1990

University of Copenhagen: International Business Studies   Denmark
International student exchange program

LANGUAGES

English (mother tongue), French (proficient), Spanish (basic)

OTHER EXPERIENCE

1991-1994

Mary Manning Walsh Nursing Home, New York
Volunteered monthly classical piano concerts for residents

1991-1994

New York and Paris Wellesley Alumnae Clubs; appointed New York
Alumnae Council Representative for 1993-1994

1990 and 1994

Actively campaigned during elections of Maryland's House of Delegates

(Continued)

Exhibit 7.1   *(Continued)*

8 SHAKER CIRCUITS (A)

After rocking the car back and forth to free it from the snow, David Gray and Peter Mellin were finally on their way. As they admired the Christmas decorations on Public Square in Cleveland, they contemplated the rather odd meeting they had just concluded with Steve Trevor, owner of Shaker Circuits. David and Peter had been in negotiations to buy Shaker Circuits for the last eight weeks. When Steve called this meeting, David and Peter expected that it was just to renegotiate some deal point. Much to their surprise, Steve informed David and Peter that if they did not purchase Shaker Circuits by December 31, 1989, Steve was going to close the business!

David said, "I think he was spooked by the EPA problems he had last year." "I know," replied Peter, "but, after all, he did what they wanted and got a clean report in March." David thought for a moment, "I'm sure that investigation was like a visit to the proctologist!"

THE ENTREPRENEURS

After graduating from St. Lawrence University in 1984, David Gray took a job with Kuehne & Nagel, an international freight forwarding company. The job involved conducting business in many time zones and required long hours. It was extremely stressful at times, but David was a nonexempt worker,° so he received overtime pay. He made more money than most of his peers fresh out of school.

This case was prepared by Scott Wipper with assistance from Dan D'Heilly under the direction of Professor William Bygrave. Partial funding provided by the Ewing Marion Kauffman Foundation. Copyright © 1995 Babson College. All rights reserved.
° All employees had a compensation classification of exempt or nonexempt. Nonexempt workers were paid overtime and typically had fewer management responsibilities. Exempt workers tended to be on salary.

143

David received several raises over the next 18 months, and the time went quickly. When he began to focus on long-term career opportunities, it became apparent that it would be extremely difficult to break into the upper management ranks of Kuehne & Nagel, a European firm managed by Europeans. After several failed attempts to come to terms with his superiors, and much to the dismay of his manager, David decided to leave Kuehne & Nagel.

David did not have a difficult time finding another position. He was soon accepted into the brand management program at Procter & Gamble (P&G). He had heard that P&G's training program was terrific, and thought he would learn a great deal from the other people who had made it through P&G's difficult screening process.

After six months with P&G, David decided to leave the corporate world and strike out on his own. But first he wanted a better management and entrepreneurship education, so he enrolled in the Graduate School of Business at Babson College beginning in the fall of 1987. David focused on manufacturing management and entrepreneurial studies.

David received his MBA in May 1989. He was eager to get started in a business of his own. Although David didn't have direct manufacturing experience, he believed that he could create a quality product and be successful managing a manufacturing operation.

Peter Mellin had been a close friend of David's since high school, and they had kept in touch over the years. After graduating from Middlebury College in 1985, Peter worked for a couple of brokerage firms in New York. He enjoyed selling and was quite successful. The day after the stock market crashed in 1987, Peter was on the phone making cold calls to prospective clients! He was one of the firm's top salespeople in 1987. In 1988, Peter decided that he wanted to do more than push paper—he wanted to sell a tangible product. He left the stock market and went into industrial sales as a territory manager for Phineaus Plastics of Akron, Ohio.

David and Peter had often talked about starting their own business. They shared a vision of becoming successful by producing and marketing quality products. In June 1989, David approached Peter with a plan—buy a manufacturing plant, improve its products, and sell, sell, sell. David would manage operations and manufacturing, and Peter would be the sales engineer. The timing was right to pursue their dream. They began searching for a small manufacturing business in July 1989.

THE SEARCH

David and Peter wanted to find the best opportunity on the market, so they threw out a broad net seeking leads in several industries. They told family, friends, bankers, and business brokers that they were in the market for a small to medium-sized manufacturing company. They did not think that the particular industry was important.

The heyday of steel in Cleveland was over, and in its place were many small firms serving the automobile, telecommunications equipment, medical instrumentation, and computer industries. Politicians and business leaders had successfully conducted an aggressive campaign to bring high-tech firms to the area, so the local economy was host to many small firms in emerging markets by the late 1980s.

Partially as a result of this, many of the leads that David and Peter generated involved high-tech manufacturing firms that had only been in business for a short time. However, Shaker Circuits had been in business for 15 years and had a solid, prosperous feeling. The contact with Shaker Circuits came from a business broker who called David and Peter after hearing about their interests through the grapevine.

SHAKER CIRCUITS

Shaker Circuits was founded by Steve Trevor in 1974 as a manufacturer of prototype PCBs. Typically, the run-size of any one design was well below 100 units. Most jobs larger than this were handled by high-volume manufacturers. Its market was geographically centered on firms in, and around, Cleveland.

In 1988, Shaker Circuits had sales of approximately $1.2 million. Although 1989 was a more difficult year, Shaker Circuits still had sales of $850,000 and showed a net income of $85,000. Originally, Steve asked $1.2 million for the business, but the disclosure that he intended to close the doors lowered the price that David and Peter were willing to pay. The five-year financials of Shaker Circuits are shown in Exhibits 8.1 through 8.3.

Shaker Circuits' daily operations were supervised by a husband and wife management team under Steve's direction. Over the last several years, he had become involved in a number of other businesses and had increasingly left the day-to-day operations of the company to Ed and Cindy Kesner. In addition to Ed and Cindy, Shaker Circuits employed 10 skilled workers. Steve checked in several times a month; by most standards, he was an absentee owner.

The Kesners had been in the industry for 20 years and had mastered Shaker Circuits' manufacturing processes. Ed and Cindy knew PCB manufacturing and their experience included working for a large PCB manufacturing firm in the 1970s. David was confident that they would play a major role in the reengineering of Shaker Circuits.

One testament to their success was the level of repeat business enjoyed by Shaker Circuits. Shaker Circuits did not employ a salesforce and did little advertising. The major marketing event of the year was Christmas when they sent calendars to 45 of their best customers. They also gave calendars to employees—any remaining calendars were sent to prospective customers. Peter could hardly wait to take over sales and marketing.

The business was located in a 4,000 square foot commercial building attached to a two-story, single-family home located 50 yards from the Cuayahoga River. The building was large enough to accommodate growth, and Steve Trevor was willing to sell the building, too. The business had been operating out of this location for the entire time it had been in business. The selling price included all of the manufacturing equipment but not the building. Ed and Cindy had both agreed to work for the new owner of the business.

The Industry

PCBs are used in practically every segment of the electronics industry. PCBs have two primary functions. First, they are the substrate to which the integrated circuits (IC) are attached. Second, they contain the pathways over which one IC communicates with another. Shaker Circuits, using engineering diagrams provided by their customers, cuts the boards to size and prints the pathways on the boards using photoengraving and chemical treatment processes. PCBs are the hard-wiring that electronic components required for processing information.

Standard double-sided circuit boards are manufactured from thin sheets of fiberglass with a full copper laminate bonded to both sides. After the panels are cut to rough size, holes are drilled into the panel to accommodate the electrical components that will be installed onto the circuit board.

After drilling the holes, the boards are run through a series of aggressive chemical baths containing sulfuric acid and hydrogen peroxide to remove any organic contaminants. The result is a clean copper surface on the faces of the circuit board. The boards are then dipped into a proprietary formaldehyde chemical bath to sensitize the fiber walls of the drilled holes so that they will accept a thin coating of electroless copper.

The next step in the process is to create the pathways, or "traces," so that the array of chips that are placed on each board can communicate with one another. This is done using an ultraviolet light (UV)-sensitive photo polymer called dry film resist. After heat laminating the dry film to the copper, the panel is placed under a phototool. The phototool is a clear piece of film that contains a laser plot of the desired traces. After exposure to UV light, the areas not under the traces undergo a chemical reaction called polymerization which makes them impervious to the developing chemicals of the copper electroplating process. The copper electroplating process deposits copper over the entire surface including the drilled holes. The boards are racked manually and placed into a 380-gallon copper electroplating tank. The copper-plating tank contains a solution of copper sulfate, sulfuric acid, brightener, and hydrochloric acid. After this step, the boards are rinsed, inspected, and prepared for the tin/lead plating process.

After going through an acid-cleaning tank to remove oil and grease, the copper boards are placed in a dilute sulfuric acid solution to micro etch the surface. The next step is a treatment in a fluroboric acid solution just prior to tin/lead plating. The boards are then placed in a 380-gallon tank containing fluroboric acid, stannous fluroborate, lead fluroborate, and a proprietary brightener. The boards are then washed.

After tin/lead plating, the dry film resist must be removed by running the panels through a conveyor system that sprays a dilute caustic solution to break down and

EXHIBIT 8.1   Shaker Circuits income statement.

	1989	1988	1987	1986	1985
Revenue (annual)					
Computer manufacturers	$125	$ 160	$150	$145	$160
Power supply manufacturers	320	450	330	210	185
Electronic instrument manufacturers	175	340	170	150	140
Automotive industry	230	290	225	175	145
Total revenue	$850	$1,240	$875	$680	$630
Variable costs					
Materials COGS, manufactured	298	440	306	245	227
Design	47	62	48	34	32
Outside services	13	12	13	14	6
Total variable costs	$357	$ 515	$368	$292	$265
Contribution (gross margin)	$493	$ 725	$508	$388	$365
(%)	58%	59%	58%	57%	58%
Fixed costs					
Salaries	$170	$ 186	$131	$ 75	$ 57
Phone	6	7	6	5	4
Utilities	4	6	4	3	3
Rent	60	55	52	50	50
Office equipment leases	13	12	9	7	6
Warehouse equipment leases	21	25	18	14	13
Travel	11	12	9	7	6
Postage/shipping	9	12	9	7	6
Legal/accounting fees	13	12	13	10	9
Insurance	13	12	10	10	9
Total fixed costs	$319	$ 341	$260	$187	$165
Total costs (fixed & variable)	$676	$ 856	$628	$480	$429
Income before interest, taxes,					
& depreciation	174	384	247	200	201
Depreciation	19	19	16	12	10
Interest	13	10	9	10	9
Income before taxes	$142	$ 355	$222	$178	$182
State income taxes	7	18	11	9	9
Federal income taxes	50	124	78	62	64
Net income	$ 85	$ 213	$133	$107	$109
	10.0%	17.2%	15.2%	15.7%	17.3%

EXHIBIT 8.2   Shaker Circuits balance sheet.

	1989	1988	1987	1986	1985
Assets					
Cash & marketable securities	$185	$132	$83	$104	$106
Accounts receivable	153	196	134	94	79
Inventory	89	129	92	73	66
Total current assets	$427	$457	$308	$272	$251
Property plant & equipment	286	278	241	179	125
Accumulated depreciation	(99)	(80)	(61)	(45)	(33)
Property plant & equipment (net)	188	198	180	134	92
Other assets					
Total assets	$615	$656	$488	$406	$343
Liabilities					
Accounts payable	107	112	72	55	50
Short term debt	11	11	7	6	5
Total current liabilities	$118	$124	$ 79	$ 61	$ 54
Long term debt	130	100	90	100	90
Total liabilities	$248	$224	$169	$161	$144
Owners equity					
Common stock	150	150	150	150	150
Retained earnings	218	283	169	96	49
Total equity	$368	$433	$319	$246	$199
Total liabilities & equity	$616	$656	$488	$407	$344

remove the resist. This produces an alkaline polymer sludge, which must be chemically neutralized and dried prior to being hauled away by a certified hazardous waste hauler.

The boards are then run through a conveyor etcher. The etching process removes the exposed copper areas by chemically degrading the copper coating down to the fiberglass substrate of the board. The ammonia-based etching solution does not attack the tin/lead plating. This leaves the copper traces under the tin/lead plating intact and the rest of the board exposed fiberglass. The ammonia-based solution of dissolved copper must be removed by an authorized hazardous waste hauler.

The tin/lead is then chemically stripped from the pathways exposing the copper traces. A photosensitive epoxy ink, called solder mask, is applied to the boards to cover the traces but leave the holes and surface mount pads exposed.

The boards are then run through hot air solder leveling to coat the exposed holes and surface mount pads. This is accomplished by running the boards through a curtain of liquid tin/lead and then blowing off the excess solder with extremely hot air knives. After hot air leveling, an epoxy-based nomenclature ink is applied to the

EXHIBIT 8.3   Shaker Circuits cash flow.

	1989	1988	1987	1986	1985
Operations					
Net income	$ 85	$213	$133	$107	$109
Depreciation	19	19	16	12	10
Accounts receivable decrease/(increase)	43	(63)	(39)	(16)	2
Inventory decrease/(increase)	39	(37)	(19)	(7)	(5)
Accounts payable (decrease)/increase	(5)	40	17	6	4
Net cash from operations	$ 181	$173	$108	$102	$120
Investing					
P P & E decrease/(increase)	(9)	(37)	(61)	(54)	(15)
Net cash from investing	$ (9)	$(37)	$(61)	$(54)	$(15)
Financing					
Increase/(decrease) in short-term debt	(1)	4	2	1	5
Increase/(decrease) in long-term debt	30	10	(10)	10	5
Issues of common stock					
Common dividends	(150)	(100)	(60)	(60)	(60)
Net cash from financing activities	$(121)	$(86)	$(68)	$(49)	$(60)
Beginning cash balance	132	83	104	106	61
Net cash flow	52	50	(22)	(2)	45
Ending cash balance	$ 185	$132	$ 83	$104	$106
Operating cash flows + common dividends	$ 331	$273	$168	$162	$180
Discount rate	15.0%				
NPV of operating cash flows	$ 787				

boards to aid in component placement. The final step in the process is to rout the boards to their final dimensions using a CNC router.

PCBs were a member of the electronic components industry. In 1988, the value of shipments in the parent industry were approximately $57 billion dollars. This represented a 25 percent increase over the value of shipments in 1987. United States PCB production was over $4.5 billion in 1989. Most industry analysts felt that the growth would be modest for a few years then pick up significantly in the early to mid-1990s. Demand in the consumer electronics and defense industry would weaken, but would be offset by strength in the computer and telecommunications sectors. By most accounts, electronic components shipments were estimated to increase by over 10 percent in 1989 and 1990.

For the PCB market, 1988 was a good year. Demand from computer, telecommunications, instrumentation, and automotive markets was strong. Unit shipments of PCBs were growing and the market was demanding improvements in technology.

PCB sales to computer manufacturers made up over 40 percent of the revenue of independent PCB manufacturers. Over 15 percent of revenues came from telecommunications customers, and OEMs were relying more and more on independent PCB manufacturers.

There were approximately 1,500 independent companies producing PCBs in the United States in 1989. More than 90 percent of these companies had sales below $10 million. Independent PCB manufacturers accounted for approximately 65 percent of the market production. An additional 1,500 companies produced PCBs as a step in their overall manufacturing process. Shaker's competitors were the independent PCB prototype manufacturers in New England with sales under $10 million.

The Deal

David and Peter had very little savings to put into financing the deal. They planned to get the bulk of the financing from two sources: David's uncle Hubert and Steve Trevor. David's wealthy uncle Hubert agreed to contribute the down payment and provide working capital as needed. Steve Trevor would receive the down payment, then accept the balance of the purchase price in installment payments spread out over a three-year period.

Hubert was investing in his nephew, "David, I trust your judgment on this one. God knows I have no clue about what goes into making a circuit board, but I'm confident that you and Peter have what it takes to make this thing work." Hubert agreed to act as Shaker's bank during the reorganization, and accept their notes as debt at prime plus 1 percent. His decision to finance cash flow was based in part on the business plan, but more importantly, his decision sprang from a desire to see his nephew succeed.

The ownership structure did not reflect the financial investment. Hubert did not want an equity position in the company because he wanted to function as the bank and not be tied into making ownership decisions. David and Peter split the equity evenly as 50/50 partners.

While Steve Trevor's numbers could justify his asking price, their spreadsheet argued for at least a 25% discount. In addition to wanting to bring the price down, David and Peter wanted Steve to bear some of the financial risk of the acquisition. They wanted Steve to accept payment over time as a sign of good faith.

When Steve resisted lowering the price and the co-financing proposal, David and Peter decided to force the issue. "Let's sit tight for the rest of the year. By January 1, Steve will be so interested in selling that we will pay $0.25 on the dollar for the equipment," commented David. Peter agreed but did have some concerns about the customers. "What will they think about the new management if they can't get their circuit boards?" All considered, David and Peter took Steve's threat to close the business at the end of the year as a tremendous opportunity to acquire Shaker Circuits for substantially less than they had been prepared to spend.

PREPARATION QUESTIONS

1. What is your valuation of Shaker Circuits? Use several valuation methods in your preparation. Which method is the most appropriate?

2. What factors should David and Peter consider in order to decide whether or not to make an offer to purchase Shaker Circuits? Should they make an offer?

3. If David and Peter decide to make an offer to purchase Shaker, what is the maximum price they should pay?

4. How should they structure the deal? What terms and conditions should they negotiate?

9 DIAMOND TECHNICAL GROUP (DTG)

Albert Villa, 54, worked with a team from DTG, including Ben Garvey, their Director of Corporate Development, as an outside consultant. Their particular responsibility was to help DTG, a high-tech contract research firm, bring its long-term fiber-optic sensor project to market. Al had managed manufacturing groups for a Fortune 500 corporation and handled the acquisition and divestiture of divisions. In the early spring of 1991, Al met Tom Landis, who had recently been appointed president of Pyron, Inc. (He was a founder and had previously been director of Product Development.) Pyron manufactured ultrasonic sensors for industrial glass process control. Both Al and Tom thought there was potential for a joint venture in the sensor field.

Pyron had experienced severe financial setbacks in 1988 (Exhibits 9.1 to 9.3), however the potential for growth still existed. It was estimated that more than 4,000 domestic specialty glass processors, and at least half as many similar businesses outside of North America, spent an estimated $470 million in 1990 (with growth to $700 million expected by 1995) on instrumentation to increase the yield and efficiency of their processing and molding operations.

Pyron's System III was used primarily by large corporations and research departments and listed for $55,000 in its most popular configuration. Its smaller system 1000, with a sales price of $25,000 per unit, was the only instrument that could directly measure and control the properties necessary to guarantee 100 percent properly manufactured parts. The Minisystem 1200/QC was a quality assurance instrument designed for industrial use.

Pyron had expanded its revenue base by licensing aspects of its technology to the Instrumentation Group (IG) of a major chemicals corporation, now spun off

Written by Professor Edward Marram in collaboration with Abbey Hansen and Jennifer Starr. Copyright © 1993 Edward Marram, revised 5/96. All rights reserved.

EXHIBIT 9.1 Statement of income and retained earnings (in thousands of dollars) for Pyron, Inc.

FYE October 31	1984	1985	1986	1987	1988 Audited	1989 Audited	1990
Net sales	$275	$659	$928	$1,063	$1,649	$2,297	$1,619
Costs and expenses							
Cost of sales	198	235	260	344	512	759	605
Selling, general and administrative	81	249	374	679	1,128	1,424	1,247
Research and development	81	115	182	300	226	302	357
Total costs and expenses	$360	$599	$816	$1,323	$1,866	$2,485	$2,209
Operating profit (and loss)	$ (85)	$ 60	$112	$ (260)	$ (217)	$ (188)	$ (590)
Other income (expense)							
IG royalty income	—	—	300	300	10	46	55
Net interest income	27	18	4	14	(1)	(10)	(44)
Loss on sale of trade receivables	—	—	—	—	—	—	(80)
Total other income (expense)	$ 27	$ 18	$304	$ 314	$ 9	$ 36	$ (69)
Profit (loss) before taxes	$ (58)	$ 78	$416	$ 54	$ (208)	$ (152)	$ (659)
Income tax benefit (provision)	(1)	1	(107)	(5)	68	7	—
Profit (loss) before change in accounting principle	(59)	79	309	49	(140)	(145)	(659)
Cumulative effect of change in accounting principle	—	—	—	—	36	—	—
Net income (loss)	$ (59)	$ 79	$309	$ 49	$ (104)	$ (145)	$ (659)
Retained earnings (beginning)	$ 2	$(72)	$ 5	$ 313	$ 360	$ 258	$ 114
Retained earnings (ending)	(72)	5	313	360	258	114	(544)

EXHIBIT 9.2 Balance sheet (in thousands of dollars) for Pyron, Inc.

FYE October 31	1984	1985	1986	1987	1988 Audited	1989 Audited	1990
Assets							
Current assets							
Cash	$163	$150	$350	$96	$ 86	$ 176	$ 74
Accounts receivable	76	136	285	331	402	342	218
Income taxes recoverable	—	—	—	96	76	11	—
Lease payments receivable	—	—	29	—	—	—	—
Inventory	85	107	161	220	229	380	350
Other current assets	—	10	7	13	11	4	126
Total current assets	$324	$403	$832	$756	$ 804	$ 913	$768
Property, plant, & equipment							
Property, plant, & equipment°	50	66	196	289	331	362	159
Accumulated depreciation	—	—	(66)	(123)	(126)	(177)	—
Total property, plant, & equipment	$ 50	$ 66	$130	$166	$ 205	$ 185	$159
Other assets	11	11	15	12	45	38	33
Total assets	$385	$480	$977	$934	$1,054	$1,136	$960
Liabilities & equity							
Liabilities							
Notes payable—bank	—	—	5	—	130	—	—
Short-term borrowing	—	—	—	—	—	—	588
Accounts payable	10	21	73	64	59	181	52
Customer deposits	4	—	—	6	—	—	—
Accrued expenses†	9	20	140	42	142	144	132
Total liabilities	$ 23	$ 41	$218	$112	$ 331	$ 325	$772

Stockholders' equity							
Common stock	$ 59	$ 59	$ 61	$ 63	$ 65	$ 75	$ 75
Additional paid-in capital	375	375	385	398	431	652	666
Retained earnings	(72)	5	313	361	259	114	(544)
Subtotal	$362	$439	$759	$822	$ 755	$ 841	$197
Deferred compensation	—	—	—	—	(22)	(30)	(9)
Stock subscriptions Receivable	—	—	—	—	(10)	—	—
Total stockholders' equity	$362	$439	$759	$822	$ 723	$ 811	$188
Total liabilities & equity	$385	$480	$977	$934	$1,054	$1,136	$960
Shares issued and outstanding	59,125	59,125	61,825	63,305	65,421	72,721	75,033

* No breakdown of cost versus depreciation available for 1984, 1985, and 1990.

† Includes:

FY 1986 state excise tax payable, federal income tax payable, deferred income tax payable.

FY 1987 deferred income tax payable.

FY 1988 deferred income taxes.

FY 1989 deferred rent.

EXHIBIT 9.3 Statement of cash flows (in thousands of dollars) for Pyron, Inc.

FYE October 31	Actual 1988	Actual 1989 audited
Cash flows from operating activities		
Net loss	$(102,055)	$(144,219)
Adjustments to reconcile net loss to net cash		
Depreciation and amortization	51,320	54,849
Cumulative effect of change in accounting principle	(36,468)	—
Deferred compensation expense	4,881	18,636
Deferred income taxes	(5,000)	(7,240)
Decrease (increase) in accounts receivable	(71,191)	59,881
Increase in inventory	(8,969)	(151,569)
Decrease in other current assets	22,093	72,861
Decrease (increase) in other assets	(22,056)	2,477
Increase in accounts payable and accrued expenses	87,833	131,240
Net cash provided by (used by) operating activities	$ (79,612)	$ 36,916
Cash flows from investing activities		
Capital expenditures	(41,790)	(30,916)
Capitalized software costs	(15,534)	—
Net cash used in investing activities	$ (57,324)	$ (30,916)
Cash flows from financing activities		
Net borrowings (payments) under revolving credit loan	130,000	(130,000)
Issuance of common stock	—	203,713
Stock subscription received	—	10,150
Repurchase of common stock	(2,848)	—
Net cash provided by financing activites	$ 127,152	$ 83,863
Net increase (decrease) in cash	$ (9,784)	$ 89,863
Cash at beginning of year	$ 96,387	$ 86,603
Cash at end of year	$ 86,603	$ 176,466

as IG, Inc. The IG license generated $300,000 a year in both 1986 and 1987, and $50,000 a year from 1988–1991. Royalty payments under the license were expected to continue until 2001.

To reach a broad manufacturing market, the existing instruments needed to be upgraded to include a multichannel option. Pyron had designed prototype electronics for such a multichannel sensor and made plans to introduce it within the year.

Pyron was privately held by more than 25 stockholders. Its principal stockholder was Professor Robert Fontaine, founder and chairman. Other stockholders were the other founders, family, friends, and board members.

ORIGINS OF PYRON, INC.

Professor Fontaine had conducted government-sponsored research at Great Western University on the ultrasonic measurement of the crystalline/amorphous structure of glass since the mid-1970s. The technology that grew from this research combined sensors and computer components to evaluate the properties of glass in its molten or solid state. The commercial potential of this technology seemed highly promising. Aerospace and automobile manufacturers could use it to check the impact resistance of windshield glass; eyeglass manufacturers could install it in their factories to analyze lens blanks; manufacturers of windows for office buildings could apply the technology to the production of sheet glass for window panes; and the basic components (sensors, chips, and software) could certainly be modified for other industrial applications.

The technology inspired interest at scientific and technical conferences where Professor Fontaine frequently gave presentations. Professor Fontaine's team was a cadre of his graduate research assistants, including Master's degree candidates Chu Li ("Charlie") Lam, William Woods, Alec Smith, and post-doctoral fellow Tom Landis. Charlie recalled:

> Bob and Tom Landis went to a big scientific conference in 1981. Afterwards, a lot of people came up to them asking whether they could get an instrument like the one we had developed in our lab. That planted the seed in their minds that we should start a company. I remember talking with William Woods and saying, "Sure, maybe we'll make some money, but the main thing is to have fun."

In January 1982, they incorporated as Pyron, Inc. They obtained the right to sell their technology by leasing it from Great Western University with a nonexclusive license. After discussing contribution and ownership, Bob and his four graduate students pooled $25,000 in personal funds for start-up costs. Bob owned 57 percent of the stock with the remainder distributed among his graduate students. Bob continued his professorship at Great Western, so conflict of interest rules limited the time he could spend at the company. All of the graduate student-founders were board members.

Tucked right under the roof of an old brick factory building, Pyron's space had no interior walls, just partitions. Charlie recalled building the first products:

> Tom Landis and I worked 70 hours a week. It got incredibly hot in the attic that summer. We would take off our shirts as we worked with our soldering irons. I also soldered and even ironed computer boards in my kitchen at home. The whole thing had a typical graduate student aura.

SOME ISSUES OF STRATEGY

The company's marketing strategy was to begin selling to R&D scientists, among whom it already had a network, mostly from the many conference papers that Bob and Tom had presented. After establishing their reputation in this market, Pyron would sell to technical personnel in manufacturing companies, and further expand into Quality Assurance (QA) and Quality Control (QC) in mass market manufacturing. Its ultimate objective would be to sell process control products for the production lines in the manufacturing market.

Another aspect of the strategy was to build a reliable market in the re-supply of ultrasonic sensors, which had to be replaced with each use. The longer term strategy also included augmenting the existing market for its products with new product lines using ultrasound technology. Here, the emphasis would be on high volume industries like automobile and sheet-glass manufacturers. The strategy also called for developing spin-off instrumentation products for medical markets and exploiting other capabilities of ultrasound technology in related sensor markets.

Pyron raised additional funds, not by approaching the venture capital community, but by selling stock privately. The offering document, a Private Placement Memorandum, summarized 1982–1983 gross revenues as $43,000 and projected sales of 6 research instruments in FY 1984, citing formal and informal quotations that Pyron had issued to major research laboratories; serious discussions with 5 aerospace companies; and requests for quotations from universities in the United States and Europe. Sales were forecast to grow from $250,000 in 1984 to $1 million by 1986.

The 1983 Private Placement Memorandum estimated the domestic market for Pyron's ultrasonic instruments at about 300 research units ($12 million), plus about 1,300 units for process control ($26 million). Foreign markets could increase each total by about 25 percent. While there was no directly comparable device on the market, the basic measurements could be made with other methods. Only one small (under $1 million annual revenues) equipment manufacturer offered a product for laboratory use. On the down side, it warned of the difficulties of marketing an unfamiliar technology. It would require some customer education about ultrasonic glass monitoring technology to penetrate even the easiest market, R&D. Marketing process control instruments to industry would be more difficult, it would require education and cooperation from prospective customers for new product development.

In August 1983, Pyron offered 25,000 shares of private stock at $16/share. The Pyron founders raised $400,000 from friends, extended families, and at least one major instrument manufacturer company. Out of a total of 59,125 shares, Bob Fontaine and his family held 20,750. President-designate Joseph De Cordova and his family held 4,325. Tom Landis held 4,000. Charlie Lam and his family held 4,625. Alec Smith and his family held 4,125. William Woods and his family held 4,625.

STAFFING

The 1983 Memorandum called for Pyron to function with three full-time employees. Tom Landis would be vice president for Technology, Charlie Lam would be operations manager and director of Sensor Design Engineering, and the third full-time employee would be a full-time president-treasurer: Joseph De Cordova. Pyron had advertised for a president in the local newspapers, but family contacts introduced Bob and Joe. Joe De Cordova was a 54-year-old with a strong personality, Ph.D. in physical chemistry, and 25 years experience in technical marketing and management in the chemical, aerospace, and aircraft industries. Joe had just taken early retirement from Boeing. He was good at one-on-one sales and had a broad network in government and aerospace.

PRODUCT DEVELOPMENT

Pyron's first research unit products, "System I's," were bulky, and their sensors were so delicate they sometimes had to be handled with tweezers. Each unit consisted of ultrasonic sensing devices, which had to be in physical contact with the glass being tested, plus cabling to attach the sensors to computer units housed in large cabinets. Installations were tricky, as Charlie explained:

> The glass was being processed in autoclaves big enough to drive a Volkswagen into. Our instrument needed 8 wires, but the autoclaves were designed for 2 wires and could only be drilled in a distant location. Since customers didn't want to ship their 20-ton autoclaves around the country, we redesigned our cabling to get our wires through the existing ports. At first, we had to be on site every time one of our systems was used.

Tom was surprised to see people "driving over our cables with forklifts" at sites where System I's were being used. This made him appreciate the need to spend time and money on low-tech problems like ruggedizing cabling, "something I never thought I'd have to worry about when I was a graduate student." He and Charlie traveled to users' sites, learned their technical problems, and returned to the company to simulate the customers' conditions and redesign Pyron's units for their sites.

PYRON'S EFFORTS TO GROW

In March 1985, Bob's son Chris, a recent Stanford graduate with a degree in East Asian studies, came to work at Pyron. At first he was a go-for, with some bookkeeping responsibilities because he had taken an accounting course in college. But Chris learned the technology and business so quickly that he became business manager, operations manager, and eventually, vice president for Sales and Marketing.

Answering an ad in a local paper for someone with experience in technical instrumentation marketing, Beth MacCaffrey, 29, joined the company in 1985. She came with a Master's degree in chemistry, eight years as an applications engineer, product line manager, and marketing manager, and experience in the technical marketing of analytical and process instrumentation.

Beth summarized Pyron's approach to sales in 1985:

> Joe was sales-oriented. I went on sales calls with him and he taught me to find out who has the authority to sign for capital expenditures and sell to that person. But he was pitching the product with long slide presentations, like advanced engineering lectures. He used to show three slides about the characteristics of a sine wave. A typical sale took nine months.

Beth streamlined the sales presentation and reduced turnaround to about four months. She even managed to get a few sales in a week or less. With Beth, Tom, Joe, and Chris paying attention to marketing and sales, and Bob giving demonstrations to potentially important customers and publicizing the technology at scientific conferences, Pyron's revenues grew to $659,000, finally earning a profit in 1985.

Chris put time and effort into making the technology more commercially attractive. He observed that, although the company had little difficulty selling what were essentially "ugly tan boxes that measured the properties of glass being processed" to the aerospace market because there was a lot of cash in that market, the company had to develop a more professional looking product to deal with increasing competition and shrinking customer budgets in other markets. The device was now housed in a more elegant box, with a Pyron logo on it, and supported with professionally printed literature and an interesting slide show.

Chris also opened a completely new market for Pyron: foreign sales. He began by following up on contacts with about thirty European and Asian companies whose representatives had asked for quotations on Pyron's products at trade shows. Chris obtained State Department authorization to sell the instrument as a computer, which allowed the company to sell overseas. In the process, he taught himself international marketing.

RIDING HIGH

Pyron had now grown to nine full-time employees. The company had upgraded its first product, System I, into a more rugged, more professional, looking unit, System II; FY 1985 gross sales had increased 240 percent from FY 1984 to $659,000; and the company was now profitable. Most gratifying, the company's list of customers included top aerospace firms and blue chip chemical conglomerates.

Pyron's was not the only ultrasonic measuring device on the market. One competitive product was called the "Ultramet," it was priced from $15,000 to $30,000, depending on options. Tests showed this instrument to be less sensitive under extremes of temperature and pressure than Pyron's. Another competitive product was developed by a professor at the University of Chicago, but it gave readings in a narrower range than Pyron's. Researchers could also use commercially available sensors and computer components to develop their own ultrasonic devices to measure the crystalline/amorphous structure of glass. But Pyron's engineers found that such systems were less reliable for glass in the solid than in the molten state—a drawback for industrial process control and quality assurance applications. Only Pyron's instruments rendered accurate measurements on both molten and solid glass.

The company was now attracting attention. The Instrumentation Group of a Fortune 100 chemical company was said to be considering acquiring Pyron because it wanted to add an ultrasonic analyzer to its own R&D line, and it might be cheaper to buy Pyron for the sake of its technology than to develop an instrument from scratch. Beth, for one, was upset by the prospect of Pyron's being acquired by a big corporation. She liked the small company "because of its informal, creative culture." Others at Pyron shared her aversion to being acquired. The team decided to craft a licensing agreement to exploit IG's interest in such a way as to bring in cash and gain prestige and publicity for Pyron, while simultaneously limiting IG's ability to compete with Pyron for major sales.

The deal was signed in mid-1986, as Beth recalled:

> We restricted IG to R&D lab sales, which were onesie-twosies and expensive. It all came down to cable length. I knew from factory visits that manufacturers needed at least 50 feet of cabling to connect their samples to their computers. So we wrote the licensing agreement to limit IG to 10 feet of cabling, just enough to run an experiment in a laboratory fume hood.

The deal gave Pyron two $300,000 payments and a further $400,000 for consulting, plus a non-exclusive license with a prospective royalty stream of $2,000 per equipment sold for a period of 15 years in amounts not less than $40,000 per year for the first two years, $50,000 per year for the following six years, and $25,000 per year thereafter.

REACTIONS TO THE ROYALTY DEAL

Opinions at Pyron were divided about what to do next. Pyron had just made money and seen its technology validated by a major company. Charlie remembered the discussion:

> Beth MacCaffrey and Tom Landis felt that we had money and were now worth something, so it was a good time to sell or raise capital. We discussed whether to go out and raise more capital or try to go it alone.

Chris, who was in the outer circle of employees at the time, recollected a general feeling of buoyancy, "Sales were good and we thought we had just beaten a Fortune 100 company at the negotiating table." He also took it for granted that Pyron would put money into enhancing its product. There were at least two reasons for doing so: advances in computer design were making Pyron's System II obsolete, and competitors now had Pyron's technology and could be expected to upgrade it.

POSITIONED FOR GROWTH

Pyron seemed to be on the threshold of new growth. Bob Fontaine announced a near-term financial goal: to grow Pyron from a $1 million company to a $5 or $10 million company in 1987, using lower and lower technology to get products into bigger and bigger markets. Charlie commented, "We all talked about major growth, but we focused on making different products with ultrasonic technology."

The pressure to upgrade Pyron's well-received System II ultrasonic instrument created waves of hiring. A transition team from manufacturing, engineering, and marketing was formed to get System III ready for release by March 1, 1988. In addition to instituting a System III Program, Pyron stepped up efforts to develop new product lines: new chips for its existing sensors, a fiber optic device, and other kinds of sensors for the process control market.

From 1986 to 1987, Pyron grew from 9 to 16 employees. New hires included a product development engineer, a manufacturing technician, an associate engineer, an inside sales engineer, and a customer service coordinator. In 1987, sales revenues rose almost $1.4 million, including $300,000 from the IG deal (Exhibits 9.1 and 9.2). Beth McCaffrey and Tom Landis gave Bob their opinion, "It's time to sell. It looks good now, but the future is not as clear cut." Beth projected losses in the next few years based on new product development and increased marketing efforts. But when she told Bob her projections, he said, "That's not good enough."

In March 1988, Pyron entered into a revolving-loan credit agreement with a regional bank that allowed the company to borrow up to $250,000, depending upon the availability and eligibility of accounts receivable and inventory. The interest rate was 11.5 percent (1.5% above prime), secured by all of the assets of the company. The agreement also called for Pyron to maintain a specified compensating balance ($25,000 plus 10% of average borrowings) and certain debt to equity ratios. As a further condition, the company could not incur losses in two consecutive quarters. Tom Landis recalled, "We got the line of credit early on, as a matter of prudence, because we thought we might have a lot of purchase orders and need to borrow against the orders or receivables for parts to build things."

Instead of too many purchase orders, there was a lag in the demand for glass processing equipment. Chris described the economic climate:

> All budgets were constricting. Even our customers' travel budgets were down, but we didn't notice it because our revenue from Japanese and German sales masked it.

The aerospace market, in which Pyron had found its biggest initial success, was producing less than 30 percent of its sales, while the foreign markets that Chris had opened up accounted for over 50 percent. For Bob, the basic lesson was that "aerospace was a lousy market." This had implications for Joe's tenure as president. His primary contacts were in the aerospace industry; and there had been a chill in the air between him and the rest of the board of directors for the past two years, during which he had not produced a business plan for further development of the company.

A consultant's report to the Chairman of the Board of Directors in February 1988 made the following observations:

1. Even though there is a formal chain of command (though quite convoluted by multitasking of individuals), there is no person or group of people at the company to serve as the visionary or torch bearer to lead the company into the future.

2. At Pyron, there doesn't seem to be any strategic planning at all. From an operational standpoint, company staff is in a reactive mode for production, sales, and planning, with no clear vision of the future or to where their efforts should lead.

3. Pyron is at the point where it must develop a plan for survival and growth in its defined business area. The first priority of this plan must be to boost sales

through increasing market awareness (with IG's help), and by pushing the current product, or its close derivative, into new but similar markets.

In March 1988, Bob sent Joe a letter saying that, "The board of directors voted at its meeting on Saturday, March 5, to terminate immediately your appointments as president and treasurer." Beth commented, "The board could have urged Bob to sell me the company but they didn't. They looked for a new president instead."

As before, Pyron placed ads in local newspapers and interviewed candidates. One applicant was Leonid ("Leo") Vlasik, 46, who had emigrated from Russia in the early 1970s with Master's degrees in electrical engineering and physics, and experience as an assistant professor of Electrical Engineering at Moscow Scientific Institute. In California, Leo earned an MBA and embarked upon a broad-based career in high-tech management. He had functioned as project design engineer in a high-tech industrial firm, and also held executive positions in Operations, Manufacturing, Engineering, Business Development, Strategic Alliances, Corporate Venturing, and Product Development at a well-known Silicon Valley software company, where he had been a vice president for five years. Bob favored Leo because "He was very intelligent, had executive experience, and spoke finance. He looked like someone who knew how to raise money."

Beth recalled a board member, Aram Hovanessian, managing director of a leading international investment banking firm, warning Bob to avoid the common mistake of going to the opposite extreme from the previous president's qualities. She commented:

> Joe was a good salesman but couldn't plan; Leo was a planner, but didn't know what was going on from day to day. He had credentials, but no manufacturing, human resources, or marketing experience. He was the opposite of Joe.

Tom Landis remembered another candidate's reaction in the job interview:

> The most analytical person we interviewed wasn't interested in us. He said the structure of our instrument and the market made it impossible to make money. Our cost of sales was high because we had to educate the customer, show that this science really worked, and demonstrate its value. Financially, we were always living on the hairy edge.

During the search, Beth, Tom, and Chris ran the company. Beth and Tom were in their mid-thirties, Chris was 26. "Neither Tom nor I wanted to be president," Beth said, "but we didn't want Chris to be either." Tom commented, "Chris, Beth, and I could have made the company work without a president. Beth is good at her job and Chris is very smart. His age was sometimes hard for various people in the company to take, including myself, but he could have stepped in as president."

The board hired Leo Vlasik as president in September 1988. Beth remembered that it took about $30,000 in legal fees to finalize his contract. In addition to his $90,000 salary, he received a company car, stock ownership, and his own personal secretary, who was paid a salary of $36,000. Leo also added a CFO/treasurer for $60,000 with accounting and credit management experience who had held similar responsibilities at a high-tech company for the last 5 years. Shortly after coming to Pyron, Leo asked Charlie Lam and William Woods to leave the board. Charlie recalled:

> We didn't dispute Leo's wishes. We were in engineering, focused on the development of product. Maybe he was uncomfortable with an open board and wanted to institute some hierarchy. But we would have liked to watch the meetings and learn about running a business.

SG&A expenses grew in other ways too. The company moved to larger quarters: 6,000 sq. ft. in nearby Technology Park. The domestic sales force also expanded. Beth thought the company was getting top-heavy (Exhibit 9.4).

In August 1988, five months behind schedule, Pyron began shipping System III, its third generation laboratory product, still priced in the $40,000 range. By November 1988, the Company had an installed base of nearly 100 units, primarily in the aerospace, automobile, and glass industries.

UNEXPECTED SETBACKS

The company hired a new manufacturing manager in February 1989 to help Chris, who was then functioning as operations director. The new manager, James Wesley, held both an MBA and certification from the American Process and Inventory Control Society (APICS), which indicated special training ("somewhat like being a CPA," as he explained) in manufacturing. Further because James had worked for a $4 to $5 million instrument division of a $150 million company and a technical company in Palo Alto, he brought training and relevant experience to Pyron.

When James arrived, Charlie recalled, Pyron's operations function was running from "fire to fire." Assemblers would run out of parts with equipment half built, and would come to Charlie to order the necessary pieces. Even more disturbing, Charlie recalled:

> In January 1989, we released our new System III's after a several month delay and shipped units to three waiting customers—we needed to generate income. All three of the units came back because of a defect in the PC board.

James helped Pyron discover the cause of this upsetting development: problems with vendors. Charlie commented:

> James brought Pyron a knowledge of the things that can go wrong in manufacturing, especially due to vendors' mistakes, and the idea that you should visit vendors in order to look at what they're doing.

Charlie had little time to visit vendors because he was busy putting out fires, but James's visits revealed important problems. He discovered one, in particular, with inadequacies in cleanliness. When another Pyron employee, an engineer, examined the PC boards with a microscope, he found fine cracks which were causing connections to fail when the temperature dropped. Pyron switched vendors for these parts, and the repaired instruments functioned correctly, but the episode had been embarrassing.

In March 1990, amidst a national banking crisis and general tightening of government regulations on commercial lending, the bank called Pyron's loan. Pyron had incurred a loss in two consecutive quarters, and the economic climate precluded leniency on the part of the bank. They now had 30 days to pay off the debt.

Additional debt was accumulating: to the landlord, to vendors, and to lawyers (Exhibit 9.5). Although Leo's mandate was to raise over $400,000 by the end of 1989, he had raised just over $200,000 through a private placement, some as a result of Chris' connection with a Japanese client. This was hardly enough to keep the company afloat. An executive remembered how Bob Fontaine was averse to the idea of bankruptcy because bankruptcy would place creditors ahead of stockholders; and the stockholders included friends and relatives. Others speculated that Bob didn't want to declare bankruptcy because that would have meant loss of control since the court would decide whether the company would have to liquidate; and Bob didn't want to lose control.

PAYING OFF THE BANK: PYRON ENTERS INTO A FACTORING ARRANGEMENT

In April, 1990, because of pressure to repay the bank loan, Bob Fontaine turned to a different source of capital: West Coast Financing Inc.(WCFI) a factor, with whom Pyron entered into a complex financing arrangement.

The agreement of April 3, 1990, called for all of Pyron's accounts receivables to go directly to the factor with an 80 percent advance to Pyron. When WCFI collected a receivable from a customer, it withheld the 80 percent previously forwarded to Pyron, plus a 6 percent fee for WCFI's services and forwarded the remaining 14 percent to Pyron. On June 28, 1990, Pyron agreed to a note to WCFI for $588,000 secured by Pyron's receivables and inventory, which would become a demand loan at

EXHIBIT 9.4   1991 unaudited income statements Q1–Q3, projected Q4 (in thousands of dollars) for Pyron, Inc.

	Q1	Q2	Q3	Q4 Projected	FY 1991 Projected
Net revenues	$ 189.6	$360.2	$416.4	$450.0	$1,416.2
Cost of goods sold (excluding direct labor)	38.5	65.2	69.0	74.1	246.8
Royalty expense	2.3	4.7	4.5	4.6	16.0
Gross margin	$ 148.8	$290.3	$342.9	$371.3	$1,153.3
Expenses (including direct labor)	389.7	249.6	295.0	320.0	1,254.3
Operating profit (loss)	$(240.9)	$ 40.7	$ 47.9	$ 51.3	$ (101.0)
Royalty income	5.5	12.5	12.5	12.5	43.0
Net interest/factoring expense	(37.3)	(43.2)	(54.5)	(55.0)	(190.0)
Pre-tax profit (loss)	$(272.7)	$ 10.0	$ 5.9	$ 8.8	$ (248.0)

EXHIBIT 9.5   Unaudited balance sheet as of 7/31/91 for Pyron, Inc.

Current assets	
Cash	$155,000
Accounts receivable trade	49,000
Royalty receivable	22,000
Factoring holdback	59,000
Inventory	351,000
Pre-paid expenses	28,000
Total current assets	$664,000
Total fixed assets	123,000
Other assets	
Deposits and capitalized expenses	30,000
Total other assets	$ 30,000
Total assets	$817,000
Current liabilities	
Accounts payable (see notes)	138,000
Factoring note payable (see notes)	588,000
Royalty payable	30,000
Reserves	18,000
Accrued factoring interest (see notes)	30,000
Deferred rent and other accruals	60,000
Total current liabilities	$864,000
Capital	
Common stock	75,000
Paid-in	679,000
Equity legal expenses	(9,000)
Deferred compensation	5,000
Retained earnings	(544,000)
Earnings year-to-date	(253,000)
Total capital	$ (47,000)
Total liabilities & capital	$817,000

EXHIBIT 9.5 *(Continued)*

FINANCIAL NOTES

Current financial statements: FY91 Income Statement information for Q1, Q3 and Balance Sheet information for 7/31/91 are based upon management's best current analysis, and are presented UNAUDITED. Pyron historically undergoes an annual audit, and prepares interim financials for informational purposes only. The figures presented are thus subject to subsequent adjustment.

Tax-loss carry-forwards: As of 10/31/90, Pyron had approximately $640,000 in loss carry-forwards that expire in 2005. In addition, the company has R&D tax credits of approximately $40,000 that also expire in 2005. The use of such carry-forwards by Pyron's acquirer may be subject to certain limitations under the tax reform act of 1986.

WCFI/note: Pyron currently owes WCFI a note that has a net obligation value of $529,000. According to a prior letter of understanding, that note has been accruing interest at a rate of 30 percent per year since April 1, 1991. It is unclear whether the 30 percent rate is enforceable, and good faith negotiations that used an 18 percent rate have been suspended. Therefore, the actual amount of the debenture is unclear, as is the appropriate interest rate expense for Q2, Q4. It has been plugged into the financial statements at 18 percent.

WCFI/factoring: Pyron is currently factoring all receivables through WCFI at a rate of 6 percent of invoice face value. The current deal expires in FY93. Pyron believes that upon settlement of the WCFI Note that an unconditional release from factoring would be forthcoming. For conservatism sake, however, factoring expense is shown in financial projections through FY93.

Vendor debt: Pyron's current obligations/accounts payable include a certain amount of past due vendor debt, all of which is under a negotiated settlement with the other party. All relationships with vendors are cordial, and all strategic vendors have been retained. The components of vendor debt are as follows:

Landlord:	$33,000 (Note, maturing December 1993)
Vendor 1:	$17,124 (Installment pay-down through March 1992)
Vendor 2:	$7,650 (Installments through May 1992)
Vendor 3:	$1,678 (Installments through October 1991)
Vendor 4:	$1,409 (Installments through October 1991)
Fontaine:	$1,567 (Installments through November 1991)
Vendor 5:	$25,061 (Pay-down as percentage of Revenue > $120,000)
Lawyer 1:	$16,122 (Pay-down as percentage of Revenue > $120,000)
Lawyer 2:	$1,656 (Pay-down as percentage of Revenue > $120,000)
Total:	$105,267 (Included in A/P value from balance sheet)

(Continued)

EXHIBIT 9.5   *(Continued)*

Severance liability: Pyron negotiated a severance arrangement with L. Vlasik, formerly President, which originally amounted to $50,000, and at the moment has depleted to $39,500, payable in twelve equal installments going forward. This severance does not show on the balance sheet, and is treated as a period expense in the Income Statement projections.

Contingent liabilities: In order to encourage employees to stay during an enforced salary reduction to 33 percent of nominal base salary, a long-term incentive plan was put in place which calls for a repayment of "lost" salary in the event of company recapitalization. The maximum value for this contingent liability stands at $103,000.

Current salary reduction: In Q3 and Q4, salaries have been paid at only 70 percent of nominal base salary. Due to incentive payments, actual salary expenses during this period approach 85 percent of nominal base. It is anticipated that a salary re-adjustment toward 100 percent of nominal base will be required upon recapitalization. Current financial information suggests that the reduction in interest/financing costs will more than offset the net increase in salaries.

Near-term expense increases: Given the precarious financial position of the company, incremental expenditures have been largely curtailed. Management has identified areas of exposure which would be well served by strategic investment for growth. The most immediate recommendations would address:

> Marketing: Proactive marketing and product launch expenses.
> Sales: The addition of two salesmen, one with European potential.

New sensor business opportunity: Pyron currently has under option a new sensor technology which shows tremendous potential. The revenue potential for this new sensor and its associated electronics is conservatively estimated to be ten times larger than Pyron's ultrasonic products. While initial product definition and technical exploration is underway, substantial additional capital will be required to bring this product to market. Neither capital investment nor revenue/operating costs associated with the new sensor business opportunity have been included in the financial information presented. A separate business plan for this product is under development, and can certainly be discussed at a future meeting.

the rate of 30 percent per year if unpaid by March 31,1991. Leo and Bob signed the factoring agreements. Tom Landis recalled the employees' general reaction to the deal, "Relief. The factor paid our debt to the bank."

Working under these conditions, the company was able to operate and make sales, although the effect on its bottom line was significant. During 1990, cash proceeds to Pyron from the sale of its receivables to WCFI amounted to $1,055,000 and WCFI withheld fees of $79,657. Even in this critical state, James Wesley recalled:

> A group of employees thought they could go on. The company's products were beginning to find acceptance in the automobile, printed circuit board, and bathroom fixtures industries; and Chris believed Pyron could improve its sales efforts.

TURBULENCE IN THE COMPANY

The past two years had been a bumpy ride. In mid-1989, Beth became pregnant and encountered medical complications that made an extended maternity leave inevitable. She told Leo to replace her, but he didn't. While Beth was on leave, Chris also went in and out of the employment picture. He had planned to go to business school; and once the new president was in place, he felt that he could go to school full-time and cover the foreign marketing function part-time. In 1990, Beth returned from leave and, in her words, "Leo came into my office and said, 'Help me, my back is against the wall. Sales are horrendous, we're dying. I need to restructure and lay off.'" Beth laid off employees, although some continued to work for the company as outside contractors.

Beth was uncomfortable. To her, the current situation felt "underhanded, gray, and very political." It also disturbed her that, "Bob cut himself off" from the employees and seemed to filter all communications through Leo. She commented, "Maybe that was a demand that Leo made, but it was really strange." Sales picked up a bit, but Leo asked Beth for another round of layoffs. She was upset, "They hadn't told me the severity of the situation." Despite liking her job and most of her colleagues at Pyron, Beth resigned. Her loss created a functional vacuum in marketing. Chris left business school to return to the company and managed to get revenues up to $175,000/month by July.

Amid this turmoil, the company brought out its first product designed for the factory floor: a compact, highly efficient "Minisystem." In sales calls, Chris discovered unexpected obstacles to achieving the company's long anticipated goal of getting its products onto the factory floor. Many supervisors, wary of Pyron's unfamiliar technology, were resistant to the new product, especially because installing its sensors required drilling into existing molds. Supervisors, Chris learned, were highly reluctant to touch the production line. Even the prospect of decreased waste and increased productivity failed to persuade them. In some cases, increased productivity further dissuaded them because a higher volume of glass components might unbalance the flow of production. Chris responded by positioning the new product in the Quality Assurance area "before the line."

FURTHER CRISES

In the summer of 1990, Pyron's sales went from $175,000/month in July, August, September, and October, to $29,000 in November and $4,000 in December. Some attributed this falling off to Saddam Hussein's invasion of Kuwait, which had sent shock waves through heavy industry and seemed to cause a generally negative effect on purchases.

Pyron's planning group saw no recourse but to cut expenses. Through expansions and contractions, the company had endeavored to keep employees in its network, sometimes by working out part-time consulting relationships. In January 1991, Pyron went through another round of layoffs, cutting staff from twenty to twelve. With the understanding that salaries would rise as soon as possible, and lost pay would be restored in the event of a recapitalization, all remaining permanent employees accepted deep salary cuts. The chairman's monthly fees were reduced to zero. Employees' monthly pay was now ⅓ of what it had been on December 1, 1990, subject to a minimum of $1,000/month and a maximum of $2,500/month. Half-time work was required. Normal commissions and revenue sharing plans continued unchanged.

In April 1991, Pyron negotiated a severance deal with Leo Vlasik. The deal included $50,000 in severance pay, the company car that Pyron had bought for him, and continued membership on the board.

WHO SHOULD LEAD?

Bob, Chris, Charlie, and Tom again faced the question of whom to designate as president. Tom recalled:

> Chris was a real possibility. His high intelligence, competence, energy, achievements within the company, and tenacity all spoke for him. On the other hand, his youth, and the nepotism issue, argued against him. Somebody had to become president. Bob suggested me. I talked with Chris about it. I didn't really want to do it, but I said I'd give it a go. I didn't think I could bear it if Chris were president. It was just a psychological thing about his age. What a president does is scramble. I spent 70 percent of my time dealing with the factor, trying to get a break. There were threats back and forth. We wasted $25,000 to $30,000 in legal bills and so did he. We could have used the money better.

In 1991, Pyron was operating on a factoring deal, with a skeleton crew, part-timers, and outside consultants. All remaining employees had taken severe pay cuts. At various times during the year, they received anywhere from 30 percent to 70 percent salary. But the company went on. In August, Bob's letter to stockholders mentioned that the company had just finished its first full quarter since the major reorganization with encouraging results. He cited unaudited revenue of over $400,000 in the quarter, mentioned a "small profit," and noted that the Minisystem for process control had generated favorable comments and press coverage at a recent technology fair. And the company had two new products: a new software package for the System III and a Quality Control version of the Minisystem. Bob's letter ended, "We are trimmed down and focused as never before in company history." The Pyron team had stuck together through tough times, and cost cutting measures reduced losses significantly.

THE ACQUISITION QUESTION AGAIN

Four years earlier, Pyron had deflected IG's acquisition offer and turned it into a lucrative licensing arrangement. In 1990, things had changed; Pyron was seeking suitors. A letter from Bob to the stockholders announced the engagement of a consultant to help search for a suitable equity partner. A German firm that bought Pyron's instruments had once looked like a potential acquirer. Chris described this company's interest as a long-term, on-again off-again proposition. This company took another look at Pyron in 1990, but, according to Beth, "The fiasco was our numbers. They just weren't good enough to get financing."

In June 1991, another potential buyer entered the picture. Diamond Technical Group (DTG) was a Bay area high-tech contract research firm whose management wanted to diversify into manufacturing. Ben Garvey was particularly impressed by two factors: their grasp of what it took to commercialize a technological device, and their dedication to keeping a business going in difficult circumstances. Both Pyron's technology and its people struck him as a potentially good fit with DTG's needs. Chris and Tom showed Ben a chart detailing their sales pipeline which seemed to include enough cash to cover the expenses of doing the acquisition deal and bringing the company into DTG as a division. Ben directed Al Villa, a veteran manufacturing executive whom DTG employed as a consultant to identify companies as acquisition candidates, to open a discussion with Pyron. Tom Landis recalled, "When Al Villa called and asked, 'Would you perhaps be interested in being bought?' I said, 'Would we!'"

DTG and Pyron started discussing an acquisition deal. But complications multiplied when IG, now spun off by its parent company as an independent instrumentation firm, prepared its own acquisition offer for Pyron. Suddenly Pyron was in the middle of a tug-of-war. In sum, both IG and DTG were willing to pay Pyron's debts plus a small sum of money to stockholders. But beyond this, the offers differed: DTG wanted to keep Pyron operating and put its employees back on full salary, while IG wanted Pyron primarily for its technology.

Charlie speculated on IG's interest in Pyron:

> IG offered to pay stockholders only after we made $1 million from sales of our process control product. That gave them no reason to develop it. They just wanted to stop having to pay royalties for the technology they had licensed in 1986. Stockholders would probably get nothing from the deal.

Not everyone on the board shared Charlie's aversion to the IG deal. Some doubted that DTG's offer would actually go through. Others developed personal animosities against DTG. Tom Landis explained how this complex situation developed:

> We renewed discussions with the German company just when DTG had sent us an exclusivity document, so we were able to tell Ben Garvey, "No, we're talking to someone else," and that also kept the door open for IG.

The German company backed out again, and both the IG and DTG agreements had urgent deadlines. Bob Fontaine decided to invite Ben to present the DTG proposal to the Pyron Board.

PREPARATION QUESTIONS

1. Given what you know by now about DTG and Pyron, should DTG invest time and energy in a careful job of due diligence for a possible acquisition of Pyron?
2. What key factors should be considered in their due diligence strategy?
3. Would you recommend that DTG acquire Pyron?
4. What do you think Pyron is worth to the players in this situation: DTG, IG, Bob Fontaine, Pyron's employees, and Pyron's customers?
5. What do you think DTG should offer for Pyron?
6. What should Ben Garvey present to the board?

10 WINSALES

Bill Pernsteiner, founder of WinSales Inc., gazed out his office window and thought about the day's events. Bill watched the traffic below slowly build into an evening commute. He put his forehead against the glass and felt the coolness. Bill founded WinSales, a sales automation software company, in April 1992. Over the past three years, he had worked through many problems, but none seemed to weigh on him as much, or elude him as persistently, as the marketing dilemma which he faced now. He walked to the desk, reached into his briefcase and pulled out the sales report again. "If things don't start to happen soon, I'm out of business," Bill thought. He shut his briefcase with a snap, and the quiet returned.

THE MEETING—MARCH 1994

Bill had just finished meeting with Torrey Russell, his sales and marketing consultant. Under Torrey's tutelage, Bill and Lisa Wiley, his business partner and wife, were becoming sales professionals. They had learned how to qualify prospects, handle objections, and ask for the order. Bill had been pleased with Torrey's coaching, and slowly, sales were improving. This was part of why he wanted to bring Torrey on full-time. WinSales' marketing plan was generating an increasing number of prospects, but the closing rate was still too low and he knew that Torrey could do much better.

Until this meeting with Torrey, Bill thought that the advertising campaign he designed with Lisa was working (e.g., had the right creative, media, reach, and

This case was prepared by Dan D'Heilly and Jeff Selander under the direction of Professor William Bygrave. Funding provided by the Ewing Marion Kauffman Foundation. Copyright © 1996 Babson College. All rights reserved.

frequency). Bill was surprised by what had become the main topic of their meeting. Torrey had said: Bill, I think we need to stop advertising. We're spending $3,000 a month on ads that don't generate good leads. Bill had replied, "If we're getting too many unqualified leads, shouldn't we adjust and fine-tune what's working, so it will work better?"

Torrey had paused for just a moment:

Bill, this product could prevail in any market, so you've got to decide who to target. The issue is how to find a cluster of early adopters because that's what matters when you're in start-up mode with a high-tech product. You're not going to attract early adopters with magazine ads. We should target our message better. If I accept your job offer, my first act as director of sales and marketing will be to cancel our ads.

Bill had stopped and looked closely at Torrey. Bill had known Torrey for about six months now, since November of last year when Torrey had begun to meet weekly with Bill and his two-person sales staff. Bill had been impressed with his sales acumen and marketing creativity, but stop advertising? Lisa had a BA in marketing from the University of Puget Sound, and they had drawn up the marketing plan knowing there would be a lag between ads and revenues. She had said that they would have to be patient and Lisa thought that, if anything, they should increase their advertising budget. "All of our competitors advertise. How are we going to get customers if we don't advertise?" Bill thought. He leaned back and thought about the conversation again. Bill was pleased that Torrey was willing to join WinSales, but stop advertising?

Torrey closes sales better than any of us, but what about the preliminary work? Before you can close the sale you've got to get the lead. And that takes advertising—prospects don't just appear; we need to make impressions on a regular basis. We've been spending $3,000 a month and I'm afraid that we'll lose our foothold in the market if we stop now. We shouldn't just abandon our strategy and change course, should we?

SALES AUTOMATION INDUSTRY

Sales Automation Software (SAS) customizes the complex and data-intensive sales process. Since its inception, software has played a key role in improving business processes. Word processing, simple spreadsheet programs and later, accounting programs changed the way businesses operated. Sales has been the last major function to become computerized in most organizations.

In the early eighties, just before emergence of the PC market, SAS products were written only for large computer systems. These programs were difficult to effectively integrate into the routines of the corporate salesforce, and they were unavailable for most sales organizations. Implementation was time-consuming, labor-intensive, and often unsuccessful as corporate managers had to convince their salesforces to use a confusing, new technology.

The first PC software for the salesforce was essentially an electronic rolodex, and the product category was called contact management software. These products allowed users to keep track of a large number of prospects and clients. Like SAS

EXHIBIT 10.1   SAS firm financials (000s).

	1992	1991	1990	1989
Symantec (ACT!)				
Revenues	$216,635	$133,761	$83,367	$61,162
Net income	18,703	9,006	8,822	5,229
Total assets	122,817	70,578	51,101	26,245
Total liabilities	47,175	30,444	25,845	12,150
Modatech (Maximizer)				
Revenues	$ 3,407	$ 1,956	$ 2,308	$ 1,338
Net income	372	(4,635)	(168)	76
Total assets	2,220	1,202	4,151	1,963
Total liabilities	930	937	1,052	829

programs for large organizations, they were also complex, difficult to learn, and weren't readily accepted by sales professionals.

As PC technology evolved, so did SAS products. Programs like ACT!, TeleMagic, and Maximizer emerged (see Exhibits 10.1 and 10.2). These products had increased functionality, such as the ability to prepare mass-mailings and to create electronically scheduled reminders. They began showing up at local computer stores, available off-the-shelf at reasonable prices ($75 to $250 per license).

Due to a large installed customer base, a market-leading product like ACT! or TeleMagic was not readily ported to newer technology and could not offer some of the sophisticated new features. In part, these products were limited by their initial design, which used a flat-file database system written in DOS. A flat-file system has some limited database features, such as the capacity to sort data on two axes, such as a spreadsheet. These products would not support a high degree of automated one-to-one marketing.

Some SAS developers targeted the high-end of the market, designing and implementing complex systems for large clients, while others concentrated on off-the-shelf packages to appeal to the mass-market. High-end software companies spent much more time on training, implementation, and consulting than off-the-shelf firms.

SAS imposed cultural changes on the salesforce, so implementation was one of the greatest difficulties encountered by these new software packages. Once organizations had successfully adopted sales software, it was generally difficult to persuade them to switch to a new SAS product even when better products became available. SAS training tended to be long, and a reward/punishment system was often required before new users would embrace sales automation software.

From a management standpoint however, SAS had many advantages. Sales managers had always been frustrated by the loss of "the institutional memory" and the threat to customer loyalty that occurred with sales personnel turnover. Vital information about contacts left with departing salespeople. This created two large problems:

1. Sales organizations had difficulty recapturing this data to maintain customer relationships, and

Exhibit 10.2 ACT advertisement.

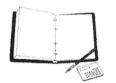

2. Former sales employees often joined the competition who gained an advantage when they used contact information against the company that paid for gathering the data.

With SAS, the data was stored electronically and both problems were alleviated to some degree.

In addition, sales automation software impacted sales activities in a couple of ways. First, SAS handled the large amounts of data processed daily in many sales departments (e.g., prospect status, referral sources, call-back dates). A large part of many sales professionals' day was occupied with paperwork. SAS transformed the documentation process.

Second, SAS could be used to coordinate the sales process. To achieve the most efficient sales cycle required elements from sales, marketing, accounting, inventory management, shipping, and receiving. When it brought these elements together efficiently, an SAS package could bring order to a sometimes chaotic process. Sales automation software helped to bring science to the art of sales.

Finally, SAS products allowed a sales manager to keep in closer contact with sales activities in the field. Since information is electronic, the system could report on such things as the distribution of sales literature, call-back dates, customer complaints, and so on. If properly maintained, the sales process could be handled with increased accountability and profitability.

As the 1990s arrived, the sales automation industry was poised for rapid growth. The information revolution was increasing the power and portability of computers while simultaneously reducing costs. By the early 1990s, computer technology finally seemed ready to serve the least computer-literate segment of the skilled workforce—sales. Worldwide market figures in 1990 placed the SAS market at $166 million. This jumped to $259 million in 1991, and by 1997, total sales worldwide were projected to exceed $2.5 billion. Projected to grow at 40 percent annually, industry analysts predicted that sales and marketing software would be the fastest growing segment of business software through the year 2000.

The reason SAS sales were projected to soar was the bottom line: in 1994, U.S. sales reps who described their use of sales automation software as "extensive" increased their revenue by 20 percent to 30 percent. This gain was equivalent to an additional two full days of selling time each month. With individual performance improvements such as these, SAS was quickly becoming more popular.

Microsoft did not release Windows 3.1 until the early 1990s, and most computers were running contact management software developed on MS-DOS with a flat-file architecture. It was under these market conditions that WinSales, a Windows-based, relational database program, would be introduced.

BILL PERNSTEINER

Bill Pernsteiner grew up in Spokane, Washington, a large town on the plains between the Rockies and Cascade Mountains. He was raised in an entrepreneurial family at a time when computers were just beginning to enter the mainstream of everyday life:

> I come from a family of entrepreneurs. My dad, brothers, and sisters, they have all started their own businesses at one time or another. We all held jobs in high school and developed a strong work ethic. I guess you could say that from early on I have always had sort of an entrepreneurial bent. Computers give power to an individual, so getting into computers was a natural.

As a teenager, Bill discovered that he had a natural ability with computers. One day in his junior year, Bill's math teacher told the class that a computer had been donated to the school. Since no one knew anything about computers, it was still in the box. Bill offered to try to get it running and soon he was computerizing all sorts of things—attendance records, assignments, tests—it was fun.

Soon after, Bill began taking computer classes at a local university, and upon graduating from high school in 1977, he entered college as a computer science major. However, Bill realized that he already knew enough for on-the-job training, so he dropped out of college to become a computer programmer.

After three years of programming in a town known for agricultural wealth, Bill moved West across the Cascade Mountains to Seattle, the home of Microsoft and Boeing. The Puget Sound region was fast becoming a Mecca for software programmers. Bill started a computer systems development business in 1983 and contracted with firms on a per project basis.

Bill met Lisa Wiley in the mid-1980s, and they were wed in April of 1987. They had met through a friend several years earlier while Lisa was still working on her BA in marketing and management at the University of Puget Sound. After their marriage, Lisa continued to work in industrial sales for a chemical company until the birth of their first son in 1990.

In 1987, Bill went to work for CNA, a small systems developer which also performed software contracting services. When Bill joined, there were only eight people in the company. Then Microsoft contracted with CNA for assistance in developing for direct mail, order entry, inventory, and telemarketing software. During his four years on the Microsoft contract, Bill's group grew to 50 people and he was promoted to director of technology at CNA.

Bill had the opportunity to work with the latest software tools available at Microsoft. In fact, he frequently worked with leading-edge software while Microsoft was still testing it, before it was publicly available. Bill participated in the beta testing of many early Microsoft products, including Windows 3.0 and Visual Basic, a programming language that turned out to become an industry standard:

> I had a special opportunity. How often do people get to see the future before it arrives? Visual Basic allowed me to create code that did things that really couldn't be done before, and Windows just made sense. I knew I should be able to spin this combination into gold.

WINSALES INC.

By 1991, Bill had grown tired of the contract programming services business. He didn't like being a "hired gun," providing services on an as-needed basis. Bill wanted to use his experience at Microsoft to develop a software product that would be on the cutting-edge of technology. With a product, he would be paid for value created, not just a day's work.

It was during this time that Bill went to dinner with a fellow programmer and started talking about the things they could do with the new tools being developed by

Microsoft. About four hours later, Bill had a blueprint for WinSales on the back of a napkin—a sales automation package that could be easily customized. One of the problems that Bill often encountered was the inflexibility of software programs:

> It seemed like every time we installed a customized program, someone would walk in the next day and say, "We need to have another feature." Then I would have to tell them that they couldn't have it. I wanted to build a product that could be changed on-the-fly without having to take everyone off-line—that was the plan.

Bill began developing WinSales in his spare time and, in April 1992, he quit his job at CNA to devote his time to WinSales. By this time, Bill was getting close to the beta test and needed money. Bill and Lisa went to friends and family and were able to raise about $75,000 in equity capital. They did not want to take on any debt.

Bill figured that between the money he and Lisa had saved and the seed capital, they could get by for about a year. By then Bill hoped WinSales would start to stand on its own, if not, Bill would do some outside work to support his growing family. Bill and Lisa already had one son, Stuart, and another baby was due shortly. Bill had planned to work full-time out of their home, but Lisa had a different plan. Lisa found an office about a mile from the house and on May 16, 1992—exactly 12 hours before their second child was born—they signed the lease:

> I told Bill, "You have to rent an office." It wouldn't be fair to Stuart, our first son, for Bill to work at home. He wouldn't understand why Daddy was home all day, but couldn't play with him. Bill needed to be out of the house.

WinSales was written for Windows and it was based on state-of-the-art database technology—the relational database. Relational databases operate on a three dimensional scale, allowing users to correlate information between more than just two fields. This type of system could be more than just a contact management system: It allowed users to develop custom-applications in ways that were not possible under the old architecture of the DOS-based systems.

Having developed software for sales organizations on several occasions, Bill knew that there was a wide range of sales information needs. He contacted SAS guru Rich Boehm for advice. Rich was a proponent of adding a selling strategy component to sales automation software. Rich tested WinSales and suggested that he meet with Jim Cecil about how to systemize client communications, what they called "drip irrigation marketing."

In the end, Bill developed a customizable, "smart information path" for WinSales that he called an "action plan." An action plan allowed a sales representative to guide a prospect through the steps most likely to optimize the relationship. Basically, an action plan was a decision tree of contact options based on segmentation data: industry, title, interest level, company status, and other factors. One company using WinSales could have as few as two action plans (e.g., the world would be divided into two types of people: prospects and customers), where another might have a complex segmentation resulting in a couple dozen action plans (e.g., media—advocate, prospect—skeptic, customer—CEO, etc.). In addition, contacts could have multiple action plans (e.g., when a customer's birthday was known, that customer would be assigned to the birthday action plan, see Exhibit 10.3). Each new contact would

Exhibit 10.3   WinSales action plan screen shot.

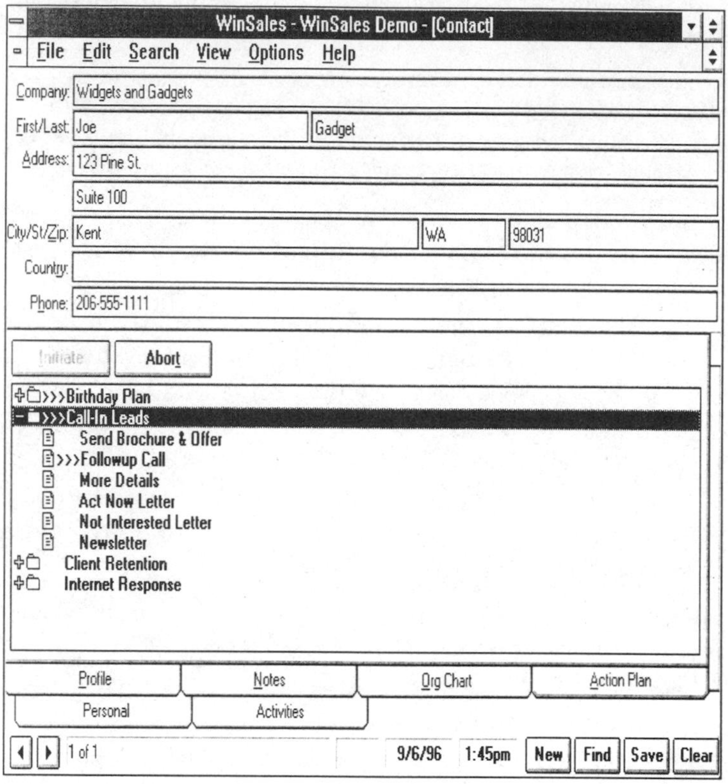

be assigned to an action plan or plans that would automatically map out the next step in the relationship. Once selected, an action plan could be in place indefinitely, or change with changes in status, depending on the applied wisdom of the sales management team.

The first step of an action plan for prospects might be to send a product brochure and a letter informing the prospect to expect a phone call "later this week." Then later in the week, WinSales would generate a phone list indicating which accounts were promised a phone call. Action plans allowed management to take a lot of the unpredictability out of the sales process. Management could make sure letters were sent, that complaints were resolved, and that contacts were prioritized according to company standards. The most important benefit was that the sales manager could segment the market, then customize action plans to focus his expertise on each type of relationship. The use of the action plan allowed a firm to move away from mass-marketing to mass-customization, or one-to-one marketing.

Bill handled the technical aspects of developing WinSales, and Lisa handled everything else: from dealing with beta site users to managing the office. As the product evolved, it began to look very promising. The concept was new and no other contact management software was as powerful—there really wasn't anything else like it out in the market. It was difficult to determine where this product would fit in, but as the release date drew near, Lisa recalled planning to market the product:

> We started trying to find out how contact management software was sold. We knew we couldn't get shelf space, so we actually went to the library looking for magazines advertising comparable products. Where did our competitors advertise? We knew that we had a product that was competitive with Goldmine and ACT! but we had no idea how they marketed their products. It was by sheer luck that Bill was sitting in a doctor's office and happened to pick up a magazine called *Personal Selling Power*. Our competitors were advertising in this magazine! Bill came back to the office so excited, saying, "I found it! I found it!" That is where we first started advertising.

Their first advertisement came out in December of 1992. They placed a quarter page display ad in the back of the *Personal Selling Power* (see Exhibit 10.4 for a copy of the ad that appeared in the November/December 1993 issue of *Personal Selling Power*.) In April of 1993, WinSales was launched with ads in a variety of magazines. But by late-1993, sales were not as brisk as Bill and Lisa had hoped. Bill spoke about some of the obstacles that WinSales was facing at the time:

> WinSales had very low name recognition and people who knew the name didn't know what to make of the product. We were a brand new technology in a fairly new industry running on a platform that was not yet widely accepted. This was in 1993 remember, and the mainstream computing world was still running on DOS. Microsoft Windows 3.1 wasn't out yet, and Windows wasn't widely accepted at the time. To add to our problems, we were competing against highly successful, widely recognized products like ACT! and Goldmine, which were still running on a DOS platform.

WinSales ads generated quite a few phone calls because the product had a good bundle of benefits, but not many calls were turning into sales. Bill and Lisa were worried about their poor closing rate. They were wasting precious time without generating much revenue. Lisa felt that the answer was to advertise more, in a focused direction. In addition to advertising in *Personal Selling Power,* she wanted to purchase the magazine's mailing list and implement a direct marketing campaign. She felt that directly targeting these subscribers would increase WinSales' brand recognition and give them the edge over the competition. They knew they had a great product, but WinSales needed to start making money soon. They needed to generate a better return on the advertising dollars spent: their bank account was shrinking. They also knew they had to hire a full-time salesperson right now, and they hoped their sales trainer/marketing consultant Torrey Russell would join the team.

TORREY RUSSELL, THE WIZARD OF OZ

Torrey Russell received his MBA from Babson College in 1978. Upon graduation, Torrey accepted a job in a small New England, hi-tech firm as director of sales and marketing. The company grew exponentially, but Torrey discovered that he had liked the job better when it was still a small company. He sold his stock options and took a similar job with another struggling high-tech start-up. Sales grew from under $100,000 to over $2 million in two years as he had become quite skilled at bootstrap marketing.

Exhibit 10.4   November 1993 page from *Personal Selling Power* magazine.

He had a falling out with the founder, so he left and founded his own company—as a competitor to his former employer. Again, Torrey had no problem finding the market's pulse and sales revenues grew rapidly:

> I like to create the Wizard of Oz effect for companies who need to market on a real tight budget—I make them appear to be larger than they really are. It's what I do best. I prefer performing tricks in a biplane to commanding a 747. It's just what I was built to do.

In the early 1990s, Torrey started a family and decided to move West, which he thought was a more wholesome place to raise children. He sold his business and set out to find a high-tech start-up opportunity in Seattle. He met Bill and Lisa in the Fall of 1993. Torrey had written a business plan for a mutual friend, who introduced them. The relationship was informal at first, with Torrey offering sales and marketing advice, but he quickly saw the potential of WinSales and decided to help with sales training.

Exciting things were happening at this time, despite the lagging sales. Action Plans made WinSales unlike any other contact management software. They had a great product, but Bill recalled that its uniqueness created problems:

> Our product was much better than the competition. If ACT! was like Marketing 101, WinSales was like Marketing 501, but no one knew it. We were too far ahead of the market. The market didn't know what to think about us.

Torrey was concerned that WinSales was not well enough understood. He was also concerned with the number of unqualified leads that were being generated. He knew Bill and Lisa wondered about this, but he worried that maybe they didn't see the cause of the problem. To him, the problem was the ads. Running advertisements in a magazine generated leads, but were they educated leads? Action plans were something completely new to the market. In Torrey's mind, running ads did not educate their potential clients to the real technological advantages of WinSales. How could it? The ads were small and run in the same magazines as their competitors! Why would anyone believe that WinSales was superior to ACT! and Maximizer when WinSales paid for the advertisements making the claims? To the prospect, they were all out of the same mold, and Torrey wanted to break the mold.

One of the first changes Torrey had insisted upon after the relationship became formalized in November of 1993 was using WinSales better. They weren't effectively managing their own database. They committed to putting all their leads into WinSales:

> Here we were, trying to sell people on this wonderful sales tool that would allow them to keep their prospects from falling through the cracks, and we weren't even using it ourselves! We weren't following up with each lead, and few got placed onto action plans! If we weren't using our product effectively, how could we expect others to see the benefits of using our product?

Implementing SAS was never easy, even at WinSales, Inc. Torrey ran into the same resistance faced by sales managers everywhere: contact activity slipping through the cracks. Bill was the worst. Lisa finally threaten to fire him if he took one more phone call that didn't get recorded in WinSales.

Soon all incoming leads were placed into the database. They began by looking at each prospect's history, evaluating where they were in the sales cycle, and then placing them on an appropriate action plan. The importance of this issue became apparent as they started to sort through the piles of old leads. As they added up the names, more than half of the prospective clients in their database had never received a follow-up contact.

TORREY'S PROPOSALS

Bill sat in his office and pondered his most recent meeting with Torrey Russell. While Torrey's proposed course of action seemed too extreme, Bill was impressed with the ideas that Torrey had offered as alternatives to traditional advertising. "Torrey said it was just drip irrigation marketing but would it work without advertising?"

Torrey wanted to purchase a list of editors and place them all on action plans. "We are selling a relationship marketing tool, so why not use it to educate opinion leaders and get free press?" Bill recalled Torrey saying. They would design a media communications plan to motivate editors to write stories about WinSales. By developing relationships with the press, Torrey believed WinSales would generate more product awareness and credibility than through print ads, and at less cost.

Another idea that Torrey talked about involved trade shows. Bill thought this idea was especially intriguing: Torrey wanted to stop "attending" trade shows, he said:

> We need to work trade shows differently. We will go around to all the booths and pick up business cards, ask for the name of the VP of Marketing and write it on the back. We will hand them our business card, and say, "I'm sorry, no time, just send me your literature, thanks." We'll go through the whole show in about an hour. We will leave with a stack of cards, and enter them into action plans that evening. The first letter will go out three days later and say, "I gave my card to someone at the show, at your booth, and we haven't received your literature. By the way, we're wondering what you are doing with all of those leads in front of you, because you could be using a product just like this!" Then we will describe action plans and one other feature that would appeal most to that prospect and end the letter with, "Please see the enclosed brochure."
>
> All those that don't respond will get another letter five days later, saying, "It has now been eight days since I attended this show. What have you done with my literature—I still don't have it!" Of course, the cards will still be sitting on their desk and by now they'll be embarrassed. By the third letter they will be on the phone wanting to buy WinSales. We shouldn't attend trade shows, we should attack them! Guerrilla marketing warfare! To advertise in the back of a magazine and wait for people to call is no way to create the Wizard of Oz effect.

Another of Torrey's ideas involved seminars. Torrey suggested giving seminars to groups of early adopters. As he explained it, WinSales would generate business by arranging for a speaker on a hot subject like "networking," for instance:

> By providing a speaker that uses WinSales, we will be able to arrange for virtually cost-free exposure of our product to a highly focused group of prospects. If done correctly, WinSales will be able to co-sponsor these events with other groups that would be willing to trade-out the costs of producing the seminar in exchange for free product. This will allow us to produce events with minimal cost and maximum benefits.

As Bill reviewed his notes from the meeting, he realized that Torrey might be right. It was evident Torrey believed that he could make WinSales profitable through this type of promotion, but Bill was still unsure as to how he felt about this approach. He didn't want to try to act like the Wizard of Oz and instead, end up looking like the sorcerer's apprentice.

Bill placed his notes back in his briefcase and stood up. He walked over to his window and stared down at the traffic below. Lisa had made suggestions, too—sales were finally starting to pick up—a little bit. She wanted to increase the marketing budget to go after the people who read *Personal Selling Power* magazine. After a year of advertising, maybe WinSales was beginning to gain a foothold in the market:

> Torrey told us that we have a 6- to 8-month sales cycle, so maybe we are about to start reaping the rewards of our advertising. On the other hand, maybe Torrey is right about drip irrigation marketing. He has some great ideas, and we certainly need him to man the phones. I also have to admit that we need to educate the market better. Lisa's suggestion of a direct mail campaign might be the answer to educating the market, but then again, it might not. If it doesn't work, our financial situation will become even more critical. But I am afraid that if we stop advertising now, it could be the end of my company as well.

11 CLEARVUE

Brooks O'Kane sat in his chair on the front porch staring at a bottle of ClearVue glass cleaner. He was wondering in what direction he should go with this product. He had taken it from being mixed once a week in a vat in his father-in-law's warehouse to a $4 million business in direct competition with the nation's top glass cleaners.

As the success of ClearVue grew, Brooks' choices narrowed. In a short time, Brooks had done wonders marketing the product in two different categories. Distribution was spilt 50/50 between regional grocery accounts and national automotive accounts. However, with each marketing success he achieved, he learned there were many other variables that must be considered if success was to continue, and the product was to compete nationwide in either distribution channel.

ClearVue's prosperity was remarkable given the company's human-resource overhead. Due to a large order from Wal-Mart, the company had been forced to outsource production and transportation, in effect, making ClearVue, a virtual corporation with sales of $2 million per employee.

As he sat on his front porch, Brooks thought about the challenges of marketing ClearVue. The grocery market had needs quite unlike the automotive market. Both markets demanded his full attention across the board: public relations, advertising, packaging, product development, direct sales, and marketing. Something had to give, and Brooks knew his decisions weren't as clear as the bottle of glass cleaner before him.

This case was prepared by Dan D'Heilly, Andrea Alyse, and Carole Guarante under the direction of Professor William Bygrave. Funding provided by the Ewing Marion Kauffman Foundation. Copyright © 1996 Babson College. All rights reserved.

BROOKS O'KANE

Brooks had graduated from a New Hampshire state college in 1983, with a degree in marketing. He then worked as an account executive in one of the area's larger advertising agencies before moving to a smaller agency where he felt he would have more creative input, but that agency went out of business in the late 1980s. Brooks then focused his energy on renovating investment properties until a subsequent industry downturn:

> The real estate market died. I didn't make a dime. I didn't lose a dime, but I probably wasted two years of my life.

At about this time, Brooks' father-in-law and president of Lawrence Plate Glass, Walter Demers, Jr., approached him about becoming the marketing director of his small family-run glass business in Lawrence, Massachusetts (see Exhibit 11.1). Brooks became the Lawrence Plate Glass Company's director of marketing in 1989. His first priority had been developing a consistent image. The company had six locations, and they all had different letterheads, logos, and signage. One day, several months later, Demers appeared in the doorway of Brooks' office and asked him to "take care of ClearVue," the company's $60,000 a year, glass-cleaning product. Brooks got the distinct impression that this was not considered an important assignment.

GLASS CLEANER INDUSTRY

The $160 million glass-cleaner segment of the cleaning-products market was dominated by three major players in the early 1990s: Windex, Glass Plus, and SOS Glass Works. Windex, the industry leader, with a marketshare of almost 45 percent, was wholly owned by Bristol-Myers Squibb. Glass Plus, owned by Dow Chemical, and SOS Glass Works, owned by Miles Inc., a subsidiary of Germany's Bayer conglomerate, each

EXHIBIT 11.1   Lawrence Plate Glass Co.—1989 profile.

Total sales: $18 million
Employees: 150

Branch locations:

Lawrence, MA (3 locations)	Beverly, MA
Haverhill, MA	Manchester, NH
Lowell, MA	Lewiston, ME

Business segment breakdown:

Residential Glass & Repair	$5,000,000
Wholesale Glass Division	3,000,000
Contract Glazing Division	8,000,000
Garage Door Division	2,000,000
ClearVue Glass Cleaner	60,000

had approximately a 15 percent marketshare. The remaining 25 percent of the market was mostly made up of private-label and regional brands.

Because total industry sales in this market were flat, allotted grocery shelf-space in this category remained constant, and competition had intensified. Brooks recalled the competitive response when ClearVue gained a regional marketshare of only 4.5 percent:

> The deals and promotions were incredible. The Cinch product came out and Procter & Gamble spent a fortune on it. Then they came out with another product that was the same exact product and called it Mr. Clean . . . exact same bottle, different color. This made me mad because they were trying to dominate the shelves, and keep people like me off—and they had the money to do it.

However, increased competition also resulted in the creation of niche segments. Industrial-strength, environmentally friendly, private-label, and regional cleaning products such as ClearVue, were a growing segment in this otherwise mature industry. In addition, throughout the 1990s, consumers became increasingly price-sensitive to the cost of cleaning products and more willing to substitute a regional or private-label brand, sometimes saving as much as 50 percent.

Although the automotive cleaning-products segment was dominated by players such as Armor-All and Turtle Wax, the automotive glass-cleaning segment remained fragmented through 1995. Total after-market retail sales in the automotive cleaning-products segment grew almost 84 percent from 1994 to 1995, from $270 million to $322.4 million. Retailers averaged a 47.4 percent gross margin on sales of these products in 1995, slightly lower than the 1994 average gross margin of 51.5 percent, and projected a 6.3 percent growth in this category for 1996. Automotive chains and discount stores were the best channels for glass cleaner in 1995, but nonauto retailers and department stores also achieved success in selling automotive glass-cleaning agents.

Opportunity Knocks: ClearVue

Walter Demers Sr. founded Lawrence Plate Glass in 1918. In about 1950, he developed ClearVue because he needed a product that cleaned glass better and more cheaply than those already available on the market. A low-tech operation, it was mixed by an employee on Saturday mornings in a corner of his plant in a 300-gallon tub. Originally, he had no intention of selling it, but people asked what he used at the shop, so Demers packaged ClearVue for sale:

> It became popular by word of mouth. People loved it. When people vacationed in Boston, or moved from Boston, they took ClearVue with them across the country. ClearVue never advertised, but it developed a loyal, cult-like following.

When Brooks became director of marketing, ClearVue was still being made in a tub in the back of the company's warehouse by a guy named Bert. Brooks' father-in-law gave him an old accounts receivable ledger and a file of ClearVue fan letters from around the world. Brooks became convinced that there was additional market potential for this product:

I knew right then and there—I had to do something with this. It amazed me that people would write fan mail about a glass cleaner. I knew I had a terrific product and a great story. Then I thought about this guy Bert out back with an oak paddle. I thought, "I've got Bartle and James, the Keebler Elves, and Ben & Jerry all rolled into one. I can do something with this."

But before Brooks would tell the story, he wanted to refine his presentation.

Clearly Superior Packaging

One of Brooks' first moves was to improve the old ClearVue package because he knew that sometimes people sampled new products simply because they liked the way they looked. After meeting with a package designer who wanted a hefty $25,000 to redesign ClearVue, Brooks knew he had to find a creative solution. He decided instead to work on the design project with the graphic artist who had done his newspaper advertisements:

> My whole objective was to have a label that looked as good as the product worked. I wanted clean, crisp, different, top-shelf all the way, but I couldn't pay top-shelf prices. I paid $2,500 and we won three national packaging awards. All of it was decided by gut feelings and talking with people—no focus groups or any market research. It was bootstrap marketing at its finest.

The "quality first" strategy also applied to the bottle Brooks chose for ClearVue, which had previously been in a drab white plastic bottle. The glass-cleaning industry was already using PVC (a clear plastic material), but Brooks decided to use PET (a higher grade of clear plastic than PVC). Although $.01 more per bottle, PET is both easier to recycle and clearer in appearance—setting ClearVue's packaging apart from the rest. Also, his competitors were dyeing their liquids blue, while ClearVue remained true to its name—clear. Since then, competitors have adopted many of ClearVue's strategies:

> Now everyone is using the best PET plastic and clear liquid. We caught the front end of a trend.

To further emphasize the high quality appearance, Brooks decided to use special labels that allowed him to print on both sides, so that consumers could read the story of Bert on the back of the label—right through the liquid in the bottle.

PPG Industries

Demers, however, didn't initially share his son-in-law's enthusiasm. He did not want Brooks to grow ClearVue. He simply wanted to free up the person who was managing it, so that person would have more time for other things. As a result, Brooks wore two hats for a couple of years. In addition to being the marketing director of Lawrence Plate Glass, he was the sole person marketing ClearVue:

> For a long time, it was kind of like I was making phone calls when he (Demers) wasn't looking. I gradually wore him down. I had some early successes that opened his eyes. The key one was PPG (Pittsburgh Plate Glass) Industries, the world's largest glass

company. When I told my father-in-law I was going after it—he literally laughed in my face—but I got their business.

In 1989 Brooks called the local PPG branch that Lawrence Plate Glass dealt with to get the corporate number. He was lucky. Within ten minutes of picking up the phone, he was talking to the PPG sundries and accessories buyer in their corporate office, who told him, "Brooks, your timing is perfect. We need a better glass cleaner." At the buyer's request, Brooks sent samples to 100 PPG warehouses along with a questionnaire about ClearVue. Within four months, they had a contract with PPG. PPG became ClearVue's exclusive glass industry distributor in North America:

> PPG is a $7 billion glass company. If I knew at the beginning what I know now, I would never have done it. I would have been too smart. I would never have picked up the phone and asked. It's like the pretty woman not getting any dates because everyone is too intimidated to ask. I learned you can pick up the phone and call anyone. Don't assume anything—just do it. The PPG sale is what opened my father-in-law's eyes to the potential of ClearVue.

ClearVue became a separate company at the end of 1989, with Brooks owning a majority of the stock. There were three other stockholders, two family members and one key employee of Lawrence Plate Glass.

Distribution

While looking at old sales records, Brooks noticed that ClearVue had one grocery store client—so why not go after others? He successfully landed a couple of small accounts, but was advised to get a food broker if he wanted to pursue larger ones.

Brooks was referred to Chase, Kolbin, and Allen, one of the largest food brokers in New England, which managed national accounts like Coca Cola and Clorox. Brooks called and asked to speak directly to senior partner Freeman Chase, who was impressed with Brooks' enthusiasm and passed his name along to an account manager. However, Brooks was not satisfied with being assigned to an account manager, so he asked Chase to attend his presentation to the account management team. Everyone, except Brooks, was surprised when Chase showed up at the ClearVue account meeting:

> Freeman became my mentor and personally managed the ClearVue account. You go in with a regular account manager and you talk to associate buyers. With Freeman, we went in three levels up—he knows people who make the real decisions. This was a huge advantage. I came in with a lot of credibility.

Freeman advised Brooks, "Don't make price a barrier for people sampling the product—there's always time to raise the price down the road." As a result, Brooks set the price 30 cents cheaper than national brands, such as Windex, in the grocery stores.

Prohibitive slotting fees were an obstacle to ClearVue's grocery distribution. Stop and Shop's fee at that time, for instance, was $25,000 per item. Brooks creatively negotiated around slotting fees, mostly with agreements that included payment-in-kind. Sometimes he would offer a pallet of product at wholesale in lieu of cash for most of the slotting fee, then about 10 percent of the fee in cash. He also negotiated deals that induced grocers to actively promote ClearVue. For example, he negotiated one slotting fee that consisted of a 5 percent discount per case for the first six months, with a cash guarantee at the end of six months if the additional profit fell short of the slotting fee. However, if the store sold more than the fee would have generated, it was theirs to keep, thereby motivating them to give ClearVue good placement and promotion.

Initially, Brooks estimated it would take a good three years to get grocery distribution in New England. However, he made presentations to Stop and Shop, Star Market, and Purity Supreme and they all signed deals the same day. In three months, ClearVue had achieved an 80 percent New England market penetration.

Braced by his success with PPG and the New England grocers, Brooks went after Wal-Mart. He tried letters and phone calls to Wal-Mart buyers, all without success, so he sent a handwritten note to the top decision maker, Sam Walton: "Sam, I need your help . . . I'm a young guy just starting out and I've got the best glass cleaner in the world . . ." Soon after, a household buyer from Wal-Mart called Brooks to order 15,000 cases of ClearVue as a test. Although ClearVue held its own against the other glass-cleaner giants, it did not earn a permanent place in the household section. Next, Brooks called Wal-Mart's automotive buyer and convinced him that ClearVue would attract women shoppers to the automotive department. Brooks had created a new market niche, complete with national distribution.

When Wal-Mart ordered those 15,000 cases, they didn't know that ClearVue had produced only 72 cases at any one time. Not only had ClearVue grown beyond grocery store aisles and into automotive, it had also outgrown Bert's paddling in the back room. Unable to fulfill the order, Brooks stopped producing ClearVue and hired a New Hampshire contract bottler.

Getting the ClearVue Word Out

Brooks knew how to get free publicity from his days in advertising. He collected magazine and newspaper editorial schedules, then contacted editors to fit the ClearVue story into their publications. Every time a story ran, people would call him with ideas about everything from chemical suppliers to food brokers to package designers. Consultants began coming to Brooks instead of his having to track them down. He also made use of other innovative marketing to get the ClearVue word out. He told the folksy, fun ClearVue story wherever and whenever he could, gave out samples everywhere he went, and personally answered every fan letter with a handwritten reply:

> If someone's wacko enough about my product to write me a letter, I not only want to keep that person as a customer, I want to turn them into a salesperson. That's why I take the time to write them a handwritten note and send them coupons. It's something the big guys can't duplicate.

Brooks also pens an annual newsletter, which is sent to anyone who has a connection with his product (see Exhibit 11.2). It was sent to 7,500 people in 1995!

In addition to having many articles written about ClearVue, Brooks has also appeared on the television show *Chronicle* with the ClearVue story. It took him a

Exhibit 11.2   ClearVue newsletter.

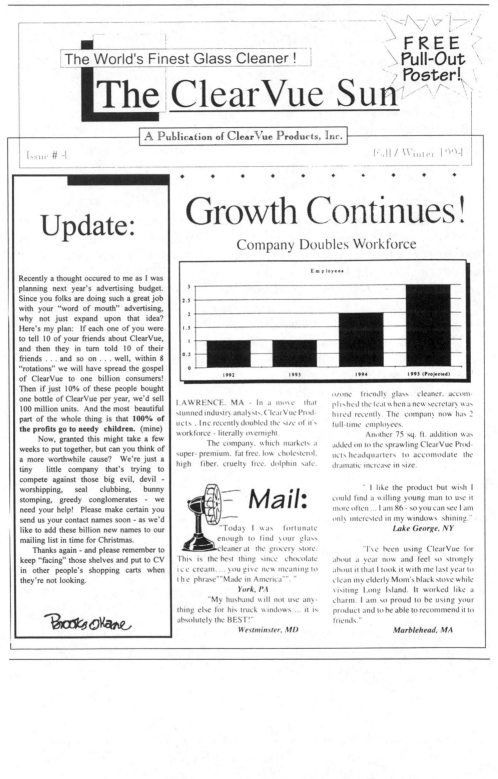

The World's Finest Glass Cleaner !

FREE Pull-Out Poster!

The ClearVue Sun

A Publication of ClearVue Products, Inc.

Issue # 4   Fall / Winter 1994

Update:

Recently a thought occured to me as I was planning next year's advertising budget. Since you folks are doing such a great job with your "word of mouth" advertising, why not just expand upon that idea? Here's my plan: If each one of you were to tell 10 of your friends about ClearVue, and then they in turn told 10 of their friends . . . and so on . . . well, within 8 "rotations" we will have spread the gospel of ClearVue to one billion consumers! Then if just 10% of these people bought one bottle of ClearVue per year, we'd sell 100 million units. And the most beautiful part of the whole thing is that **100% of the profits go to needy children.** (mine)

Now, granted this might take a few weeks to put together, but can you think of a more worthwhile cause? We're just a tiny little company that's trying to compete against those big evil, devil-worshipping, seal clubbing, bunny stomping, greedy conglomerates - we need your help! Please make certain you send us your contact names soon - as we'd like to add these billion new names to our mailing list in time for Christmas.

Thanks again - and please remember to keep "facing" those shelves and put to CV in other people's shopping carts when they're not looking.

Brooks O'Kane

Growth Continues!

Company Doubles Workforce

LAWRENCE, MA - In a move that stunned industry analysts, ClearVue Products , Inc recently doubled the size of it's workforce - literally overnight.

The company, which markets a super-premium, fat free, low cholesterol, high fiber, cruelty free, dolphin safe,

Mail:

"Today I was fortunate enough to find your glass cleaner at the grocery store. This is the best thing since chocolate ice cream. ... you give new meaning to the phrase""Made in America"". "
York, PA

"My husband will not use anything else for his truck windows ... it is absolutely the BEST!"
Westminster, MD

ozone friendly glass cleaner, accomplished the feat when a new secretary was hired recently. The company now has 2 full-time employees.

Another 75 sq. ft. addition was added on to the sprawling ClearVue Products headquarters to accomodate the dramatic increase in size.

" I like the product but wish I could find a willing young man to use it more often ... I am 86 - so you can see I am only interested in my windows shining."
Lake George, NY

"I've been using ClearVue for about a year now and feel so strongly about it that I took it with me last year to clean my elderly Mom's black stove while visiting Long Island. It worked like a charm. I am so proud to be using your product and to be able to recommend it to friends."
Marblehead, MA

Exhibit 11.2 *(Continued)*

The ClearVue Sun

Current Accounts

· · · · · · · · · · · · · · · · · · · ·

We get a tremendous amount of calls and letters from consumers looking for a supply of ClearVue. Even though we still have a long, long way to go in having truly national distribution, most consumers can get their hands on a bottle. Much of the reason for this is the fact that we landed the Wal-Mart account **(in the <u>automotive</u> section)** several years ago. They pretty much cover 48 of the 50 states.

Below is a listing of some of our major accounts around the country.

Note: Any account with an "A" next to it signifies an <u>automotive</u> store or that it would appear in the <u>automotive section</u> of that particular chain. If you can't find it, please call us (508) 794-3100.

New England:
Stop & Shop
Shaws
Star Mkt.
BJ's Wholesale Club
DeMoulas/Mkt. Basket
A&P / Foodmart
Finast/Edwards
Shop & Save
Purity Supreme
Almacs
Bradlees (A)
Auto Palace (A)
VIP Discount Auto (A)
Spags
Aubuchon Hardware
Ames (A)
Hills (A)
Caldor (A)
The Fair
Ann & Hope
Christy's Mkt.

New England (cont.)
Big Y
Victory Markets
Big D
Benny's
Ann & Hope

PA/NJ:
Weis Mkts.
Acme Markets
Genuardi Mkts.
Clemens
Giant Food
Fox's Markets
Jamesway (A)
Pep Boy's (A)
Clover (A)
Scott Grocery
R&S (A)

Florida:
Pep Boy's (A)
Wal-Mart (A)
Discount Auto (A)
BJ's Wholesale Club
Rose Auto (A)

IL:
Pep Boys (A)
Wal-Mart (A)
Straus Auto (A)

MI:
Murray's Automotive

Texas / AZ:
Pep Boys (A)
Wal-Mart (A)

California:
Pep Boys (A)
Wal-Mart (A)
FEDCO (A)

New York:
Price Chopper
Tops Markets
Shop n' Save
Wheels (A)
Great American/Victory
Aid Auto

Who Uses What?
Recent Poll Very Revealing

| Windex | ClearVue |

(Continued)

Exhibit 11.2 *(Continued)*

The ClearVue Sun

ClearVue Organizational Chart

Duties Re-defined in Restructuring

> Brooks O'Kane
> President

> Michelle Ordway
> Secretary

O'Kane   Ordway

Job Duties /Descriptions:

O'Kane - Customer golf and ski outings, writes company newsletter, schmoozes with other high-powered CEO types, selects "Employee of the Month", waters plants and a whole lot of other **really important** stuff.

Ordway - New business development, vendor relations, finance, marketing/advertising, logistics, market research, inventory control, production, office management , chemical engineering and customer service.

... fan mail

"I was at the hardware store and the lady working there strongly recommended ClearVue ... have never been so pleased ... telling everyone I know about it".
Roanoke, VA

"I can't believe how good your glass cleaner works ... everything sparkles with very little effort."
Indianapolis, IN

"As soon as our monsoons subsided, I went to our Wal-Mart and cleaned out their stock of ClearVue."
Park Ridge, IL

"I'm hooked on ClearVue...it is the product of my dreams!"
Tenants Harbor, ME

"in my 62 years of washing windows, this is by far the very best cleaner I've ever used."
Chittenango, NY

"I LOVE IT!!!"
Woodbury, MN

"Help - I need ClearVue... I'll travel anywhere within 40 miles of Detroit to get some."
Detroit, MI

Strange Uses for ClearVue

Over the years we've received letters from some of our customers touting CV's effectiveness at cleaning surfaces other than glass, mirrors, windshields etc.

Among the more unusual submissions:

- Cleans golf balls, clubs and shoes
- Shines military boots
- "Spray my chandelier with it."
- " gets the St. Bernard slobber off my car windows".
- Cleans Poodle pee off the floor.
- Removes tree frog guts from sliding doors.
- Eliminates puppy "nose art"
- Uses as a nail polish remover
- Bug killer
- Mace Substitute
- Cleans Iguana spit
- Carpet Cleaner
- Cleans Marine Corp Sword
- Jewelry Cleaner
- Automotive wheel cleaner
- Chalkboards
- "Great for cleaning computers !"
- "clean my best crystal with it"
- Bowling Balls

NOTE: We do not recommend using CV on carpets, shoes, wood, painted surfaces or plastics.

Exhibit 11.2   (Continued)

Misc. Tidbits

• Visiting Lawrence, MA? Well why not take a tour of ClearVue Products World Headquarters? FREE tours are offered Mon. - Fri. 8:00 AM - 5:00 PM. Due to space constraints tours are limited to one person each.

• The geniuses at Windex recently added a "Potpouri" scented glass cleaner to their product mix. *(Now, that deserves a Nobel prize.)*

• We will sell approximately 350,000 gallons of ClearVue this year - or to put it another way, enough glass cleaner to fill 350,000 one gallon containers. *(I think)*

• If you are dead or have recently relocated, please let us know so that we can update our mailing list.

CV Makes Mag Cover
Spring Edition of "Your Company"

Note: Thanks to my Mom this issue of "Your Company" was a complete sellout. She still has several thousand copies if anyone needs one.

... fan mail

"ClearVue is absolutely terrific ... really is great ... I saw you on TV the other night - hurrah for the little guy."
Yonkers, NY

"... it really does a superior job ... God bless you!"
Hauppauge, NY

"I used to buy Windex, but was never satisfied ... ClearVue is GREAT! ... it's the only one that doesn't leave streaks."
Crown Point, IN

"Nothing like doing the windows once and not having to worry about streaks."
Vernon, CT

"I am a day care Mom ... ClearVue is the best!"
Pasadena, MD

ClearVue Products, Inc.
P.O. Box 567
Lawrence, MA 01842

TO:

Our Favorite Customer!

The World's Finest Glass Cleaner

couple of years of lobbying the show's producers to get his chance in the spotlight. At one point, he had a plaque made and sent to the producers, inscribed "I do hereby declare on April 1, that I will appear on *Chronicle* before Dec. 31." Then, through his newsletter, he organized a write-in campaign for supporters to help him get on the show.

Initially, Brooks didn't have enough money to pay for advertising. However, as revenues increased, he decided to buy time on talk radio because "people don't push those buttons" and ClearVue appealed to the talk radio audience—women over 35 years old.

NEW ROADS: NEW CHALLENGES

Brooks' problems with automotive and grocery vendors were not the same:

> What's becoming an issue, and I'm surprised it's not more of an issue on the grocery side, is being a one-SKU vendor. Automotive departments are constantly wanting to reduce the number of vendors and items they carry.
>
> I had an advantage initially because there weren't any auto-glass cleaners out there—now they are coming out of the woodwork. Why would they want to buy an auto glass cleaner from me when they can buy it from Armor-All or Turtle Wax or someone like that, when they are already buying 50 other items from them? Why have to cut another purchase order and have to set me up as another vendor?
>
> The grocery stores were more concerned with promotional support and slotting fees. First you pay your way in, then they want you to produce coupons and FSIs, so you have to pay to keep your spot.

The biggest decision Brooks pondered while sitting on his porch was: Should he align himself with automotive or grocery? He needed to find someone who could provide an automotive product line, or a food distributor who could help finance his national expansion. He felt compelled to find a distributor for one line or the other:

> I need to be focused. I don't have the resources, personnel, or money to be good at the automotive, the hardware, the club stores, the grocery stores . . . I can't do it all—it's too sophisticated. The one SKU thing is a problem, and I don't have the resources to have a broad product line on both the grocery and automotive sides.

While Brooks and his secretary had run the ClearVue show, he was now considering hiring a marketing professional to help him expand. Brooks thought that ClearVue was generating enough cash to grow (see Exhibit 11.3).

EXHIBIT 11.3 ClearVue operations—1995.

Sales	$4,000,000
Cash	85,000
Accounts receivable	535,000
Inventory	329,000
Total current assets	$ 975,000
Accounts payable	412,000
Total current liabilities	$ 418,000
Gross profit	39%
Net profit	6%

OPPORTUNITY KNOCKS (AGAIN): RED CROSS NURSE

Brooks was leaning toward grocery because another product opportunity had just about fallen in his lap. The 68-year-old owner of Red Cross Nurse (RCN), a household cleaning product, was looking to retire and had approached Brooks about the possibility of selling the company to him:

> He sees my distribution and sales expertise. I have access to the Wal-Marts and Kmarts; a royalty on my sales is more than he's making now.
>
> Basically, its like a no-money-down real estate deal: I pay a token payment up front of $2,500, guarantee of a couple of thousand a month as a base, and 5 percent of sales for 10 years. The total payment is capped at $500,000. Then I own the brand outright—I would own the name, "Red Cross Nurse!" I can't even guess at how much the name *Red Cross* is worth.

A few days after the owner of RCN approached him, Brooks was visiting one of his major supermarket accounts when his buyer told him RCN was a very good product. RCN had been around since 1869. Previously a well-established brand, its sales peaked at $500,000 in 1990, but had declined precipitously (see Exhibit 11.4 on page 198). Brooks had heard from a friend that disinfectants were a good market. He felt that if he bought RCN, not only could he could turn the company around, but, in addition to having two grocery items, he could basically put any product under his brands—as long as it cleaned or killed germs—to build a grocery product line:

> The owner of RCN has a lousy package, and he doesn't do any promotion or advertising. I think RCN has great potential—this could be even bigger than ClearVue.

PREPARATION QUESTIONS

1. Compare and contrast Brooks O'Kane's entrepreneurial methods with those prescribed in classical marketing texts.
2. What are your recommendations to Brooks as he contemplates the future of his company?
3. Should Brooks buy Red Cross Nurse?
4. If you think he should buy Red Cross Nurse, recommend a marketing strategy for the product.

**EXHIBIT 11.4   Red Cross Nurse income statement,
March 31, 1994.**

	3/94	4/93–3/94
Income:		
Sales	$16,959	$227,100
Sales discount	(197)	(3,477)
Net sales	$16,762	$223,623
Cost of goods sold:		
Beginning inventory	0	(2,892)
Purchases alcohol	5,132	20,333
Purchases oils	3,974	11,981
Purchases boxes	0	2,643
Purchases bottles	671	22,345
Purchases sprayers	4,160	12,325
Purchases chemicals	117	1,981
Ending inventory	(8,812)	(346)
Total cost of goods sold	5,243	68,369
Gross profit	$11,519	$155,254
Expenses:		
Salaries	3,950	53,578
Payroll taxes	313	4,268
Advertising	31	1,815
Auto expense	674	6,852
Bank service charges	12	263
Commissions	970	6,240
Coupons	185	3,099
Dues & subscriptions	40	1,018
Pesticide registration	0	1,133
Delivery expense	270	2,269
Insurance	2,573	30,258
Miscellaneous expense	0	83
Office expense	390	6,968
Professional fees	0	1,060
Rent	1,000	12,000
Repairs & maintenance	(33)	1,328
Sub-contractor	249	2,227
Taxes	0	4,425
Entertainment	36	1,344
Travel	0	143
Utilities	390	5,617
Total expenses	$11,052	$145,987
EBIT:	468	9,267
Interest expense	764	8,256
Net income	$ (296)	$ 1,011

12 SEAFAX (A)

Neal Workman thought about his company, SeaFax (a seafood credit and collections company), as he watched his wife sleep. She knew things were tough, but if she knew how close they were to losing their home, her sleep might have been less peaceful. Neal had put their life savings (personal and corporate) on the line to buy a computer system that he believed would revolutionize the way seafood was purchased. Mike Waters, his CFO, thought the system cost much more than they could afford. He was so vehemently opposed to this investment that he threatened to resign in protest.

Maybe Mike was right. As of December 6, 1990, SeaFax was nearly out of cash, and big bills were already past due. If revenue didn't get flowing immediately, all was lost.

NEAL WORKMAN

The second of seven children, Neal followed his own drummer from an early age. In fact, he was expelled from a Jesuit-run high school for being a disruptive class clown. As he recalled, "If the well-traveled road went right, I went left."

Neal landed a position with Dun & Bradstreet at the age of 22. Three years later, he earned "Salesman of the Year" honors, and did so again the following year. No one at Dun & Bradstreet had ever done this before, yet they only awarded him a small, crystal box in recognition of his accomplishment. Dun & Bradstreet never regained Neal's loyalty, and after seven years, he left to work for himself.

This case was prepared by Dan D'Heilly under the direction of Professor William Bygrave. Copyright © 1995 Babson College. All rights reserved.

Neal quit Dun & Bradstreet for several reasons: the restrictive corporate culture, the lack of suitable career opportunities, and the lasting sting from receiving a little glass box when he set a new corporate benchmark for excellence. He kept it on his desk for many years, to remind him that, "It's better to give nothing than to give something too small."

In February 1985, when Neal started the company that would become SeaFax,[*] he didn't have a business plan or even a clear idea of how he was going to earn a living. Neal started a company that reflected his skills, needs, and attitudes. He had bill collecting, credit analysis, and sales skills. He lived in Portland, Maine, a town with high unemployment. His wife was pregnant with their first child, but he saw an opportunity—lobstermen had far too many bad debts. With confidence born of successful credit and collections experience, he set out to find his first customer.

THE SEAFOOD CREDIT AND COLLECTIONS INDUSTRY

The value of seafood sold for human consumption in the United States was between $13 and $18 billion through the late 1980s. Less than 20 percent of these products originated in Asia, South America, and Europe; a little over 20 percent was harvested by Canadians; and the remaining 60 percent was produced by U.S. fishermen.

Seafood was primarily harvested from the ocean. Aquaculture was beginning to emerge as a significant source, but still played a minor role. Some companies, especially ones that were foreign-owned, were vertically integrated with fleets that served their own packers and distribution systems. However, most seafood was sold to middlemen when the ships arrived at the docks.

Seafood Products

Seafood products for human consumption could be divided into three major categories: frozen, fresh, and canned. Revenues were split—approximately 55 percent frozen, 25 percent fresh or live, and the remaining 20 percent miscellaneous (see Exhibit 12.1). Depending on the product (e.g., shrimp vs. swordfish), seafood had to be frozen somewhere between 6 and 72 hours after being brought to the dock in order to produce top-quality products. Once frozen, it could be sold to processors, brokers, or retailers within the next 6 to 10 months.

Fresh products, however, had the best profit margin. The same seafood was usually worth twice as much fresh as frozen, but fresh products lasted only 5 to 10 days. Selling fresh products was more difficult, because their perishability required quick sales cycles. But because fresh products earned top dollar, distributors sometimes delayed freezing the catch if there was a reasonable prospect of selling it fresh.

When fresh seafood wasn't sold in time, it was only good for fertilizer. However, fertilizer prices were frequently too low to even pay freight costs, so leftover fresh products were often dumped back into the sea as a complete loss.

---

[*] The original name of the company, Debt Management Services, was changed to SeaFax in 1990.

EXHIBIT 12.1   Fresh/frozen seafood.

	1985	1986	1987	1988	1989	1990 (projected)
Annual catch (mil. lbs.)	3,294	3,393	3,946	4,588	6,204	7,041
Revenue ($000,000)	2,198	2,641	2,979	3,362	3,111	3,366

Source: U.S. Dept. of Commerce, Fisheries Statistics Division.

Seafood Distribution

The seafood distribution network consisted of traders, processors, and wholesale distributors. The processors and wholesale distributors purchased fish dockside, almost always in cash transactions. The majority of middleman trading occurred through wholesale distributors. These firms had the warehouse space, established customers, and the product specialization needed to buy in bulk and find profitable opportunities for reselling their inventory. The second largest segment of the market, with perhaps 20 percent of the transactions, was the processors. Typically, they cleaned, processed, and distributed their own seafood products.

Traders, on the other hand, didn't purchase directly from fishermen and seldom took direct possession of the seafood. They arranged deals to take advantage of market disequilibriums and accounted for approximately 10 percent of the deal flow. In addition, some distributors would engage in trading when they saw a good buy outside of their usual product categories.

In 1980, most seafood distributors shared similar problems:

1. Commodity products,
2. A constant need to evaluate new customers, and
3. Poor quality credit information.

They operated in a volatile market, where product differentiation was negligible within categories, terms were negotiable, and creditor default was too common.

A problem common to all distributors was unpredictable profit margins. This problem was attributed to the commodity nature of the market—the prices changed every day. Fortunes were made and lost based on the timing of a purchase. When market prices rose after a purchase, profit margins improved. But when prices dropped, a distributor could be left holding inventory with a book value significantly higher than the market value.

Many retail buyers (e.g., restaurants, fish markets, airlines) shopped without loyalty, because the products were interchangeable, and they could negotiate the same terms with many distributors. There was sufficient supply for buyers to go elsewhere for their next purchase, so they negotiated from strength. Essentially, they could delay and deny some accounts payable without serious negative repercussions.

Seafood distributors also faced credit problems, because many of their primary customers (e.g., restaurants and fish markets) had high management turnover and failure rates. In seafood wholesaling, buyers frequently defaulted on agreements made in good faith because they didn't have the ability to pay. Also, a surprising number of retailers went bankrupt—leaving bad debts—and created new seafood businesses financed in part by fresh vendor credit.

The lack of reliable credit information about retailers was a big problem. There were two types of theoretically avoidable bad debts: those owed by firms that couldn't pay according to agreed-upon terms, and those owed by retailers who never intended to abide by the terms—in fact, some never intended to pay at all. With better credit information, most of these sales would never have taken place.

Another common problem was maintaining price points. Buyers sometimes lowered the price-per-pound on their invoices if the commodity price at the time of delivery was lower than the market price when they placed their order. All they had to do was claim the seafood had been damaged during shipment. Seafood distributors often didn't have a lot of leverage.

Sellers of fresh seafood also had a transactional urgency created by product perishability. This created difficulties in the area of collections. Frozen products could often be repossessed for nonpayment, but there was no obvious recourse when fresh seafood distributors weren't paid. As a result, credit and collections services were critical for fresh seafood distributors.

Bad debt losses were high for seafood distributors in general, and they were particularly bad for fresh seafood distributors. Approximately 0.77 percent of the transactions in the seafood market had to be written off. This was in sharp contrast to most industries, where bad debts occurred with fewer than 0.5 percent of accounts receivable. This gap created the potential for a seafood credit and collections niche market.

Until 1980, no specialized seafood credit and collections services were available—there was no seafood credit and collections industry. The only national seafood credit and collections services were offered by Dun & Bradstreet. However, the frequency and depth of its reporting was designed for more stable industries. With seafood credit problems half again as serious as those of typical markets, Dun & Bradstreet's services were insufficient.

Dun & Bradstreet checked credit references annually. During that investigation, its policy called for contacting two references, and these references were usually selected by the business under investigation. While Dun & Bradstreet had a seafood market presence, its seafood segment revenues were too small for it to consider a vertical niche in this market (see Exhibit 12.2).

SEAFOOD CREDIT CORP.

In 1980, Seafood Credit Corp. was founded by Frank Martino, a former credit manager for Empress Seafoods. Frank had several years of credit analyst experience prior to entering the seafood industry. When Frank joined Empress Seafoods, he overhauled its credit operations, and its losses plummeted. Soon, Frank found himself providing credit advice to other seafood sellers on a daily basis. These associates urged him to go into business and start a seafood credit bureau.

Seafood Credit Corp. relied primarily on word-of-mouth advertising to develop its market. It had a small inside salesforce and no outside sales presence. Although it offered both credit and collections services, collections never generated substantial revenues.

Seafood Credit specialized in analysis. Frank was a credit guru and every credit report Seafood Credit Corp. published carried a Frank Martino credit-line recommendation. He positioned his service as *the* credit consulting authority for the seafood industry. Thus, the seafood credit and collections industry was launched.

One common characteristic of firms that used credit services was their size: only larger firms could afford credit services. The average annual revenue of a credit customer was over $5 million. Ten percent of the firms accounted for 70 percent of industry revenues: this was Seafood Credit Corp.'s customer base.

Between 1980 and 1985, the seafood credit industry grew rapidly as Seafood Credit Corp. extended its market. However, with annual losses worth over a hundred million dollars, it appeared that seafood distributors were not being fully protected by Seafood Credit Corp. In retrospect, the types of opportunities missed by Seafood Credit Corp. could be characterized as marketing and market-definition issues.

Marketing

1. Many firms were unaware of their services.
2. Many firms who heard about Seafood Credit Corp. weren't actively solicited.
3. Some firms knew about them and wanted better credit information, but didn't appreciate the value enough to pay for professional credit services.

Market Definition

1. Seafood distribution companies needed professional collections services. Collections are a natural adjunct to credit services, yet Seafood Credit neglected the development of their collections business.
2. Fresh products were more at risk from poor credit information, yet Seafood Credit focused on the frozen seafood sector, and didn't deliver information fast enough for the quick decisions needed in the fresh product market.

SEAFAX

At the age of 29, Neal Workman started SeaFax, a collections agency, in the basement of his home (see Exhibit 12.3). Originally, SeaFax focused on helping New England's

EXHIBIT 12.2   Credit/collections.°

	1985	1986	1987	1988	1989	1990 (projected)
Revenue ($ mil.)	168.6	161.9	171.3	166.5	186.4	195.7

° Predicasts' Basebook.

Exhibit 12.3   SeaFax flyer.

WE ARE SEAFAX

*F*ounded in 1985 as a credit information and collection service with a unique focus on seafood, SeaFax® has grown to become the foremost provider of financial and credit information to the seafood industry worldwide. The company stakes its reputation on delivering complete, accurate and timely information to its clients. Utilizing leading-edge telecommunications technology, SeaFax is able to respond rapidly to client needs, providing a wide variety of customized financial reports and other products.

SEAFAX BUSINESS REPORTS

Detailed company-specific business profiles including SeaFax Credit Appraisal and Credit Limit Guide Line. Subscribers are automatically notified of any change in SeaFax Credit Appraisal for a period of 12 months from report delivery date.

PRE-SCHEDULED DELIVERY

Register your accounts for Pre-Scheduled Delivery and receive a full updated SeaFax Business Report every 120 days. For the cost of 3 reports, you will automatically receive 3-4 updates per year.

SEASCAN BULLETIN

Compiled and released 17 times annually, this is the industry's most comprehensive company-specific publication of delinquencies, NSF check data and collection experiences. Hundreds of seafood companies report their slow-paying accounts to SeaFax every 3 weeks, allowing you to track how your customers pay their other suppliers.

FLASH REPORTS

Issued 3 to 5 times a week. Flash Reports contain the most critical, time-sensitive credit/collection data sourced by our analysts and field staff daily.

BANKRUPTCY CREDITOR INDEX

Published six times a year, this publication identifies the unsecured creditors of industry bankruptcies, receiverships and assignments for the benefit of creditors industry-wide. SeaFax sources information directly from bankruptcy courts, trustees, receivers and assignees. Company-specific creditor listings are also available upon request.

DEBT SEARCH

On a company-specific basis, Debt Search scans our entire database of Seascan, Flash Report and Bankruptcy Creditor Index records to retrieve a 24-month historical profile of any negative experiences.

SEAFAX FIRST NEWS

A single-page summary of seafood industry collection placements, credit appraisal changes, work-in-progress investigations, and business news compiled and faxed to our clients daily.

SEAFAX SEAFOOD INDUSTRY REFERENCE GUIDE

Lists over 10,000 buyers and sellers of fresh and frozen products throughout North America.

SEAFAX ON-LINE

On-line system delivery of SeaFax Business Reports, Debt Search and Flash Reports via personal computer.

DEBT COLLECTIONS

Our highly successful and aggressive team of professionals is ready to meet your needs.

*F*or more information on our products and services, please call the following toll-free number:

1-800-777-3533

 SEAFAX

P.O. Box 15340
Portland, Maine 04112-5340

The Industry's Network for
Receivables Management Worldwide

---

lobstermen collect their bad debts. In 1985, the first year of operations and his only year as a sole proprietor, he generated $41,000 in revenue (see Exhibit 12.4). He soon realized that this target market of live seafood (lobsters) was too narrow. The entire fresh seafood industry was underserved, so he expanded his marketing to include fresh seafood resellers. He marketed SeaFax aggressively, and revenues increased to almost $400,000 in 1986. In 1987, growth slowed to 100 percent, and SeaFax generated over

EXHIBIT 12.4 SeaFax financial information.

	1985	1986	1987	1988	1989	1990 (projected)
Revenue ($000)	41	384	819	844	1,519	2,098
% Change	n/a	837	113	3	80	38
DMS	41	384	713	844	1,250	1,383
SeaFax	n/a	n/a	106	—	269	714
Profit ($000)	n/a	30	(9)	43	61	(98)
DMS	n/a	30	3	43	62	(62)
SeaFax	n/a	n/a	(12)	—	(1)	(36)

$800,000. Revenue increases slowed after 1988, as market size started to become a limiting factor.

Between 1985 and 1990, the seafood credit and collections market multiplied several times. The combined revenues of Seafood Credit Corp. and SeaFax climbed from approximately $0.5 million to over $3 million over that six-year period.

COMPETITIVE STRATEGY

Neal's initial challenge was to show lobster distributors that he could help them reduce the number and size of their bad debts. Neal asked for a retainer up front, which made the initial sale harder. This required prospective clients to trust that SeaFax would be in business and effective when needed. Many distributors were skeptical, but Neal's credentials as a top Dun & Bradstreet agent gave him enough credibility to get started, and his well-publicized successes convinced other fishermen that they should try this new approach to collecting bad debts.

There were numerous anecdotes of his ability to collect bad debts. One story recalls the time Neal visited the gruff owner of a Houston restaurant who owed $5,000 to New England lobstermen. The owner told Neal to get lost. Neal purchased a bull horn and went into the restaurant to describe the owner's bad-faith business practices to his patrons. The owner threw him out, but when Neal returned later, a check for payment-in-full was waiting.

As he came to understand the fresh seafood industry, Neal realized that this market needed very high-quality credit and collections services. He believed that the current market leader's credit services were accurate, but that delivery was too slow for fresh seafood in particular, and that Seafood Credit Corp. was generally nonresponsive to market opportunities.

For example, Seafood Credit did not concentrate on collections services. From prior experience, Neal knew that credit and collections were usually packaged together. The records created while collecting debts produce extensive credit data, so he decided to use collections as his entry to the credit market.

Neal saw an industry that had not come into the electronic age, and he constantly looked for ways to use technology effectively. He read business books for recreation, and would regularly introduce ideas taken from Michael Porter, Tom Peters, Peter Drucker, or a similar business guru, into the workplace at SeaFax. For example, he paid $1,000 a quarter to the employee who put the worst serious idea in the company suggestion box, an idea taken from a book by Tom Peters. "Imitation is the kindest complement," he said.

Neal was a natural salesman, and a superior collector of debts. He was also a talented leader and motivator, but he was new to this market niche. Despite his newcomer status, Neal's ability to collect debts gave him an opportunity to establish relationships with Seafood Credit's clients. An important factor in SeaFax's success was its ability to cross-sell°; it often gained a new credit customer shortly after it signed a new collections client.

Through his collections activities, Neal also learned who sold to whom, and which buyers were deadbeats. So when he made sales calls for his credit bureau business, he selected distributors who he knew probably had bad debts outstanding.

Neal encouraged traditions that celebrated successes and cultivated team spirit. One custom that acknowledged the contribution of back-room skills to front-line sales performance was the victory dance. Because a SeaFax sales presentation included offering one free business report (Exhibit 12.5) to demonstrate product quality, the sale was considered a joint accomplishment of the salesperson/credit analyst team. So whenever a sales rep signed a major new customer, the company would gather to applaud and watch the analyst do the victory dance.

The victory dance used trade advertisements to celebrate winning a customer from Seafood Credit. The ads of SeaFax customers were pinned to one wall of the main meeting room; ads for Seafood Credit customers were pinned to the opposite wall. When a new client was signed, the successful salesperson summoned coworkers by striking a gong. The salesperson would then announce the name of the new customer and acknowledge the credit analyst. As the company cheered, the analyst would remove that customer's advertisement from the Seafood Credit wall and pin it onto the SeaFax wall after comically dancing across the room.

PUBLISHING CREDIT INFORMATION

To provide quality debt-management services, Neal needed accurate credit intelligence. Neither Dun & Bradstreet nor Seafood Credit provided the timely and inexpensive information that Neal wanted, so he began publishing credit information during his first year in business. Neal produced business reports that were mailed to customers upon request, and on a periodic basis after the request to update the mailed information. SeaFax's reports differed from those produced by Frank Martino's Seafood Credit Corp. in several ways:

1. *Research Methodology:* Neal's recommendations came from numerous reference checks, while Frank typically recommended a credit line based on fewer references, but always included financial statement analysis.

° Cross-selling is the act of urging a current customer to buy additional products or services.

Exhibit 12.5 SeaFax business report.

Date Printed: 08/15/9X

```
SEA BASKET, LTD.                    Established      : 1956
17 SPOKE AVE.                       Business Type    : CORPORATION
RODALE, FL  12345                   Date Incorporated : 06/09/61
Tel: (555)-123-4396                 Incorporated In  : FLORIDA
FAX: (555)-456-3041
                   ------------------------------------
                   SEAFAX Credit Appraisal: RECOMMENDED
                   ------------------------------------
```

Principals	Title	Ownership
BARNEY BRIDGESTONE	PRESIDENT	SEE BELOW
AMY CANNONDALE	VICE PRESIDENT	
MARK COLONGO	VICE PRESIDENT	
FRANK KONA	TREASURER	

Business Summary - (06/16/9X)
Business Description: WHOLESALE DISTRIBUTOR, IMPORTER

Product Line: FULL LINE SEAFOOD

Accounts Sold: WHOLESALE DISTRIBUTORS, RESTAURANTS, CHAIN STORES,

                     RETAIL MARKETS

Number of Accounts: 1,100

Number of Employees: 49

Territory: UNITED STATES, EUROPE

Sales: $66,000,000 ESTIMATED 199X

History - (06/16/9X)
```
    SEA BASKET, LTD. WAS ESTABLISHED IN 1929 BY MAVIC BRIDGESTONE.
    THE SECOND AND THIRD GENERATIONS OF THE BRIDGESTONE FAMILY MEMBERS,
    WHICH INCLUDES THE CURRENT PRINCIPALS, TOGETHER OWN 100% OF THE
    CORPORATE STOCK. ALL OFFICERS ARE INVOLVED IN DAILY OPERATIONS.
```

Antecedents - (06/16/9X)
```
    BARNEY BRIDGESTONE       BORN 1944. ATTENDED COLORADO UNIVERSITY
                             AND INDIANA UNIVERSITY. JOINED THE
                             COMPANY IN 1959.
```

Page Number: 1   SEAFAX File: 101010

(Continued)

2. *Speed:* Neal automated his credit information, so he could quickly publish up-to-date information.

3. *Market Responsiveness:* Neal was constantly searching for new ways to satisfy customer needs (i.e., SeaFax reports were typically presented in an easy-to-read style).

Neal's strategy for developing a quality credit service was to listen to customers. Once, when he felt that the pace of innovation was too slow, he sent all 28 SeaFax employees on the road to interview all 300+ customers. Over a 14-week period, he spent $18,000 sending secretaries to Seattle and accountants to Atlanta. The interview included a 10-point questionnaire, and the SeaFax employees weren't supposed to end

Exhibit 12.5 *(Continued)*

SEA BASKET, LTD.   Date Printed: 08/15/9X
RODALE, FL

Operations - (06/16/9X)

SEA BASKET, LTD. OPERATES AS A WHOLESALE DISTRIBUTOR AND
IMPORTER. SEAFOOD REPRESENTS 100% OF TOTAL SALES AND IS SOLD 50%
FRESH AND 50% FROZEN. PRIMARY PRODUCTS SOLD INCLUDE SALMON,
SWORDFISH, AND SHELLFISH. PRODUCT IS IMPORTED WORLDWIDE, AND ON A
LIMITED BASIS, EXPORTED TO EUROPE. THE COMPANY OPERATES FROM A
27,000 SQ.FT. FACILITY. FREEZER AND COOLER ARE LOCATED ON SITE.
THE COMPANY SELLS PRODUCT UNDER THE BRAND NAME "BARNEY'S". THREE
VEHICLES AND COMMON CARRIER SERVICES ARE UTILIZED FOR PRODUCT
DISTRIBUTION.

BANKING REFERENCES

Checking Information

Bank Name:	CODA BANK	Average Balance:	MED 5 FIGURES
Telephone:	(555) 123-2012	Account Opened:	01/01/66
Ref. Date:	06/02/9X		
Comments:	YEAR-TO-DATE AVERAGE BALANCE.		

Credit Line Information

Bank Name:	CODA BANK	Date Issued:	05/21/9X
Telephone:	(555) 123-2012	Credit Line:	MED 6 FIGURES
Ref. Date:	06/02/9X	Outstanding Balance:	MED 5 FIGURES
Secured:	UNSECURED	Monies Available:	NOT QUOTED
		Renewal Date:	06/01/9X
Comments:	HANDLED AS AGREED.		

Loan Information

Bank Name:	CODA BANK	Date Issued:	02/9X
Telephone:	(555) 123-2012	Loan Amount:	MOD 5 FIGURES
Ref. Date:	06/02/9X	Outstanding Balance:	MOD 5 FIGURES
Secured:	UNSECURED	Loan Type:	TERM
Comments:	PAYS AS AGREED. MATURES 02/9X.		

Page Number: 2   SEAFAX File: 101010

an interview until they had three answers to Question 10. Question 10 asked the customer for complaints about SeaFax. The results generated many innovations and a very high level of employee buy-in. The ideas were vigorously implemented—employees at SeaFax exuded team spirit and concern every time they talked with a customer. The relationship factor differentiated SeaFax from Seafood Credit—SeaFax built relationships with its customers using every means at its disposal.

In response to a customer's suggestion, Neal began producing a newsletter, *SEASCAN* (Exhibit 12.6). *SEASCAN* was a rubber sheet° published every three weeks, listing delinquencies, bounced checks, and accounts placed in collection (as

---

° A rubber sheet is a list of creditors who have: (1) bounced checks, (2) paid late, (3) defaulted on accounts payable, or (4) filed for bankruptcy with debts unpaid.

Exhibit 12.5 *(Continued)*

SEA BASKET, LTD.   Date Printed: 08/15/9X
RODALE, FL

EXPANDED TRADE PROFILE

	Date	Frequency	High Credit	Outstanding Balance	Selling Since	Summary
(U)	06/9X	N/QUOTED	$ 20,000	$ 20,000	1 MONTH	N/30, TOO NEW TO RATE.
(U)	06/9X	MONTHLY	$ 24,000	$ 3,700	7 YEARS	N/30, 10 TO 12 DAYS SLOW.
(U)	06/9X	WEEKLY	$ 49,000	$ 37,000	N/QUOTED	N/21, PROMPT.
(U)	06/9X	WEEKLY	$ 150,000	$ 103,000	8 YEARS	N/30, 15 DAYS SLOW.
(U)	06/9X	1 SALE	$ 12,000	$ 0	1 SALE	N/30, PROMPT. LAST SALE 03/9X.
(U)	06/9X	2X WEEK	$ N/QUOTED	$ N/QUOTED	4 YEARS	N/21, PROMPT. LAST SALE 05/9X.
(U)	06/9X	MONTHLY	$ N/QUOTED	$ 1,600	9 MONTHS	N/30, PROMPT.
(S)	06/9X	2X WEEK	$ 36,000	$ 13,000	4 YEARS	N/15, 2 TO 18 DAYS SLOW.
(U)	06/9X	WEEKLY	$ N/QUOTED	$ 0	1 YEAR	N/30, PROMPT. LAST SALE 05/9X.
(U)	06/9X	WEEKLY	$ 92,000	$ 92,000	6 YEARS	N/30, 10 TO 14 DAYS SLOW.
(S)	06/9X	N/QUOTED	$ 800,000	$ 430,000	14 YEARS	N/30, 7 DAYS SLOW.
(U)	06/9X	MONTHLY	$MOD 6 FIGS	$ LO 5 FIGS	6 YEARS	N/30, 5 TO 7 DAYS SLOW.
(U)	06/9X	WEEKLY	$ 150,000	$ 60,000	3 YEARS	N/30, PROMPT.
(U)	06/9X	SPORADIC	$ 42,000	$ 28,000	10 MONTHS	N/30, PROMPT.
· (U)	06/9X	1 SALE	$ 9,000	$ 0	1 SALE	N/30, TOO NEW TO RATE. LAST SALE 03/9X.
(U)	06/9X	SPORADIC	$ 340,000	$ 0	4 YEARS	N/30, 4 DAYS SLOW. LAST SALE 04/9X.

*-Non-Seafood Reference   (U)-Unsolicited Reference   (S)-Solicited Reference

Page Number: 3   SEAFAX File: 101010

(Continued)

reported by his clients). As customers began using *SEASCAN*, they wanted to read the urgent news more quickly. SeaFax responded by developing *FLASH Reports* (Exhibit 12.7), a fax publication sent out two to five times a week when critical new information arrived. Several years later, Seafood Credit followed suit, first with an industry rubber sheet and then with regular updates between newsletters.

In 1990, SeaFax planned to invest heavily in computerization so that customers could access SeaFax's reports online. This was the fastest solution yet, Neal explained:

In 1986, we promised customers that we would give them a verbal credit-worthiness answer by phone within an hour, and then get them a hard copy of the business report through the mail within five working days. There was no way we could do it more quickly

Exhibit 12.5 *(Continued)*

```
SEA BASKET, LTD.                              Date Printed: 08/15/9X
RODALE, FL
                        PAYMENT TREND INDEX
                         SEA BASKET, LTD.
                            RODALE, FL
                          Average Days Slow
Report  # of  |===|====|====|====|====|====|====|====|====|====|====|====|
Period  Refs. 1   5   10   15   20   25   30   35   40   45   50   55  60+

06/9X    15   **** (4)

02/9X     9   *** (3)

10/9X    11   ****** (6)

06/9X    11   ***** (5)

02/9X    10   **** (4)
```

The above information is an analysis of payment experience reported by trade
suppliers of the subject company over a period of up to 18 months and
represents an average number of days past normal credit terms. Averages do not
include accounts placed for collection.

```
                     PERSONAL  VISIT  PROFILE
-----------------------------------------------------------------------
| SeaFax Employee  :   PHIL CHIRRELLO        Date of Visit: 01/25/9X  |
-----------------------------------------------------------------------
```

SEAFAX Credit Appraisal:
RECOMMENDED

Recommended for credit
relationship. Please refer to
Trade Summary for credit
limit guidelines.

SEAFAX Trade Summary:
SEAFAX Credit Limit Guideline

Average High Credit: $ 182,187
Average Amount Due: $ 83,450

at a reasonable price. But as soon as a customer asked for a fax, we bought a fax machine. Later, we began blast-faxing° SEASCAN and FLASH Reports by the thousands.

SEASCAN and *FLASH Reports* were distributed to all of SeaFax's subscribers. But the primary reason that SeaFax customers subscribed was to receive business

---

° "Blast-fax" is a term used to describe large-scale fax transmissions. SeaFax contracts with a former telex firm in New Jersey to deliver tens of thousands of faxes to SeaFax's customers each month.

Exhibit 12.6   Seascan® bulletin.

AMEAD GRILL & BAR WENWICK, MT				
Collection:	$1,246.20	Status: PP - $211.40		

ANDREW SEAFOOD, INC. SAN JUAN, TX				*New Listing*
Collection:	$8,000.00	Status: DISPUTED		

ANEL'S SEAFOOD, INC. NORTH CHESTER, WI				*New Listing*
Collection:	$18,033.20	Status: PP - $3,000.00		
	$10,427.05	PP - $8,049.00		
NSF Check:	$500.00	Check Date: 05/19/95	Bank: MOLLUSK BANK	
	$250.00	05/19/95	MOLLUSK BANK	
	$1,000.00	07/21/95	MOLLUSK BANK	
	$1,000.00	07/14/95	MOLLUSK BANK	
DBA: JOHNNY'S MARKET				

ANIESSO WELICA MILAN, ITALY				
Delinquent:	$9,140.00	Terms:	30 Days Past Term: 360	

ANTHONY NEW FOODS SCOTSDALE, IN --SEE-> NEW, ANTHONY				

AQUATICA LISBON, ME				
Delinquent:	$8,830.00	Terms:	30 Days Past Term: 365	

ARBOR GOOD FOOD KEARSIGE, UT				
NSF Check:	$227.50	Check Date: 04/25/95	Bank: SOUTH CONCH BANK	

ATLANTA PURVEYORS, INC. MACOMB, GA				*New Listing*
Delinquent:	$4,700.00	Terms:	30 Days Past Term: 19	
DBA: INSTITUTIONAL SUPPLIERS				
X.Y.Z.				
A.B.C.				
FIVE POINTS TRADING				

ATLANTIC CLAM HOUSE & MARKET, INC. MUANATUA, HI				
Collection:	$17,778.29	Status: NO PAYMENT		

reports—detailed, company-specific, debt-history research papers. Typically, SeaFax customers would review a business report before shipping products to their new and less creditworthy customers.

Publishing a business report involved a relatively large investment in research up front, then smaller maintenance costs to keep the information current. Each report then generated revenue every time it was sold. Thus, profitability lay with focusing on reports in high demand and selling each report as many times as possible.

The sale of business reports became increasingly important to SeaFax's growth, but publishing operations basically remained a basement production through 1989. Originally, the company updated each business report as it was ordered. Clients also wanted to know if credit circumstances had changed since they

Exhibit 12.7   SeaFax credit report.

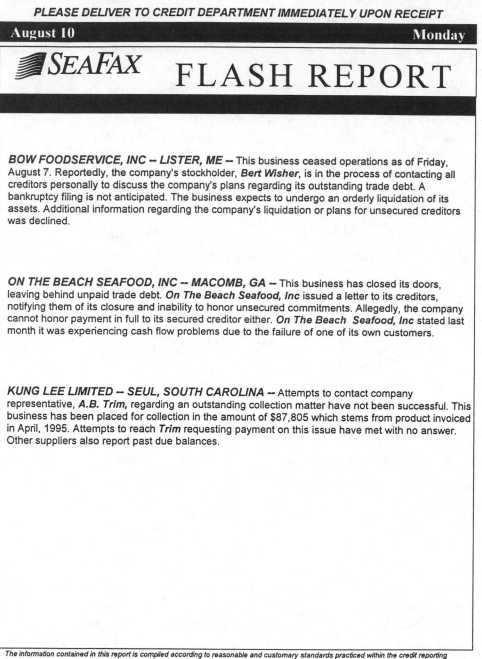

PLEASE DELIVER TO CREDIT DEPARTMENT IMMEDIATELY UPON RECEIPT

August 10   **Monday**

≋SEAFAX   FLASH REPORT

BOW FOODSERVICE, INC -- LISTER, ME -- This business ceased operations as of Friday, August 7. Reportedly, the company's stockholder, *Bert Wisher*, is in the process of contacting all creditors personally to discuss the company's plans regarding its outstanding trade debt. A bankruptcy filing is not anticipated. The business expects to undergo an orderly liquidation of its assets. Additional information regarding the company's liquidation or plans for unsecured creditors was declined.

ON THE BEACH SEAFOOD, INC -- MACOMB, GA -- This business has closed its doors, leaving behind unpaid trade debt. *On The Beach Seafood, Inc* issued a letter to its creditors, notifying them of its closure and inability to honor unsecured commitments. Allegedly, the company cannot honor payment in full to its secured creditor either. *On The Beach Seafood, Inc* stated last month it was experiencing cash flow problems due to the failure of one of its own customers.

KUNG LEE LIMITED -- SEUL, SOUTH CAROLINA -- Attempts to contact company representative, *A.B. Trim,* regarding an outstanding collection matter have not been successful. This business has been placed for collection in the amount of $87,805 which stems from product invoiced in April, 1995. Attempts to reach *Trim* requesting payment on this issue have met with no answer. Other suppliers also report past due balances.

received their last report, so SeaFax kept hard copies on file to compare manually with current reports. As a result, post-sale tracking and support for these products was very expensive. The expense was so high that Neal discontinued publishing for most of 1988, but he began again in 1989. This time, it was with a renewed commitment to efficiency—part of the decision to buy a sophisticated computer system sprang from a desire for smoother publishing operations. Publishing supplied over one third of SeaFax's annual revenues by 1990.

SeaFax's revenue grew 70 percent in 1990, and most of that growth occurred in the publishing business. The complexity of gathering, analyzing, and distributing this information created serious operational problems. The cost of producing reports was too high, and the company's inability to share information electronically—both at the office and in the field—created major quality issues.

COMPUTERIZATION

Neal decided to build a computer network, upgrade its database capabilities, and offer credit information online. This investment could revolutionize the way they did business. It would also provide SeaFax with a new way to distinguish its service from Seafood Credit. The differentiation between the two firms was becoming increasingly based on personal relationships—important, but not a lasting competitive advantage. Neal believed that the new computer system would help save customers so much money that SeaFax's sales would increase substantially.

Unfortunately, the computer systems cost more than Neal could raise through long-term debt or equity financing, and he had no angel in the wings, so he used short term debt. SeaFax received short-term bank debt by securing the loan with all its accounts receivable, property, and equipment, and with personal guarantees from Neal and his wife. SeaFax was risking insolvency, and the Workmans were risking impoverishment. Neal was betting that SeaFax could make the computer payments with the lower overhead and additional sales that the improved service would generate.

Certain covenants in the revolving line-of-credit agreement would allow the bank to call the loan. Among these provisions were several financial-ratio limits. SeaFax was in breach of the debt-to-equity ratio provision as of December 6, 1990. Thus, the bank was within its rights to call the loan and push SeaFax into bankruptcy anytime.

Neal thought the predicted sales spurt would begin as soon as he announced the computer purchase, but unfortunately, both cost savings and new revenues materialized slowly. The information was online, few customers were actually using the service. The seafood industry was taking a "wait and see" approach to SeaFax's online credit information service. Unless things quickly turned for the better, SeaFax couldn't make payroll—and the bank might view missing a payroll as sufficient justification to call the loan.

As he lay in bed, sleepless from the stress, Neal pondered SeaFax's dilemma. The chosen computer system cost more than his CFO considered feasible, but Neal thought the benefits of improving their service justified the risk. He was sure that this advanced computer system would provide an unparalleled level of timeliness, accuracy, and customer responsiveness. With this system, SeaFax's leadership position should be unassailable.

PREPARATION QUESTIONS

1. Evaluate Neal's decision to buy the new computer system.
2. How urgent is SeaFax's cash flow crisis? How much cash does it need, and how soon is it needed?
3. What must Neal do in the short term to get through this crisis?
4. What do you recommend for the long-term?

13 FJORD TRADING COMPANY (A)

On November 29, 1994, Carl Olson, Olaf Olson, and Juan Gomez paused at the end of another hectic day to discuss the status of their quest for additional capital. Shoehorned into their 450-square-foot office in a building on Seattle's fishing docks, the three executives of Fjord Trading Company were getting anxious to hear back from a group that had expressed interest in their growing business.

Carl Olson had founded Fjord Trading in early 1992 to export a variety of canned foodstuffs to Norway. By the end of 1994, however, the flow of trade was entirely in the opposite direction, as Fjord was becoming a major importer of fresh Norwegian seafood for resale to other wholesalers, distributors, large restaurant chains, and supermarkets. Based in Seattle, Fjord Trading initially focused on local customers but had expanded distribution throughout the Northwest and was considering expansion into the midwest. Sales for its second six months of operation, from January to June 1994, had increased more than 200 percent over the first half-year period, reaching a total of over $2 million (Exhibits 13.1–13.3). The second half sales growth benefited from the strong demand for fish during Lent, the 40 days preceding Easter, when many of the region's Catholics traditionally gave up or reduced their consumption of meat.

In addition to the strong seasonal demand, sales growth was driven by other external industry factors and by several initiatives that Fjord Trading instituted to differentiate its product from the commodity status of the fish available from U.S. domestic and Canadian distributors. A growing number of regular customers were eager to purchase Fjord's Norwegian fish due to its freshness and quality and because of innovations in the way the company portioned and packaged its products. These

---

This case was prepared by Sam Perkins under the direction of Professor William Bygrave. Copyright © 1996 Babson College. All rights reserved.

EXHIBIT 13.1   Fjord Trading Company income statement (historical).

	6/1/93–12/31/93	Ratio
Total sales revenue	$655,604.33	100.00%
Purchases	557,263.68	85.00
Direct item expenses		
Trucking domestic	21,259.09	3.24
Airline domestic	—	0.00
Samples expense start promotion	—	0.00
Sales discounts customer	339.69	0.05
Customs broker	15,518.60	2.37
Total cost of goods sold	$594,381.06	90.66
Gross profit	$ 61,223.27	
Selling expenses		
General commissions	188.00	0.03
Olaf commissions	—	0.00
Carl commissions	—	0.00
Lief commissions	—	0.00
Travel and entertainment	1,600.00	0.24
Total selling expenses	$ 1,788.00	0.27
General administration expenses		
Advertising	523.12	0.08
Overnight mailing services	444.25	0.07
Legal fees	—	0.00
Bad debt expense	3,929.00	0.60
Credit card charges	50.00	0.01
Bank checking charges	851.00	0.13
Bad fish expense	—	0.00
Depreciation	3,260.70	0.50
Sales discounts	266.60	0.04
Vehicle insurance	200.00	0.03
Notes interest	4,903.40	0.75
Office supplies	1,260.20	0.19
Office rent	4,845.00	0.74
Warehouse rent	122.08	0.02
Repair and maintain vehicles	507.86	0.08
Repair and maintain various equipment	138.25	0.02
Telephone	3,893.46	0.59
Utilities	461.14	0.07
Factoring expenses	5,835.61	0.89
Interest expense for inv. factor	314.19	0.05
All other factoring expenses	105.10	0.02
Vehicle excise tax, registration	260.00	0.04
Outside consulting expense	360.00	0.05
Truck rentals and lease	447.65	0.07
Petty cash account, etc.	126.09	0.02
Warehouse cash expense	6,937.50	1.06
Total general & administration	$ 40,042.20	6.11
Total expense	$636,211.25	97.04
Net income before taxes	$ 19,393.07	2.96

EXHIBIT 13.2   Fjord Trading Company income statement (historical).

	1/1/94–6/30/94	Ratio
Total sales revenue	$2,052,958.53	100.00%
Purchases	1,576,637.37	76.80
Direct item expenses		
Trucking domestic	$ 36,200.08	1.76
Airline domestic	1,782.55	0.09
Samples expense start promotion	43,930.49	2.14
Sales discounts customer	43,336.53	2.11
Customs broker	28,380.06	1.38
Total cost of goods sold	$1,730,267.08	84.28
Gross profit	$ 322,691.45	
Selling expenses		
General commissions	103.50	0.01
Olaf commissions	13,617.26	0.66
Carl commissions	7,073.13	0.34
Lief commissions	300.00	0.01
Travel and entertainment	3,005.81	0.15
Total selling expenses	$ 24,099.70	1.17
General administration expenses		
Advertising	955.00	0.05
Overnight mailing services	1,472.35	0.07
Legal fees	50.00	0.00
Warehouse supplies	4,666.92	0.23
Credit card charges	200.00	0.01
Bank checking charges	1,184.00	0.06
Wire charges metro & eastern	810.00	0.04
Bad fish expense	2,763.84	0.13
Depreciation	10,224.13	0.50
Sales discounts	144.50	0.01
Vehicle insurance	4,245.98	0.21
Notes interest	16,350.00	0.80
Office supplies	3,448.84	0.17
Office rent	6,324.00	0.31
Warehouse rent	6,831.60	0.33
Repair and maintain vehicles	10,913.28	0.53
Metro credit search/in house	780.18	0.04
Repair and maintain various equipment	3,338.91	0.16
Telephone	15,694.76	0.76
Utilities	1,023.76	0.05
Factoring expenses	16,643.37	0.81
Interest expense for inv. factor	15,446.21	0.75
All other factoring expenses	313.50	0.02
Vehicle excise tax, registration	3,048.14	0.15
Outside consulting expense	10,110.00	0.49
Outside truck driver contractor	18,658.95	0.91
Truck rentals & lease	8,010.58	0.39
Gasoline and highway tolls	9,086.02	0.44
Petty cash account, etc.	18,765.19	0.91
Warehouse cash expense	1,583.50	0.88
Total general & administration	$ 193,085.49	9.41
Total expense	$1,947,452.27	94.86
Net income before taxes	$ 105,506.28	5.14

EXHIBIT 13.3   Fjord Trading Company income statement (proforma).

	7/1/94–12/31/94	Ratio
Total sales revenue	$2,296,930.42	100.00%
Purchases	1,875,890.86	85.00
Direct item expenses		
Trucking domestic	36,197.08	1.64
Airline domestic	1,782.00	0.08
Samples expense	5,000.00	0.23
Sales discounts customer	10,000.00	0.45
Customs broker	28,378.22	1.29
Total cost of goods sold	$1,957,248.16	88.69
Gross profit	$ 249,682.26	
Selling expenses		
Olaf commissions	25,000.00	1.13
Carl commissions	25,000.00	1.13
Lief commissions	12,000.00	0.54
Travel & entertainment	3,005.79	0.14
Total selling expenses	$ 65,005.79	2.95
General administration expenses		
Advertising	955.00	0.04
Overnight mailing services	725.00	0.03
Legal fees	2,000.00	0.09
Bad debt expense	3,000.00	0.14
Warehouse supplies	4,000.00	0.18
Credit card charges	150.00	0.01
Bank checking charges	1,184.00	0.05
Wire charges metro and western	750.00	0.03
Bad fish expense	2,500.00	0.11
Depreciation	10,000.00	0.45
Vehicle insurance	5,250.00	0.24
Notes interest	16,350.00	0.74
Office supplies	3,448.81	0.16
Office rent	2,000.00	0.09
Warehouse rent	6,831.00	0.31
Repair and maintain vehicles	10,912.99	0.49
Metro credit search/in house	3,000.00	0.14
Repair and maintain various equipment	3,338.88	0.15
Telephone	9,000.00	0.41
Utilities	1,200.00	0.05
Interest expense for inv. factor	9,200.00	0.42
Vehicle excise tax, registration	500.00	0.02
Outside consulting expense	10,109.77	0.46
Outside truck driver contractor	8,000.00	0.36
Gasoline	9,000.00	0.41
Highway tolls	6,250.00	0.28
Accounting fees	2,000.00	0.09
Trade subscriptions	900.00	0.04
Software expense	550.00	0.02
Warehouse cash expense	2,000.00	0.09
Business loan consultant fees	10,000.00	0.45
Total general & administration	$ 145,105.45	6.57
Total expense	$2,167,359.39	98.21
Net income before taxes	$ 39,571.03	1.79

factors enabled the company to charge slightly more, and at better terms, than its competitors. By the fall of 1994, the partners faced the task of satisfying, rather than creating, demand and were in need of additional financing. Lack of money was constraining the growth of the business, and Fjord risked missing the opportunity to capitalize fully on the success it had generated. In addition to equipment and working capital needs, the funds were necessary to eliminate the use of factors, which Fjord was using to handle its receivables.

Juan Gomez joined Fjord as a consultant, then became general manager in March 1994. By September, he had completed a business plan to use both for internal planning and as a marketing tool in the search for financing (see Exhibits 13.1–13.5 for financial statements). The company had secured an SBA-guaranteed loan for $100,000 in October, but needed an additional $500,000 to fund projected growth. Venture capital contacts had produced several leads, including one from three private investors with whom Juan and Carl had met several days before and had discussed possible financing arrangements. The private investors were seeking a company in which they could both invest and actively participate in its management. The lead investor, Jack Calhoon had recently resigned from a senior marketing position at Nabisco. His co-investors were Larry Butcher, an entrepreneur who had just sold his own business, and Ira Goldstein, a tax attorney. The trio had indicated that they would send a formal proposal by the 29th, but it was 6:00 P.M. and no proposal had arrived. Carl, Olaf, and Juan gave up waiting and left the office.

FAMILY BACKGROUND

The Olson family, headed by Lief Olson, emigrated in 1968 from Norway to California, a land as distant from the homeland climatically and culturally as it was geographically. Lief, a carpenter/builder by trade, left Norway when depressed economic conditions in the building industry forced more than 300 Norwegian construction workers out of work and out of the country. While most settled in Denmark and Sweden, Lief ventured to California at the suggestion of a cousin living there who had contacts in the construction industry. Encouraged by Lief's scouting reports of plentiful job opportunities, several builders and their families followed him to California. The Olsons arrived with two children, Olaf and Carl, and had two more, Lief Jr. and Evangeline, several years later.

Lief joined the carpenters union in California and soon landed a job as a supervisor of 60 workers building an underground aqueduct and control station. At the conclusion of that two-year effort, he received an offer from the Luly Construction Company but turned it down in favor of buying a garment-production operation. Although the change in occupations was significant, the venture was not Lief's first business. Intimations of his entrepreneurial spirit were evident much earlier when, at age 18, halfway through his four-year carpentry apprenticeship, he started his own woodworking shop and home building business, which employed five people by the time he received his contractors license.

EXHIBIT 13.4 Fjord Trading Company projected cash flow statement (12 months) 1/1/95 to 12/31/95 (in thousands of dollars).

	Jan.	Feb.	Mar.	Apr.	May	Jun.	Jul.	Aug.	Sept.	Oct.	Nov.	Dec.
I. Collections & purchases worksheet												
(1) Sales (gross)	480,000	550,000	580,000	550,000	410,000	220,000	195,000	210,000	200,000	210,000	220,000	380,000
Collections:												
(2) During month of sales: (.70) (months sales)	336,000	385,000	406,000	385,000	287,000	154,000	136,500	147,000	140,000	147,000	154,000	266,000
(3) During first month after sales: (.30) (previous months)	123,000	144,000	165,000	174,000	165,000	123,000	66,000	58,500	63,000	60,000	63,000	66,000
(4) Total collections = (2 + 3)	459,000	529,000	571,000	559,000	452,000	277,000	202,500	205,500	203,000	207,000	217,000	332,000
Purchases:												
(5) 0.85 (next month's sales)	467,500	493,000	467,500	348,500	187,000	165,750	178,500	170,000	178,500	187,000	323,000	467,500
(6) Payments (1-month lag)	408,000	467,500	493,000	467,500	348,500	187,000	165,750	178,500	170,000	178,500	187,000	323,000
II. Cash gains or loss for month												
(7) Collections (section I)	459,000	529,000	571,000	559,000	452,000	277,000	202,500	205,500	203,000	207,000	217,000	332,000
(8) Payments for purchases (from section I)	408,000	467,500	493,000	467,500	348,500	187,000	165,750	178,500	170,000	178,500	187,000	323,000
(9) Wages and salaries	12,000	13,750	14,500	13,750	10,250	10,000	10,000	10,000	10,000	9,800	9,500	9,500
(10) Rent	2,000	2,000	2,000	2,000	2,000	2,000	2,000	2,000	2,000	2,000	2,000	2,000
(11) Other expenses	36,900	43,200	49,500	52,200	49,500	36,900	19,800	17,550	18,900	18,000	18,900	19,800

	(1)	(2)	(3)	(4)	(5)	(6)	(7)	(8)	(9)	(10)	(11)	(12)
(12) Taxes	—	—	15,778	—	—	11,564	—	—	5,929	—	—	7,938
(13) Construction payment	—	—	—	—	—	—	—	—	—	—	—	—
(14) Total payments	458,900	526,450	574,778	535,450	410,250	247,464	197,550	208,050	206,829	208,300	217,400	362,238
(15) Net cash gain (loss) (Line 7 – Line 14)	100	2,550	(3,778)	23,550	41,750	29,536	4,950	(2,550)	(3,829)	(1,300)	(400)	(30,238)
III. Cash surplus or loan requirements												
(16) Cash of start of month if no borrowing is done	1,000	1,100	3,650	(128)	23,422	65,172	94,708	99,658	97,108	93,279	91,979	91,579
(17) Cumulative cash (cash at start, + gain or –loss = (line 15 + line 16)	1,100	3,650	(128)	23,422	65,172	94,708	99,658	97,108	93,279	91,979	91,579	61,341
(18) Target cash balance	50,000	50,000	50,000	50,000	50,000	50,000	50,000	50,000	50,000	50,000	50,000	50,000
(19) Cumulative surplus cash or loans outstanding to maintain $50,000 target cash balance: (line 17 – line 18)	(48,900)	(46,350)	(50,128)	(26,578)	15,172	44,708	49,658	47,108	43,279	41,979	41,579	11,341

EXHIBIT 13.5   Fjord Trading Company balance sheet as of 6/30/94.

Assets	
Current assets	
Western Bank checking	$ (5,339)
Metro factors reserve	(271,244)
Cash total	(276,583)
Notes receivable effing	395,420
Accounts receivable	392,985
Import fish inventory	(2,649)
Other current assets	116,764
Total current assets	$349,354
Other assets	
Vehicles	77,140
Accumulative depreciation vehicles	(7,789)
Vehicles net 69,351	
Computer	7,710
Accumulative depreciation equipment	(771)
Equipment net	6,939
Effing barter assets (suspense)	6,303
Pending export front money	935
Land, vehicles, equipment, buildings	83,528
Total other assets	$243,346
Total assets	$592,700
Liabilities	
Current liabilities	
Western Bank loan payable Nissan	28,696
Notes payable 1995 Ford truck	30,835
Accounts payable	32,503
Total current liabilities	$ 92,034
Long term liabilities	
Notes payable links financial	112,118
Notes payable Citibank Visa	0
Total long term liabilities	112,118
Total liabilities	$204,152
Equity	
Carl Olson start equity	55,173
Olaf Olson start equity	0
Lief Olson start equity	0
Total investors' equity	$ 55,173
Retained earnings	
Retained earnings	227,869
Current earnings	105,506
Total retained earnings	$333,375
Total equity	$388,548
Liabilities and equity	$592,700

According to Lief, his decision to buy the firm was driven largely by his wife's desire to extend her interest in making clothing into owning and running a garment business, a yearning frustrated by her limited fluency in English. In 1971, the couple purchased a small garment shop where she was employed as a seamstress. The operation, which was owned by an Indonesian friend, produced T-shirts and employed 15 people. Over the next 12 years, Lief and his wife grew the shop into a 150-person business, relocating twice to larger quarters and transitioning from T-shirts to women's sportswear and fashion apparel. As a sideline, Lief also started and ran a company called Dylon that imported industrial sewing goods from Hong Kong and eventually operated out of a storefront in downtown Los Angeles.

The garment business was successful but demanding, requiring "12 to 16 hour days, 6 and sometimes 7 days a week," and when the company's major customer suddenly went out of business, Lief and his wife decided to sell the factory and "take it easy for a while." They remained in California for two more years, running Dylon and enjoying the gains of their years of hard labor. Then in 1985, homesick and eager to see relatives and old friends, the family took a trip to Norway. The two younger children, born in California, were fascinated by the ancestral homeland they'd never seen, and the family decided to turn the vacation into a year-long stay. Ten years later, Lief and his wife still hadn't left, though the children had grown, traveled, and worked abroad.

CARL OLSON, FOUNDER

Carl Olson, the younger of the first two children, was three when the family arrived in California. He grew up in the city of Camarillo, where he attended and graduated from high school in 1984. During their high school years, both brothers worked in the family garment business as drivers. Following graduation, Carl went to work full-time at Dylon, where his older brother Olaf was also employed as a sales associate. During the first year of work, Carl took general business classes at Moorpark College, but did not complete a full course of study. He continued at Dylon for several years as the operations manager, handling the receivables and payables accounts and negotiating sales contracts. He remained at Dylon until the family's decision to remain in Norway necessitated a sale of the company. From 1985 until 1988, Carl followed his father's early vocational path, working in construction in a friend's small but prosperous house-framing company. When the booming California real estate industry came to a halt in the late 1980s, Carl headed back to Norway to join his father in a series of successful business ventures inspired by the chance sale of a single pool table.

ENTREPRENEUR IN TRAINING

When the Olsons decided to stay in Norway for a year, they arranged to rent their house in California. Eventually, as the one year grew to two and three, Lief had most of the furnishings, including a pool table, packed up in a container and shipped over.

Unable to fit the pool table in their smaller Norwegian house, Lief advertised it in the newspaper and sold the table sight-unseen to the second caller for $2,000, more than five times the original price. The calls from interested buyers continued, however, forcing Lief to take the phone off the hook for much of the following two weeks. Within a month, Lief arranged to purchase and ship a container-load of pool tables from the United States to Norway. The 30 tables were manufactured in Taiwan and came complete with balls, racks, and cues, "the works for about $400 each." They sold out immediately at prices ranging from $2,000 to $3,000, and although a 120 percent luxury import tax raised the cost substantially, the venture proved to be immensely profitable. And it was only the beginning. With long, cold nights providing ideal conditions for the adoption of the indoor sport, pool table sales "took off like gangbusters."

From pool tables, Lief branched into snooker, a relative of pool and billiards. Snooker is favored in England, and Lief became a dealer for Rowlan, one of the oldest snooker table manufacturers in the United Kingdom. Carl, who had joined his father's venture after leaving California, spent two months in England learning how to erect and repair snooker tables. To promote their products, the Olsons brought in professional snooker players to give live and televised exhibitions, and they set up tournaments for local players. Soon, the family enterprise was setting up and running entire clubs for the games. The largest one featured a pub in the basement, 14 pool tables on the first floor, 8 snooker tables on the second, and a disco on the third. Over a four-year period, Lief and Carl established and then sold more than 50 such clubs. Then, almost as rapidly as it had flared, the pool/snooker craze died out. The country was saturated with tables, and newspapers were full of ads for used equipment.

As the gaming business was slowing down, Lief bought into Astrid Imports, the oldest sporting goods company in Norway with such prestigious dealerships as Barington Firearms and Warwick Fishing Equipment. From early 1990 to February 1992, Carl worked as the purchasing manager for Astrid. Although based in Norway, he traveled frequently to the United States to look for merchandise and establish contacts with vendors. Carl enjoyed the travel and liked the import/export business, and he became intrigued with the idea of starting his own trading venture with his father between the United States and Norway. The challenge was to find the right products or market niche:

> We were looking for something that we could either send to Norway or something in Norway that we could send out here. We'd always been fiddling with the idea of water from Norway. Fish don't take quite as much money.

START OF FJORD TRADING

In late 1991, a friend of the family approached Lief about importing foodstuffs from the United States. A bookkeeper by profession, the friend had a wholesale food business on the side and sought to enlist the Olsons' help because of their contacts and experience doing business in the United States. With the outline of a business plan in place, Carl moved to Seattle in early 1992 to start Fjord Trading, which was to export food products to the bookkeeper's new business. Carl chose Seattle as the base of operations because of his roots on the West Coast and because of an existing relationship with a steamship company that the Olsons had used to import pool tables.

Initially Fjord Trading shipped canned and dry foods from the United States to Norway. Carl purchased items from wholesale clubs and food distributors such as Monarch and JP Food Service, relying on his own instincts about what would sell in Norway rather than on objective data about market demand. He sent 40-ton containers filled with as many as a hundred different items at one time, everything from spaghetti mixes to spices in one or two case lots. Eventually Carl expanded into frozen seafood, which Lief sold through a wholesale distributorship he established to handle those products. Although the business grew, various factors conspired to restrain the rate of growth and the success of the venture. Differences between United States and European product packaging, sizes, and styles limited consumer acceptance of the canned and dry food goods, and growth in any one product was severely limited by the natural demand constraints of Norway's small population.

At its peak in 1992, the dollar amount of all goods shipped to Norway reached $30,000 a month. Yet, just as growth in this area started to stall, a chance inquiry in late 1992 initiated the start of more promising trade in the other direction. According to Carl:

> One of the wholesalers from whom I was buying frozen seafood said he was looking for fresh seafood, and I mentioned that I thought I could bring in fresh fish from Norway. They started ordering and soon we were bringing in more stuff than we were sending out. We phased out exporting to Norway in mid-1993, though I still get calls occasionally from people there looking for certain products.

IMPORTING FRESH NORWEGIAN SEAFOOD

Carl passed the query about Norwegian seafood along to his father. Although the family's business and trading experience did not include dealing with fish, it seemed a natural product to consider. Norway, as Lief explained, "lives and thrives on fish." Fishing was by far the largest industry, comprising 80 percent of Norway's exports, and more than half of its gross national product. The industry was tightly regulated by the government, which controlled "who can fish where, how much can be caught by what methods, and what areas to leave alone." The Norwegian government also sponsored considerable research into fish demographics, projecting population sizes and growth rates, as well as other industry issues such as processing and packaging. Regulation and research enabled the industry to remain relatively healthy, especially compared to the fishing industries in the United States and Canada. Although the total catch had fallen from a high of 346 thousand tons at its peak to 200 thousand tons in 1994, the decline was far less than for Norway's North Atlantic competitors.

Because of Norway's distance from its export markets, more than three quarters of the seafood exported to the United States was frozen. After processing in Norway, the fish was packaged, frozen and shipped in freezer containers by surface transportation. Importing fresh fish to the United States required the expense and logistical complexities of air freight and the challenge of delivering a product that would remain fresh long enough to reach retail consumers.

Ignorant himself in the ways of selecting and buying fish, Lief Olson turned for help to an industry insider, a snooker table customer who had become a good friend. The man had grown up in the fishing industry and had worked for 25 years for the largest fish auction. He knew the individual boats, their owners, and the quality of their catch. With a couple of phone calls, the first order for fresh fish was placed and filled, then air-freighted to Seattle. The wholesale customer liked the product and increased the size of his next order. Although Carl initially considered the fresh fish orders to be a chance sideline to the main business of exporting foodstuffs, to his surprise within a few months Fjord Trading was importing more fresh fish than it was sending out canned, dry, and frozen. Carl found the relative simplicity of the product and the economics of the new line compelling:

> So it was: buy the groceries, handle hundreds of different items, carry inventory, get paid in 45 to 60 days; or buy fish, deal in just a few kinds, and get paid in 7 to 10 days. It seemed a lot easier and it was growing fast.

EARLY CHALLENGES

In spite of the apparent promise of selling fresh Norwegian seafood in the Northwest, Fjord Trading faced a variety of difficulties as it pursued this new course. Carl had broad experience in the ins-and-outs of importing and exporting, but prior to this venture he had never dealt with fresh fish and the particular challenges engendered by one of the most purely competitive markets in the world. Except for bans on fishing in certain areas for environmental reasons, there is far less government or industry control over levels of production (harvest) and prices for fish than for such commodities as grains and dairy products. Although prices of other commodities may be subject to significant swings due to such factors as unseasonable weather and storm damage, they are sufficiently stable to allow trading on a commodities futures market. The variability of local conditions and harvests in the fish industry, however, precludes a futures market for fresh fish. Prices fluctuate too widely and too quickly. (There is futures trading in frozen fish, the price of which is loosely tied to fresh but doesn't change as rapidly or to as great a degree.)

In the Northwest market, prices of fresh fish were determined not only by the size and timing of the harvests of the local fishing fleet, but also by the conditions of the Canadian fishing industry. As Carl explained:

> Usually the Canadian stuff is cheap, and that brings down the Norwegian prices. The price will go as low as $2.75 and as high as $5.00, and that can happen within one week. You can have a Canadian truck come down with 100,000 pounds of fresh fish and they'll be unloading that for 2 to 3 days and flood the market. Then the older the product gets, the cheaper the price gets, so maybe its $3.50 to start and then it'll start dropping. In the meantime, you're sitting with Norwegian at $4.00 a pound and you have to ride the storm out unless you want to drop your pants and start selling at $3.00.

Although local conditions were the primary determinants of prices for regional markets, with the growth in export/import of fresh fish, such dramatic short-term price changes were having increasingly strong impacts on distant markets.

Though it often took several days for the prices to ripple through, a glut in Canada would eventually cause prices in Norway and Europe to fall also. Norwegian fish was relatively less expensive at auction than local U.S. domestic fish but the high transportation costs and the longer time lag between order and shipment created riskier conditions due to price swings that could occur between purchase and delivery. The rapid price changes and the short shelf-life of fresh fish combined to make the industry "notorious" for canceled or modified contracts and "credits" for unacceptable or unwanted product.

To minimize its exposure to the extreme price fluctuations, Fjord Trading initially functioned as a broker for the fresh Norwegian fish business. In theory that role should have reduced the company's risk while also requiring less working capital than if it worked as a wholesaler. In practice, however, the company ended up bearing most of the risk anyway with limited upside potential. According to Carl:

> Wholesalers didn't take any responsibility for the product. There were no guarantees. You give them a price, and they say "fine" and you ship the product and they say: "We're having a little problem with the product and have some left or we weren't able to move as much as we thought. We're going to have to start lowering our price." So right away that comes off the selling price. The price agreement is essentially meaningless.

Fjord's risk in this early stage was magnified by the fact that it was doing increasingly large amounts of business with relatively few customers. If one big account suddenly reduced its requested shipment quantity, there were few alternative venues for unloading excess product. Thus, in the early months, Fjord experienced some losses on large orders that were rejected or that it had guaranteed at too low a price given the market conditions in Norway at the time of purchase. One of the reasons for the variations in customer order, according to Carl, was that many people in the seafood business really were not equipped to handle fresh fish, even though they thought they were:

> Handling fresh and handling frozen are two very different things. So sometimes customers found they weren't able to handle as much as they thought, and they cut the size of their orders at the last minute.

Added to the risks of price fluctuation and customer fickleness was the challenge of preserving freshness and quality while moving the product two thousand miles through an inefficient and expensive transportation channel. Fjord's fish was flown out on Norwegian Airlines into one of several West coast cities—except Seattle, into which NA did not fly. Although Los Angeles was the most common port, shipments occasionally came via San Francisco, from where they were transferred and flown up north or driven in refrigerated trucks. Compounding the routing problems was the fact that Norwegian Airlines' planes were too small to permit containerized cargo handling. Each box of fish was individually loaded and unloaded, a system known as "belly freight." Renting space in refrigerated trucks also proved problematic; the different produce shipped in one carrier required different ranges of temperature. Instead of being the 28 to 30 degrees needed for fresh fish, the trucks could be as high as 40 degrees, effectively reducing the shelf life of the fish. In mid-1994, when volume justified the expense, Fjord purchased it's own truck.

CREATING DIFFERENTIATION IN A COMMODITY MARKET

As the fresh fish importing business quickly displaced foodstuffs exporting, Carl and his father took several steps to reduce risk from market factors and to gain more control over the operation. In both Norway and Seattle, they switched from doing business as brokers to becoming wholesalers. Lief had initially bought most of the fresh fish from a processor and had to take product the way it was conventionally cut and packaged. As the business grew he started his own processing company, Effing Ltd., which enabled him to buy at auction and manage the processing operation. Being in direct contact with the suppliers enabled better information on prices and on the status of the fishing fleet, "What's coming in; how many boats are out; who's on vacation." As a wholesaler on the sales end, Carl accepted a small degree of increased risk but also benefited from price swings in his favor. The most significant changes, though, were in the way Fjord portioned and packaged its fresh fish. The innovations allowed it both to differentiate its product from commodity catch and to reduce risk from extreme short-term price movements.

MODIFIED ATMOSPHERIC PACKAGING (MAP)

Traditionally, fresh fish was packed in a bed of ice in a cardboard box, a method that was messy and left the product susceptible to spoilage and contamination. In late 1993, with the support of the Norwegian government, Lief began experimenting with modified atmospheric packaging (MAP). MAP used specialized equipment to draw air out of a plastic package and replace it with carbon dioxide, nitrogen, and a small amount of oxygen, and then seal the package. Depending on the initial quality of the product, MAP could extend shelf-life between 50 and 100 percent. For fresh fish, such a product-life extension could mean an extra 14 days for a superior quality product.

Modified atmospheric packaging had been available for many years and was used for produce such as Dole salad mixes, but since the late 1960s there had been a moratorium in the United States on its use for fresh fish. The restriction was triggered by a 1968 incident in which an entire family that had consumed MAP-packed smoked mackerel had died of salmonella poisoning. The Norwegian government, however, had been testing and experimenting with MAP for fresh fish since 1982 in an effort to encourage its adoption, but as yet its use was not widespread. No one had figured out how the technology could add value to their business. Each species required a different mixture of gases and the industry considered the process too complicated and too expensive. Wholesalers saw no gains from MAP that could justify the extra cost, and the competitive marketplace prevented the costs from being passed along to customers.

Lief Olson could not remember precisely when or where he heard about MAP, but he quickly saw its potential application to Fjord's business:

> I probably came across it in some articles and got interested in it as a way to solve problems with freshness and short shelf life. It costs more but increases our range of customers and helps take out the ups and downs in the market.

Fjord began using MAP in early 1993 after conducting additional testing on cod and haddock—the two principal fish it handled. The USFDA initially remained neutral on the issue but then tested Fjord's product and officially approved MAP for use with fresh fish sold at wholesale. The new packaging method gave Fjord Trading several advantages over purveyors of fresh fish packed in ice. The most fundamental benefit was the ability to weather short-term excess supply conditions that pushed the price of fresh fish below acceptable levels. MAP allowed Fjord to wait out dips in price for longer than would otherwise be possible and then sell its product when the market rebounded. MAP also helped Fjord ameliorate some of the increasing transportation complexities by enabling fewer and larger shipments and thus better scheduling of flights and destinations.

While MAP provided direct benefits to Fjord Trading, its value to Fjord's customers varied substantially depending on their place in the value chain and the nature of the end users they serviced. Some distributors, such as Cristo (the largest food distributor to restaurants in the United States, offering over 7,000 items) did not have the ability or inclination to handle large quantities of fresh fish packed in the conventional manner with the attendant mess and risks of deterioration and loss of quality. MAP enabled such customers to expand the selection and availability of their own offerings, thereby also increasing demand for Fjord's products. As Carl explained:

> MAP gives us an extreme advantage to get people into the seafood business who otherwise couldn't because of the short shelf life and distribution time and the mess of the water and ice and the stink. Cristo thought they couldn't be in the fresh seafood business in a significant way, but with this kind of packaging, they can now offer fresh fish widely. They love it.

While MAP enabled Fjord Trading to differentiate its product and charge a premium to some distributors, the innovative packaging did not provide much added value to customers such as supermarkets. Restricted by law and inhibited by consumer demand from selling MAP-packaged fish at retail, wholesalers could not differentiate the product from local catch or imported fish packaged in the conventional manner and saw no particular gain from paying extra for MAP-packaged product. Thus Fjord did not attempt to emphasize MAP as a differentiating factor to such customers and often repackaged their fish to avoid confusion among customers who did not understand the MAP process.

PORTIONING AND LABELING

In conjunction with MAP, Fjord Trading also differentiated its product by offering consistent portioning, another innovation that was of value to certain types of customers. A typical ice-packed shipment from most distributors comprised a 25-pound box of fillets in varying sizes. Restaurants then had to recut and weigh the fish to appropriate meal portions. Through its strategic alliance with Effing Ltd., Fjord arranged to have fillets cut to standards that would be useful without recutting. For example, haddock usually came in 8 to 10 ounce portions for lunch or 12 to 16 ounce portions for the dinner menu. The fillets were packed in a 10-pound box that was easier to handle than the 25-pound containers and were untouched from the time of packing in Norway until they were taken out to be cooked. By eliminating steps and reducing restaurants' food preparation time, the combination of portioning and MAP provided benefits for which end-users were willing to pay more. Fjord further leveraged the value of the innovative packaging and standard sizes by offering customers the ability to have their own labels put on the packages of fillets. The private labeling enabled customers to extend the reach of their brand, another differentiating quality with tangible value to discount retailers such as BJ's and Sam's wholesale clubs.

NORWEGIAN VERSUS DOMESTIC SEAFOOD

While Fjord Trading employed innovative techniques—MAP, portion consistency, and labeling—to differentiate its products, it had to contend with a more subtle challenge in differentiating the fresh fish on the basis of its origin. Norwegian seafood faced mixed perceptions from buyers. Although all the fish comes out of the same ocean, fresh Norwegian fish usually sold for more than Canadian but less than local Northwest domestic stock. Such perceptions often led to sudden changes of identity. As Carl explained, "There's a lot of repackaging in the industry. Often Norwegian is sold as domestic and Canadian is sold as domestic."

In spite of the sometimes inferior perception of Norwegian seafood, there was the strong potential to differentiate Norwegian quality on the basis of Norway's environmental conditions, governmental supervision, and industry practices. The clean, cold waters around Norway provided superior conditions for healthy, high-quality fish, and government oversight and management of fishing methods and catch sizes helped to ensure preservation of this asset. Norway was also far ahead of the United States in its adoption of a rigorous inspection program. For 11 years, Norway had required HAACP inspections of fish handling and processing operations, a protocol which is on a par with USDA inspections of meat and poultry. Similar tight controls are planned for implementation in the U.S. fishing industry by 1998.

CUSTOMER DIFFERENTIATION

The differentiating qualities of product source, portion sizing, packaging, and attention to customer needs, such as private labeling, permitted Fjord Trading to establish customer relationships based on factors other than price and increasingly to de-emphasize the commodity-based business and customers:

> What we're trying to do is to stay away from the day-to-day seafood guys that are looking for today's price, order 100 pounds, and then ratchet it up to 200 or down to 50, depending upon where prices are headed. Instead, we're building programs with people who order every single day, regardless of what the domestic price is, regardless of short-term industry conditions, regardless of whatever else is going on.

By late 1994, Fjord's biggest accounts were with QFC and Albertsons. Although grocery chains often placed large orders for advertised specials, they were more prone to try to pull back from accepting shipment if a sale was not moving the product as fast as anticipated.

ECONOMICS AND EXTERNAL FACTORS

Carl financed the start of Fjord Trading with the proceeds of a house he had owned in California and sold at the time of his move to Seattle. The initial purchases of dry and canned foodstuffs were small enough to handle with a combination of available cash and store credit. When the sales of fresh fish started in earnest, Lief, working through his industry friend, opened a line of credit for $50,000 with the auction. The terms of the fresh fish trade were typically net 14 days, though Carl figured it took a total of about 21 days, including time for check clearing, to be able to use the funds for another order. With business expanding rapidly, Carl turned to the use of factors in October 1993 to provide financing for the growing accounts receivable.

According to Carl, the cost of using a factor in the fresh fish business far exceeded the nominal expenses. The factor charged: (1) $1 to generate each invoice, (2) the prime rate plus 2 points on the outstanding accounts receivable balance, and (3) a 1 percent factoring commission on each invoice. By Carl's calculation, the fees totaled about 3 percent to 4 percent of revenue but represented only a portion of the true cost. All checks and invoices went through the factor, which sent Fjord Trading a monthly statement detailing all activity. Customers notified the factor, but not Fjord Trading directly, of deductions and credits, and by the time Fjord received the information it was too late to resolve the issues. Instead of being able to negotiate with customers over alleged problems with orders when the fish was still there to examine, Fjord had to take most of the losses:

> It got out of control. We weren't getting the information we needed back from the factory, as far as deduction and credits were concerned. Everything was without recourse because the information was so late. We saw on a monthly report what had happened, but we couldn't go back to the customer 30 to 40 days later and resolve issues. The cost of not knowing what was going on was getting too high. We needed to stop factoring to get back control over the operation.

In addition to eliminating the use of factoring, Fjord Trading urgently required more capital to finance its rapid expansion. New large customers projected increasing volume orders and wanted assurance that Fjord had the capability to service their growing accounts. Some of these customers were regional divisions of national organizations and offered the potential for substantial increased business in other parts of the country. Additionally, during the busy season around Lent, which was due to start within a few months, Fjord could sell virtually all the fish it could buy, usually at a higher margin. Finally, the owners were eager to move to larger offices with more owned storage space and they needed capital to finance the move, which would involve facility improvements and new equipment.

PROPOSAL

At 11:15 on the morning of November 30, a phone call from Jack Calhoon preceded the arrival of a one-page fax containing a proposal to finance expansion of Fjord Trading and reorganize the management team of the company (Exhibit 13.6). Juan, Carl, and

**EXHIBIT 13.6   Proposal to finance expansion of
Fjord Trading Company.**

TO: Juan Gomez, Business Manager/Fjord Trading Company
FROM: Jack Calhoon, Larry Butcher, and Ira Goldstein
DATE: 29 November 1994
RE: Providing funding in order to expand the business

PROPOSAL

We propose as a group to provide funds up to $500,000 for Fjord Trading Company to use as
a basis to expand their purchasing power in the fresh fish business. Jack Calhoon will come
into the company immediately and act as president of operations/marketing director on a day
to day basis; he will be overseeing the cash flows and become directly involved in processing
new accounts and helping in any way to supervise any already existing accounts. Jack Calhoon
will work daily with Juan Gomez, Carl, and Olaf Olson, officers of the present company. Jack
Calhoon will be empowered to help direct the flow of finances for receivables, and make adjustments and business decisions on operating the company on a day-to-day basis that involves
any and all decisions with regard to the handling of present accounts and future accounts.

Larry Butcher and Ira Goldstein will take initially more of a business consultant role(s) with
regard to the day to day overseeing of the operating of the business. All principals currently
involved will have ownership and management positions in the new corporation that will be
formed and their percentage of ownership and management in the new corporation that will
be formed and that will take the place of the current DBA ownership structure. The structure of this infusion of funds proposal is for a 50 percent share of the present company that
will then be converted into a 50 percent share of stock in the new corporation that will be
formed.

This proposal is what has been discussed among the principals over the last several weeks and
is contingent upon the UCC filing being completed and in place prior to the transfer of all the
funds.

Submitted this day, November 29, 1994 for the group:

_____
Jack Calhoon

Agreed _____
        Carl Olson

Olaf read the memo through several times. They had not anticipated such terms and
were unsure how to respond. Juan suggested seeking assistance to evaluate the offer.
Who should they ask? Was half the company worth $500,000? or more? Were they
willing to relinquish operational control if that was necessary to secure the financing?
The opportunities created by the infusion of capital seemed clear, but the men sus-
pected that they did not fully comprehend and appreciate the potential risks inherent
in such an arrangement.

14 ENOX TECHNOLOGIES

In early 1993, Voislav (Voit) Damevski and Stanley Rich, cofounders of ENOX Technologies (a mechanical-engineering research firm), conferred on the future of their relationship with Burton Engine Company, one of the world's leading manufacturers of diesel engines. They had just completed a rancorous conference call with the Burton project manager over interpretations of the performance/payment thresholds in their contract. Stanley, as usual, was outspoken in his criticism:

> I can't work with those people anymore, Voit. They're unreasonable and manipulative, and it's not worth it. We ought to terminate our contract and focus on the natural gas market.

Voit was equally frustrated by the experience of dealing with Burton but less quick to conclude that ending the relationship was in the best long-term interest of ENOX. He tried to temper Stanley's outburst:

> But Stanley, there is tremendous long-term potential in the diesel market, and it may make sense to keep a hand in it. In spite of the strings it attaches, Burton has come up with a lot of money, and it's well connected to the government R&D funding pipeline. Besides, the stationary gas compressor market is finite. Eventually we'll need to find new markets.

Since 1990, ENOX Technologies, formerly PlasMachines, had been doing research for Burton on a technology that used electrical plasma to reduce nitrogen oxide in diesel exhaust emissions, a major concern due to impending change in environmental regulations. By 1993, Burton had provided ENOX more than $200,000 of its own

This case was prepared by Sam Perkins under the direction of Professor William Bygrave. Funding provided by the Ewing Marion Kauffman Foundation. Copyright © 1996 Babson College. All rights reserved.

233

funds and had also served as the conduit for an additional $300,000 in research money from the U.S. Department of Energy (USDOE) and state environmental organizations. Additionally, ENOX had secured Small Business Innovation Research (SBIR) grants from the U.S. Environmental Protection Agency (USEPA) to work on the plasma device. Given the high level of government and private interest in finding effective ways to reduce nitrogen oxide and the proven efficacy of this technology, continued funding for research and eventual product development seemed assured.

Soon after beginning the work for Burton, however, Voit and Rich started to investigate other applications for the underlying electronic technology they had developed to create the electrical plasma. One promising concept was to use the device as an ignition system to improve the firing of spark plugs in gasoline engines, an approach which both enhanced fuel efficiency and reduced nitrogen oxide. The ignition was well suited to the task of retrofitting older stationary engines used to run the compressors on natural gas pipelines, and by 1993, ENOX had secured several contracts to perform tests of the ignition systems on these large engines. The effort to pursue the natural gas market however, and to continue research on the exhaust technology was straining ENOX's finances, manpower, and strategic focus, and the founders were struggling with the issue of balancing short and longer term market opportunities and resources.

The Founders

Voit Damevski grew up in Rochester, New York, and graduated from Syracuse University in 1985. As a youth, Voit was passionate about auto mechanics: beginning at the age of five, he spent most of his free time tinkering with engines and later, racing motorcycles. A serious accident at 21 convinced him to stop racing, but he continued the tinkering. The son of a doctor, Voit went through the motions of following in his father's footsteps by majoring in biology and planning a career in medicine. However, a month before he was due to start medical school, he decided to pursue his own vision of manifest destiny:

> It (medicine) was nothing I ever really wanted to do. Instead, I wanted to be in business. From when anyone can remember, I've always done my own thing, had my own businesses. I paid my way through school by having a painting company, importing cars, all sorts of strange jobs, and always on my own.

Voit enrolled in a local MBA program but left after one semester, disillusioned by the school's emphasis on finance. He'd wanted a program that would nurture his entrepreneurial instincts. A friend had recommended Babson College and after further investigation, Voit felt that the college's focus on entrepreneurship studies would be perfect for his needs. Voit also read, *Business Plans That Win Dollars,* by Babson professor Stanley Rich. Disdaining Stanley's advice that "cold calls get cold responses" Voit phoned him one night at 10 o'clock to praise the book and discuss his desire to get an MBA. Stanley's response was encouraging, and the call proved to be the genesis of a friendship and business partnership.

Exhibit 14.1   Exhaust after-treatment with chemical additive.

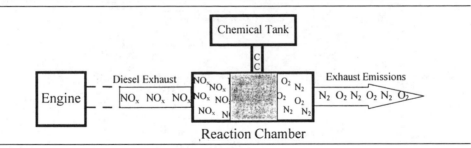

Stanley Rich was an inventor and habitual entrepreneur, who had more than 500 international patents to his name and had started a half-dozen companies. By his own admission Stanley was a "good starting pitcher"* who liked best to develop new technology and prove a marketable application that could create a business opportunity, but he had little interest in the details of building a business or running a company. As Voit described, "The everyday management, building sales, and marketing, all of those things were functions that in Stanley's mind would just happen." He became an adjunct member of Babson's Entrepreneurial Studies department in 1986, but continued to consult with outside companies about technology development.

Opportunity Assessment—The Problem of Nitrogen Oxide

Voit enrolled in Babson's MBA program, and in late 1988, while Voit was finishing the program, Stanley Rich enlisted his services to help with an opportunity assessment for Burton Engine Company of a technology for reducing nitrogen oxide in diesel engine exhaust. The technology used a powdered chemical, injected into a diesel exhaust stream, that caused the nitrogen oxide to come apart and be discharged as harmless constituent elements, nitrogen and oxygen (Exhibit 14.1). Although the technology achieved its purpose, Stanley and Voit quickly concluded that the requirements of its use—filling up with the chemical at every fuel stop—would be too onerous to make it acceptable to most truckers. Voit recalled their research:

> Stanley picked up the phone and called six or seven truck operators and asked them how would they feel about pulling up to a gas station and not only filling up with diesel, but filling up with a powdered chemical. The first three hung up the phone on him. That was kind of an easy one to figure out.

In spite of the lack of application for that particular technology, Damevski and Rich were intrigued by the opportunity of finding a way to reduce nitrogen oxide, one

---

* This is an analogy to the game of baseball, which normally has nine innings. The starting pitcher rarely completes all nine innings. He usually leaves before the game is finished and is replaced by the relief pitcher (a reliever).

Exhibit 14.2   Exhaust after-treatment with electrical plasma.

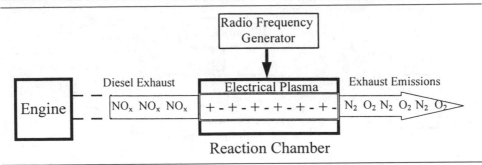

of several engine emissions that were being targeted by the USEPA for reduction.° The two kicked around a lot of ideas, drawing on Stanley's formal training as an electrical engineer and Voit's informal pastime and years of experience tinkering with engines. Emerging from their verbal peregrinations came the theory of passing the exhaust through an electrical discharge of plasma, created with a radio frequency generator. The plasma would "excite" the exhaust gases in a reaction chamber, causing the unstable compounds, such as nitrogen oxide, to decompose into their components (Exhibit 14.2). At a meeting in January 1989, Rich ventured the idea to Burton engineers, who liked the concept, cut a check for $25,000, and said, "Here, go tinker."

The Prototype

In August 1989, Voit and Stanley formally incorporated as PlasMachines, a name Voit loved to hate:

> That name was Stanley's wonderful creation. It was probably the worst name in history. He said we're using an electrical plasma and we're building machines—so we're Plas-Machines. I said it sounds like we're in the medical instrument business. But we kept that name for quite a few years.

For the following four months the partners worked together every day, alternating between Stanley's basement and Voit's apartment. Through Stanley's extensive network of contacts, they found and hired an electrical engineer to build the prototype electronic driver for the reactor, while Voit built the mechanical components. By November, Stanley and Voit deemed the prototype complete, but, although the contraption glowed like a neon bulb when it was turned on, they had no way to test its

---

° Nitrogen oxide (NO_x) is the collective term for nitric oxide (NO_x) and nitrogen dioxide (NO_2), which are formed both from natural sources (lightning and biological processes) and from anthropogenic activities (burning fossil fuels). Approximately 90 percent of the nitrogen oxides enter the atmosphere as emissions from internal combustion engines in automobile and stationary sources, which create nitric oxide (NO) at very high temperatures. NO is rapidly converted to nitrogen dioxide (NO_2), which is a major contributor to air pollution through ozone formation, smog and acid rain. In 1989, the U.S. Congress was debating the reauthorization of the 1970 Clean Air Act (CAA), and NO_x reduction was one of the issues the USEPA was pushing for. The CAA reauthorization was passed in 1990 with each state responsible for the development of implementation plans.

functionality. They reported their status to the Burton engineers, who were astonished to hear that the plasma concept had actually been turned into a physical device, and a few days later Stanley and Voit flew to the Burton test facility in Columbus, Ohio. The team hooked up the reactor to a diesel exhaust pipe, let the engine heat up and turned on the machine. The nitrogen oxide meter gauges dropped by 50 percent. They turned off the reactor, and the reading went back up. On again and down 50; off and back up. They followed that routine—up, down, up down—for 10 minutes until the reactor burned out and melted down—there was nothing left of it. The Burton engineers were excited by the test results and the proof of concept.

For Stanley, the "starting pitcher," that proof brought him to the successful completion of four or five innings, as Voit recalled:

> Stanley jumped for joy and in his mind it was done. At that point, he was ready to sell it to Burton, and it was over and done with. There was no more work. That was his mindset. I used to say he would fly at 30,000 feet when everyone else was still walking on solid ground, because he just saw so far into the future that he lost sight of the things he had to do to turn the opportunity into something that was going to be of value.

In spite of his inclination to leave the pitching mound to a middle reliever, Stanley leveraged the test results and Burton's reaction into additional financing to continue the research and development of the plasma after-treatment technology:

> This is where the genius of Stanley came in. This is where he excelled. He turned that exciting proof of concept into a $200,000 option agreement with Burton. We created the excitement there at Burton, and he turned that excitement into a lot of money fairly quickly.

That day, Burton and the partners agreed on the basic structure of a contract that would provide PlasMachines $200,000 in seed capital to conduct further research in exchange for exclusive rights for six months to negotiate a licensing deal. Burton also pledged to secure additional funding for technology development through the USDOE and other agencies. In spite of the ease of reaching the preliminary agreement, the details took nine months to work out. According to Voit, Burton started to realize that they were negotiating with only two guys, who continued to push out the timeframe of negotiations. By mid-1990, PlasMachines had nearly run through the $45,000 advance from Burton, and the start-up was close to being broke. No cash was coming in, and expenses had increased because Stanley and Voit had moved the company out of their homes into office space in Natick, Massachusetts, negotiating a $700 per month lease for a 6,000 square-foot building with a bay and work area. At first, Voit was skeptical about taking on the extra cost and more space than they could use but was convinced by Stanley's optimistic view that they would eventually grow into it.

Finally, feeling that Burton was stringing them along with no incentive to conclude the deal, Voit and Stanley took their last cash and bought airplane tickets to visit Flint Diesel, a Burton competitor. They had gotten an appointment with CEO William Stark and his chief engineer, to whom they pitched their technology and its potential application and benefits. Mention of the association with Burton, however, immediately terminated Stark's interest, but Stanley and Voit nevertheless returned to Boston with their mission accomplished: they had secured Stark's business card. Voit then asked the Burton people to come to Natick to conclude negotiations, and the following day the president of a division, a lawyer, and three other people visited PlasMachines' nearly vacant building. During a break in discussions, Voit directed the division president to his desk to use the phone, near to which Stark's card was strategically placed—not too blatant, not too hidden. After the calls, the Burton people conferred for a few minutes, came back into the room, signed the agreement, and cut PlasMachines a check for $280,000 with more to follow.

The total funding package included money from three sources. The original option agreement with Burton was for $200,000 of which $45,000 had already been drawn. A research contract with the USDOE, secured by Burton, provided $160,000, one-third paid by Burton. It was a fraction of the $14 million in USDOE funds that Burton received annually. Finally, the state of California put in $280,000. With the toughest air quality standards in the United States, California funded research efforts in emissions reductions, financed by state gas taxes and overseen by the Southern California Air Quality Management District, the environmental enforcement agency. All the engine companies used these and other sources to fund research, but it was very difficult for a small firm to secure such moneys directly.

R&D Shop

The relationship with Burton Engine promised to provide PlasMachines with funding to develop the exhaust after-treatment technology, yet Stanley and Voit quickly recognized that the R&D work was unlikely to lead to the creation of a product-based business within the next several years. Although the 1990 Clean Air Act Amendment (CAAA) set a general target for reducing nitrogen oxide by the mid-1990s, the exact timeframe, degree of reduction, regulatory mechanisms, and differences in state plans remained to be worked out. California was considering a total restriction on diesel fuel, mandating that diesel engines run on natural gas by 1996, but other states were proposing less drastic measures. In response to these conditions, most engine companies were examining a range of technical options but delaying commitments until the uncertainties had been resolved. According to Voit, Burton hedged their bets by investing in several technologies for reducing nitrogen oxide, while tying up licensing options for as long as possible. Until there was a clear regulatory signal and schedule for implementation, however, the company was not compelled to move quickly from research to marketable product:

> The real hot button for Burton was to make sure that they had a window on all these unique technologies that were being developed. There was really no specified timeframe to develop a product. We realized that there wasn't going to be a market for a very long time. This wasn't a driver from Burton's standpoint, so they didn't have a defined goal.

The applicability and cost of the technology itself was a long way from what the market needed and would accept. Translating a relatively large and fragile technology into a rugged device that would attach to the end of an truck engine and survive half a million miles would be a significant challenge, accentuated by the need to price it at less than $700. In the absence of a clear and compelling regulatory mandate, Voit didn't see an application for the technology for a "long, long time. We're so far away that I didn't see a mechanism for how you'd get from a technology to a product."

Although the immediate financing problem had been solved, Voit soon became disenchanted with the procedures and constraints of running an R&D operation that was dependent upon one customer. It was too much like a job, rather than owning a business:

> You're doing work, you're doing monthly reports, you're submitting the monthly reports. I started to get bored. R&D is great, but it's not going to lead anywhere; it's not going to make a business. You've got one customer, and you're handcuffed. They control everything. What I wanted to do was create a business, and what Stanley wanted to do was create a business.

NITROGEN OXIDE: SAME PROBLEM—DIFFERENT ANSWER

In 1990, even as they were in the midst of negotiating with Burton and continuing the R&D work, Stanley and Voit pursued other avenues in their determination to fashion a business around their technology and the need to reduce tailpipe emissions. The route of their exploration mirrored a fundamental shift that was occurring in the environmental regulatory philosophy in the United States: preventing pollution at the source instead of treating and controlling it at the end of a process. Stanley and Voit asked the fundamental question: What could be done up front to *prevent* the creation of nitrogen oxide, rather than attempt to remediate nitrogen oxide in the tailpipe? Nitrogen oxide is created by the high temperatures that occur in an internal combustion gas engine when the air/fuel mixture is ignited by a spark plug (Exhibit 14.3).

Exhibit 14.3   Internal combustion engine.

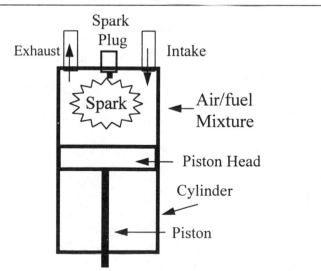

The exhaust emissions, including nitrogen oxide, are a function of the ratio of air to fuel, the temperature and the efficiency of the combustion, which, in turn, is a function of the quality and timing of the spark. A poor spark produces poor combustion and more misfires, which generate higher levels of emissions. Stanley and Voit hypothesized that the electronics they had developed to create the wave form for the plasma might also be applied to enhancing the performance of an engine's ignition system by improving the firing of the spark plug. More consistent ignition would improve the efficiency of the engine and reduce misfires, thereby reducing levels of contaminants in the exhaust emissions.

For Voit, who had a strong affinity for spark plugs, ignition coils, and related electronics, the logic of the approach was clear and appealing. To augment his experience and intuitive sense of the subject, he spent much of the following six months at a library at MIT, combing through the Society of Automotive Engineers (SAE) journals for information about leading edge research and applications in the field of automotive ignitions. Voit found two competing schools of thought that were developing along diametrically opposing lines. The Detroit-based approach posited that the best method of ignition was to spark the spark plug as fast as possible, concentrating the energy to maximize the precision of the timing in igniting the fuel/air mixture in the cylinder. In the other automotive capital of the world, Japan, engineers pursued the opposite path, theorizing that a long, slow release of energy to the spark plug would ensure a higher probability that the mixture would ignite, thereby maximizing the overall performance of the engine, even if the individual spark plug firings were underperforming the optimum. The PlasMachines device offered the potential to satisfy both methods of firing. It dumped a lot of energy very rapidly at the start and then sustained it for a long period of time (Exhibit 14.4).

Voit and Stanley were encouraged by the theoretical benefits of using the device for an ignition system, but they lacked a gasoline engine to test it until Voit had his parents load his 1974, 500-horsepower Firebird onto a flat-bed truck and ship it

Exhibit 14.4 Ignition system comparison.

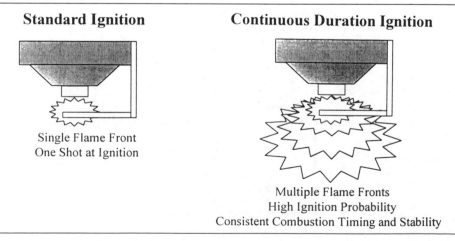

Standard Ignition	Continuous Duration Ignition
Single Flame Front One Shot at Ignition	Multiple Flame Fronts High Ignition Probability Consistent Combustion Timing and Stability

to Boston. Testing the mechanism on the car proved that it worked as an ignition system but didn't offer any insights into its effectiveness at reducing nitrogen oxide or other contaminants, nor did it provide any measure of potential increased operating efficiency. With a moonlighting engineer to help them at night, Stanley and Voit worked on refining the design, drawing on their experience and expertise in electrical engineering and mechanics. Without a lab or equipment to test their ideas and technical refinements empirically, much of their effort relied on dialectical theorizing. As Voit described the process:

> During the day, Stanley and I would spend an enormous amount of time sitting and talking and thinking stuff through and playing what-if games. That worked very well for us. Playing these games back and forth without having a lot of equipment at our fingertips allowed us to go through the thing conceptually. Stanley was a very good electronics engineer but didn't really understand engines. He didn't understand how the system worked mechanically. So we would sit there and go back and forth. He'd say one thing, I'd say, "no it can't work that way—it's got to work this way." We did a lot of talking about what was going to be the best way to optimize the electronics for an ignition system.

Voit's initial perception of a potential market for the ignition system was the automobile racing industry, where enhanced engine performance was critical and cost considerations relatively minor. He knew the industry fairly well from his former racing days and believed its interest in experimenting with new technologies would make it a logical arena to try out the system. At the point where Voit and Stanley thought they had a functional ignition system, they shared the concept with engineers at Burton, who liked the technology even though it had no application for their own diesel engines.° In spite of that apparent drawback, Stanley and Voit succeeded in convincing Burton to give them an additional $20,000 to take the prototype to Southwest Research Institute† for a week's worth of testing on a small single-cylinder General Motors engine.

The results bettered expectations. The ignition system eliminated misfires, enabling a smoother operating engine with lower levels of emissions due to the reduction of unburned fuel in the exhaust. Further enhancing the benefits of the technology was its ability to allow an engine to operate with a leaner fuel mixture, a process known as "extending the lean limit of operation." A gasoline engine operated optimally at a ratio of 14.7 parts air to 1 part gasoline. A leaner mixture had a higher concentration of air to gas. With a conventional ignition system, increasing the ratio of air to gas produced more misfiring because a leaner mixture was more difficult to ignite. The PlasMachines system, however, was able to achieve stable ignition of mixtures up to 22 to 1 without misfires. The leaner mixture lowered the temperature in the cylinder, which in turn reduced the formation of nitrogen oxide, whose production was directly variable with the temperature level. At a 22–1 mixture, nitrogen

---

° In diesel engines, the pressure created in the cylinder ignites the air/fuel mixture, eliminating the need for an ignition system using spark plugs.

† The Southwest Research Institute is a third-party independent testing organization with a staff of 3,000 located in San Antonio, Texas. Known worldwide as the premier test organization for automobile developments, it is used by the automotive industry as an R&D center.

Exhibit 14.5   Nitrogen oxide physics.

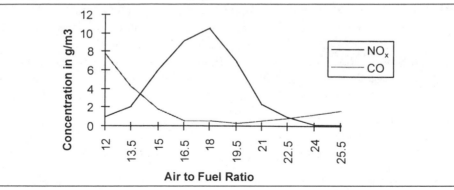

oxide was reduced 95 percent (Exhibit 14.5). In addition to the reduction in emissions, the absence of misfiring and the leaner fuel mixture both contributed to a 4 percent increase in fuel efficiency, above the threshold that automobile companies considered valuable.

The people at the Institute were duly impressed: "Wow that is really interesting, that's really unique technology. No one's ever seen that before" were some of the responses. As Voit recognized, however, unique technology didn't automatically translate into a marketable product on which one could build a business:

> At that point we were still dealing with the circuit board that was about 2′ by 2′ square and cost several thousand dollars. For an automobile ignition system, if it didn't cost about $35, no one was even going to be interested in it. So it was really neat but it was still big bucks.

Voit and Stanley had some preliminary discussions with Ford and General Motors, both of whom expressed an interest in the technology, but the difficulty of dealing with the large, bureaucratic organizations, and their nonnegotiable demands, precluded continuation of the initial contacts. Even before they would agree to start serious negotiations, the big auto companies wanted all rights to any outcome of design and development. The two partners discovered that it was essentially impossible for a two-person firm to deal on anything approaching equal footing, especially where they had no patent protection. Initial patent applications had been filed but not granted and second applications had not yet been completed because Stanley and Voit were still trying to figure out exactly what it was they wanted to patent.

The technology was proven but there was no visible path to a market application. The partners saw the situation very differently:

> Stanley and I got along on everything except where business was headed. In his mind again, we had this great technology and the world ought to be beating a path right to the door. They ought to be lining up. That's really not what occurs because you are dealing with very large industries with a pervasive "not invented here" syndrome, where change doesn't come quickly because it has to be reliable and it has to be very cost effective. So you can't just walk in with this big giant thing and say "here it is, it

does a better job," and expect them to say, "Okay, great." You've got a long way to go to where the technology becomes viable for application to building millions of automobiles a year. It's a leap of faith that's tremendous. Stanley could make the leap of faith, but I never did. I always said, "Boy, that's so far away that you've still got to find a way to make a business out of this. You have to find markets where you can sell the technology that you have today. Where are we going to sell it? How are we going to price it and who is going to buy it?" We really didn't know. This is when luck has to play a role.

From Automotive Engines to Natural Gas Compressors

In spite of confidentiality agreements with the Southwest Research Institute, word of PlasMachines' ignition system leaked out, spread around, and eventually found its way to somebody associated with the natural gas pipeline industry. In early 1991, several months after the week of testing, Stanley and Voit received a phone call from an executive at Centram Natural Gas, who was interested in learning more about the technology. The natural gas industry used large stationary engines to run compressors in order to maintain a constant pressure to transport the gas through the transmission lines. The threat of more stringent environmental regulations that would lower the level of permissible emissions from the engines was forcing the natural gas companies to investigate pollution control and prevention alternatives. It offered a potential market for the ignition system that Voit was wholly unaware of:

> I had no idea what the guy was talking about. I had no idea what a stationary engine was, had never seen a natural gas transmission map and had never even thought about how natural gas gets into a house. I had no idea but I said, "Sure, no problem, let's talk."

The Centram executive flew to Boston and drove with Voit and Stanley to eastern New York state to visit one of the compressor stations. Voit wasn't prepared for what he saw: "the biggest engines in the world—gigantic."[*] The engines were so large because they needed to generate a tremendous amount of torque[†] to drive the compressors, and they operated at very low speeds—200 to 300 rotations per minute (rpm)—because they needed to be extremely reliable. The majority of gas pipeline compressor engines still working were built in the 1940s and 1950s, though some dated from the 1920s. The engines were based on old German-designed diesel ship engines, and, when properly maintained, were capable of running virtually forever. Voit described the simple engines as "like looking under the hood of a '57 Chevy; there's nothing to them." The problem with the engines was their tendency to misfire almost 25 percent of the time, due to the difficulty in getting the spark from the spark plug to ignite the mixture in a 20-inch diameter cylinder. Every misfire sent another cylinder-full of unexploded fuel into the atmosphere, and the typical engine emitted more than 200 tons of nitrogen oxide per year, at the rate of 15 grams per brake horse power.

---

[*] A typical engine was the size of a two-car garage.
[†] Torque is the tendency of a force to produce rotation around an axis.

Compressor stations built after the early 1960s used smaller, more efficient turbine engines that didn't pose the same environmental problems. Because the cost of replacing the older models with the turbine type was so great, however, the gas companies were looking for ways to modify the old engines to achieve the emissions reductions that were likely to be mandated in the implementation of the Clean Air Act.° Prior to the development of the PlasMachines ignition system, the primary alternative available to gas companies was a major rebuild of the engines, including new cylinders, new cylinder liners, new connecting rods, turbo chargers, and manifolds. The modification would create a smaller pre-ignition chamber in which a rich fuel mixture would be ignited by the spark plug, and this explosion would ignite a leaner fuel mixture in the main combustion chamber. Fewer misfires and lower combustion temperatures would reduce nitrogen oxide emissions. Centram had a proposal from the engine manufacturer to rebuild and modify 65 engines at a cost of $1.2 million each.

Given the simplicity of the forty-year-old engine, Voit considered the ease of hooking up a PlasMachine ignition system to be a "slam dunk." For $40,000 upfront, Voit and Stanley agreed to build a prototype system for Centram. They took their one circuit board that had been tested at the Southwestern Institute and found an engineering firm in Waltham, Massachusetts, to make six copies (one for each cylinder of the engine) for $27,000. Within three months the system was ready for testing, which Voit performed on a home-made engine simulator—a piece of metal with six evenly spaced magnets that spun around to simulate the timing mechanism for the six spark plugs. In mid-1991, they installed the prototype on a Centram engine and ran it continuously for 2,500 hours without mishap. Simply by eliminating the misfires the system reduced nitrogen oxide emissions by 67 percent.

At that point in early 1992, Voit and Stanley realized they had found the niche market where their technology was currently applicable and cost effective. Although the market wasn't growing, it had many favorable characteristics. There were a known quantity of engines, (approximately 10,000 in the United States and an equal number worldwide), relatively few variations in engine type and only a handful of potential customers, all of whom had the same regulatory mandate. Price wasn't an issue because the only alternative was so much more expensive. The technology didn't require miniaturization, as would have been necessary for the automotive market. The challenges involved the introduction of new technology into a staid industry and the development of credibility for a small start-up among large corporations. The walls of Voit's office started to fill up with natural gas transmissions maps of the United States, showing 600,000 miles of pipelines.

Looking for a customer closer to home, Voit and Stanley approached Dunbar Natural Gas in late 1992. Dunbar had 13 engines in New England, which they had budgeted $16.7 million to overhaul. They were eager to explore less costly

---

° The target levels were dependent upon the geographic location of the compressor station but were likely to be in the range of less than 1 gram per brake horse power.

alternatives. Pulling a figure out of thin air, Voit proposed installing the PlasMachines ignition systems for $150,000 per engine, and after several months of negotiation, they eventually secured a $100,000 payment up front to test the system on an engine in Rhode Island. Voit spent most of the summer of 1993 working around the clock, commuting between the Natick office, where he spent days, and the Rhode Island plant, where he and four engineers from Dunbar performed the testing at night. To produce as lean a mixture as possible, they modified the air intake, rented eighteen 500 horsepower compressors and plumbed them all together to blow air into the huge engine. The results were positive: They were able to reduce nitrogen oxide to a level 60 percent lower than the state requirements and equal to California code, the lowest in the country. After two months of testing, Voit had completed a comprehensive map of the engine's operations, emissions levels, fuel efficiency, and costs, creating documentation that Dunbar could use to negotiate optimal targets and timetables with state regulators.

FROM REGIONAL TO NATIONAL MARKETS

Dunbar showed the test results to its parent company, Hallet Western, which was intrigued by the technology and decided to assume control of the project. Voit and Stanley flew down to Houston to discuss a contract and soon discovered the inbred nature of the natural gas industry and "how business is done in Houston":

> The culture is very conservative. It's an old-boy network like I've never encountered in my life. It's based in Houston; it's bred in Houston. You've got to be cut from Texas A&M in order to survive. I've gotten down to too many meetings where I've been pegged as a Yankee from Boston who supports Ted Kennedy. It is unreal. It's relentless. Bring your cowboy boots. You can go in and give them the best pitch in the world on why fundamentally and economically it makes sense, and they may turn around and give the business to their friend that they have been doing business with for 20 years on a handshake deal because that's the way it's done.

Voit proposed to run tests with the ignition system on each of the four types of engines that Hallet used for a total price of $400,000. The Houston executives responded with the suggestion that the $400,000 be coupled with a firm price on future product to be installed after the testing was completed. Voit realized that dealing with these senior people was very different than what he was used to:

> We didn't know what it would cost us. I had no clue. We didn't have a product.

At that point, PlasMachines had five employees, only two of whom were being paid cash. In addition to Voit, who was involved both in technology development and efforts to raise capital, George Arnos headed up the sales effort, and Ray Caldwell, whom Stanley had brought in from the automotive industry, was president. Both received most of their compensation in the form of stock options. Two salaried engineers were also employed full-time. Stanley's own involvement had become significantly limited by 1993, due to declining health.

INDUSTRY DEREGULATION

Until 1993, evolving state regulations had been the principal driver behind gas companies' interest in the PlasMachines ignition systems, which enabled the companies to meet increasingly stringent emissions standards. Other benefits of the device, such as increased fuel efficiency and reduced maintenance were largely irrelevant to the gas companies. As participants in a regulated utility, they simply passed along incremental costs to consumers in a rate increase. Whether the engine fuel cost $100,000 or $125,000 annually didn't matter to their financial bottom line. This situation changed in 1993 when the natural gas industry was deregulated by the Federal Energy Regulatory Commission (FERC) in a document entitled FERC Order 636. Instead of owning the gas they shipped, pipeline companies became solely transportation companies, and they were suddenly forced into a competitive environment where controlling costs became very important.

Having customers who had spent a long period as a regulated industry and then suddenly transitioned to deregulation had several significant implications for PlasMachines, which in 1993 changed its name to ENOX Technologies. The primary driver—emissions reduction—took a back seat to the efficiency benefits. While the environmental advantages remained important, ultimately they were a less compelling justification for many companies than saving money. Most businesses waited until the last moment before complying with a regulatory mandate, and as the pendulum of environmental compliance seemed to start a reverse swing in the mid-1990s with the arrival of the GOP-controlled Congress, the threat of tougher emissions levels lost its edge. According to Voit: "Our customers that were lining up (for emissions reduction reasons) now had sort of slacked off." Soon after deregulation, ENOX started to sell their technology on the basis of economic value:

> We were quantifying the savings and selling on cost savings in fuel and the decreased amount of hours that people needed to spend. The interval between servicing the engines had increased. The availability of the engine, the number of hours it was available in a given month or in a given operating season had dramatically improved. All of those had a dollar cost associated with them.

One of the challenges, however, in calculating and illustrating the economic gains was the lack of accurate cost information on which to base the savings. As part of a regulated utility, the gas companies had no incentives to manage costs and thus no need to capture or understand them on a level that would be useful for evaluating operations. While a company might know the total fuel cost for all transmission plants in the country, it typically had no ability to track the costs of operating a specific engine at a particular pumping station. Part of ENOX's job became educating their customers about the need to understand their costs in order to realize how significant the potential savings could be if the engines were made to operate more efficiently.

The long period of regulation followed by sudden deregulation had another profound implication for ENOX and its ability to respond to the needs of the market. Because regulation stifled innovation and technological sophistication, ENOX encountered only minor competition from the gas companies internally to enhance engine efficiency and automate. As one example, Voit explained:

Their idea of automation is to install an alarm to signal low oil pressure instead of a red blinking light. There's no examination of why the oil pressure is low, or why the engine's misfiring or why the fuel rate went down or why the emissions are higher. For us it's pretty much virgin territory.

With deregulation, however, came the need to cut costs, and many companies, who didn't understand their operating costs, cut where it was easiest, operations and maintenance personnel. The combination of lack of internal technical sophistication and loss of experienced mechanics provided ENOX with a two-pronged advantage. After several years of intimate work enhancing the efficiency of different types of engines, ignition systems, and fuel mixtures, ENOX had more expertise with these systems than anyone else in the country.

RELATIONSHIP WITH BURTON ENGINE COMPANY

Throughout the period of developing its expertise with natural gas transmission engines, ENOX continued its work with Burton Engine on the electric plasma device for reducing nitrogen oxides in exhaust emissions. In 1993, Stanley Rich received a patent on various components of the after-treatment technology. Concerns about the relationship with Burton and the value of continuing the research mounted in proportion to the growing promise of the gas pipeline market. The personalities of the people involved and the different cultures of the organizations inhibited their ability to collaborate effectively. Stanley was particularly outspoken and tended to grate against the more reserved, corporate types who inhabited the Burton bureaucracy. The absence of personal affinity between the parties was exacerbated by the conditions Burton attached to their contracts. As ENOX started to generate more cash flow without strings from several different customers, the Burton deals looked increasingly less attractive. Moreover the technology remained a long way from being applicable. By Voit's calculations, it would have taken an order of magnitude improvement in efficiency for the device to be cost effective, because many of the components of the automotive electrical system—alternator, battery, wires—would have needed to be upgraded to generate the electrical charge to create the plasma. That increase would have required a substantial investment.

Nevertheless there continued to be significant interest in the technology due to the size of the potential market, and there promised to be continued research funding available. Voit debated the issue:

> It was R&D. It was paying some overhead, and there was a large potential market down the road. But it was also really taking away a lot of the focus in the company.

PREPARATION QUESTION

Outline a 5 year strategic plan for ENOX. Your plan must consider the resources that would be needed to implement your plan. How could ENOX obtain these resources?

15 MIKE BELLOBUONO

Mike Bellobuono knew he had a lot to consider. It was a very exciting time for the bagel industry. Industrywide sales had exploded, and his company, Bagel Boys, a Connecticut-based bagel chain, had established seven retail locations in three years. There was tremendous opportunity for growth, but Mike knew that the company needed to achieve growth quickly or risk being faced with an inability to compete against larger players.

The company was at the point where the four-member management team had to decide whether to begin selling franchises or to remain as a fully company-owned operation. There was a lot at stake in this decision for president Joe Amodio, vice president Wes Becher, territory development manager Jamie Whalen, and director of operations Mike Bellobuono. Originally, they had planned on remaining as a fully company-owned operation but then had met Fred DeLuca, who suggested franchising and offered financing. Fred, founder of Subway, a multimillion dollar sandwich franchise, had the potential to be a tremendous asset for Bagel Boys. He had access to large amounts of capital, an array of resources such as advertising and legal support, and most of all, experience: his company had more locations in the United States than any other franchiser. However, Mike knew that Joe and the team didn't want Bagel Boys to simply become an extension of Fred's empire. The four were used to operating as members of a small, closely knit team and weren't sure if partnering with Fred would result in their losing control of the whole operation.

If they decided to franchise, Mike wondered if they would be able to find franchisees that had the finances, motivation, and ability to successfully run a Bagel Boys

This case was prepared by Andrea Alyse with assistance from Dan D'Heilly under the direction of Professor Stephen Spinelli. Funding provided by the Ewing Marion Kauffman Foundation. Copyright © 1996 Babson College. All rights reserved.

store. He had also heard many stories about conflicts arising out of franchiser-franchisee relationships. True, some of these conflicts were preventable, but inevitably there would be difficulties, probably ending in legal challenges. This greatly concerned him; he knew that disgruntled franchisees would poorly represent the company, and he wasn't sure if accelerated growth was worth the headaches and the possibility that unhappy franchisees would damage the company's reputation. He was also worried about maintaining the high standard of operations in franchisees' stores that Bagel Boys had put into place in its seven company-owned stores. He knew how difficult it was to build a name and how one bad incident could destroy it beyond repair. He thought about what happened to Jack-in-the-Box, a large, fast-food franchise company. In January 1993, a customer had gotten sick and died from bacteria in an under-cooked hamburger. Following this incident, the company hired independent inspectors to review every single franchise and ensure that all complied with the Board of Health's regulated cooking process. Not one additional violation was found in any of the hundreds of locations but nonetheless, following this incident, franchises experienced declines in revenues of up to 35 percent.[*]

On the other hand, if they decided not to franchise they risked being locked out of certain geographical areas by the competition. Bruegger's Bagels was opening units all over New England (Exhibit 15.1), and Manhattan Bagel, a new industry player, had gone public giving the company access to large amounts of capital for expansion. Operating as a chain store, as Bagel Boys was currently doing, constrained the company's potential growth rate. If the company decided against franchising, the team wondered if Bagel Boys would be able to withstand the onslaught of competition that was sure to occur. They wanted to make the right decision, but there was much to consider, and the offer to partner with DeLuca would not stay on the table for long. The bagel wars were heating up and Mike knew that they had to develop a superior growth strategy.

MIKE'S BACKGROUND

Mike graduated from Babson College with a BS in May 1991. He was working for a lawn service, but he and his college friend Jamie Whalen were looking to find a career in a hot market. Specifically the two were looking at bagels and chicken franchises. Although neither of them had any previous food-franchise experience, as part of a class project during Mike's senior year, they had done an in-depth study of the food-service industry (see Exhibit 15.2). Based on this research, they believed that the industry would experience continued growth, and that bagels and chicken would be the next high-growth segments.

It was then that Mike first met Wes Becher and Joe Amodio. The two had opened a bagel store one year earlier by the name of Bagel Boys, and business had gone so well that they had opened a second store and set their sights on developing

---

[*] "E-Coli Scare Deals Blow to Seattle Burger Sales," *Restaurant Business,* March 20, 1993 and "Fallout of E-Coli Episode Still Troubles Foodmarket," *Nation's Restaurant News,* March 20, 1995.

Exhibit 15.1   Bruegger's Bagels growth statistics.

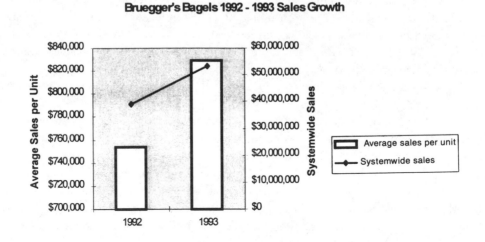

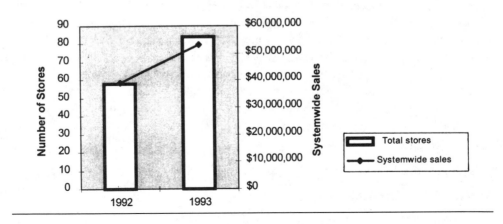

additional locations in the near future. (See Exhibit 15.3 for Bagel Boys's Income Statement.) Mike was very impressed with Bagel Boys's operations and the possibility of getting in on a ground floor opportunity. After considering alternatives such as Cajun Joe's, Boston Chicken, and Manhattan Bagel, he decided he liked both the company and the taste of Bagel Boys's bagels best.

Jamie's father, who had originally approached Mike about the possibility of Mike's becoming a partner with Jamie, was extremely supportive of the decision. Mike and Jamie had grown up in the same neighborhood and been friends as far back as they could both remember. Through the years, Mr. Whalen and Mike had become so close that Mike thought of him as his second father, and Mr. Whalen looked at Mike as the perfect business partner for Jamie. He eagerly endorsed Mike's idea and

Exhibit 15.2 Foodservice industry growth.

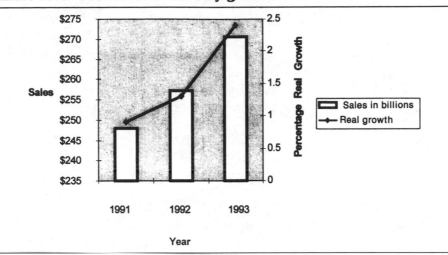

even felt that Jamie should leave school one year early to do this. Mike's father, how-ever, was somewhat less than enthused at first:

> My father wanted me to go to law school or work for Aetna, where I had a job offer, but to me, working for someone else was never an option. When I told him about Bagel Boys he said "Bagels? You went to business school and now you're going to sell bagels?" He wasn't exactly convinced that I was making the right decision, but he supported my decision anyway.

DUE DILIGENCE

Mike first approached Bruegger's about opening bagel stores in Connecticut, but they felt that there was no market potential there. He then considered Manhattan Bagel. He liked their analysis of the bagel market, and they also agreed that Connecticut was a viable market. However, in the end Mike decided to invest in Bagel Boys because he felt that Bagel Boys had several distinct competitive advantages. First there was Irving Stearns. Irv, Bagel Boys's chief bagel-maker, had been in the business for more than 20 years and knew everything there was to know about bagels. He baked a product that tasted better than any Mike had ever eaten, and he could quickly develop new products. There simply wasn't anyone else like Irv. Mike also liked the flexibility of Bagel Boys's management. They were quick to spot and react to new market trends and directions. For example, Bagel Boys offered customers five different kinds of flavored coffees before flavored coffees became popular—at a time when all their competitors only offered regular and decaffeinated. Finally, with Bagel Boys, he was on the ground floor.

EXHIBIT 15.3   Bagel Boys per store earning claims 1993 (estimate).

	Weekly	Annually	Percent of Total Revenue per Store
Total revenue per store	$8,000.00	$416,000.00	100.00%
Cost of goods sold			
Salaries and wages	2,000.00	104,000.00	25
Food	1,680.00	87,360.00	21
Beverages	800.00	41,600.00	10
Paper supplies	320.00	16,640.00	4
Total cost of goods sold	$4,800.00	$249,600.00	80
Gross profit on sales	$3,200.00	$166,400.00	40
Operating expenses			
Payroll tax	136.00	7,072.00	1.70
Payroll service	20.00	1,040.00	0.25
Rent	480.00	24,960.00	6.00
CL&P	200.00	10,400.00	2.50
CNG	120.00	6,240.00	1.50
Telephone	24.00	1,248.00	0.30
Advertising	200.00	10,400.00	2.50
Local advertising	80.00	4,160.00	1.00
Insurance	80.00	4,160.00	1.00
Linen and laundry	16.00	832.00	0.20
Repairs and maintenance	80.00	4,160.00	1.00
Rubbish removal	40.00	2,080.00	0.50
Office supplies	40.00	2,080.00	0.50
Uniforms	16.00	832.00	0.20
Professional fees	40.00	2,080.00	0.50
Miscellaneous	20.00	1,040.00	0.25
Total operating expenses	$1,596.00	$ 82,992.00	19.95
Total income from operations	$1,604.00	$ 83,408.00	20.05

Note: All figures have been estimated based on industry data and do not necessarily represent the actual financial performance of a Bagel Boys store operation.

BAGEL BOYS

Mike and Jamie contacted Joe and Wes about buying a franchise. They soon found out that companies that franchised were required to adhere to the U.S. Federal Trade Commission (FTC) Disclosure Rule. The Rule stated that franchisers must disclose certain, specified information to all prospective franchisees, in a format approved by the FTC (see Exhibit 15.4). Most franchisers used a Uniform Franchise Offering Circular (UFOC) format to comply with FTC regulations. A UFOC document contained information including: a description of the business, estimated development costs, fee schedules, franchisee and franchiser obligations, other businesses affiliated with the franchise, and pending lawsuits. Additionally, 13 states required franchisers to file a

EXHIBIT 15.4   Summary of the U.S. Federal Trade Commission's disclosure rule.

I. Rule Overview

  A. Basic Requirement: Franchisors must furnish potential franchisees with written disclosures providing important information about the franchisor, the franchised business and the franchise relationship, and give them at least ten business days to review it before investing.

  B. Disclosure Option: Franchisors may make the required disclosures by following either the Rule's disclosure format or the Uniform Franchise Offering Circular Guidelines prepared by state franchise law officials.

  C. Coverage: The Rule primarily covers business-format franchises, product franchises, and vending machine or display rack business opportunity ventures.

  D. No Filing: The Rule requires disclosure only. Unlike state disclosure laws, no registration, filing, review or approval of any disclosures, advertising or agreements by the FTC is required.

  E. Remedies: The Rule is a trade regulation rule with the full force and effect of federal law. The courts have held it may only be enforced by the FTC, not private parties. The FTC may seek injunctions, civil penalties and consumer redress for violations.

  F. Purpose: The Rule is designed to enable potential franchisees to protect themselves before investing by providing them with information essential to an assessment of the potential risks and benefits, to meaningful comparisons with other investments, and to further investigation of the franchise opportunity.

  G. Effective Date: The Rule, formally titled "Disclosure Requirements and Prohibitions Concerning Franchising and Business Opportunity Ventures," took effect on October 21, 1979, and appears at 16 C.F.R. Part 436.

II. Rule Requirements

  A. General. The Rule imposes six different requirements in connection with the "advertising, offering, licensing, contracting, sale or other promotion" of a franchise in or affecting commerce:

    1. Basic Disclosures: The Rule requires franchisors to give potential investors a basic disclosure document at the earlier of the first face-to-face meeting or ten business days before any money is paid or an agreement is signed in connection with the investment (Part 436.1(a)).

    2. Earnings Claims: If a franchisor makes earnings claims, whether historical or forecasted, they must have a reasonable basis, and prescribed substantiating disclosures must be given to a potential investor in writing at the same time as the basic disclosures (Parts 436.1(b)-(d)).

    3. Advertised Claims: The Rule affects only ads that include an earnings claim. Such ads must disclose the number and percentage of existing franchisees who have achieved the claimed results, along with cautionary language. Their use triggers required compliance with the Rule's earnings claim disclosure requirements (Part 436.1(e)).

    4. Franchise Agreements: The franchisor must give investors a copy of its standard-form franchise and related agreements at the same time as the basic disclosures, and final copies intended to be executed at least 5 business days before signing (Part 436.1(g)).

    5. Refunds: The Rule requires franchisors to make refunds of deposits and initial payments to potential investors, subject to any conditions on refundability stated in the disclosure document (Part 436.1(h)).

(Continued)

EXHIBIT 15.4 *(Continued)*

6. Contradictory Claims: While franchisors are free to provide investors with any promotional or other materials they wish, no written or oral claims may contradict information provided in the required disclosure document (Part 436.1(f)).

B. Liability: Failure to comply with any of the six requirements is a violation of the Franchise Rule. "Franchisors" and "franchise brokers" are jointly and severally liable for Rule violations.

1. A "franchisor" is defined as any person who sells a "franchise" covered by the Rule (Part 436.2(c)).

2. A "franchise broker" is defined as any person who "sells, offers for sale, or arranges for the sale" of a covered franchise (Part 436.2(j)), and includes not only independent sales agents, but also subfranchisors that grant subfranchises (44 FR 49963).

III. Business Relationships Covered

A. Alternate Definitions: The Rule employs parallel coverage definitions of the term "franchise" to reach two types of continuing commercial relationships: traditional franchises and business opportunities.

B. "Traditional Franchises": There are three definitional prerequisites to coverage of a business-format or product franchise (Parts 436.2(a)(1)(i) and (2)):

1. Trademark: The franchisor offers the right to distribute goods or services that bear the franchisor's trademark, service mark, trade name, advertising or other commercial symbol.

2. Significant Control or Assistance: The franchisor exercises significant control over, or offers significant assistance in, the franchisee's method of operation.

3. Required Payment: The franchisee is required to make any payment to the franchisor or an affiliate, or a commitment to make a payment, as a condition of obtaining the franchise or commencing operations. (NOTE: There is an exemption from coverage for required payments of less than $500 within six months of the commencement of the franchise (Part 436.2(a)(3)(iii)).

C. Business Opportunities: There are also three basic prerequisites to the Rule's coverage of a business opportunity venture (Parts 436.2(a)(1)(ii) and (2)):

1. No Trademark: The seller simply offers the right to sell goods or services supplied by the seller, its affiliate, or a supplier with which the seller requires the franchisee to do business.

2. Location Assistance: The seller offers to secure retail outlets or accounts for the goods or services to be sold, to secure locations or sites for vending machines or rack displays, or to provide the services of someone who can do so.

3. Required Payment: The same as for franchises.

D. Coverage Exemptions/Exclusions: The Rule also exempts or excludes some relationships that would otherwise meet the coverage prerequisites (Parts 436.2(a)(3) and (4)):

1. Minimum investment: This exemption applies if all payments to the franchisor or an affiliate until six months after the franchise commences operation are $500 or less (Part 436.2(a)(iii)).

2. Fractional Franchises: Relationships adding a new product or service to an established distributor's existing products or services are exempt if: (i) the franchisee or any of its current directors or executive officers has been in the same type of business for at least two years, and (ii) both parties anticipated, or should have, that sales from the franchise would represent no more than 20% of the franchisees sales in dollar volume (Parts 436.2(a)(3)(i) and 436.2(h)).

EXHIBIT 15.4 *(Continued)*

3. Single Trademark Licenses: The Rule language excludes a "single license to license a [mark]" where it "is the only one of its general nature and type to be granted by the licenser with respect to that [mark]" (Part 436.2(a)(4)(iv)). The Rule's Statement of Basis and Purpose indicates it also applies to "collateral" licenses [e.g., logo on sweatshirt, mug] and licenses granted to settle trademark infringement litigation (43 FR 59707-08).

4. Employment and Partnership Relationships: The Rule excludes pure employer-employee and general partnership arrangements. Limited partnerships do not qualify for the exemption (Part 436.2(a)(4)(i)).

5. Oral Agreements: This exemption, which is narrowly construed, applies only if no material term of the relationship is in writing (Part 436.2(a)(3)(iv)).

6. Cooperative Associations: Only agricultural co-ops and retailer-owned cooperatives "operated 'by and for' retailers on a cooperative basis," and in which control and ownership is substantially equal are excluded from coverage (Part 436.2(a)(4)(ii)).

7. Certification/Testing Services: Organizations that authorize use of a certification mark to any business selling products or services meeting their standards are excluded from coverage (e.g., Underwriters Laboratories) (Part 436.2(a)(4)(iii)).

8. Leased Departments: Relationships in which the franchisee simply leases space in the premises of another retailer and is not required or advised to buy the goods or services it sells from the retailer or an affiliate of the retailer are exempt (Part 436.2(a)(3)(ii)).

E. Statutory Exemptions: Section 18(g) of the FTC Act authorizes "any person" to petition the Commission for an exemption from a rule where coverage is "not necessary to prevent the acts or practices" that the rule prohibits (15 U.S.C. § 57a(g)). Franchise Rule exemptions have been granted for service station franchises (45 FR 51765), many automobile dealership franchises (45 FR 51763; 49 FR 13677; 52 FR 6612; 54 FR 1446), and wholesaler-sponsored voluntary chains in the grocery industry (48 FR 10040).

IV. Disclosure Options

A. Alternatives: Franchisors have a choice of formats for making the disclosures required by the Rule. They may use either the format provided by the Rule or the Uniform Franchise Offering Circular ("UFOC") format prescribed by the North American Securities Administrators' Association ("NASAA").

B. FTC Format: Franchisors may comply by following the Rule's requirements for preparing a basic disclosure document (Parts 436.1(a)(1)-(24)), and if they make earnings claims, for a separate earnings claim disclosure document (Parts 436.1(b)(3), (c)(3), and (d)). The Rule's Final Interpretive Guides provide detailed instructions and sample disclosures (44 FR 49966).

C. UFOC Format: The Uniform Franchise Offering Circular format may also be used for compliance in any state:

1. Guidelines: Effective January 1, 1996, franchisors using the UFOC disclosure format must comply with the UFOC Guidelines, as amended by NASAA on April 25, 1993. (44 FR 49970; 60 FR 51895).

2. Cover Page: The FTC cover page must be furnished to each potential franchisee, either in lieu of the UFOC cover page in non-registration states or along with the UFOC (Part 436.1(a)(21); 44 FR 49970-71).

3. Adaptation: If the UFOC is registered or used in one state, but will be used in another without a franchise registration law, answers to state-specific questions must be changed to refer to the law of the state in which the UFOC is used.

EXHIBIT 15.4 *(Continued)*

4. Updating: If the UFOC is registered in a state, it must be updated as required by the state's franchise law. If the same UFOC is also adapted for use in a non-registration state, updating must occur as required by the law of the state where the UFOC is registered. If the UFOC is not registered in a state with a franchise registration law, it must be revised annually and updated quarterly as required by the Rule.

5. Presumption: The Commission will presume the sufficiency, adequacy, and accuracy of a UFOC that is registered by a state, when it is used in that state.

D. UFOC vs. Rule: Many franchisors have adopted the UFOC disclosure format because roughly half of the 13 states with franchise registration requirements will not accept the Rule document for filing. When a format is chosen, all disclosure must conform to its requirements. Franchisors may not pick and choose provisions from each format when making disclosures (44 FR 49970).

E. Rule Primacy: If the UFOC is used, several key Rule provisions will still apply:

1. Scope: Disclosure will be required in all cases required by the Rule, regardless of whether it would be required by state law.

2. Coverage: The Rule will determine who is obligated to comply, regardless of whether they would be required to make disclosures under state law.

3. Disclosure Timing: When disclosures must be made will be governed by the Rule, unless state law requires even earlier disclosure.

4. Other Material: No information may appear in a disclosure document not required by the Rule or by non-preempted state law, regardless of the format used, and no representations may be made that contradict a disclosure.

5. Contracts: Failure to provide potential franchisees with final agreements at least 5 days before signing will be a Rule violation regardless of the disclosure format used.

6. Refunds: Failure to make promised refunds also will be a Rule violation regardless of which document is used.

V. Potential Liability for Violations

A. FTC Action: Rule violations may subject franchisors, franchise brokers, their officers and agents to significant liabilities in FTC enforcement actions.

1. Remedies: The FTC Act provides the Commission with a broad range of remedies for Rule violations:

a. Injunctions: Section 13(b) of the Act authorizes preliminary and permanent injunctions against Rule violations (15 U.S.C. § 53(b)). Rule cases routinely have sought and obtained injunctions against Rule violations and misrepresentations in the offer or sale of any business venture, whether or not covered by the Rule.

b. Asset Freezes: Acting under their inherent equity powers, the courts have routinely granted preliminary asset freezes in appropriate Rule cases. The assets frozen have included both corporate assets and the personal assets, including real and personal property, of key officers and directors.

c. Civil Penalties: Section 5(m)(1)(A) of the Act authorizes civil penalties of up to $10,000 for each violation of the Rule (15 U.S.C. § 45(m)(1)(A)). The courts have granted civil penalties of as much as $870,000 in a Rule case to date.

d. Monetary Redress: Section 19(b) of the Act authorizes the Commission to seek monetary redress on behalf of investors injured economically by a Rule violation (15 U.S.C. § 57b). The courts have granted consumer redress of as much as $4.9 million in a Rule case to date.

EXHIBIT 15.4 *(Continued)*

  e. Other Redress: Section 19(b) of the Act also authorizes such other forms of redress as the court finds necessary to redress injury to consumers from a Rule violation, including rescission or reformation of contracts, the return of property, and public notice of the Rule violation. Courts may also grant similar relief under their inherent equity powers.
  2. Personal Liability: Individuals who formulate, direct, and control the franchisor's activities can expect to be named individually for violations committed in the franchisor's name, together with the franchisor entity, and held personally liable for civil penalties and consumer redress.
  3. Liability For Others: Franchisors and their key officers and executives are responsible for violations by persons acting in their behalf, including independent franchise brokers, sub-franchisors, and the franchisor's own sales personnel.
  B. Private Actions: The courts have held that the FTC Act generally may not be enforced by private lawsuits.
  1. Rule Claims: The Commission expressed its view when the Rule was issued that private actions should be permitted by the courts for Rule violations (43 FR 59723; 44 FR 49971). To date, no federal court has permitted a private action for Rule violations.
  2. State Disclosure Law Claims: Each of the franchise laws in the 15 states with franchise registration and/or disclosure requirements authorizes private actions for state franchise law violations.
  3. State FTC Act Claims: The courts in some states have interpreted state deceptive practices laws ("little FTC Acts") as permitting private actions for Rule violations.
  VI. Legal Resources
  A. Text of Rule: 16 C.F.R. Part 436.
  B. Statement of Basis and Purpose: 43 FR 59614-59733 (Dec. 21, 1978) (Discusses the evidentiary basis for promulgation of the Rule, and shows Commission intent and interpretation of its provisions - particularly helpful in resolving coverage questions).
  C. Final Interpretive Guides: 44 FR 49966-49992 (Aug. 24, 1979) (Final statement of policy and interpretation of each of the Rule's requirements - important discussions of coverage issues, use of the UFOC and requirements for basic and earnings claims disclosures in the Rule's disclosure format).
  D. Staff Advisory Opinions: Business Franchise Guide (CCH) 6380 et seq. (Interpretive opinions issued in response to requests for interpretation of coverage questions and disclosure requirements pursuant to 16 C.F.R. §§ 1.2–1.4).

UFOC prior to selling franchises. Producing this document was an expensive and time-consuming process but without complying with the FTC's Disclosure Rule, Joe and Wes weren't legally permitted to sell franchises. However, Mike and Jamie persisted until Joe and Wes agreed to sell them a store as a limited partnership:

> I looked at a partnership as giving me greater control over my own destiny. If we didn't form a partnership, and I just opened up stores for them, I would have no control over any changes they decided to make; having this control was extremely important to me.

Mike and Jamie opened the Manchester store in December of 1991. Then Wes, impressed by Mike and Jamie's dedication, approached the two about becoming full partners in the company. Wes explained to Mike that, although he had several prospective investors, he was interested in offering the two a partnership because he and Joe were looking for investors who would work for the company, not simply finance it. To buy into the company, Jamie and Mike arranged financing through their fathers, and the two became full partners the next year. Mike, Wes, Jamie, and Joe handled all aspects of the partnership. Each store was visited by one of the four members of the team on a daily basis to ensure that operations were running smoothly and to solve any difficulties that arose. Wes, Jamie, and Mike focused on the day-to-day operations, and Joe on growing the company:

> Joe was the leader and a fly-by-the-seat-of-the-pants type of guy. Joe would point in a direction, and we three would make it happen. Joe had an incredible talent for sales-manship, a kind of way about him that enabled him to achieve the seemingly impossi-ble. One Christmas we were in New York City, and we were in this restaurant. The owner was depressed because the restaurant was empty. Joe said he could fill the restaurant if the owner sat him by the window. He proceeded to put on quite a show, performing in the window, carrying on, gesturing, and waving droves people in who wanted to see what all the excitement was about. And you know what? He filled the restaurant in under an hour. But Joe wasn't finished yet. He then got the entire place to sing "The Twelve Days of Christmas," and when people forgot the words of a section of the song, he had them running out into the street asking people if they knew the words and could help out—I mean strangers, in the middle of New York City. It was unbeliev-able! Even the ending was like a fairy tale: as the crowd got to the twelfth day of Christmas, Joe was tipping his hat at the door and making his exit. To this day when-ever he goes into that restaurant his dinner is free; the owner never forgot what Joe did for him.

By 1993, Bagel Boys had seven stores with the goal of saturating the entire state of Connecticut by the year 2000. Bruegger's wasn't there yet, and Manhattan only had a few locations, but Mike knew they were coming:

> We were Bagel Boys, and we wanted to make Connecticut our turf, so that you knew that if you were going to go into Connecticut, you would have to fight us.

THE BAGEL INDUSTRY

Although the exact origin of the bagel is not fully known, legend maintains that the first bagel was created for the king of Poland, as a celebration bread, when the king's army repelled a 1683 Turkish invasion. Jewish immigrants introduced the bagel in the United States, and for decades bagels were perceived as a strictly ethnic food, with limited mass-market appeal.

Traditionally, bagels were made from water, flour, yeast, and salt, combined and formed into a ring shape. These rings were boiled in water to create the crust and shiny appearance, and then baked in brick ovens to produce a crispy outside and soft, chewy inside, considerably denser than most breads. As bagels gained mass-market acceptance across the country, the industry grew at an accelerating rate. Modern-day bakers often use machine-formed bagels and large stainless steel ovens, complete with rotating racks for faster, more uniform baking. As competition between bagel shops has increased in the United States, the traditional bagel recipe has been adapted to increase the variety of flavors (e.g., egg, salt, garlic, onion, poppy seed, sesame seed, blueberry, chocolate chip, corn, and cheddar cheese).

Lender's, now a division of Kraft General Foods, first successfully marketed a mass-produced, frozen, supermarket bagel in 1962. Before this time, bagels had only been sold as fresh. By 1991, Lender's had grown to sales of $203 million, and Sara Lee, Lender's closest competitor, who had entered the frozen bagel market in 1985, had sales of $22.4 million (Exhibit 15.5).

In the 1980s, Lender's and Bagel Nosh opened bagel shops nationally, but both companies failed, never able to attract enough customers. By the early 1990s, bagels were gaining mass-market acceptance across the country. However, the industry was growing most notably on the East Coast where, as of mid-1992, more than half of all bagel sales in the United States (51%) came from 15 east-coast cities. Consumption of bagels was expected to increase between 3 and 3.5 percent in 1993. Exhibit 15.5 illustrates the increase in per-capita bagel consumption. Frozen supermarket bagels achieved sales of $211.9 million in 1992, an increase of 4 percent over the previous year, but fresh bagels, the most rapidly growing segment, increased sales to $95 million, up 28 percent from 1991. Consumer awareness of bagels had increased steadily, but most dramatically throughout the past decade. Breakfast accounted for 65 percent of all bagel sales, and with the trend toward increased consumer-health awareness, bagels had become a natural, low-fat, high-carbohydrate alternative to other menu items, such as doughnuts and muffins.

Exhibit 15.5   Bagel consumption.

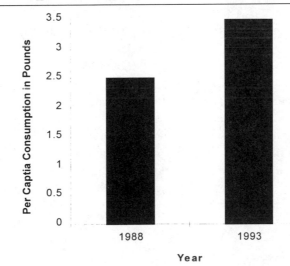

FRED DELUCA

In the spring of 1993, the Bagel Boys team was contacted by Fred DeLuca, founder of Subway, a large sandwich franchise. A vendor that sold luncheon-meat slicers to both Bagel Boys and Subway had told Fred about Bagel Boys's operation, and Fred decided that he wanted to tour the plant and meet the team. Fred was well-known in the franchise industry. While still in college, he had opened his first Subway location in 1965. Nine years later he began franchising, and by 1995, Subway had grown to more than 10,000 locations. In addition, *Entrepreneur Magazine* rated Subway the number-one franchise in their annual franchising 500, six times between 1988 and 1994:

> We never thought that he wanted to do business with us. We were just excited to meet him. When we realized he was interested in making a deal, we were astonished.

It was then that the team first seriously considered franchising.

TO FRANCHISE OR NOT TO FRANCHISE?

Fred had offered to buy into Bagel Boys and turn them into a world class franchise, but first he wanted to be sure that the bagel team was fully aware of, and ready to meet, all potential difficulties involved with franchising:

> Fred wanted to know why we wanted to franchise. He said, "do you know what you are getting yourself into? Are you sure you really want to deal with all the problems that arise from franchising?"

The team weighed both the pros and cons of becoming a franchiser. They evaluated two basic strategies: either to grow rapidly throughout Connecticut as a chain, or to franchise and grow nationally. They thought they could probably get to 40 stores as a company-owned chain. That would be enough to compete in Connecticut. But could they really get to 40 stores? Did they have the management talent, the money, and the time?

They were afraid of losing control if they franchised, but knew it would be difficult to grow quickly without franchising. They were also afraid they wouldn't be able to lock out the competition: Manhattan Bagel planned to expand into Connecticut and Bruegger's had been named one of the 50 fastest growing U.S. restaurants (see Exhibit 15.6). Last, Mike and the team feared that Fred DeLuca would lose interest. After all, they had already been negotiating for six months and hadn't reached an agreement. Then Subway began receiving increasing amounts of negative publicity regarding the company's support of its franchisees. One, particularly disturbing article appeared in *The Wall Street Journal* (see Exhibit 15.7) and Mike and the team began to wonder if aligning with Fred could ultimately have a negative effect on Bagel Boys. They knew, however, that time was running out and they needed to decide the best future direction for Bagel Boys.

EXHIBIT 15.6 Fifty fastest growing restaurants 1992–1993.

Name of restaurant	City and state	Type of restaurant	Does the company franchise?	Proj. 1992–1993 % change in systemwide sales	Proj. 1992–1993 % change in units	Proj. 1992–1993 % change in average unit sales
1 Boston Chicken	Naperville, IL	Fast Food	Y	261.0	161.4	9.2
2 Lone Star Steakhouse & Saloon	Wichita, KS	Casual Steakhouse	Y	136.3	95.7	3.6
3 Italian Oven	Latrobe, PA	Casual Italian Dinnerhouse	Y	126.2	60.0	11.7
4 Romano's Macaroni Grill	Dallas, TX	Casual Italian Dinnerhouse	N	107.7	86.7	0.2
5 Hooters	Atlanta, GA	Casual Dinnerhouse	Y	87.2	16.0	25.0
6 Papa John's	Louisville, KY	Delivery/Take-out Pizza	Y	80.4	81.8	8.7
7 Outback Steakhouse	Tampa, FL	Casual Steakhouse	Y	77.9	71.8	6.7
8 Checkers Drive-in	Clearwater, FL	Drive-thru Hamburgers	Y	68.1	81.2	5.2
9 Taco Cabana	San Antonio TX	Patio-style Mexican	Y	65.1	87.7	-4.2
10 Hot 'n Now	Irvine, CA	Drive-thru Hamburgers	N	54.0	80.9	3.6
11 Wall Street Deli	Memphis, TN	Self-serve Deli and Buffet	N	56.2	26.4	5.0
12 Mick's	Atlanta, GA	Casual Dinnerhouse	N	53.8	50.0	1.5
13 Applebee's	Kansas City, MO	Casual Dinnerhouse	Y	50.5	44.4	5.3
14 Starbucks	Seattle, WA	Coffee Specialist	N	50.0	63.7	6.7
15 Grady's American Grill	Dallas, TX	Casual Dinnerhouse	N	45.1	52.6	1.2
16 Bertucci's Brick Oven Pizza	Woburn, MA	Casual Italian Dinnerhouse	N	45.0	42.9	5.9
17 Fresh Choice	Santa Clara, CA	Self-serve Buffet	N	44.4	63.6	4.9
18 Miami Subs Grill	Fort Lauderdale, FL	Fast Food	Y	42.9	23.2	3.5
19 Stacey's Buffet Largo, Fla.	Largo, FL	Self-serve Buffet	Y	39.0	50.0	-5.3
20 Longhorn Steaks	Atlanta, GA	Casual Steakhouse	Y	37.4	32.5	-2.8
21 Panda Express	S. Pasadena, CA	Fast Food Oriental	N	36.8	40.0	2.9
22 Bruegger's Bagel Bakery	Burlington, VT	Fast Food	Y	36.5	44.8	9.5
23 California Pizza Kitchen	Los Angeles, CA	Casual Dinnerhouse	N	26.4	51.7	5.6
24 Old Country Buffet	Eden Prairie, MN	Self-serve Buffet	N	33.7	28.6	4.3
25 Sfuzzi	Dallas, TX	Casual Italian Dinnerhouse	N	33.3	25.0	3.0

(Continued)

EXHIBIT 15.6 *(Continued)*

Name of restaurant	City and state	Type of restaurant	Does the company franchise?	Proj. 1992–1993 % change in systemwide sales	Proj. 1992–1993 % change in units	Proj. 1992–1993 % change in average unit sales
26 Claim Jumper	Irvine, CA	Dinnerhouse	N	33.3	30.0	4.3
27 Nathan's Famous	Westbury, NY	Fast Food	Y	31.4	20.3	-4.0
28 Morton's of Chicago	Chicago, IL	Upscale Steakhouse	N	31.1	20.0	9.2
29 The Cheesecake Factory	Redondo Beach, CA	Casual Dinnerhouse	N	29.9	60.0	1.2
30 Au Bon Pain	Boston, MA	Bakery Cafe	Y	28.8	11.0	5.5
31 Ruby Tuesday	Mobile, AL	Casual Dinnerhouse	N	28.2	25.6	6.2
32 Schlotzsky's Deli	Austin, TX	Fast Food	Y	27.0	17.7	2.9
33 Blimpie	New York, NY	Fast Food	Y	26.6	27.9	0.0
34 Cracker Barrel	Lebanon, TN	Family Restaurant	N	25.1	20.7	3.7
35 The Cooker Bar & Grille	Columbus, OH	Casual Dinnerhouse	N	24.5	45.0	0.0
36 Subway	Milford, CT	Fast Food	Y	22.7	13.9	6.0
37 The Spaghetti Warehouse	Garland, TX	Casual Italian Dinnerhouse	N	21.7	37.0	11.5
38 Dunkin' Donuts	Randolph, MA	Fast Food	Y	21.3	16.6	4.5
39 Sirloin Stockade	Hutchinson, KS	Budget Steakhouse	Y	21.3	7.6	15.0
40 Cinnabon	Seattle, WA	Fast Food	Y	21.2	8.6	5.2
41 T.G.I. Friday's	Dallas, TX	Casual Dinnerhouse	Y	20.2	18.3	0.0
42 Don Pablo's	Bedford, TX	Casual Mexican Dinnerhouse	N	19.8	47.4	2.7
43 Rally's	Louisville, KY	Drive-thru Hamburgers	Y	19.6	20.0	-4.5
44 Chili's	Dallas, TX	Casual Dinnerhouse	Y	19	15.5	3.2
45 Damon's-The Place for Ribs	Columbus, OH	Casual Dinnerhouse	Y	18.3	4.0	2.9
46 Red Robin	Irvine, CA	Casual Dinnerhouse	Y	18.1	19.0	-3.5
47 Bain's Deli	King of Prussia, PA	Fast Food	Y	17.9	8.0	10.3
48 On the Border Cafe	Dallas, TX	Casual Mexican Dinnerhouse	Y	17.9	46.7	0.0
49 Bojangles	Charlotte, NC	Fast Food	Y	17.2	20.3	5.7
50 Ruth's Chris Steak House	New Orleans, LA	Upscale Steakhouse	Y	17.1	8.8	4.8

Source: Restaurant Business, July 20, 1994.

EXHIBIT 15.7   Franchise Realities: Sandwich-Shop Chain Surges, but to Run One Can Take Heroic Effort.

By Barbara Marsh

MILFORD, Conn.—The dream of owning one's own business has few better salesmen than Frederick DeLuca, co-founder of Subway Sandwich Shops. His company enables would-be entrepreneurs to start a business fairly inexpensively, and thousands have. Subway has 7,000 franchises world-wide, nearly four times the number five years ago. "For the last five years, we've been the fastest-growing franchise in the world, and I think, the history of the world," Mr. DeLuca says.

For Subway, this is a comfortable arrangement. Each new sandwich shop brings the company that Mr. DeLuca and a partner own thousands of dollars in initiation fees, and then a hefty cut of sales.

For franchisees, it's a quite different situation. A substantial number of Subway franchises are scarcely profitable. Indeed, after laying out up to $70,000 to get started, investors who run their own shops often find that about all they have done is buy themselves a low-paying job with long hours.

Others give up and sell. Company documents filed with state regulators show that within three years, about 40% of the 2,300 Subway shops listed as open or preparing to open at the end of 1987 either changed hands, relocated, closed down, or never opened. And Mr. DeLuca estimates that half of resold units are priced at either break-even or a loss to the owner.

As out-of-work middle managers and others jump into franchising in record numbers these days, the Subway story provides a simple but timely reminder that the interests of a franchisee and franchiser don't necessarily coincide. Often the primary financial goal for the franchiser is growth: The more outlets, the more royalties and fees the franchiser collects, regardless of whether the individual outlets become successful businesses on their own. That's a risk borne largely by the franchisee.

A typical Subway shop is a 1,000-square-foot space with yellow decor and fake plants, doing mostly takeout business but also providing booths for customers. Counter staff make submarine sandwiches to order, slashing buns and stuffing them with cold cuts or hot meat fillings, plus fixings. Salads, soda pop, chips, and cookies complete the short menu. The payroll can range from one to 20 people, depending on the store's volume.

Subway doesn't monitor the earnings performance of its franchisees in any systematic way, unlike, for instance, McDonald's Corp. Mr. DeLuca estimates that 300 Subway outlets don't break even and can't afford to pay an owner/manager's salary of $20,000. An additional 1,000 franchises, he guesses, can afford to pay no more than $35,000. This amount, by his way of figuring, is the business's profit before debt expense.

But Mr. DeLuca says he believes that most franchisees are satisfied. "No system can grow to over 6,000 stores without having a fundamentally good business," he says.

And, to be sure, many Subway franchisees do well. The company points to Thomas Neal, who says he expects to earn about $100,000 this year on his Subway in Gainesville, Fla. "I'm glad I made the investment," he says.

Dane Banks and Nancy Kessler feel otherwise. They say their Subway in Olathe, Kan., lost money from the day it opened in 1989 until the franchiser took it back 18 months later. Subway had told them the shop would break even if weekly sales averaged $4,000, they say, but their sales averaged only $3,500. The mounting losses meant that Mr. Banks, who had taken a $68,000 mortgage on his home to open the store, couldn't meet personal debts. He lost his home and his car, and amid the stress, the partners broke off their marital engagement. Now in litigation with Subway, Mr. Banks says: "If I just get back what I lost I'd be happy."

A new Subway costs the franchisee about $45,000 to $70,000 up front, depending on costs of leasehold improvements, interior renovations, seating and equipment. (A company owned

(Continued)

EXHIBIT 15.7 *(Continued)*

by Subway Shops' owners holds the lease and sublets to the franchisee.) That makes a low-priced Subway cheaper than 70% of more than 1,000 franchises listed in Entrepreneur magazine, and even a high-priced store still costs less than half of them. Subway offers financing for restaurant equipment worth up to $32,000.

William Bygrave, professor of entrepreneurship at Babson College in Wellesley, Mass., has analyzed a Subway-shop investment. Using Subway's most recent cost and revenue estimates, he figures that the typical Subway franchisee would have to work extremely long hours and take no vacation to earn $49,000 before taxes (and excluding disability insurance or retirement savings). That assumes a good location. With a poor location, Dr. Bygrave says, "You probably won't make it and you stand to lose all that initial investment."

Mr. DeLuca says he doesn't dispute the professor's calculations. Mr. DeLuca and his partner, Peter Buck, charge $10,000 for each new franchise, $2,500 for each additional Subway opened by existing franchisees and $5,000 each time a store changes hands. They take an 8% cut of franchisees' revenue—one of the highest in the fast-food industry. They also take an added 2.5% of revenue for advertising. And they collect a rental fee on leased equipment.

In exchange, they provide, among other things, a two-week training course, store design, over-the-phone business advice, and a weekly newsletter. They give a cut of their revenue to "development agents" who sell franchises.

Subway expects to collect revenue this year of $150 million, and while its two owners won't disclose profits, outsiders estimate that Subway has supplied the two men with a fortune of more than $100 million. Whatever the case, Mr. DeLuca lives modestly, while Mr. Buck, who is 61 and retired, owns glider planes and various residences, including a ranch in Brazil.

Growth has been a religion for the partners ever since 1965, when Mr. Buck, then a 34-year-old nuclear engineer, gave $1,000 to Mr. DeLuca, who was a 17-year-old family friend, to open a sandwich shop in Bridgeport, Conn. When sales sputtered, they took the unusual measure of opening a second store, to create the appearance of success. Mr. DeLuca, a college psychology major, says, "Nobody knew we weren't successful, because nobody was in the stores."

After years of steady growth, the company started expanding aggressively five years ago. Mr. DeLuca attributes the growth mostly to "energetic franchisees." But Rieva Lesonsky, editor in chief of Entrepreneur, credits Mr. DeLuca's "very aggressive marketing campaign" and "fairly low" initiation fee.

In any case, Subway's growth has occurred at a rate that experts call hard to manage. "It's very difficult" to open 1,000 units a year, says Edward Kushell, a Los Angeles franchising consultant. "There tend to be holes in the training, the legal compliance, the representations you make to franchisees—all the things that could cause problems down the line."

Maintaining control is all the trickier for Subway because it farms out to development agents a lot of services often performed by franchisers. Selected from the ranks of franchisees, they get commissions to recruit new franchisees, help pick store sites, negotiate leases, decide which owners will be granted new locations and conduct quality-assurance inspections that can result in an owner's being blocked from buying another outlet.

The arrangement not only allows Subway to expand without employing a team of salespeople; it has also enabled Subway to disclaim responsibility for sales claims not consistent with its franchise prospectus.

Richard Pitta says he bought a franchise after hearing a development agent tell of a franchisee who had more than doubled his money in a year by selling his unit, and hearing another agent tell him to expect weekly sales of $5,000 to $6,000. But Mr. Pitta's unit, in Elizabeth, NJ, never rose above his break-even point of $3,400. He fell behind on his payments to Subway, he says, then got an offer from Subway to buy him out for $7,500, after

EXHIBIT 15.7 *(Continued)*

he had invested a total of about $85,000. The offer angered him, but he says he accepted it because he couldn't afford to sue.

The biggest complaint at Subway is one common at rapid-growth franchisers: poor site selection. John Melaniphy, a Chicago consultant on restaurant sites, says Subway has "some very, very poor locations" and is "selling too many franchises too close together."

When Charles Innes left his $46,200-a-year job as a Hewlett-Packard Co. manager, he says he depended on a Subway agent to review and, if appropriate, disapprove his selection of a site. "That's why you buy a franchise," he says. "In theory, you are paying for their knowledge and experience to possibly save you from getting into business trouble."

But the site that he chose and that his agent approved, in Martinsburg, Md., was in a bad neighborhood and had poor visibility from the street, he says. Mr. Innes says that despite working 100-hour weeks, he walked away from it after 18 months, losing his $70,000 investment. Subway bought his equipment for about $10,000 and, conceding that his location was poor, closed the site and opened another one on the affluent side of town, he says.

Mr. DeLuca says that Messrs. Innes and Pitta didn't stick long enough with Subway. "Sometimes success takes time," he says.

In its zeal to expand, franchisees say, Subway has also sometimes sold franchises too close together. Chi Jones says his Northbrook, Ill., store was doing annual sales of nearly $600,000 until Subway franchised another store a little over a mile away. Then his sales fell about 15%.

Some franchisees contend agents pressure them to expand in a way that cannibalizes their own sales. Richard Dudak says he was prospering as the only Subway operator in Moon Township, Pa. Then, he says, a Subway development agent told him of plans to sell another in a new shopping center a bit over a mile away. "I was sort of given the impression that, 'If you don't buy it, we'll give it to someone else,'" Mr. Dudak says.

The agent, Tim Tolmer, doesn't dispute this impression. Mr. Tolmer says his staff is trying to help Mr. Dudak boost sales.

Though Mr. Dudak thought the second franchise was too close, he bought it. Weekly sales at the first store immediately dropped 28% to $3,200, he says.

Paul Landino, chairman of Subway's agent advisory board, says he can't deny that new openings occasionally cause a permanent drop in sales at existing locations.

Nick Janotta, a Chicago landlord, says that to protect franchisees in space he owns, he included in his lease a prohibition against Subway's opening new outlets within a certain radius. But Mr. Janotta says Subway, which holds the leases at all franchised locations, put three stores within the prohibited area, and as a result, the shop in his space has had a series of different owners, all complaining of poor business.

Mr. DeLuca agrees that Subways have opened within Mr. Janotta's area but says he "wouldn't want to draw a conclusion" about whether Subway violated the lease.

Messrs. DeLuca and Buck have created separate companies that hold the leases. Subway Sandwich Shops' parent, Doctor's Associates Inc., of Milford, Conn., has typically disclaimed responsibility for leases signed by these leasing companies.

Frank DeLeonardis, owner of a commercial building in Mount Vernon, NY, that contained a Subway shop, got a judgment in 1987 in New York state court in White Plains against a leasing company, Subway Sandwich Shops Inc., for $30,000 in unpaid rent, says his lawyer, B.T. Canty. Mr. Canty says the leasing company didn't pay, so his client sued again, in state court in Milford, Conn., to enforce the judgment. But when he tried to collect from the leasing company's bank account, he found less than $100 there, says Mr. Canty. Meanwhile, he asserts, $18,000 had been transferred to Doctor's Associates.

Mr. Canty then sued Doctor's Associates in Milford, alleging that the leasing company was its alter ego and alleging "fraudulent conveyance" and unfair trade practice. He says he accepted a settlement for $25,000 in 1991.

(Continued)

EXHIBIT 15.7 *(Continued)*

Mr. DeLuca says he won't comment on settled litigation but does say the leasing companies now routinely offer to settle unpaid leases. Subway has added language in its leases specifically stating that Doctor's Associates and its owners aren't liable for leasing-company obligations.

Some former franchisees charge that Subway will grant franchises to anyone with enough cash to buy one, including people incapable of reading, writing, or doing simple arithmetic. Mr. DeLuca says the company doesn't wish to prejudge people. "Very few of our people were voted most likely to succeed in high school," he says. "And I wasn't either."

Source: Wall Street Journal, September 16, 1992.

16 TAKE A BREAK TRAVEL

A FORK IN THE ROAD: SUMMER OF '95

Greg Raiff and Mario Ricciardelli sat in their Boston office discussing how to manage the extraordinary growth they were creating at Take A Break Travel. Their spring break travel businesses went from sole proprietorships with no employees prior to the merger on July 23, 1993, to 13 employees (including Greg and Mario) for the 93/94 season. In their second year after the merger, they grew to 38 employees when they created a data processing department. Now, they contemplated creating a national salesforce and going to 53 employees for the 95/96 season.

It they made this step, they would face several critical issues. First, they would hire and manage decentralized employees—a difficult challenge under the best of circumstances. These new hires would be located in 16 different states. In addition, hiring 15 employees at once would reduce the amount of time available for training and supporting any single new employee. Finally, they would be entering a new market niche: high school spring break travel. Although it had many of the same fulfillment issues as their current business, the customers were very different.

They wouldn't be considering this market now except that college spring break travel was a seasonal business and there were large peaks and valleys in the workload of their new data processing department. They either had to find something for them to do in the off-season, or layoff some twenty-plus trained employees and recreate the department every year.

This case was prepared by Dan D'Heilly, Jim Foster, and William Mayfield under the direction of Professor Edward Marram. Funding provided by the Ewing Marion Kauffman Foundation. Copyright © 1996 Babson College. All rights reserved.

If they invested in a national salesforce and it didn't work out, they could be in trouble. The company would be taking on a lot of overhead. But, if they were going to do it, they believed that the time to act was now.

TAKE A BREAK TRAVEL—A COLLEGE BUSINESS

Take A Break Travel was founded in 1987 by Mario Ricciardelli and Scott Tomkins[°] in their junior year at Babson College where they were majoring in Entrepreneurial Studies. They ran the business out of their dorm room. Scott and Mario were among the hundreds of students around the country reselling spring break vacation packages. They resold products developed by a wholesaler who purchased and packaged hotels rooms and airline tickets for college students. Scott and Mario earned "free" spring break vacations, a couple thousand dollars each, and the annual Babson Student Business Initiative Award. But when they considered doing it again their senior year, neither was enamored enough of the business to go for it again. Mario cited poor service as a major reason for staying away, "the wholesaler made promises that he didn't keep."

When graduation arrived in May 1989, Mario had an attractive offer from a land developer, but he wanted to start his own business immediately, "before I need to deal with some of the financial and family constraints that came with age." He didn't have a business in mind, so he asked entrepreneurship professor Bill Bygrave for advice. Professor Bygrave told him to select an industry, get experience working for someone else, then start a business in a field he knew. However, Mario reasoned that he already had experience in the spring break industry, so he resurrected Take A Break Travel in the summer of 1989.

TAKE A BREAK—PART II

Located in downtown Boston, Take A Break Travel specialized in college spring break vacations to Mexico, the Caribbean, and Florida. Approximately 75 percent of Take A Break's retail business was made up of air/land packages to Jamaica, Cancun, the Bahamas, and land-only packages to Florida. (See Exhibit 16.1 for brochure cover.)

Most of his competitors were lifestyle entrepreneurs, content to manage companies that would never grow. As a result, their businesses had no harvest potential. Mario wanted to create a company that he could sell in five years to someone like American Express, and this business didn't seem to have that potential.

The new business was successful, but frustrating for many reasons. First, the wholesalers were very unreliable. In addition, he never had enough field agents commit to working again in the coming year, and worst of all, he wasn't sure how to grow his business. The good news was that he consistently made better money than most of

---

[°] The "Scott Tomkins" case series was written in 1987 and 1989 by William Bygrave, Copyright © Babson College.

Exhibit 16.1   Brochure cover.

his classmates were earning, and he only worked full-time nine months each year. (See Exhibit 16.2 for 1993 Income Statement.)

The weakest link in his business was poor service from the wholesaler. His wholesaler put students in the wrong hotels and even on the wrong flights. In fact, some tickets were never delivered to his customers, although payment had been received by the wholesaler. While investigating customer complaints, he became friends with a distant competitor, Greg Raiff. They talked on the telephone about how to handle complaints and avoid these problems in the future.

HEAT WAVE VACATIONS

Greg Raiff also owned and operated a college student travel business, Heat Wave Vacations. Heat Wave was located in Vermont, a three-hour drive from Boston. Greg got started by organizing a high school trip. Heat Wave was featured in a newsletter sponsored by American Express in 1988 (See Exhibit 16.3).

Heat Wave Vacations helped pay for Greg's education at Middlebury College in Vermont. However, upon graduating in 1993, he did not want to continue on the same path. He wanted a high-potential venture, and he needed to add a wholesale component to the business if he was going to realize that goal. But running Heat Wave, and simultaneously creating a wholesale operation was more than one person could do. Greg needed a partner. He was determined to grow the business or get out of the student travel industry.

THE INDUSTRY

Prior to the 1980s, students made spring break vacation plans through travel agencies or just got in their cars and went on roadtrips. However, airline deregulation changed wholesale and retail distribution channels by allowing airplane charter companies to flourish. Spring break charter operations sprang up in areas with large student populations like Boston and Chicago within a couple of years and prices dropped. By the 1990s, a typical spring break package cost $500, less than half what it cost a decade earlier.

Although some travel agencies sold spring break packages, their volumes were low, so gross margins for their packages were typically between 15 percent and 20 percent. By contrast, spring break wholesalers had high volumes and gross margins in the 25 percent to 30 percent range.

Mario speculated that there were essentially no air/land packages prior to deregulation; Cancun and Nassau—two of the most popular destinations in 1995—didn't even exist as touring options. There were approximately 5,000 student-customers in 1985, but by 1995 there were over 100,000 students taking low-cost spring break vacations each year.

Spring break charter companies were classified as either wholesale or retail operations. Wholesale operators purchased travel services (e.g., airplane charters, hotel

EXHIBIT 16.2 Heat Wave/Take A Break International combined income statement—prior to merger—for the years ending December 31, 1992 and 1993.

	Take A Break International Dec. 31, 1992	Heat Wave, Inc. Dec. 31, 1992	Combined income statement Dec. 31, 1992	Take A Break International Dec. 31, 1993	Heat Wave, Inc. Dec. 31, 1993	Combined income statement Dec. 31, 1993
Travel sales	$1,347,763	$536,732	$1,884,495	$1,026,053	$1,620,372	$2,646,425
Allowances and refunds	(16,815)	(13,669)	(30,484)	(12,704)	(35,035)	(47,739)
Net sales	$1,330,948	$523,063	$1,854,011	$1,013,349	$1,585,337	$2,598,686
Cost of travel	1,080,274	406,806	1,487,080	848,833	1,399,073	2,247,906
Commissions	29,214	—	29,214	23,249	19,807	43,056
Gross profit	$ 221,460	$116,257	$ 337,717	$ 141,267	$ 166,457	$ 307,724
Operating expenses:						
Salary and wages	13,092	7,929	21,021	19,976	3,914	23,890
Temporary wages	—	4,325	4,325	—	1,356	1,356
Advertising	10,645	9,536	20,181	18,167	1,708	19,875
Amortization	200	—	200	—	—	—
Bank service charges	—	698	698	3,040	1,407	4,447
Bad debt expense	—	—	—	—	35	35
Casualty/theft (recoveries)	—	—	—	(10,224)	—	(10,224)
Depreciation	6,288	10,263	16,551	1,945	4,444	6,389
Dues and subscriptions	—	—	—	300	44	344
Insurance	6,279	—	6,279	2,189	—	2,189
Market research	—	—	—	1,200	—	1,200

(Continued)

EXHIBIT 16.2 *(Continued)*

	Take A Break International Dec. 31, 1992	Heat Wave, Inc. Dec. 31, 1992	Combined income statement Dec. 31, 1992	Take A Break International Dec. 31, 1993	Heat Wave, Inc. Dec. 31, 1993	Combined income statement Dec. 31, 1993
Meals and entertainment	1,616	565	2,181	25,118	634	25,752
Miscellaneous expenses	12,087	3,023	15,110	1,887	486	2,373
Office expenses	16,278	4,088	20,366	2,368	9	2,377
Office supplies	—	—	—	—	54	54
Photocopy expenses	—	—	—	483	343	826
Postage and shipping	3,896	7,057	10,953	3,408	37,550	40,958
Professional fees	8,428	2,389	10,817	3,233	1,508	4,741
Rent	7,779	2,525	10,304	7,030	3,248	10,278
Repairs and maintenance	1,715	—	1,715	1,662	—	1,662
Sales promotion	2,786	—	2,786	583	6,727	7,310
Stationery and printing	18,082	—	18,082	13,474	2,334	15,808
Payroll taxes	7,002	345	7,347	3,503	190	3,693
Corporate taxes	456	150	606	912	—	912
Taxes and licenses	—	425	425	—	—	—
Travel expense	15,035	4,026	19,061	—	—	—
Telephone	16,853	12,301	29,154	14,512	12,617	27,129
Utilities	—	—	—	828	—	828
Total operating expenses	$ 148,517	$ 69,645	$ 218,162	$ 115,594	$ 78,608	$ 194,202
Net operating income	72,943	46,612	119,555	25,673	87,849	113,522
Interest income	2,356	1,581	3,937	843	281	1,124
Net income	$ 75,299	$ 48,193	$ 123,492	$ 26,516	$ 88,130	$ 114,646

Exhibit 16.3   Newsletter.

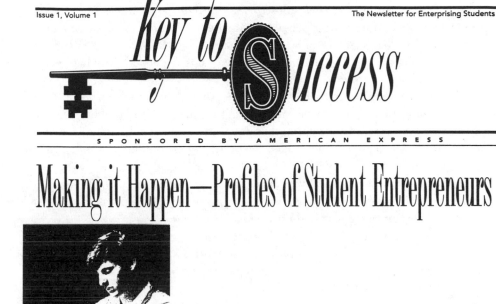

Issue 1, Volume 1

Key to Success

The Newsletter for Enterprising Students

SPONSORED BY AMERICAN EXPRESS

Making it Happen—Profiles of Student Entrepreneurs

Making waves – Gregory Raiff.

Taking Off With HeatWave Vacations

"HeatWave Vacations" travel services was founded by Middlebury student Gregory Raiff whose mission is to provide fun spring break trips at a good value, for students who are dissatisfied with trips purchased elsewhere. As a student representative for a travel company, he became disillusioned selling students trips organized by executives who lacked the dedication and know-how to provide a quality product suited to a student's needs. Raiff realized he could do better. Thus "Heat-Wave Vacations" was incorporated.

Currently, Raiff organizes trips to Cancun (his specialty), Jamaica, and Bahamas for High School and College students. In his first year Raiff boasted 1,900 participants! He recently traveled to Europe to research and negotiate expansion opportunities. He is planning Ski trips to the Alps targeted to college students and recent graduates and teen tour trips for Junior High School students.

Raiff's high integrity company philosophy works. Although campus reps promote his trips for commission, Raiff is quick to reward individuals whose sales results do not reflect their genuine efforts with a bonus. Besides the rep system, Raiff relies on networking and personal contacts for direct mail campaigns and classified advertisements.

Raiff's success results from hard work and perseverence. He saved every penny from part time jobs while in school to raise capital to launch "HeatWave Vacations."

Becoming incorporated at a young age and dealing with the related legal issues was no easy feat. Even if Raiff loses money in the end, he says he would consider it "tuition" for everything he's learned. Running a business, negotiating with lawyers, dealing with accountants, even ordering office supplies has been a priceless and valuable education.

accommodations, tours) in bulk and developed inexpensive packages to fun destinations. These packages were then sold directly to students through a new sales channel, independent contractors known as field agents.

Field agents were usually college students working part-time for extra cash and a "free" spring break vacation. Typically, agents would receive one free trip for every 20 trips sold, and a commission of less than 5 percent of the selling price. The field agents found customers by talking to friends and by posting fliers around campus. Although the best agents could earn as much as $8,000 for a couple of months of part-time work, they often proved unreliable. Most field agents only sold travel services for one year, and many quit before earning their free vacation.

The marketing unit for this industry was the college or university. Packages were developed based on college schedules, field agents were recruited on-campus, and sales were tracked by school of origin. Because of the annual field agent turnover, sales at each college were highly unpredictable. Sales depended on what the new year's field reps would produce.

The industry had other problems. College students were not an ideal market segment because they often booked late, had a poor image with hoteliers, and were extremely price sensitive. Also, spring break vacations occurred during customers' college years, so the main product lacked long-term repeat potential. Finally, the industry was like the ski industry in the sense that it was strongly affected by the severity of the winter weather. A warm winter meant a low interest in spring break travel. However, college students often traveled in groups, referred friends, and came back to the same operator the next year if they had a good time.

Activity in this industry was based on the academic calendar because most of the effort was required between September to April. During this period, students became field agents, formed travel groups, selected destinations, reserved packages, and took their vacations. Customer service requirements could be high, as groups of students learned to plan and organize a group vacation. It was also an on-going effort to keep the student-entrepreneur salesforce organized and motivated.

During spring break, on-site activities were extensive. The Take A Break staff met incoming planes, sometimes even sleeping at the airport, and coordinated local events. This was necessary to orient the students. The logistical demands at vacation destinations were strenuous, so Take A Break began carrying cellular phones in 1995.

The academic calendar was when operations were hectic, but package development was finished by mid-fall. Foresight in developing packages was critical because last year's hot destination was not always this year's best seller. Hotel rooms and airplane seats reserved for resale were referred to in the industry as "inventory." To reserve inventory, a deposit was required by the airline or hotelier. Wholesalers frequently had excess inventory at some destinations, and they often didn't have enough inventory at the most popular spots.

The charter travel industry was regulated by the Department of Transportation (DOT), however, since the spring break charter business was just emerging, it hadn't received much attention from regulators although they would have a significant impact if implemented. First, regulations stipulated that all charter flights must register with the DOT. The DOT then issued a charter number for that flight and required that it be published in advertisements. Second, the DOT also required that operators secure all inventory before marketing the charter. Finally, the DOT allowed revenue from future charter flights to be used for deposits on hotel rooms and airplane charters, but required that all remaining cash be placed in separate escrow accounts until after services were delivered. Prior to 1995, no spring break charter operator fully complied with DOT regulations.

These escrow requirements provided a tremendous safeguard for consumers, but they placed a heavy burden on seasonal charter operators. Most business processes and marketing expenses were incurred between July and March, but could not be funded by present cash flow unless the charter company also operated non-air travel business. Given these constraints, most spring break charter operators did not have the resources necessary to create sophisticated transaction processing operations, fund large-scale marketing programs, and/or had been out of compliance.

Many wholesalers hedged their risk by purchasing fewer seats and rooms than they thought they would need. Charter companies were required to carry a surety bond. A typical surety bond might be $200,000, and it would be collateralized at 75 percent, so a charter company could have $150,000 sitting in the bank in case of failure. They planned to purchase a more complete inventory when end-user demand was better established. Sometimes wholesalers ended up substituting inventory between hotels as they ran out of space. This unethical tactic was not uncommon among spring break wholesalers. Sometimes wholesalers simply canceled trips at the last minute when they couldn't fulfill orders.

Greg and Mario got to know each other as field reps handling complaints about these wholesaler practices. They would call each other to identify unscrupulous wholesalers, and to find other sources of inventory for their customers. They were so-called "friendly competitors," and discussions often turned to improving their businesses.

THE MERGER

While trading notes about how to manage wholesalers, Greg and Mario discovered that they shared a common goal for their companies: growth and harvest. However, sales for each company had plateaued below two million dollars and both were discouraged about the prospect of achieving their goals as retail operators.

Greg was traveling down from Vermont to Boston to visit friends, and both wanted a chance to meet "the competition," so Greg and Mario met at a restaurant for dinner. They liked each other instantly and created their first business plan on the back of a napkin.

In a nutshell, their plan called for market domination as an integrated wholesaler/retailer within five years. If they generated huge customer volumes and created a reliable wholesale operation, they should dominate the industry. Operationally, Mario would manage marketing, while Greg would create the wholesale operation. They intended to maintain their SG&A at a fixed cost per destination, so once a large enough volume of passengers were booked to a given destination, additional passengers contributed straight to the bottom line.

Greg and Mario decided to generate high sales volumes by always having the lowest price. They called this their "Spaghetti-O's strategy." This was a commitment to offering the lowest prices in a very price-sensitive market. This price-leader strategy worked for local discount retailers and they were confident that it could generate a large spring break market share. As Mario explained it:

> We're young and it doesn't cost us much to live. We'll lower our margins and eat Spaghetti-O's° every night if we have to, but we'll never lose on price.

° Spaghetti-O's are an inexpensive canned pasta dish.

They believed that the demographics of their customers (the segment of the college market with discretionary income for spring break travel) were very attractive to many companies (e.g., American Express). If Take A Break could build a stable operation with a large market share, they should reach their dream of a rich harvest.

Before merging, Greg and Mario hired attorney and Babson professor Richard Mandel to help craft their partnership agreement. The competitors needed to be able to trust their new partnership. One key issue was how to join assets while avoiding unknown past liabilities (i.e., a lawsuit stemming from a previous season). They did this by capitalizing the new entity, R&R International, with the assets of the prior companies in an asset-only transaction and they each contributed $100,000 for the first year's working capital (they still had not secured a line of bank credit by the fall of 1995).

Two of the other main points addressed in the stockholder agreement (See Exhibit 16.4 for the Stockholder Agreement Checklist) were an escape clause and a valuation formula. They created an escape clause that would allow either partner to simply call it quits on the one-year anniversary of the merger. A preset valuation formula (with terms and conditions for various contingencies) was also established to alleviate potential disagreements in any future change in ownership. Mario reflected on the process:

> Drafting the partnership agreement was some of the best money we ever spent. It was $10,000 to get all the BS out of the way. We really hammered each other for 3 weeks.

EXHIBIT 16.4   Stockholders' agreement checklist.

1. Required investment of each stockholder: equity versus debt; future commitments, if any.
2. Equipment or real estate leases from stockholders.
3. Who will serve on the board of directors?
4. Who will serve as the officers of the corporation?
5. Employment issues: job descriptions; time commitments; compensation rates; bonuses; fringe benefits.
6. Disposition of stock upon death of a stockholder: purchase by corporation or other stockholders; mandatory or elective.
7. Disposition of stock upon disability of a stockholder: purchase by corporation or other stockholders; mandatory or elective.
8. Disposition of stock upon disability of a stockholder: purchase by corporation or other stockholders; mandatory or elective; penalty for premature termination, termination for cause or without adequate notice?
9. Restrictions on resale of stock.
10. Formula for valuation of stock for any of the above situations.
11. Payment terms for stock repurchase: fund with life insurance; policies held by escrow agent; promissory note; term, downpayment, interest rate; secured by pledge of stock repurchased.
12. Responsibilities with regard to proprietary information.
13. Noncompetition obligations.
14. Provisions for breaking deadlocks (for 50–50 stock distributions).

Source: Professor Richard Mandell, Babson College, 1996. Professor Mandell is a partner in the law firm, Bowditch & Dewey.

By the time we worked through all the issues Mandel raised, we knew that the deal covered every contingency. We had full confidence in our partnership, so we were ready to dig in and conquer the world.

Finally, there was also deadline pressure: Mario wanted the deal done before he got married, or not at all. On July 23, 1993, the day before Mario's wedding, Greg Raiff and Mario Ricciardelli signed a merger agreement creating R&R International. They were poised to take on the college spring break travel industry.

PACKAGE DEVELOPMENT

When Mario and Greg decided to merge in the summer of 1993, they did not know how to wholesale travel packages. As a result, they made mistakes forecasting demand, evaluating inventory deals, and preparing for customers at vacation sites.

Greg was a talented negotiator and he was largely successful at securing the inventory that he and Mario wanted. The difficulty lay in forecasting demand and selecting vendors. Greg secured enough inventory for 100 percent growth, but the company's 1994 inventory demands ended up being in excess of 200 percent. Securing inventory was also a risky process. Credit information was not always available and reliable. In their first year, Take A Break gave a Mexican hotelier a $50,000 deposit which the hotelier did not honor or refund. (This issue was still being decided in the Mexican court system in early 1996.)

Take A Break manufactured and sold tourist items to incoming customers (e.g., tee shirts, tours, snorkels). Add-on sales were nonexistent in 1994, their first year operating charters. The next year they observed other charter operators selling merchandise, so they sold off-the-shelf items to customers. Add-on sales were a minor source of revenue in 1995, but two product managers were hired to develop customized items to sell on-site in 1996. Add-on sale revenue was projected to contribute an additional $200,000 for Spring Break '96. Gross margins on add-on sales were in the 60 percent to 80 percent range.

They used the company's large customer-base to economically produce specialty items (e.g., tee-shirts), and to negotiate favorable pricing from local vendors at destination attractions. An example of these local deals was the Spring Break VIP cards. The VIP card allowed the "breakers" to get into clubs without a cover charge plus they got one free drink per establishment. Take A Break developed VIP cards for all their package destinations. They sold these cards for thirty dollars, and they only cost Take A Break the sales commissions and $0.25 each to stamp the plastic.

SPRING BREAK 1994

At the time of the merger in 1993, Mario forecast that business volume would be about $3 million, but had no idea how to project the business that they would actually produce:

> We didn't have a book of business that we could combine, we had a transient customer base, it was more that I thought the synergy of working together would double our business.

In the fall of 1993, Take A Break hired six full-time regional sales managers who worked on cheap metal desks at the corporate office and managed their territories with contact management software. These regional mangers consulted with student agents about on-campus activities, provided promotional material and tried to keep the agents motivated. Total staffing at this point was Greg and Mario, six sales managers, and three student interns.

In the 1994 season, their first year in business, Take A Break sold travel packages to over 16,000 people for approximately $7 million in revenue ($140 average gross profit per passenger). This was more than double the number of passengers that Greg and Mario had expected. Take A Break became the largest operation on the East Coast, and one of the three largest in the United States.

Take A Break forced $7 million in revenue through a system that had only processed transactions worth $1.5 million in any previous season. In one week during December 1993, checks worth $1 million arrived at their office. Greg and Mario spent nights curled up on the floor trying to grab an hour's sleep between processing orders and handling crisis situations.

Greg managed backroom operations just as he'd managed them in years past. Take A Break changed inventory status from "available" to "sold" only after a ticket was issued. However, the ticket-issuing process was not tightly linked to customer payments. In most instances, checks were deposited the same day they arrived in the mail. A photocopy of the check was made for processing the ticket later. This created a time lag, so they regularly over-booked accommodations. For example, a prospective customer could call and ask if a certain hotel had rooms available. If Take A Break hadn't processed a ticket for those rooms, the answer was "yes," but a check for that inventory might already be in the bank with a photocopy waiting in the "Tickets to be issued" in-box, another check could arrive in that day's mail, and the caller's check could arrive two days later. Although their biggest problem was processing tickets, resources increasingly needed to be focused on refunding over-booked accommodations.

Take A Break was dramatically under-staffed. Beginning in December, they hired so many temporary workers (perhaps as many as 40 temps over a three-month period) that the interview process changed into an attendance policy, "If they showed up for the interview, we hired them." Take A Break had poorly trained staff handling ticketing, customer service, and check processing. They budgeted half a million dollars for overhead; but they spent almost twice that figure. (See Exhibit 16.2 for Operating Expense data.) Mario described this as the most troubling ongoing problem:

> It was a constant problem to find affordable, talented, and motivated people. We needed to systemize our human resource function.

Salaries and refunds weren't the only unexpected expenses. Mario found out that one of these poorly trained employees, who turned out to have a criminal record, was embezzling funds:

> He did get some cash. . . . People ask, "Why didn't you check his references?" But I was much too busy, he walked in and I said, "Here's a ticket, start typing."

When spring break '94 was past and they reconciled the books, deposit slips were the best revenue records, and the company checkbook was the best source of operating expense data for the December to April period. Many customers took advantage of the confusion to receive unwarranted refunds. The worst of these came to be known as "triple bangers," they (1) received a cash refund, (2) canceled their credit card payments, and (3) took the trip when their tickets arrived:

> They never believed us when we said the tickets are in the mail, and we never imagined that so many people would rip us off.
>
> We proved that the price-leader strategy works. Sales soared because we guaranteed that our price would be the lowest available. . . . Unfortunately, gross revenues are unimportant. Our fulfillment systems made us unprofitable.

Greg and Mario had a decision to make; their agreement had a one-year no-fault dissolution clause and the year was up. The thrill of generating $7 million convinced them to remain partners, but something needed to be done to professionalize their business.

GROWTH? SYSTEMS!

When Mario and Scott Tomkins started Take A Break in 1987, their due diligence included talking to industry insiders. It was time to pull out the old business cards. Mario called Joseph Newman at TNT, a computer expert whom he talked to when first putting the company together in 1988. He called TNT after reading the Steve Belkin° case in an entrepreneurship class. Joseph strongly recommended a computer system called Tech 7 that was designed for the charter business. Tech 7 was used by many charter companies including Garber Travel Services, Thomas Cook Vacations, and All About Travel.

They had driven sales without calculating how much they could deliver; now it was time for the back office to catch up. Take A Break hadn't made much profit in their first season, and Tech 7 cost $50,000, but there was little doubt that they needed a sophisticated system to grow their business. After some soul searching, Greg and Mario committed to buying this state-of-the-art system:

> It was almost like buying a franchise, because Tech 7 said, "No, this is the way you have to do it. You can't do it another way. If you want to make your own rules, you'll have to reprogram the system and it will cost you $10k." So we figured out how to run our business the Tech 7 way. It taught us how to do charter operations.

It was also a system that took time to learn. They wouldn't be able to bring in untrained temporary workers from this point forward: they needed a system manager to train staff, and to troubleshoot exceptional situations. This was a problem because most of their cash became available during the eight weeks of spring break.

Greg and Mario reorganized their staff into six functional departments to professionalize their operations. Take A Break's 37 employees were organized into six

---

° Steve Belkin founded TNT, a charter travel company.

departments: information systems, 25 employees; sales, 6 employees; product development, 2 employees; operations, 1 employee; graphic arts, 1 employee; and accounting/finance, 2 employees. (See Exhibit 16.5 for Organization Chart.) In addition to the full-time staff at corporate, they still had seasonal field staff who met customers as they arrived and coordinated activities on the ground.

Superimposed on the departmental structure were two additional managers who managed staff at the corporate office. They found highly qualified people to manage finance and reservations. Their controller came from Price Waterhouse, a big 6 accounting firm. Her role was to manage escrow accounts, cash flow, bank and supplier relations. This was critical if they were to establish and maintain economies of scale. They also found a manager with Tech 7 experience to head up their new information systems department.

Telephony was another system that received attention. During the height of the spring selling season, the phones lines had been filled many times. There was no way to know how much business they lost as a result. They also bought an 800 line, so the demands on the phone system were expected to increase.

SPRING BREAK 1995

Gearing up for the coming season and the new hires, Greg and Mario refurbished the offices by buying plants, painting, and putting candy dishes on all the desks. On the Monday that new employees were due to begin training, a fire tore through their office at 7:30 A.M. and it was "burned to a crisp." To make matters worse, they were under-insured. Still sitting on Mario's desk was a note from his insurance agent asking if he wanted to increase his coverage. The corners of the note were curled and black from the flames. They conducted training sessions at a local hotel and within two weeks they had set up a new office. Fortunately, they were able to salvage most of the equipment.

Exhibit 16.5   R&R International, Inc. organization chart.

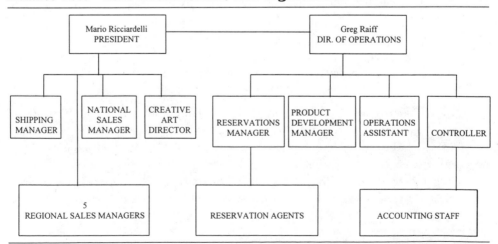

For 1995, Greg and Mario set two major goals: zero passenger-volume growth, and expansion into the southern United States. This moved their focus to operations management and risk reduction. Tech 7 and their new operations center worked almost perfectly, and the new markets were also a successful effort (see Exhibits 16.6–16.10 for financial statements).

The gross margins were about the same for southern college town packages, but the cost, sales, and inventory risk structures made this a very attractive move:

1. There was little additional overhead cost.
2. Adding these markets lessened Take A Break's reliance on unpredictable northern markets.

EXHIBIT 16.6   R&R International balance sheet as of May 31, 1994.

ASSETS	
Current assets:	
Cash—BayBank	$ 28,854
Cash—FNB	309,223
Cash—NBRO CD	200,000
Cash—NBRO restricted	11,567
Due to/from affiliates	1,033
Prepaid expenses	13,998
Total current assets	$564,675
Total property and equipment	34,076
Total assets	$598,751
LIABILITIES AND EQUITY	
Current liabilities:	
Notes payable	$ (3,129)
Lease	11,652
Deferred revenue (94)	(217)
Due to/from affiliates	20,000
Loans payable (March)	50,000
Loans payable (GMR)	65,000
Loans payable (other)	20,000
Total current liabilities	$163,306
Long term debt	—
Total liabilities	$163,306
Equity:	
Common stock	$ 100
Additional paid capital	39,900
Retained earnings	(164,390)
Distributions	(22,712)
Net income (loss)	582,547
Total equity	$435,445
Total liabilities and equity	$598,751

EXHIBIT 16.7 R&R International, Inc. balance sheet as of December 31, 1994.

ASSETS

Current assets:

Cash	$ 63,772
Cash—restricted escrow (NBRO)	392,391
Certificate of deposit	120,000
Prepaid expenses	168,500
Total current assets	$744,663

Property and equipment—at cost:

Computer and office equipment	15,402
Furniture and fixtures	20,527
Leasehold improvements	5,013
Software systems	12,847
Telephone system	15,150
Less accumulated depreciation	$(13,684)
Property and equipment—net	$ 55,255
Total assets	$799,918

LIABILITY AND STOCKHOLDERS' EQUITY

Current liabilities:

Accounts payable	$ 88,534
Capital lease obligations	5,657
Note payable to shareholder	15,000
Deferred sales revenue	593,073
Total current liabilities	$702,264

Other liabilities:

Due to predecessor affiliates	20,000
Customer deposits	100,000
Total other liabilities	$120,000
Total liabilities	$822,264

Stockholders' equity:

Common stock, ($.01 par value; 10,000 shares authorized, issued and outstanding including $39,900 of paid in capital	40,000
Accumulated deficit	(62,346)
Total stockholders' equity	$(22,346)
Total liabilities and stockholders' equity	$799,918

EXHIBIT 16.8   R&R International, Inc. statement of cash flows for the year ended December 31, 1994.

CASH FLOWS FROM OPERATING ACTIVITIES

Net income	$ 102,540

Adjustments to reconcile net income to net cash from operations:

Depreciation and amortization	$ 10,821
Increase in prepaid expenses	(130,366)
Increase in accounts payable	92,702
Increase in deferred sales revenue	258,476
Increase in customer deposits	100,000
	$ 331,633
Net cash provided by operating activities	$ 434,173

CASH FLOWS FROM INVESTING ACTIVITIES

Additions to property and equipment	$ (29,139)
Investment in certificates of deposits	(312,391)
Net cash used by investing activities	$(341,530)

CASH FLOWS FROM FINANCING ACTIVITIES

Net change in due from affiliates	$ 15,121
Payment of loan from officers	(255,000)
Distributions to shareholders	(3,358)
Increase in loans payable	306
Decrease in capital lease obligations	(8,835)
Net cash used by financing activities	(251,766)
Net decrease in cash	(159,123)
Cash, January 1, 1994	222,895
Cash, December 31, 1994	$ 63,772

SUPPLEMENTAL DISCLOSURE OF CASH FLOW INFORMATION

Cash paid during year for:

Massachusetts corporate excise tax	$ 456
Interest expense	$ 3,824

3. There was less down-side risk in southern charters because shorter distances meant that airplane inventory was 30 percent to 40 percent cheaper.

Take A Break successfully marketed packages in many new markets including Nashville, Atlanta, Orlando, Richmond, and Raleigh:

> It was very satisfying. For the first time since either of us had been in this industry, the wholesale operations were not a problem. We put together packages and delivered them as promised.
> The number of actual passengers was the same or even a bit more than in 1994, and the margins were about the same. We decided not to increase the number of passengers . . . We grew expenses and the number of cities served. We wanted to stabilize

EXHIBIT 16.9 R&R International, Inc. natural business cycle income statement June 1994–May 1995

	Five months ended May 31, 1994	Twelve months ended Dec. 31, 1994	June 1, 1994– Dec. 31, 1994	Five months ended May 31, 1995
Travel sales	$8,863,732	$9,382,252	$ 518,520	$5,919,706
Allowance and refunds	(671,756)	(789,913)	(118,157)	(210,307)
Net sales	$8,191,976	$8,592,339	$ 400,363	$5,709,399
Cost of travel	7,272,287	7,497,864	225,577	3,572,849
Commissions	27,214	79,906	52,692	272,232
Credit card fees				30,909
Gross profit	$ 892,475	$1,014,569	$ 122,094	$1,833,409
Operating expenses				
Sales and wages	$ 84,235	$ 196,991	$ 112,756	$ 164,605
Temporary wages	14,397	23,474	9,077	6,569
Advertising	34,366	117,985	83,619	47,523
Bank service charges	5,650	11,549	5,899	7,768
Bad debt expense	—	993	—	7,795
Casualty/theft/losses	16,872	34,556	17,684	—
Computer support	—	400	—	23,034
Dues and subscriptions	723	1,913	1,190	928
Depreciation	—	10,821	—	—
Insurance	2,017	21,687	19,670	5,127
Interest expense	215	3,824	3,609	—
Legal settlement	—	9,520	—	—
Miscellaneous expense	8,113	10,015	1,902	—

Office expense	27,302	49,888	22,586	19,287
Photocopy expenses	6,976	7,804	828	—
Postage and shipping	39,633	62,653	23,020	25,538
Legal and accounting	9,994	162,487	152,493	23,735
Rent	10,000	13,900	8,900	10,726
Rental of equipment	1,057	7,296	6,239	15,766
Repairs and maintenance	367	12,619	12,252	435
Stationery and printing	7,678	27,386	19,708	—
Payroll taxes	18,740	21,017	2,277	20,295
Corporate taxes	—	—	—	456
Taxes and licenses	1,455	1,470	15	701
Training expenses	249	249	—	—
Travel expense	—	8,943	—	19,563
Telephone	27,449	101,328	73,879	106,672
Utilities	2,729	—	(2,729)	3,406
Total operating expenses	$ 320,217	$ 925,768	$ 605,551	$ 509,929
Net operating income (loss)	$ 572,258	$ 88,801	$(483,457)	$1,323,480
Interest income	10,289	13,739	3,450	12,163
Net income (loss)	$ 582,547	$ 102,540	$(480,007)	$1,335,643

EXHIBIT 16.10 R&R International D/B/A Take A Break Travel Statement of assets, liabilities, and equity as of May 31, 1995.

ASSETS

Current assets:

Cash	$ 63,199
Accounts receivable	12,247
Marketable securities	1,002,298
Prepaid expenses	59,730
Total current assets	$1,137,474

Property and equipment:

Leasehold improvements	5,862
Furniture and fixtures	43,437
Machinery and equipment	41,567
Computer equipment	19,142
	$ 110,008
Less: Accumulated depreciation	13,684
	$ 96,324

Other assets:

Cash, restricted	120,216
	$1,354,014

LIABILITIES AND STOCKHOLDERS' EQUITY

Current liabilities:

Accounts payable	$ 52,701
Loans from affiliates	18,967
Total current liabilities	$ 71,668

Stockholders' equity:

Common stock	$ 100
Additional paid in capital	39,900
Retained earnings	1,242,346
	$1,282,346
	$1,354,014

operations so we could get our reservations center up and running, hire a controller, and then grow aggressively again in 1996.

The High School Group Travel Market

Although pleased with Tech 7's performance, Greg and Mario were concerned about how to keep their permanent workers busy during the slack summer season—about 12 weeks a year. Mario had looked into the corporate travel and the high school markets briefly in 1989, but neither market was attractive at the time. Now the high school senior graduation trip market seemed like a good idea. They projected millions of dollars in additional revenues with just an incremental increase in operating costs.

The total market was estimated to contain 2 million high school seniors. These trips had marketing cycles which ran almost entirely in the second and third quarters. By contrast, college marketing occurred mostly in the fourth and first quarters. However, high school trips required more planning and preparation than college student trips. The parents were also more involved than with the college students.

In addition, this market required professional sales representatives; a high school student salesforce was not a viable option. Colleges were a mass marketing operation: fliers on campus, newspaper advertising to enlist hundreds of field agents. However, high schools travel groups needed the professional consulting that a structured direct salesforce could provide. Quality came at a price: the commission for these agents would be in the 10 percent range.

Unfortunately, Greg and Mario had no experience with the high school market. They also had little experience with professional sales or remote employee management. What support would high school groups need? What additional demands would this initiative make on their operations and cash flow? What kind of unexpected growing pains would they face in this new arena? Maybe they should just trim their sails and take a break during the off season.

PREPARATION QUESTIONS

1. What is Take A Break's "growth strategy?" Do you agree or disagree with this approach?

2. What resources does Take A Break's strategy require in calendar year 1996? Please quantify.

3. Is their harvest expectation realistic? Evaluate the fit between their goal of a five-year buyout and the corporate structure they are creating. How big do they need to get before they become attractive: revenues, number of employees, passengers, other?

17 BAGELZ

Bagel Boys was a Connecticut-based bagel chain, with seven established retail locations. In 1993, Mike Bellobuono and team members Joe Amodio, Wes Becher, and Jamie Whalen were approached by Subway sandwich franchise co-founder Fred DeLuca. He offered to buy into the company and turn them into a world-class franchise, but reaching a deal wasn't easy. Negotiations continued for six long months, during which time Bagel Boys stopped opening additional stores, and in late 1993, an agreement was finally reached. Fred DeLuca and Peter Buck (Fred's Subway partner) purchased a 50 percent stake in the franchise company. Mike, Jamie, Joe, and Wes retained the other 50 percent, and 100 percent of the commissary—a separate company founded by the four which supplied Bagel Boys franchisees with bagel dough and cream cheese.

Aligning with Fred offered numerous competitive advantages as a franchisor. Franchising offered Bagel Boys a high-growth opportunity—essential to compete against other industry players such as Bruegger's and Manhattan Bagel (see Exhibit 17.1). But the Bagel Boys team was concerned because as the company expanded, the likelihood of franchisee problems also increased. They wondered how they could best defend against this and thought that perhaps some changes were in order. Although they were unsure what that would entail, the team thought they needed to reassess at least two factors: (1) the way they selected franchisees and (2) the company's internal management structure. Furthermore, they needed to evaluate all alternatives to determine the company's best strategic direction.

This case was prepared by Andrea Alyse with assistance from Dan D'Heilly under the direction of Professor Stephen Spinelli. Funding provided by the Ewing Marion Kauffman Foundation. Copyright © 1996 Babson College. All rights reserved.

Exhibit 17.1   Comparison of Bruegger's Bagel Bakery and Manhattan Bagel.

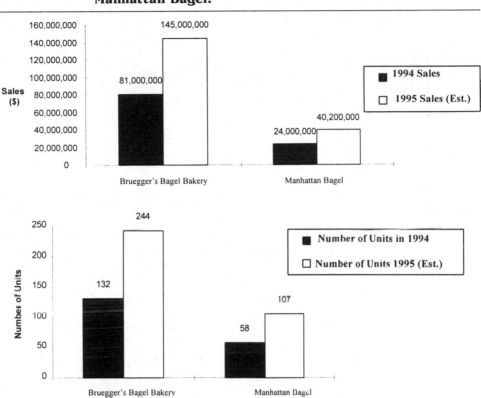

Source: *Nation's Restaurant News*, July 17, 1995, *Restaurant Business*, July 1, 1995, and *BusinessWeek*, May 21, 1996.

FRANCHISING OPERATIONS

Attempts to officially register the Bagel Boys name revealed that another company had already filed for the exclusive rights to use that name. Mike and the team named the new company Bagelz. Bagelz was registered as a franchise company in December 1993 and began selling franchises in the summer of 1994. As Mike recalled:

> When we began to franchise, many people thought we were already doing it because a lot of people didn't know the difference between a chain and a franchise. We had gotten dozens of letters from people asking to buy a franchise. That was where we got our first franchisees.

Charismatic and a natural-born salesman, Joe assumed the responsibility for selling stores—a critical position since the company's development strategy focused heavily on rapid growth through franchising. Jamie, Wes, and Mike concentrated on the operational aspects of the company, consulting with Fred often:

> Fred was the one who really made it all happen. Without him we would have never franchised; we simply felt that we didn't know enough about it to do it on our own.

EXHIBIT 17.2 50 fastest growing U.S. restaurants 1994–1995.

Name of restaurant	City and state	Type of restaurant	Does the company franchise?	1994–1995 % change systemwide sales	1994–1995 % change in avg. unit sales	1994–1994 % change in units
1 East Side Mario's	Dallas, TX	Casual Dinnerhouse	Y	126.3	-2.0	59.1
2 Boston Chicken	Golden, CO	Fast Food	Y	106.7	5.8	55.2
3 Kenny Rogers Roasters	Fort Lauderdale, FL	Fast Food	Y	106.5	2.4	45.6
4 Planet Hollywood	Orlando, FL	Eatertainment	N	101.2	13.0	57.1
5 St. Louis Bread Co.	Boston, MA	Fast Food	Y	87.8	-2.8	59.5
6 Old Chicago Restaurants	Boulder, CO	Brewpub	N	82.4	-20.5	64.3
7 Hometown Buffet	San Diego, CA	Buffet	Y	71.6	-4.5	48.3
8 Johnny Rockets	Los Angeles, CA	Fast Food	Y	69.9	2.7	129.4
9 Manhattan Bagel	Eatontown, NJ	Fast Food	Y	67.5	10.0	175.9
10 Hops Grill & Bar	Tampa, FL	Brewpub	N	67.4	3.6	50.0
11 Starbucks	Seattle, WA	Fast Food	N	66.9	9.0	55.6
12 Landry's	Houston, TX	Casual Dinnerhouse	N	66.3	-6.3	60.0
13 Chesapeake Bagel Bakery	Mclean, VA	Fast Food	Y	65.7	0	122
14 Fazoli's	Lexington, KY	Fast Food	Y	64.0	2.6	72.6
15 Mozzarella's	Mobile, AL	Casual Dinnerhouse	N	62.7	-12.8	41.2
16 Don Pablo's	Bedford, TX	Casual Dinnerhouse	N	55.3	5.7	33.3
17 Bruegger's Bagel Bakery	Burlington, VT	Fast Food	Y	55.0	-0.1	84.8
18 Papa John's	Louisville, KY	Fast Food	Y	51.1	-0.9	38.9
19 Lone Star Steakhouse	Wichita, KS	Casual Steakhouse	N	52.4	1.6	39.1
20 Outback Steakhouse	Tampa, FL	Casual Steakhouse	Y	45.4	0	38.8
21 Schlotzsky's Deli	Austin, TX	Fast Food	Y	45.3	16.1	30.5
22 Pollo Tropical	Miami, FL	Fast Food	Y	44.5	4.9	23.5
23 Country Harvest Buffet	Bellevue, WA	Buffet	N	42.0	2.2	13.3

	Name	City	Category				
24	Applebee's	Kansas City, MO	Casual Dinnerhouse	Y	40.9	0	31.2
25	Damon's—The Place For Ribs	Columbus, OH	Casual Dinnerhouse	Y	39.7	10.5	26.8
26	Cheesecake Factory	Redondo Beach, CA	Casual Dinnerhouse	N	36.7	2.4	40.0
27	Papa Murphy's Take 'N' Bake Pizza	Vancouver, WA	Fast Food	Y	35.7	5.7	34.3
28	Crab House	Hollywood, FL	Seafood Dinnerhouse	N	35.5	6.7	53.8
29	Peter Piper Pizza	Phoenix, AZ	Fast Food	Y	33.3	2.5	38.9
30	Cici's Pizza	Dallas, TX	Fast Food	Y	32.8	2.6	21.0
31	Romano's Macaroni Grill	Dallas, TX	Casual Dinnerhouse	N	31.3	-3.5	40.0
32	Donatos Pizza	Blacklick, OH	Fast Food	Y	30.7	3.2	21.6
33	Blimpie	New York, NY	Fast Food	Y	30.0	2.0	54.3
34	Italian Oven	Latrobe, PA	Casual Dinnerhouse	Y	29.9	-11.4	25.7
35	Steak-Out	Huntsville, AL	Fast Food	Y	29.8	2.0	16.9
36	Ninfa's	Houston, TX	Casual Dinnerhouse	N	29.4	-10	32.1
37	California Pizza Kitchen	Los Angeles, CA	Casual Dinnerhouse	Y	27.7	24.6	22.4
38	Burgerville U.S.A.	Vancouver, WA	Fast Food	N	27.3	31.3	2.6
39	Cinnabon Cinnamon Rolls	Seattle, WA	Fast Food	Y	26.7	2.5	11.7
40	Claim Jumper	Irvine, CA	Dinnerhouse	N	26.5	8.3	13.3
41	Chammps Americana	Wayzata, MN	Casual Dinnerhouse	Y	25.3	2.9	28.6
42	Levy Restaurants	Chicago, IL	Eatertainment	N	25.0	23.2	0
43	California Cafe Restaurant	Corta Madera, CA	Casual Dinnerhouse	Y	25.0	2.0	28.6
44	Green Burrito	Newport Beach, CA	Fast Food	Y	25.0	2.3	52.4
45	Auntie Anne's	Gap, PA	Fast Food	Y	24.2	1.7	9.9
46	Rio Bravo Cantina	Marietta, GA	Casual Dinnerhouse	Y	24.0	3.0	25.0
47	Old Country Buffet	Eden Prairie, MN	Buffet	Y	23.7	-0.9	16.4
48	Chevys	Irvine, CA	Casual Dinnerhouse	Y	23.6	-3.8	28.3
49	Ruby Tuesday	Mobile, AL	Casual Dinnerhouse	Y	23.6	-4.5	18.0
50	Steak 'N Shake	Springfield, MO	Fast Food	Y	23.5	5.0	21.3

Source: Restaurant Business, July 1, 1995.

Franchising had become increasingly popular throughout the U.S. restaurant industry. In 1995, 34 of the top 50 fastest growing U.S. restaurants were franchises (see Exhibit 17.2). By 1996, twelve Bagelz franchised locations were operating and six other franchised sites were under development. Additionally, one franchisee was planning to open multiple nonbake satellite units. A nonbake location is one in which there is no oven on the premises and bagels must be supplied from another Bagelz store. The first nonbake location had been opened in Saybrook, Connecticut, in 1993, in response to a bet: a landlord challenged Mike and his team to build a store in three weeks' time, to meet the start of the summer tourist season. They accomplished this feat in exchange for lower rent, and the store became an instant success. Sales revenues were comparable to those of traditional stores, but rent, labor, and equipment costs were significantly less—as was the population needed to support the unit. Population issues were also why Mike and his team sold only site-specific locations:

> We didn't sell territories or give assurances that we wouldn't open a store next door. The problem was different population densities. For example, a mile radius in New York City could have supported many locations, but in much of Kansas, a mile just wouldn't be large enough to support even one store. Also, if there was one store on the Massachusetts Turnpike and one in the nearest town, although located in close proximity of each other, they would clearly serve two different markets of customers. We looked very carefully at each individual situation when we developed stores near each other. We weren't looking to annoy franchisees—we knew they were the key to successful development.

Franchising was expensive. As a franchisor, Bagelz needed to open a minimum of 50 locations before there existed the potential to obtain a profit. Developing stores was a cash-intensive process, and it often took as long as two years to build a steady customer-base (see Exhibits 17.3 through 17.6 for financial statements.) Additionally, Bagelz asked for a lower franchise fee than its competitors. Mike limited this fee to $10,000 because, although less income for Bagelz in the short term, he wanted to attract mom-and-pop franchisees. He felt that they were the most motivated to make a Bagelz store succeed.

To help minimize corporate costs, Mike used Subway's legal department to write the Uniform Franchise Offering Circular (UFOC)° (see Exhibit 17.7) and their architects for designing new stores. Because of this, Bagelz's corporate franchise-development costs were significantly lower than what they otherwise would have been.

° A UFOC contains information including: a description of the business, estimated development costs, fee schedules, franchisee and franchisor obligations, other businesses affiliated with the franchise, and pending lawsuits. The Federal Trade Commission requires franchisors to furnish a UFOC to prospective franchisees. Additionally, thirteen states require state office UFOC filings for franchisors who franchise in that state.

EXHIBIT 17.3   Bagelz Franchising balance sheets December 31, 1995 and 1994.

	1995	1994
ASSETS		
Current assets		
Cash	$ 3,230	$ 2,590
Accounts and other receivables	11,916	3,450
Other current assets	1,210	2,281
	16,356	8,321
Property and equipment	95,412	95,412
Less accumulated depreciation	(14,964)	(3,230)
	80,448	92,182
Other assets	88,318	44,091
Due from affiliates	12,853	16,991
Other assets	101,171	61,082
	$197,975	$161,585
LIABILITIES AND STOCKHOLDERS' EQUITY		
Current liabilities		
Accounts payable and accrued expenses	$ 44,425	$ 58,824
Due to affiliates	42,855	96,679
Other current liability	1,210	2,281
Income taxes payable	500	250
	88,990	158,034
Loans payable—stockholders	87,976	38,217
Deferred franchise fee revenue	13,000	28,700
Stockholders' equity (deficit)		
Common stock, no par value, 20,000 shares authorized, 200 shares issued and outstanding	1,000	1,000
Additional paid-in capital	194,217	56,000
Accumulated deficit	(187,208)	(120,366)
	$ 8,009	$ (63,366)
	$197,975	$161,585

JOE'S DEPARTURE

At this time, Joe left to pursue other interests:

> Joe was an entrepreneur in the truest sense of the word. We didn't want Joe to go, but his passion was starting companies. His attitude was go, go, go, and he loved to get the company going, but then, when it came to dealing with day-to-day stuff, Joe got completely bored out of his mind. He got us to grow, but he didn't want to deal with the red tape of being a franchisor.

EXHIBIT 17.4   Bagelz Franchising Corporation (an "S" corporation) statements of loss for the years ended December 31, 1995 and 1994.

	1995	1994
Revenue		
Royalties	$265,313	$(57,144
Initial franchise fees	76,700	86,300
Other revenue	16,902	6,499
	$358,915	$ 149,943
Selling, general and administrative expenses	(409,393)	(262,496)
Loss before depreciation and amortization	(50,478)	(112,553)
Depreciation and amortization	(14,372)	(5,857)
Loss from operations	$ (64,850)	$(118,410)
Other income (expenses)		
Interest income	5,350	—
Interest expense	(7,092)	(1,306)
Penalties	—	(150)
	$ (1,742)	$ (1,456)
Loss before state income tax	(66,592)	(119,866)
State income tax	(250)	(500)
Net loss	$ (66,842)	$(120,366)

The price for Joe's interest in the company was quickly agreed upon and divided equally among Mike, Wes, and Jamie. Fred and Peter's 50 percent ownership stake remained unaffected. Wes then became president, Mike, vice president, Jamie became director of training and manager of territory development.

ORGANIZATIONAL STRUCTURE

The company was growing so rapidly that each team member had to perform multiple functions, making it difficult to define an organizational structure. By 1996, however, the team wanted to develop a more formal management infrastructure. For the present time, Mike, Wes, and Jamie worked as a team with Jamie ultimately reporting to Mike more than Wes. In addition to the five partners, there were four other full-time corporate employees: a bookkeeper, a controller, a marketing director, and a receptionist.

Mike and his team called Fred for advice but maintained final authority. For example, Fred advised allowing the sale of nonbake units to franchisees who didn't already own a bake unit. He reasoned that, as a function of demand, bake units would naturally open to support nonbake ones. The team ultimately decided against allowing franchisees to own only nonbake locations. Doing so would put nonbake franchises in a potentially weak negotiating position—they would then be at the mercy of

EXHIBIT 17.5 Bagelz Franchising Corporation statement of cash flows for the years ended December 31, 1995 and 1994.

	1995	1994
Cash flows from operating activities		
Net loss	$ (66,842)	$(120,366)
Adjustments to reconcile net loss to net cash used in operating activities:		
Depreciation and amortization	14,372	5,857
(Increase) decrease in		
Accounts and other receivables	(8,466)	(3,450)
Other assets	2,571	(2,949)
Increase (decrease) in		
Accounts payable and accrued expenses	(14,399)	58,824
Other liabilities	(1,071)	—
Income taxes payable	250	250
Deferred franchise fee revenue	(15,700)	28,700
Net cash used in operating activities	$ (89,285)	$ (33,134)
Cash flow from investing activities		
Advances to affiliates	(44,227)	(44,091)
Purchase of property and equipment	—	(95,412)
Acquisition of intangible assets	—	(15,669)
Net cash used in investing activities	$ (44,227)	$(155,172)
Cash flows from financing activities		
Advances from affiliates	51,075	96,679
Capital investment	100,000	56,000
Repayment of advances from affiliates	(104,899)	—
Loans from stockholders	87,976	38,217
Net cash provided by financing activities	$134,152	$ 190,896
Net increase in cash	640	2,590
Cash—beginning of year	2,590	—
Cash—end of year	$ 3,230	$ 2,590
Supplemental disclosure of cash flow information		
Cash paid during the year for:		
Income taxes	—	$ 250
Interest	—	125
Supplemental disclosure of non-cash transactions		
Total capital investment	$138,217	

franchisees who operated bake locations to supply their bagels. Supplier-franchisees would have the power to raise wholesale bagel prices, drive nonbake franchisees out of business, and acquire the nonbake facilities. For nonbake franchise locations, franchisees were given the option of purchasing bagels from other franchisees, but all still had the ability to supply a nonbake location internally.

EXHIBIT 17.6   Bagelz per store earning claims 1995 (est.).

	Weekly	Annually	Total revenue per store
Total revenue per store			
Sales	$8,000.00	$416,000.00	100.00%
Total revenue	$8,000.00	$416,000.00	100.00
Cost of goods sold			
Salaries and wages	1,760.00	91,520.00	22.00
Food	1,520.00	79,040.00	19.00
Beverages	720.00	37,440.00	9.00
Paper supplies	320.00	16,640.00	4.00
Total cost of goods sold	$4,320.00	$224,640.00	54.00
Gross profit on sales	$3,680.00	$191,360.00	46.00
Operating expenses			
Royalties	640.00	33,280.00	8.00
Payroll tax	136.00	7,072.00	1.70
Payroll service	20.00	1,040.00	0.25
Rent	480.00	24,960.00	6.00
Electric	200.00	10,400.00	2.50
Gas	120.00	6,240.00	1.50
Telephone	24.00	1,248.00	0.30
Advertising	200.00	10,400.00	2.50
Local advertising	80.00	4,160.00	1.00
Promotions	4.00	208.00	0.05
Insurance	80.00	4,160.00	1.00
Linen and laundry	16.00	832.00	0.20
Repairs and maintenance	80.00	4,160.00	1.00
Rubbish removal	40.00	2,080.00	0.50
Office supplies	40.00	2,080.00	0.50
Uniforms	16.00	832.00	0.20
Professional fees	40.00	2,080.00	0.50
Miscellaneous	20.00	1,040.00	0.25
Total operating expenses	$2,236.00	$116,272.00	27.95
Total income from operations	$1,444.00	$ 75,088.00	18.05

* All figures have been estimated based on industry data and do not necessarily represent the actual financial performance of a Bagelz store operation.

The franchisee made up the final part of the organization. There were seven franchisees, and plans were underway to open 53 new franchises by August 1997, and 2,000 by the year 2000. Mike was aggressively recruiting new franchisees and selling multiple units to existing ones. Ultimately, the number of stores sold to a particular franchisee would depend on the number of stores that the franchisee wanted and the number the team felt the individual could efficiently operate.

EXHIBIT 17.7   Bagelz's UFOC highlights.

Estimated initial investment for a Bagelz Franchise Operation

Initial investment	Lower cost	Mid-cost	Higher cost
Initial franchise fee	$ 10,000	$ 10,000	$ 10,000
Real property	2,500	4,000	8,000
Leasehold improvements	37,000	40,000	46,000
Equipment	55,000	60,000	65,000
Security systems	1,000	1,500	2,000
Freight charges	1,700	2,100	2,500
Outside signage	1,500	2,000	2,500
Opening inventory	5,000	5,000	5,000
Insurance	1,000	1,000	1,000
Supplies	500	750	1,000
Training expenses	600	1,100	2,600
Legal and accounting	1,000	1,000	1,000
Grand opening advertising	2,000	2,000	2,000
Miscellaneous expenses	5,000	5,000	5,000
Additional funds (3 months)	23,000	41,000	54,000
Total	$146,800	$176,450	$207,600

Fees for a Bagelz Franchise Operation

Type of fee	Amount
Royalty	8% of total gross sales
Advertising	2.5% of total gross sales
Local advertising	1% of total gross sales
Opening advertising	$2,000
Audit	Cost of audit plus interest
Late payments	Interest up to the legal maximum rate
Transfer	$5,000, plus $1,000 for any satellite
Extension	$500 (does not apply to satellite location)
Location rent	Varies
Insurance	Varies
Non-compete violation	$10,000 for each competing store plus 8% of its gross sales
Confidentiality violation	Baglez's damages
Trademark violation	$250 per day
Dispute resolution	Half of mediation and arbitration fee
Equipment ordering administrative fee	Up to 4% of the equipment

OPERATIONS

Stores opened at 6 A.M. and closed at 5 P.M. during the week and 2 P.M. on the weekends. The majority of business was done in the morning, but lunch hours were a significant source of revenue. Originally, there was no dinner business, but management's goal was to extend the days to 7 P.M. To achieve this, they were first looking to develop the 2-to-5 afternoon coffee-hour business, and were testing several pastries and snack products to complement their cappuccino offerings.

The operations manual was in its fourth revision due to dramatic changes in the company's operational procedures throughout the past several years. For example, previously, bagel-making was a boil-and-bake operation, but now Bagelz had found a way to make it a bake-only operation without compromising the product's taste. To do this, they used a newly developed baking technology, able to provide the same taste as a boil-and-bake bagel without the boiling:

> In one store, we replaced the regular oven with a new type that was only being used in 17 other retail operations throughout the country. We were number 18, and after installing it, we noticed that sales continued to climb. To us, this was a clear indication our customers approved.

Boil-and-bake was a difficult process; it was a hard, hot job and the baker played an important role in store operations. This role was so critical that the management team had store alarms installed, set to alert the team member on-call, if the store wasn't opened by 3 A.M. Further complicating the situation was that baking required skilled labor. If the scheduled baker didn't show up, a skilled replacement had to fill in.

Management worked to reduce other costs for the franchisee, as well. Mike formulated a series of bagel demand charts based on sales patterns. These charts took much of the guesswork out of bagel inventory management for franchisees. The implementation of the new oven technology also reduced costs. Bagels could be made faster; therefore baking could start later in the morning. There were other benefits as well:

> Before we started installing the new ovens, they baked with the oven door open. And it was hot! In one of our stores, we were having a ventilation problem and it was so hot in the baking area that the light fixtures on the ceiling melted. After installing the new oven, baking could be done with the door closed; it was much cooler in the baking area and there was a utility savings as well: the new oven used only 25 percent as much energy.

Other improvements to production systems further reduced costs. For example, poppy seeds could cost as much as $80 for a 50-pound bag. In the past, bagels had been boiled, placed on seeded boards, seeded on the top, then baked. After baking, seeds left on the boards had to be discarded because baking seeds more than once produced a burned-tasting product. Management refined the process by dampening the bagels with a sponge, then dipping them in seed bins. Leftover seeds remained in the bin, effectively eliminating waste and reducing costs. Bagels were then defrosted and baked. Stores had a double-defrost rack and a single-bake oven because, while defrost took 30 minutes, bake only took 15. The double defrost-rack kept the production process continually flowing.

THE COMMISSARY

The commissary, which sold bagels, cream cheese, and other products to franchisees, was wholly owned by Mike, Jamie, and Wes. Franchisees were required to purchase cream cheese and bagel dough directly from the commissary, but were permitted to buy other items either from the commissary or from an approved vendor and product list. Because of the commissary's bulk-purchasing power, franchisees were unlikely to obtain a lower price, effectively discouraging them from purchasing products from outside vendors. Maintaining high quality standards was also important, because the commissary needed large orders to receive large price discounts. In early 1996, the commissary's cream cheese sales volume averaged approximately 3,500 pounds per week:

> A lot of people cut cream cheese with water; at the commissary, we don't. We also make larger bagels—four and a quarter ounces—when others use a four-ounce standard. Because of this, we will never be a cost leader, but the goal is to be seen as a product leader. You see, although you can't tell the difference between a four and four-and-a-quarter ounce bagel, the larger one has a longer shelf life, so we hope the customer will get a fresher bagel.

In the early days of the commissary, there was only one dough-producing machine. Production was started early in the day, so in the event there was a mechanical problem, it could be repaired in time. An additional machine was purchased in 1995, but production still started early in the day, so that in the event of an emergency, a store's order could still be met. As the sole source of bagel dough, the commissary had to deliver. Then in 1996, they developed frozen dough in conjunction with several large manufacturing companies:

> Originally all our stores were doing fresh dough because we weren't able to formulate a frozen dough that tasted the same. But fresh dough only has a shelf life of three days and, therefore, there was a minimal distance from the commissary that a store could be located. Because commissaries are a nightmare to set up, this in effect, limited company growth potential. Frozen dough has a shelf life of about three months, and cream cheese 30 days, so growth was no longer limited to clusters around commissaries.

Mike, Wes, and Jamie planned to eventually outsource all frozen-dough production. Some franchisees had complained about the commissary's monopoly on dough sales, but once frozen bagel production was outsourced, franchisees could then buy from the lowest-priced producer.

MARKETING

Bagelz was continually improving products and store design. Mike and the team felt that Bagelz needed better marketing. For example, to increase coffee revenues, they developed better coffee displays, sold porcelain mugs, and positioned the product with an upscale image:

> We even looked into pumping the coffee smell into the store through the air vents. You see, mine was the same exact coffee as other, higher priced coffee competitors, but these sellers displayed the product better, so people saw it as superior and as such, were willing to pay more for it.

Although they wanted to create a deli or gourmet-shop image for Bagelz, they also wanted customers to perceive it as having the convenience of fast food. To do this and speed product-assembly times, they switched to presliced meats and premixed cartons of pasteurized eggs. These processes had additional benefits: there was no chance of employee injury from a slicer blade and no threat of salmonella. Microwaved, the eggs were always uniform in taste and appearance. They also added self-serve drink fountains and refrigerators with prepacked cream cheeses.

To better market take-out products, cream cheese containers were custom printed with the Bagelz logo and put in a display case by the register—in case a customer forgot to get it from the self-serve refrigerator. Previously, a customer had to step out of line to get it, then step back into line, delaying other customers. Pressure from those waiting, to keep the service line moving, had resulted in lost sales.

One of the company's greatest advertising successes was travel coffee mugs with the Bagelz name on them. Early on, Bagelz gave them away in exchange for any competitor's mug that a customer brought into the store. Other advertising tactics included emphasizing the "Z" in the Bagelz name, even putting the Z in front of words, as in "Z sandwiches." (See Exhibit 17.8 for Bagelz's menu and Exhibit 17.9 for Bruegger's.)

> Another thing we had been advertising was something called a quarterloaf. There were a lot of people who weren't going to go in to buy a bagel because they simply weren't filling enough. For example, when I'm really hungry, I'm a grinder type of guy: extra sauce, dripping with cheese; it's a beautiful thing. Now, *that's* a sandwich! At first we were thinking of giving extra-thick bread, but others were doing it. The same with submarine sandwiches. Then we came up with the quarterloaf idea, and we knew we had a winner. No one knew what the heck a quarterloaf was, but it sounded good. And most of all, it sounded large.

The quarterloaf was one-fourth the size of a loaf of bread, shaped like a roll, and for an additional 25 cents offered the same sandwich items as a bagel. Because of this, the same sandwich-making area setup could be used for both—giving the impression that Bagelz offered many different menu items without having to coordinate extra preparation processes:

> We are constantly looking for items, like the quarterloaf, that you can do a lot with. For example, right now we have a chicken breast, but pretty soon it's going to be a chicken salad. Then it's going to be a chicken Caesar salad. We are using Franchisee Advertising Fund revenues to develop advertising campaigns for all these new products.

FRANCHISEE ADVERTISING FUND

The Franchisee Advertising Fund (FAF) was controlled by franchisees. Two and a half percent of gross sales went to the FAF, and these funds supported media advertising, coupon campaigns, and similar promotions. Discounts from vendors on products such as deli meats and paper goods were negotiated by Mike, and approved by FAF's franchisee buying cooperative. It was thought that as the number of store units increased, local FAF chapters would eventually be created. However, Mike planned to continue negotiating vendor-based pricing deals:

> We made the deals. We looked to make as large a deal as possible with suppliers. If you could fill their trucks, you would get the lowest possible price—one unit or one truckload costs the same to transport. Because we looked to develop territory clusters of stores, ordering enough to fill a truck became possible. First, we would make a deal

EXHIBIT 17.8 Bagelz's menu.

Sandwichez

Smoked Ham with Cheese and Spicy Mustard	$3.69
Turkey with Cheese and Honey Mustard	3.79
Roast Beef with Cheese and Horseradish Sauce	3.89
Nova Scotia Lox with Cream Cheese and Onion	5.69
Chicken Salad with Cheese	3.69
Tuna Salad with Cheese	3.69
B.L.T. with Cheese	3.09
Garden Veggie with Cheese and Fat Free Honey Mustard	2.99
Grilled Chicken with Cheese and Mayonnaise	4.49

(Sandwichez include Lettuce, Tomato, and Onion)

Egg Sandwichez

Egg	1.49
Egg and Cheese	1.69
Egg and Ham, Sausage or Bacon	2.29
Egg and Ham, Sausage or Bacon with Cheese	2.49

Bagel Choicez   .49 ea.   4.99 dz.

Plain, Cinnamon, Egg, Pumpernickel, Salt, Everything, Sesame, Whole Wheat, Poppy, Garlic, Onion, Cornmeal, Raisin, Daily Special

Spreadz

Butter	.89
Peanut Butter and Jelly	1.09
Cream Cheese	1.39

Gourmet Cream Cheese w/ Bagel:

Plain (Low-Cal Available)
Veggie (Low-Cal Available)
Garlic and Herb (Low-Cal Available)
Chive
Lox   1.79
Strawberry
Walnut Raisin
Daily Special

Desserts

Chips	.69
Cookies	.59
Muffins	1.09
Fat Free Muffins	1.09
Cinnamon Twists°	

Beverages

	Small	Med.	Large
Gourmet Coffee	$.99	$1.09	$1.19
Cappuccino°			
Espresso°			
Hot Chocolate	.99	1.29	1.49
Juice	.69		
Milk		1.29	
Soda	.79		
Iced Coffee			
Herbal Tea			

Platterz

(Prices upon request)
8 Sandwich Platter
12 Sandwich Platter
Bagel and Cream Cheese Platter (14 Bagels)
Bagel and Cream Cheese Platter (26 Bagels)

° Denotes products not available at this location.
Prices effective November 1, 1996 for the Fairfield, CT store location.

EXHIBIT 17.9 Bruegger's menu.

Bagel Sandwiches

Tuna Salad	$3.39
Grilled Chicken Salad	3.39
Roasted Turkey Breast	3.79
Smoked Turkey Breast	3.79
Roast Beef	3.79
Atlantic Smoked Salmon	4.39
Garden Vegetable	2.89
Muenster or Swiss Cheese	2.89
Bruegger's Humus	2.89
Peanut Butter	1.19

All Above Served with: Mayonnaise, Garlic Mayonnaise, Dijon Mustard, Honey Mustard, or Horseradish Sauce
Additional Extras (Choice of Any Two):
Tomato, Sprouts, Onion, Cucumber, Lettuce, or Green Pepper

Bagels and Cream Cheese

Plain	1.39
Honey Walnut	1.69
Garden Veggie	1.69
Chive	1.69
Bacon Scallion	1.69
Wildberry	1.69
Smoked Salmon Spread	2.09
Jalapeno	1.69
Light Garden Veggie	1.69
Light Plan	1.39
Light Herb Garlic	1.69
Light Strawberry	1.69
Butter, Margarine, Honey, or Jam	0.79

Soup of the Day

Cup	2.29
Bowl	2.59

Desserts

Bruegger's Bars	1.19
Bruegger's Cookies	0.71
Fresh Apples	0.71

Take-Out Cream Cheese

Original	1.79
Smoked Salmon	3.09
Others	1.99
Plain	
Sesame	
Cinnamon Raisin	
Sundried Tomato	
Pumpernickel	
Blueberry	

Honey Grain
Poppy
Salt
Onion
Garlic
Everything

Beverages

	Small	Med.	Large
Coffee	0.89	1.05	1.19
Flavored Coffee	0.99	1.19	1.43
Tea: Regular, Decaffeinated, or Herbal		0.79	
Milk		0.65	
Soda	0.70	0.89	0.99
Juice Spritzer		1.25	
Bottled Juice		1.39	
Orange Juice	1.19	1.43	1.67
Mineral Water		1.29	

In Season Beverages

	Small	Med.	Large
Hot Chocolate	1.19	1.39	1.59
Hot Mulled Cider	1.19	1.39	1.59
Fresh Cider	1.19	1.39	1.59

Prices effective November 1, 1996 for the Wellesley, MA store location.

with a local supplier, and then with the larger house that distributed to them. We would guarantee the supplier that we would open up a certain number of stores in an area, within a given period of time. It has worked fine so far, but if we ever miss projected store openings and usage volumes, it will become a little more difficult.

The team decided to wait on television advertising. They believed that successful television advertising for food, unlike garage or gas-station advertising, depended directly on how attractive that product looked on the screen. Achieving a high-quality, professional production was expensive and simply wasn't cost-effective for the company at the time. Instead, they saw potential for using the effectiveness of television advertising without spending FAF money by forming strategic alliances with other companies that already advertised on television. Such alliances included developing co-branded units to establish brand recognition in the highly competitive foodservice industry (see Exhibits 17.10 and 17.11).

Co-Branded Units

Co-branded units offer two different concepts, in the same location (e.g., KFC and Taco Bell). Bagelz opened their first co-branded store with Subway. A store adjoining one Subway location had gone out of business, and the site became available. Although they were able combine the seating due to Subway's existing set-up, they were not able to combine the back room—something Mike and the team hoped to eventually be able to do. They thought there would be other opportunities to develop co-branded Bagelz and Subway units:

> We were also looking to put together a breakfast program with Fred. Although he was already doing a breakfast program, he was having problems changing Subway's image

Exhibit 17.10   Foodservice industry growth statistics.

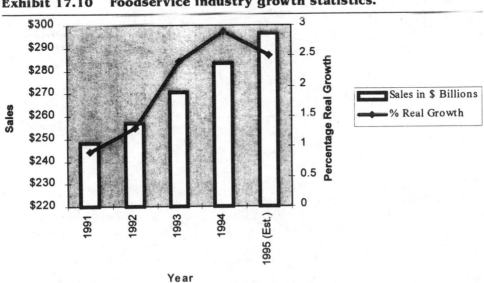

Exhibit 17.11   Food service industry statistics categorized by sector and segment.

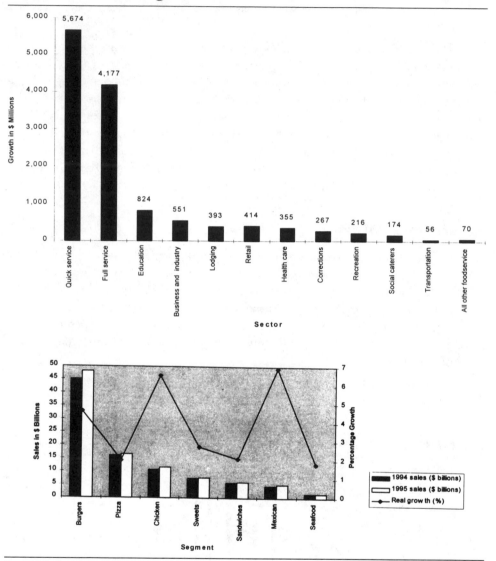

Source: Cahners Bureau of Foodservice Research and Restaurants & Institutions, January 1, 1995.

from strictly a lunch and dinner place. We were looking to use Bagelz as a morning traffic-builder, retrofitting some Subway stores—possibly changing their color scheme to differentiate the co-branded units. If this works, it opens up an enormous number of possibilities, and shared overhead would be a tremendous competitive advantage. But Subway isn't our only option—we see them as one potential brand to do business with, but there are a lot of other franchisors we could co-brand with, as well.

One company, a Mobil franchisee, had already opened a Bagelz franchise in his gas station's convenience store. The Mobil owner didn't have the room for full-sized baking facilities nor did he want to lease the space to an existing Bagelz franchisee, so management engineered a scaled-down version of necessary baking equipment. This gave the franchisee potential to open multiple, nonbake locations. The Bagelz team considered multiple-unit franchisees key for the company's success:

> If we could be three-to-one or four-to-one nonbake to bake, we would be very happy because you don't make money in the back room—you make money by setting up counters and by getting qualified franchisees to keep them operating.

FRANCHISEE RECRUITMENT—FUTURE DILEMMAS

Franchisee recruitment was a labor-intensive process, and according to a study done by Subway and several other franchisors, the national inquiry-to-approval rate of potential franchisees was a mere 2 percent. Bagelz's approval rate, about 4 percent, was twice the national average. Despite this unusually high acceptance rate, Bagelz had encountered problems with only one franchisee, who had simply abandoned the location. The Bagelz team had known that the franchisee wanted to leave the system and found a buyer willing to purchase the store, but the franchisee had gotten impatient. Not wanting to wait for due diligence, he simply pulled all his equipment out and locked the door:

> This guy was definitely a red flag. He was qualified, but there were warning signs—you can talk yourself into believing anything if you try hard enough. In the early stages of development, we talked ourselves into believing that what we needed to do was sell stores, and that little else mattered. We tried to make a deal with anyone who expressed interest. Now we're more aware of potential problems that can occur with franchisees—this is something that we're quite concerned about.

Mike and the team worried about the likelihood of franchisee problems as the company expanded. They thought that perhaps they needed to re-evaluate the way they selected franchisees and the company's management structure. After giving it some careful thought, they formulated several potential plans of action. They could either screen potential franchisees more rigorously or they could keep the screening process as it was—perhaps a small percentage of poorly performing franchisees was a price that had to be paid for continued high growth. They also could concentrate on developing an internal-management structure or possibly outsource the evaluation function. They knew they would need to carefully consider all alternatives to determine the best direction for Bagelz.

18 SOLIDWORKS

On a December afternoon in 1995, Jon Hirschtick, Michael Payne, and Victor Leventhal sat around a conference table discussing a pleasant dilemma: how much equity money should they accept? Their original goal was to raise $4.5 million, but the situation had evolved so that more than $10 million was now available at twice the anticipated share price. If they took it all, their ownership would be diluted only by the amount they anticipated when they began looking for a second round of venture capital. On the other hand, they could accept $4.5 million and halve the dilution.

They believed $4.5 million would be more than enough financing to take them to profitability, but other issues weighed in favor of taking the extra money. Their venture was in a maturing market unaccustomed to start-up companies. A richer bank account would go a long way toward reassuring prospective customers. Such an account would also send a message to competitors: "No dirty tricks, we're here to stay and we have the means to counterattack if necessary." Finally, a deep war chest would allow them to pursue opportunities not usually considered by start-ups: they could grow much more aggressively.

Did they really want such a large safety net? The $4.5 million goal already included a generous safety margin. Much of the $10 million would probably just sit in the bank as an expensive insurance policy. Besides, things were going very well: they launched at Autofact in Chicago, the biggest tradeshow in the industry, and shipped their CAD (computer aided design) software product on schedule in November. It was the hit of the show and won the Best New Product award. Sales orders were rolling in and SolidWorks was even slightly ahead of pro forma revenue projections. They didn't feel anxious. They felt fortunate.

This case was written by Dan D'Heilly under the direction of Professor William Bygrave. Funding provided by the Ewing Marion Kauffman Foundation and the Frederic C. Hamilton Chair for Free Enterprise Studies. Copyright © 1996 Babson College. All rights reserved.

ROUNDING OUT THE ENTREPRENEURIAL TEAM

Another reason for optimism was successfully bringing Victor Leventhal onto the executive management team. Landing Victor Leventhal had been quite a coup; he was a top industry professional with 28 years of experience. Vic had managed a $1 billion division of IBM for several years in the 1970s and early 1980s, then joined Computerland as executive vice president responsible for sales and marketing. At Computerland for six years, his accomplishments included creating a direct sales-force that generated over $120 million in its first year. When approached about joining SolidWorks, Vic was the CEO of a CAD systems reseller with $21 million in annual sales. The CAD reseller had grown over 200 percent in the five years Vic was at the helm.

When Vic joined SolidWorks in October 1994, Mike and Jon's biggest concern was whether they could work together—would they encounter the "too many chiefs" syndrome? However, Jon believed that the risk paid off during the search for a second round of capital:

> The management team bandwidth was really important. The fact that we had Vic, Mike, and I meant that we had enough people to think about a strategic partnership with the Japanese. We had enough brain cycles in the day. That was very important to doing this deal. If Vic hadn't been here, we wouldn't have had the management capital to do it. By having an extra, really smart, experienced person around, by moving aggressively to expand our team, we ended up able to do important initiatives that otherwise couldn't have happened. We didn't have the money when we were building our team. We chased the people, then the money chased us.

While Jon and Michael managed the product development and organizational aspects of the company start-up, Vic developed the sales and marketing plan. They worked well together on negotiating the strategic partnership, launching the product, and in dealing with the lawsuit.

THE LAWSUIT

Producing and launching the product was a smooth operation. Jon Hirschtick was an experienced CAD visionary and CEO, Michael Payne was the best in the business at delivering leading-edge CAD software on schedule, and Victor Leventhal was a CAD/CAM/CAE marketing channel guru. In addition to a hot management team, the conceptual goal was exciting so they had attracted many excellent CAD people to SolidWorks—perhaps too many.

In the fall of 1995, Parametric Technology Corp. (PTC) filed a lawsuit alleging that SolidWorks recruited PTC's employees in violation of noncompete agreements. As Jon recalled, the lawsuit became a rallying cry for SolidWorks' employees as they saw several coworkers singled out by their giant competitor:

> It really galvanized the company. People said, "If they're going to go after us like that, we want to win even more."

They were fortunate that the lawsuit was settled quickly. A protracted lawsuit could have been a significant burden for a young company.

DRIVING THE SECOND ROUND

The management team wanted to raise a pool of $4.5 million for the second round of capital. Jon began negotiating in the spring of 1995:

> After a board meeting, one of my board members took me aside and said, "You need to drive the process if you want a good valuation. Get out early and find a way to get the price up. If you wait until you need the money, the venture capitalists will set the terms."

Venture capitalists were unlikely to provide a second-round valuation as rich as the SolidWorks' management team thought was merited, so they developed a plan for getting a higher price. Michael Payne described the rationale for finding a strategic investor:

> Venture capitalists are only a tad away from bankers in that they have prescribed formulas in their minds for initial funding, and for subsequent funding. On subsequent funding, 1.2 to 2.0 times the first round if things are going well, less if it isn't. We thought the company was worth a lot more than that, so we worked to have someone else set the price. Someone with more skin in the game.

The valuation issue was only one of their concerns; total capitalization, dilution, timing, and other terms were also critical to crafting a good deal. It would require time to strike the right deal with a strategic partner.

SECOND ROUND FUNDING, PART I: STRATEGIC PARTNERSHIP

The decision about whom to court for a strategic partner was made by the executive team. There was a history of distributors investing in CAD software companies, and Michael and Vic both knew Japanese distributors who were interested in selling SolidWorks software and who had invested in past strategic partnerships. These were huge, global companies. Vic had actually been involved in negotiating a second round deal with a Japanese distributor in 1990. It takes a long time to penetrate the Japanese market, so finding a Japanese distributor early on made good marketing sense. The SolidWorks team spent minimal time considering prospective European strategic partners as Victor Leventhal explained:

> It was very uncommon in Europe to find the kind of agreement we structured. Japan was an island, but Europe was eight or nine separate countries. We didn't think we could find a European partner who could accomplish what we wanted.

SolidWorks was seeking specific characteristics in a strategic partner. The investment had to be at least $2 million, and valuation had to be generous, but Solid-Works' first priority was the partner's strength as a distribution channel.

Negotiations with Kubota began in early spring 1995 and continued for nearly nine months. This was in part because the Japanese generally take a long time to finalize deals. It was also because of the structure of Kubota. It was Kubota's venture capital entity on the West Coast that made the investment, but a distribution entity in Japan that negotiated the distribution agreement. Kubota's VC group insisted, "ROI is very important," but they couldn't make the deal without the distribution agreement, and vice versa. In the end, Kubota made the investment and secured Solid-Works' distribution rights in Japan. Jon Hirschtick recalled the negotiations:

> Kubota was very entrepreneurial in approaching this deal. They treated the investment like a venture deal. We liked that. The distribution deal also stood alone, on its own merits. In fact, the venture guys and the distribution guys never even visited Solid-Works at the same time.

The SolidWorks team aimed to maximize the terms of both deals. The valuation had to be right, but the distribution agreement had to stand on its own. Jon reported that if Kubota didn't deliver the prescribed Japanese market share, the agreement would lapse:

> We picked two goals: total dollars sold, and Japanese sales as a percentage of total revenue. Total revenue gave them a floor in case our U.S. sales skyrocketed. The percentage of revenue formula was good because we didn't know how well we would really do, but we knew how much of what we sold should come from Japan, so it was something we could agree on.

Another important point was observation rights on SolidWorks' board of directors. Kubota gained the right to be formally briefed, but did not get the right to attend board meetings. This arrangement was based largely on the advice of Axel Bichara, who led the syndicate for Atlas Ventures:

> We deal with this all the time. When a strategic investor has a board seat, they have a conflict of interest when it comes to strategic decisions. The stakes for the parent company are a much bigger concern than return on investment.
>
> The other time this is an issue is at the harvest. In an IPO, there's not much of a problem, but it can be a problem in an acquisition. The first scenario is that the strategic partner is the interested party. They go to the board meetings and know things inside out. It can be a plus, but it can also be a minus. They know the players and issues and absolutely have an inside track to picking things up at the right time. You are in a weaker position when the buyer is on the board. Even worse, potential acquirers get scared off by the strategic investor on the board, so competitors may not even bid. A big upside for us is when competitive bidding gets going, but a strategic investor can keep that from happening.

However, Axel conceded that Kubota also won many points in the negotiations:

> The Japanese used to do deals with relatively little equity and a lot of prepaid license fees, and we tried very hard to get that kind of deal. They didn't pay a penny of prepaid fees. They got a good deal.

EXHIBIT 18.1 Comparable companies: CAD industry.

Company	Year	Revenue	Valuation	Source
Autodesk	1985	$ 29.5 million	$ 173 million	Value Line
Autodesk	1994	455.0 million	1,960 million	Value Line
PTC	1989	11.0 million	131 million	Value Line
PTC	1990	25.5 million	250 million	Value Line
PTC	1994	244.0 million	2,294 million	Value Line
Rasna	1995	24.0 million	234 million	Public stock price

The first-round investors had pro rata rights° and wanted to participate in the second round. Jon's working assumption had been that the strategic partner would provide half of the second round. However, the Japanese investment model was to dominate their round of funding and Jon encouraged Kubota to make a large investment. He suggested an investment of $4 million with a 4.5 times step-up, "Why $4 million and $4.50 a share? Like any deal; you go in looking for something high, at a high price."

VALUATION

The SolidWorks management team took care of their top priority by only negotiating with strong distributors, and the $2 million investment goal was not uncommon for this kind of a deal. The contested point was SolidWorks' pre-money valuation, as Jon Hirschtick explained:

> My job is to get capital at the best price for my shareholders. How do I do that? One way is to look at companies we compare ourselves to. What are they worth today, and what were they worth right after they went public? (See Exhibits 18.1 and 18.2.) I backed that out to come up with a valuation model to justify a high valuation. Then I wrote to the Japanese, "OK, I understand you value it based on some venture formula, or cash flows, but I value it based on comparables. Take three companies no one has ever heard of, x, y, & z." I said, "Look, we expect to have this kind of revenue and this kind of valuation. We're asking you for a tenth of that valuation now." That's how I argued valuation.

It was already late in the negotiations when the Kubota VCs received authorization to make the $4 million investment. There was no room for negotiations; any other figure would have required going back through Kubota's corporate approval process. Jon knew that time was running out:

> We started the negotiations with $2.5 million in the bank, and we were down to hundreds of thousands of dollars when we closed with Kubota. It takes a long time to close an investment deal with the Japanese. One of the important things about the

---

° Pro rata rights: the right granted an investor to maintain the same percentage ownership in the event of future financing.

EXHIBIT 18.2   Comparable companies: Electrical CAD and software tools industries.

Company	Year	Revenue	Valuation	Source
Arcsys	1995	$ 6.1 million	$375 million	Public stock price
Pure Software	1995	21.4 million	470 million	Public stock price
Atria Software	1995	20.7 million	392 million	Public stock price

first round was that we had money left in the bank when we signed the deal for the second round.

Kubota agreed to a price of $4.50 a share, but stipulated that it was subject to another VC firm investing at least a token amount at the same price.

SECOND ROUND FUNDING, PART II: VENTURE CAPITAL

This agreement created a difficult situation for the VCs. On the one hand, they liked the high valuation because of its impact on their original investment. On the other hand, while they wanted to put more money into SolidWorks, they also sought a good multiple on their investment: $4.50 was just too rich. They argued that the strategic investor received more than just ROI for their investment, so naturally Kubota was willing to pay an inflated price. The VCs received nothing of strategic value, so they thought that they should be offered a discounted price to reflect the premium paid by Kubota.

Jon argued along a different line: the size of Kubota's investment took it out of the pure strategic investment category. Kubota's VC unit invested $4 million with standard ROI goals. In addition, Kubota had stipulated that no other investor would receive preferential treatment. Finally, SolidWorks raised enough money that it didn't need any investor that didn't agree to the set valuation. The VCs had to evaluate the deal on its own merits with terms as they were laid down by the strategic partnership:

Jon Hirschtick: I couldn't have gotten that valuation from American VCs, but once I had it from Kubota, they could justify it. Also, Kubota wouldn't accept anyone else getting a better deal, so the VCs had to sign on at the same price. It was their only option. The Kubota VC didn't see this as a distribution deal, he was in it for the ROI, so he wasn't about to let an insider get preferential conversion ratios° or something like that. The reality is that Kubota was getting more, but they expected to dominate this round. If others wanted to come in, the price was set.

Axel Bichara: This was a high price, but a good company. Just looking at the second round by itself, it was an opportunity to invest at a given value and the deal looked good at $4.50 in terms of multiple and IRR. I had no problem justifying a $35 million pre-money evaluation—we had a chance to make 10 times our money in 3 to 4 years. This is one of the few companies that has the potential to be $500 million within a few years and I think it's a good risk.

° Preferential conversion ratios refers to the conversion of preferred stock to common stock.

CONTEMPLATING APPROPRIATE FUNDING

Jon, Michael, and Vic let negotiations develop with a variety of prospective investors for nine months, and offers of money poured in from all sides: VCs, private investors, and employees. The total available at $4.50 was over $10 million. Jon described his negotiating strategy:

> I left things open for a long time. I was not in a rush to close the deal. We let the situation ripen, and we just said that we'd close the round when the Kubota deal closed. It was like a poker hand, sometimes you just want other people to signal their intentions first. The key was that we weren't desperate for the money.

In addition to Kubota's $4 million, Atlas Venture and Burr Egan Deleage wanted to invest about $2 million each, and North Bridge wanted to invest between $500,000 and $1 million. SolidWorks' employees also wanted to invest over half a million dollars, and there were several private investors who wanted to invest another $1 million. Jon was glad to have employee money in the pool, "There's no way I'd turn down money from someone who has the opportunity to work late and make us more profitable."

As Jon, Michael, and Vic talked about which money to take, and how much, several factors loomed large: ownership dilution, management control, employee morale, market perception, competitive uncertainty, and financing growth. The conversation was lively as they agreed on principles like, "I make money when the company is successful and goes public" and "You can't be a successful company unless you act like a successful company" only to find that they disagreed about how those principles applied to diluting ownership in exchange for a rainy day insurance policy.

19 QUICK LUBE FRANCHISE CORPORATION (QLFC)

It had been a year since Huston Oil had bought 80 percent of Super Lube, Inc., the number one franchisor of quick lubrication and oil-change service centers in the U.S.A. with 1,000 outlets. As a result of that takeover, Super Lube's largest franchisee, Quick Lube Franchise Corporation (QLFC) found itself in the position where its principal supplier, lead financing vehicle, and franchisor were the same entity. Was this an opportunity or a disaster? In April 1991, Frank Herget, founder, chairman, and CEO of QLFC was faced with one of the most important decisions of his life.

HISTORICAL BACKGROUND

Super Lube was the innovator of the "quick lube concept," servicing the lube, motor oil, and filter needs of motorists in a specialized building with highly refined procedures. It was founded in March 1979 by Jeff Martin. Frank Herget was one of the four founding members of Martins' team. After a few years, Herget became frustrated with life at the franchisor's headquarters in Dallas, Texas. He believed that the future of the Super Lube was in operating service centers. That put him at odds with founder, chairman, and CEO Jeff Martin who was passionately committed to franchising service centers as fast as possible. Martin and Herget had known each other for a long time so they sought a mutually acceptable way to resolve their differences. Their discussions quickly resulted in the decision that Herget would buy a company-owned service center in Northern California, by swapping his Super Lube

This case was prepared by Professors Stephen Spinelli and William Bygrave. Copyright © 1991 Babson College. All rights reserved.

founder's stock valued at $64,000, which he had purchased originally for $13,000. Quick Lube Franchise Corporation was founded.

Early Success and Growth

Success in his first service center inspired growth. Eventually, QLFC controlled service center development and operating rights to a geographic area covering parts of California and Washington with the potential for over 90 service centers. Herget's longterm goal was to build QLFC into a big chain of Super Lube service centers that would eventually have a public stock offering or merge with a larger company (see Exhibits 19.1 and 19.2).

Herget financed QLFC's growth with both equity and debt (see Exhibits 19.3 and 19.4). Most of the additional equity came from former Super Lube employees who left the franchisor to join QLFC in senior management positions. They purchased stock in QLFC with cash realized by selling their stock in Super Lube. A key member of Herget's team was Mark Roberts, who had been Super Lube's CFO until 1986. He brought much needed financial sophistication to QLFC.

The primary debt requirement was for financing new service centers. In 1991, the average cost of land acquisition and construction had risen to $750,000 per service center from about $350,000 ten years earlier.

Growth was originally achieved through off-balance-sheet real estate partnerships. An Oregon bank lent about $4 million and a Texas bank lent almost $3 million. However, rapid growth wasn't possible until QLFC struck a deal with Huston Oil for $6.5 million of subordinated debt. The Huston Oil debt was 8 percent interest-only for five years and then amortized on a straight line basis in years six through ten. The real estate developed with the Huston Oil financing was kept in the company. QLFC was contractually committed to purchasing Huston Oil products.

Super Lube's Relationship with Its Franchisees

Despite bridge financing of $10 million at the end of 1985 followed by a successful initial public offering, Super Lube's growth continued to outpace its ability to finance it. At the end of the 1980s, Super Lube was in technical default to its debt holders. Huston Oil struck a deal to acquire 80 percent of the company in a debt restructuring scheme. However, during the time of Super Lube's mounting financial problems and the subsequent Huston Oil deal, franchisees grew increasingly discontented.

A franchise relationship is governed by a contract called a license agreement. As a "business format" franchise, a franchisor offers a franchisee the rights to engage in

EXHIBIT 19.1   QLFC growth.

	1982	1983	1984	1985	1986	1987	1988	1989	1990	1991
Service centers	2	3	4	7	16	25	34	44	46	47
Sales ($ mil.)	.5	1.6	2.1	3.8	8.5	15.5	19	27	28	30

EXHIBIT 19.2 Quick Lube Franchise Corporation FY 1991 budget worksheet.

	Apr.	May	Jun.	Jul.	Aug.	Sep.	Oct.	Nov.	Dec.	Jan.	Feb.	Mar.	Total
Sales	$2,424,718	$2,444,629	$2,756,829	$2,816,765	$2,872,074	$2,358,273	$2,619,415	$2,435,022	$2,494,696	$2,733,469	$2,464,172	$2,795,804	$31,215,866
Cost of sales	544,689	549,348	613,728	626,809	639,126	529,542	588,628	547,137	573,063	627,574	565,836	642,144	7,047,624
Variable expenses (2)	805,251	826,956	894,782	914,050	943,260	790,276	893,236	819,709	844,626	911,313	826,811	949,576	10,419,876
Fixed expenses	358,640	349,858	351,828	363,917	371,458	366,260	371,988	391,686	378,485	388,381	399,375	393,974	4,485,890
Real estate cost	320,377	337,372	340,652	341,353	352,053	352,053	372,030	372,030	392,337	392,452	392,452	410,552	4,375,713
Store operating income	$ 395,761	$ 381,095	$ 555,839	$ 570,606	$ 565,137	$ 320,142	$ 393,533	$ 304,460	$ 306,185	$ 413,749	$ 279,698	$ 399,558	$ 4,886,763
Overhead	255,515	261,573	245,083	241,089	263,458	278,333	258,655	274,724	277,974	269,551	279,819	275,440	3,181,214
Operating income	$ 140,246	$ 119,522	$ 310,756	$ 329,517	$ 302,679	$ 41,809	$ 134,878	$ 29,736	$ 28,211	$ 144,198	$ (121)	$ 124,118	$ 1,705,549
Other income	7,392	7,392	7,392	7,392	7,392	7,392	7,392	7,392	7,392	7,392	7,392	7,392	88,704
Dropped site expense	(8,333)	(8,333)	(8,333)	(8,333)	(8,333)	(8,333)	(8,333)	(8,333)	(8,333)	(8,333)	(8,333)	(8,333)	(99,996)
Minority interest	686	613	(2,610)	(3,254)	(3,145)	2,065	511	4,529	4,346	1,290	6,564	2,459	14,054
Interest expense	(5,495)	(5,495)	(5,495)	(5,495)	(5,495)	(5,495)	(5,495)	(5,495)	(5,495)	(5,495)	(5,495)	(5,495)	(65,940)
Taxable income	$ 134,496	$ 113,699	$ 301,710	$ 319,827	$ 293,098	$ 37,438	$ 128,953	$ 27,829	$ 26,121	$ 139,052	$ 7	$ 120,141	$ 1,642,371
Income tax expense	54,921	47,253	119,971	126,613	115,680	17,885	53,211	17,790	16,727	58,652	6,880	51,779	687,362
Net income	$ 79,575	$ 66,446	$ 181,739	$ 193,214	$ 177,418	$ 19,553	$ 75,742	$ 10,039	$ 9,394	$ 80,400	$ (6,873)	$ 68,362	$ 955,009

(1) Budget revised March 21, 1990.

(2) Royalties to the franchisor equal 7% of gross sales.

EXHIBIT 19.3   **Quick Lube Franchise Corporation consolidated balance sheets.**

	Year ended March 31	
	1991	**1990**
ASSETS		
Current assets		
Cash	$ 740,551	$ 665,106
Accounts receivable, net doubtful accounts of $61,000 in 1991 and $44,000 in 1990	518,116	309,427
Construction advances receivable	508,168	137,412
Due from government agency		407,678
Inventory	1,093,241	1,074,513
Prepaid expenses other	407,578	401,562
Total current assets	$ 3,267,654	$ 2,995,698
Property and equipment		
Land	351,772	351,772
Buildings	3,171,950	2,519,845
Furniture, fixtures, and equipment	2,988,073	2,644,801
Leasehold improvements	242,434	183,635
Property under capital leases	703,778	703,778
Construction in progress	68,138	531,594
	$ 7,526,145	$ 6,935,425
Less accumulated depreciation and amortization	(1,290,565)	(854,473)
	$ 6,235,580	$ 6,089,952
Other assets		
Area development and license agreements, net of accumulated amortization	923,970	988,314
Other intangibles, net accumulated amortization	273,737	316,960
Other	151,604	208,898
	$10,852,545	$10,590,822
LIABILITIES AND SHAREHOLDERS' EQUITY		
Current liabilities		
Accounts payable and accrued expenses	$ 3,085,318	$ 3,198,694
Income taxes payable	37,224	256,293
Note payable		250,000
Current portion—LTD	203,629	174,134
Current portion of capital lease	19,655	17,178
Total current liabilities	$ 3,345,826	$ 3,896,299
Long-term debt, less current	2,848,573	3,052,597
Capital lease obligations, less current	628,199	648,552
Other long-term liabilities	731,783	483,534
Minority interest	2,602	13,821
	$ 4,211,157	$ 4,198,504
Shareholders' equity		
Common stock, par value $.01/share authorized 10,000,000 shares; issued 1,080,000 shares	10,800	10,800
Additional paid-in capital	1,041,170	774,267
Retained earnings	2,243,592	1,710,952
	3,295,562	2,496,019
	$10,852,545	$10,590,822

EXHIBIT 19.4   Quick Lube Franchise Corporation consolidated cash flow.

	Year ended March 31		
	1991	**1990**	**1989**
OPERATING ACTIVITIES			
Net income	$ 532,640	$ 764,794	$ 524,211
Adjustments to reconcile net income to net cash provided by operating activities:			
Depreciation and amortization	612,063	526,750	414,971
Provision for losses on accounts receivable	16,615	30,510	5,559
Provision for deferred income taxes	(15,045)	12,519	50,388
Minority interest in losses of subsidiaries	(11,217)	(129,589)	(83,726)
Loss (gain) on disposition of property and equipment	33,301	(420)	N/A
Changes in operating assets and liabilities:			
Accounts receivable	(225,304)	(58,700)	(135,585)
Inventory	(18,728)	(273,559)	(286,037)
Prepaid expenses and other	(6,016)	(102,117)	(34,334)
Accounts payable and accrued expenses	(113,376)	559,456	1,409,042
Income taxes payable	(219,069)	404,068	(620,434)
Due from shareholders and affiliates	N/A	N/A	(43,742)
Other long-term liabilities	263,294	167,501	84,697
Net cash provided by operating activities	$ 849,158	$ 1,901,213	$ 1,285,010
INVESTING ACTIVITIES			
Purchases of property and equipment	(599,327)	(1,922,892)	(1,922,852)
Proceeds from sale of property and equipment	374,592	8,523	782,519
Acquisition of license agreements	(44,000)	(127,000)	(117,000)
Acquisition of other intangibles	(2,615)	(327,549)	(2,500)
Change in construction advance receivable	(370,756)	593,017	(601,523)
Change in other assets	43,894	(138,816)	11,908
Net cash used in investing activities	$ (598,212)	$(1,914,717)	$(1,849,450)
FINANCING ACTIVITIES			
Proceeds from long-term borrowings and revolving line of credit	4,940,000	4,026,441	2,448,071
Proceeds from borrowings from related parties	N/A	N/A	19,600
Principal payments on long-term borrowings	(5,364,529)	(3,463,693)	(2,658,534)
Principal payments on borrowings from related parties		(19,600)	(7,216)
Principal payments on capital lease obligations	(17,876)	(38,048)	N/A
Proceeds from sale of common stock and capital contributions	266,903	97,201	19,600
Net cash provided by (used in) financing activities	$ (175,502)	$ 602,301	$ (178,479)
Increase (decrease) in cash	$ 75,444	$ 588,797	$ (742,919)
Cash at beginning of year	$ 655,106	$ 76,309	$ 819,228

a business system by using the franchisor's trade name, trademark, service marks, know-how, and method of doing business. The franchisee is contractually bound to a system of operation and to pay the franchisor a royalty in the form of a percentage of top-line sales.

The Super Lube license agreement called for the franchisor to perform product development and quality assurance tasks. Super Lube had made a strategic decision early in its existence to sell franchises on the basis of area development agreements. These franchisees had grown to become a group of sophisticated, fully integrated companies. As the franchisees grew with multiple outlets and became increasingly self-reliant, the royalty became difficult to justify. When the franchisor failed to perform its contractually obligated tasks as its financial problems grew more and more burdensome toward the end of the 1980s, a franchisee revolt began to surface.

The Huston Era Begins

The new owners, Huston, quickly moved to replace virtually the entire management team at Super Lube. The new CEO was previously a long-term employee of a Kmart subsidiary. He took a hard-line position on how the franchise system would operate and that Huston motor oil would be an important part of it. The first national convention after the Huston takeover was a disaster. The franchisees, already frustrated, were dismayed by the focus of the franchisor on motor oil sales instead of service center level profitability.

Herget decided to make a thorough analysis of the historical relationship between Quick Lube Franchise Corporation and Super Lube. Three months of research and documentation led to Quick Lube Franchise Corporation calling for a meeting with Huston Oil to review the findings and address concerns.

The meeting was held at the franchisor's offices with Herget and the franchisor's CEO and executive vice president. Herget described the meeting:

> The session amounted to a three-hour monologue by me followed by Super Lube's rejection of the past as relevant to the relationship. I was politely asked to trust that the future performance of the franchisor would be better and to treat the past as sunk cost. In response to my concern that Huston Oil might have a conflict of interest in selling me product as well as being the franchisor and having an obligation to promote service center profitability, they answered that Huston Oil bailed Super Lube out of a mess and the franchisees should be grateful, not combative.

Litigation

The QLFC board of directors received Herget's report and told him to select a law firm and to pursue litigation against Huston. QLFC's three months of research was supplied to the law firm. A suit against Huston Oil was filed three months after the failed QLFC/Huston "summit."

Huston Oil denied the charges and filed a countersuit. Document search, depositions, and general legal maneuvering had been going on for about three months when QLFC's attorneys received a call from Huston Oil requesting a meeting.

Herget immediately called a board meeting, prepared to make a recommendation for QLFC's strategic plan.

PREPARATION QUESTIONS

1. What grounds might QLFC have for filing a lawsuit against Huston Oil?
2. Why do you think Huston Oil has asked for a meeting with Herget?
3. What advice would you give Herget as he considers Huston Oil's request for a meeting with QLFC?
4. As part of that advice, how much is QLFC worth?
5. Does your answer to Question 4 depend on how QLFC is harvested?